Prentice Hall Canada Series in Accounting

Management Accounting

Canadian Second Edition

Prentice Hall Canada Series in Accounting

Management Accounting

Canadian Second Edition

Charles T. Horngren
Stanford University

Walter T. Harrison, Jr.
Baylor University

W. Morley Lemon
University of Waterloo

With
Johan P. de Rooy
University of British Columbia

Prentice Hall Canada Inc., Scarborough, Ontario

Canadian Cataloguing in Publication Data
Horngren, Charles T., 1926-
    Management accounting
Canadian 2nd ed.
First ed. (1990) as part of: Horngren, Charles T.,
1926-   . Accounting.   Canadian ed. (1991).
ISBN 0-13-037516-0
1. Accounting.   I. Harrison, Walter T.
II. Lemon, W. Morley, 1939–   . III. Title.

HF5635.H67   1993   657   C93-093279-X

Prentice-Hall, Inc., Englewood Cliffs, New Jersey
Prentice-Hall International (UK) Limited, London
Prentice-Hall of Australia, Pty. Limited, Sydney
Prentice-Hall Hispanoamericana, S.A., Mexico City
Prentice-Hall of India Private Limited, New Delhi
Prentice-Hall of Japan, Inc., Tokyo
Simon & Schuster Asia Private Limited, Singapore
Editora Prentice-Hall do Brasil, Ltda., Rio de Janeiro

ISBN 0-13-037516-0

Photo Credits
887 Toronto Works Department; **927** Dave Starett—Cove Studios; **964** Prentice
Hall Archives; **1009** Dave Starett—Cove Studios; **1056** Courtesy: Angelika
Baur; **1095** Dave Starrett—Cove Studios; **1129** Dave Starrett—Cove Studios.

Acquisitions Editor: Suzanne Tyson
Developmental Editor: David Jolliffe
Production Editor: Dawn du Quesnay
Permissions/Photo Research: Angelika Baur
Cover Design: Monica Kompter
Cover Image: © Hans Neleman/Image Bank Canada
Page Layout: Olena Serbyn

1 2 3 4 5 BG 97 96 95 94 93

Printed and bound in Canada

Original U.S. edition published by Prentice-Hall, Inc.
Englewood Cliffs, New Jersey. Copyright 1992, 1989 Prentice-Hall, Inc.

This edition for sale in Canada only.

Brief Contents

Contents

Part Seven

Management Accounting and Internal Decision-Making

*In each chapter, Assignment Material includes Questions, Exercises, and Problems (Group A and Group B).
**Extending Your Knowledge includes Decision Problems, an Ethical Issue, and Financial Statement Problems.

Appendices

Glossary   *G-1*

Index   *I-1*

Charles T. Horngren is the Edmund W. Littlefield Professor of Accounting at Stanford University. A graduate of Marquette University, he received his M.B.A. from Harvard University and his Ph.D. from the University of Chicago. He is also the recipient of honorary doctorates from Marquette University and DePaul University.

A Certified Public Accountant, Horngren served on the Accounting Principles Board for six years, the Financial Accounting Standards Board Advisory Council for five years and the Council of the American Institute of Certified Public Accountants for three years. He is currently serving as a trustee of the Financial Accounting Foundation.

A member of the American Accounting Association, Horngren has been its President and its Director of Research. He received the Outstanding Accounting Educator Award in 1973, when the association initiated an annual series of such awards.

The California Certified Public Accountants Foundation gave Horngren its Faculty Excellence Award in 1975 and its Distinguished Professor Award in 1983. He is the first person to have received both awards.

In 1985 the American Institute of Certified Public Accountants presented its first Outstanding Educator Award to Horngren. Professor Horngren is also a member of the National Association of Accountants, where he was on its research planning committee for three years. He was a member of the Board of Regents, Institute of Management Accounting, which administers the Certified Management Accountant examinations.

Horngren is the author of three other books published by Prentice Hall: *Cost Accounting: A Managerial Emphasis*, Seventh Edition, 1991 (with George Foster); *Introduction to Financial Accounting*, Fourth Edition, 1990 (with Gary L. Sundem); and *Introduction to Management Accounting*, Eighth Edition, 1990 (with Gary L. Sundem).

Charles T. Horngren is the Consulting Editor for the Prentice Hall Series in Accounting.

Walter T. Harrison, Jr., is Professor of Accounting and holds the Peat Marwick-Thomas L. Holton Chair in Accounting at the Hankamer School of Business, Baylor University. He received his B.B.A. degree from Baylor University, his M.S. from Oklahoma State University and his Ph.D. from Michigan State University.

Professor Harrison, recipient of numerous teaching awards from student groups as well as from university administrators, has also taught at Cleveland State Community College, Michigan State University, the University of Texas and Stanford University.

A member of the American Accounting Association and the American Institute of Certified Public Accountants, Professor Harrison has served as Chairperson of the Financial Accounting Standards Committee of the American Accounting Association and on the Program Advisory Committee for Accounting Education and Teaching.

Professor Harrison has published research articles in numerous journals, including *The Accounting Review*, *Journal of Accounting Research*, *Journal of Accountancy*, *Journal of Accounting and Public Policy* and *Economic Consequences of Financial Accounting Standards*. He has received scholarships, fellowships and research grants from Price Waterhouse & Co., Deloitte Haskins & Sells and the Ernst & Young Tax Research Program.

W. Morley Lemon is Associate Professor of Accounting at the School of Accountancy, University of Waterloo. He received his B.A. from the University of Western Ontario, his M.B.A. from the University of Toronto and his Ph.D. from the University of Texas at Austin.

Professor Lemon has taught at the University of Texas, the University of Illinois, McMaster University and the University of Waterloo. In addition, he has taught and prepared courses for professional accountants and accounting students in Canada and the United States.

A member of the Institute of Chartered Accountants of Ontario, Professor Lemon was elected a Fellow by that body. He is also a member of the Canadian Academic Accounting Association and the American Accounting Association, and has served as Chairperson of and on committees for all three organizations. He is Director of the Centre for Accounting Ethics, University of Waterloo.

Professor Lemon is the author of *Auditing: An Integrated Approach*, Canadian Fifth Edition, 1992 (with Alvin A. Arens and James K. Loebbecke), published by Prentice Hall Canada, Inc. He has co-authored a monograph published by the Canadian Academic Accounting Association, and has published articles in *CAMagazine*, *Contemporary Accounting Research*, and other professional and academic publications. He has received scholarships, fellowships and research grants from the Canadian Academic Accounting Association, Peat Marwick, and Ernst and Whinney.

Johan P. de Rooy is a lecturer with the Accounting Division of the Faculty of Commerce and Business Administration, University of British Columbia. He earned his B.Ed. from the University of British Columbia and his M.B.A. from Queen's University. He is both a Chartered Accountant and a Certified Management Accountant.

Mr. de Rooy is an active educator in all three professional accounting programs, having taught introductory and advanced levels of financial accounting, management accounting and auditing. He has been the national examiner for the CGA accounting theory course and the course co-author for the CGA introductory financial accounting course. Mr. de Rooy is the author of *The Uniform Final Examination, A Systematic Study Approach (Fourth Edition)*, published by Clarence Byrd Inc.

Mr. de Rooy has served on the governing council of the Chartered Accountants of British Columbia for five years and acted as chairperson for numerous provincial committees for this institute. Currently he is president-elect of the Canadian Cancer Society, B.C. and Yukon Division and sits on several provincial and national committees for the Canadian Cancer Society.

Preface

Management Accounting providers full introductory coverage of management accounting. In content and emphasis, instructors will find that the book is in the mainstream for courses in introductory accounting. This book focuses on the most widely used accounting theory and practice. This text and its supplements supply the most effective tools available for learning fundamental accounting concepts and procedures.

Clarity and Accuracy

Two themes have directed our writing of this text — *clarity* and *accuracy*. We believe that we have produced the clearest prose, learning objectives, exhibits, definitions, and assignment material for courses in principles of accounting. Students will find this book easy to study. We have assumed that students have no previous education in accounting or business.

The contributions of users of the first edition and their students and reviewers of this Canadian Second Edition have guided us in writing an accurate text. We and the publishers have sought input on our work from an unprecedented number of accounting educators and students in order to publish a book that meets your strict demands for accuracy.

This demand for accuracy did not stop with the test. The authors and publisher have taken extraordinary care and incurred extraordinary cost to ensure that the supplements are accurate.

The Business Context of Accounting

To enhance our presentation of accounting, we set out in the Canadian First Edition to create a business context for the student. As often as possible, we have integrated actual companies and their business data into our text narrative and assignment material. Students reading about companies familiar to them find the material interesting and also develop a deeper appreciation for accounting's importance in today's business world. When information drawn from real companies would be too advanced for introductory students, we illustrated the accounting point at hand by using realistic examples, building a framework of relevance that makes learning the topic more inviting to the students.

We have expanded on this approach in the Canadian Second Edition. Each chapter now opens with a description of an actual business situation. We call these vignettes, and most are drawn from the business press.

Distinctive Features of the Second Edition

Increased Assignment Material

Management Accounting, Canadian Second Edition, has increased assignment material. We have added more exercises and problems, which are now referenced to chapter learning objectives. In addition, chapters now conclude with a special feature called Extending Your Knowledge. This section includes two Decision Problems, an Ethical Issue case (new this edition), and two Financial Statement problems (double from the first edition).

Chapter-Opening Vignettes

Each chapter opens with an actual business situation. We found in the first edition that emphasis on the real-world environment of business promotes student interest and learning. Our new second-edition chapter-opening vignettes build on what we learned from the first edition.

Chapter Sequence

Management accounting chapters follow a logical order. Chapter 20 begins our study of management accounting by demonstrating how budgets are prepared. Chapter 21 intorduces a model of cost-volume-profit relationships, and important planning tool of managers. Our first two chapters on management accounting are confined to nonmanufacturing organizations. In this way, we can explore two major tools (budgets and the cost-volume-profit model) without contending with the many new terms associated with manufacturing organizations.

Chapters 22 and 23 describe manufacturing accounting systems. We discuss the value chain, cost drivers, and activity-based costing. Chapters 24, 25, and 26 pursue management accounting tools in more depth. We want students to recognize that management accounting applies ot all kinds of organizations, not just to manufacturing companies.

End-of-Book Appendices

Three appendices are presented at the end of the book:

Appendix A: Accounting for the Effects of Changing Prices
Appendix B: Present-Value and Future-Value Tables. This appendix complements the present-value coverage in Chapter 16.
Appendix C: The Financial Statements of the Schneider Corporation.

Chapter Organization _____

1. Each chapter begins with a vignette, as we have described. Learning objectives also appear at the start of every chapter. These objectives are keyed to the relevant chapter material and are also referenced to the exercises and problems.

2. Most chapters offer two Summary Problems for Your Review. Each Summary Problem includes its fully worked-out solution. These features, which generally appear at the halfway point and at the end of each chapter, provide students with immediate feedback and serve as key review aids.

3. Each chapter presents three important tools for student review. A text Summary recaps the chapter discussion. Self-Study Questions allow students to test their understanding of the chapter. The text that supports the answer is referenced by page number, and the answers appear at the end of the Extending Your

Knowledge section. Accounting Vocabulary presents the key terms introduced in the chapter, with page references. A full Glossary, keyed by page number, appears at the end of the book.

4. Assignment Material is more varied and plentiful than in completing texts. Questions (covering the major definitions, concepts, and procedures) may be assigned as homework or used to promote discussion in class. Exercises, identified by topic area and learning objectives, cover the full spectrum of the chapter text. Problems, also identified by topic area and learning objectives, come in A and B sets. The two sets allow instructors to vary assignments from term to term and to solve the A or B problem in class and assign the related problem for homework. Some exercises and problems can be solved using the Lotus R 1-2-3 templates.

5. Each chapter ends with an Extending Your Knowledge section. Under this heading are presented:

   * two Decision Problems, which help students to develop critical thinking skills. Analysis, interpretation, and determining a course of action are ordinarily required.

   * an Ethical Issue case, which presents a business scenario that challenges the ethical conduct of the accountant and asks the student to resolve the dilemma. many of these cases also challenge students' accounting skills.

   * two Financial Statement Problems (for most chapters). The first problem links the chapter's subject matter directly to the actual financial statements in the annual report of the Schneider Corporation which appears in Appendix C. Students answer the second financial statement problem using data taken from the annual report of another company.

The Supplements Package

We have a far-reaching package of teaching and learning tools to supplement the text. A team of contributors devoted hundreds of hours to perfecting the supplements. Our supplements coordinator, who is a professional accounting teacher, together with a full-time editor worked with the contributors to ensure maximum instructional value, accuracy, and consistency with the text and within the supplements package.

Resources for the Instructor

Instructor's Manual
Solutions Manual
Solutions Transparencies
Teaching Transparencies

Test Item File
Computerized Test Item File
Instructor's manuals to the Practice Sets

Resources for the Student

Study Guide with Demonstration Problems
Working Papers
Practice Sets

PHACTS Tutorial Videos
Lotus Templates

Acknowledgements to the Canadian Second Edition

I would like to thank Chuck Horngren and Tom Harrison for their encouragement and support.

Special thanks to Johan de Rooy for all his work. Thanks to Jack Hanna, University of Waterloo, for his help with the material in Appendix A on inflation accounting. Thanks also to Bob Beam, University of Waterloo and Van Hall, C.A. for their help with Chapter 11. Thanks to Carrie Mace, Julie Robson, and especially to Lynn Miske, for their work on the Solutions Manual. The work of Melanie E. Russell on the Test Item File and other supplements, and Don Rogazynski on the Working Papers is also appreciated.

I would also like to thank the following individuals for the invaluable assistance they provided in reviewing the text and supplements and for providing so many helpful suggestions:

Wayne A. Campbell, Seneca College
Ray Carrol, Mount St. Vincent University
Randy Dickson, Red Deer College
Janet E. Falk, Fraser Valley College
Harvey C. Freedman, Humber College
John Glendenning, Centennial College
Maureen Labonte, Algonquin College
Robert F. Madden, St. Francis Xavier
  University

Allen McQueen, Grant MacEwan
  Community College
Michael A. Perretta, Sheridan College
Gordon Rice, Mohawk College
Al Scherbluk, Ryerson Polytechnical
  Institute
Ralph H. Sweet, Durham College
Nora Wilson, Humber College
Leroy Wright, Fanshawe College

Many people gave very useful feedback on the first edition, including Sylvia Brown, Ian Wells, and the accounting faculty of Fanshawe College, members of the accounting faculty of Conestoga College, and the many focus group participants.

Thanks are extended to Douglas Dodds, Schneider Corporation, for permission to use the Schneider Corporation annual report. Thanks are also due to John Labatt Limited and National Trust for permission to use as exhibits a bond and a stock certificate, respectively issued by their companies.

Publications from the Canadian Institute of Chartered Accountants, the Butterworths series on Financial Statement Presentation prepared by the partners of Price Waterhouse and edited by Christina Drummond, *The Financial Post*, *The Globe and Mail*, and financial statements issued by a large number of Canadian companies have been very helpful in the writing of this book.

I would like especially to acknowledge the people of Prentice Hall Canada, especially the editorial work of David Jolliffe and the support of Yolanda de Rooy and Suzanne Tyson over the past months as the Canadian Edition took shape. I would also like to acknowledge the editorial support of Amy Lui-Ma, Dawn du Quesnay, Maryrose O'Neill and Marta Tomins. And I would like to thank Lu Mitchell, who was there at the start.

This book is dedicated to Margie, whose life and spirit have been my inspiration.
W. Morley Lemon
Waterloo, Ontario
1993

Chapter 20

Introduction to Management Accounting:
The Master Budget

SMI Industries Canada Ltd., a Quebec City manufacturer of runway sweepers and snow-removal equipment, is a classic example of all that can go wrong if proper management accounting practices are not completed. SMI's sales revenues were $7 million in 1987, $8 million by 1989, and almost $10 million in 1990. But in March, 1991, the company filed for bankruptcy. What went wrong? Well, it was certainly not the absence of sales.

It all started in 1987 when Eddy Bedard, president and majority shareholder of SMI Industries, committed SMI to a one-year, $2 million project to develop a new, all-season, road-clearing sweeper. Undercapitalized with insufficient financing, $2 million over budget, and three years behind schedule, the company eventually fell victim to its owner's grand designs. Inventory swelled, reducing the turnover to four times a year and consuming all the company's available cash flow. Parts for the new sweeper started arriving, but production had not begun. Finally, the bank refused to increase SMI's loan, and it was all over.

What is the lesson? As Chapter 20 states, two of the cornerstones of a successful business are *planning* and *control*. The best and most important example of this is a realistic and comprehensive master budget, something that SMI obviously did not prepare in 1987 and 1988. This budget provides management with critical insights into what it is doing, and where it is going. When actual results differ significantly from the master budget, management should investigate the matter. If the variance is favorable, an opportunity to out-perform the plan may be present; if unfavorable, then there is time to correct the problem before the matter gets out of control. In any case, it means the chance to affect change on a timely basis, which is one of the hallmarks of good management.

In August, 1991, Eddy Bedard and a group of Montreal investors put in a bid to buy some of the assets of SMI from the trustee. You can be sure that this time a carefully considered master budget and business plan have been prepared!

Source: Catherine Callaghan, "Inventory Avalanche Buries Snowblower Maker," *Profit* (September 1991), p. 22.

LEARNING OBJECTIVES

After studying this chapter, you should be able to

1 Use a performance report

2 Budget the components of the income statement

3 Prepare a budgeted income statement

4 Prepare a cash budget

5 Prepare a budgeted balance sheet

6 Use a continuous budget

Our study of accounting has so far focused on gathering, processing, and reporting information for decision-makers outside the business. Some of these outside parties are investors, creditors, and government agencies. Thus far we have looked through their eyes at a business's past performance and financial position. The income statement tells users the results of the company's operations. The statement of changes in financial position reports where cash came from and how it was spent. The balance sheet shows the company's current financial position. Accounting designed to report to parties external to the business is called financial accounting.

We now shift our focus. We turn to a discussion of how accounting information helps shape the business's future, and we do this through the eyes of the people who run the business. The decision-makers inside the company are called managers, and accounting designed to meet their information needs is called management accounting. Exhibit 20-1 summarizes the distinctions between management accounting and financial accounting.

Chapter 20 begins our study of management accounting by showing how budgets are prepared. We deal with the familiar financial statements: income statements and balance sheets. However, our statements will compile planned figures, not past figures, and we will evaluate performance by comparing actual results with budgeted amounts.

Chapter 21 introduces a model of cost-volume-profit relationships, a favorite planning tool of managers. Our first two chapters on management accounting are confined to nonmanufacturing organizations. In this way, we can explore two major tools (budgets and the cost-volume-profit model) without contending with the many new terms associated with manufacturing organizations. The latter appear in Chapters 22 and 23, which describe manufacturing accounting systems. Then Chapters 24, 25, and 26 pursue management accounting tools in more depth. Chapter 24 extends the coverage of budgeting to flexible budgets and standard costs. Chapter 25 covers responsibility accounting, and Chapter 26 shows how to use accounting information to make some special decisions. Above all, recognize that management accounting applies to all kinds of organizations, not just manufacturing companies.

Two Themes in Management Accounting

Two themes of management accounting are (1) the cost-benefit criterion, and (2) behavioral implications. The cost-benefit criterion is a means for choosing among alternative accounting systems or methods — how well they help achieve management goals in relation to their costs. We use this common-sense technique every day. For example, suppose you are asked whether you want cheese on your hamburger for an extra 25 cents. You weigh the benefit of adding the cheese against the cost. If the benefit exceeds the cost, you order cheese. If the benefit is less than 25 cents, you forgo the cheese.

EXHIBIT 20-1 *Distinctions between Management and Financial Accounting*

	Management Accounting	Financial Accounting
1. Primary users	Managers of the business	Outside parties (investors, creditors, and regulators) and managers of the business
2. Decision criterion	Comparison of costs and benefits of proposed action	Comparison of accounts with generally accepted accounting principles (GAAP)
3. Behavioral implications	Concern about how reports will affect employee behavior	Concern about adequacy of disclosure. Behavioral implications are secondary.
4. Time focus	Future orientation: e.g. 19X3 **budget** versus 19X3 **actual** performance	Past orientation: e.g., 19X3 **actual** versus 19X2 **actual** performance
5. Reports	Detailed reports on parts of the entity: products, departments, territories	Summary reports primarily on the entity as a whole

A business application of the cost-benefit criterion is the installation of a budgeting system. A major benefit is to compel managers to plan and thus make different decisions than would have occurred from using only a historical system. Is an accounting system a good buy? The answer depends on managers' weighing perceived benefits against additional costs.

The behavioral implications of a course of action are also critical. Managers consider the effect of the action on people's behavior. Suppose the company in our example tries to increase sales by pressuring its sales staff to meet quotas. If a salesperson fails to meet quota for three consecutive months, he or she is fired. Depending on the personalities of the people involved, such a policy may lead to increased sales. But it may also create fear and cause a decline in sales. Effective management accounting systems apply the cost-benefit criterion in light of the behavioral implications of a proposed action.

The Role of Management

How do managers use accounting information? Managers determine the company's goals, and then plan and control its operations to reach those goals. They set long-range targets by asking questions such as: What will the company's total assets be in five years? By how much can the business increase sales over the next ten years? Should the company spend $5 million on research to develop a new product line? Will it be profitable to enter the Alberta-Saskatchewan-Manitoba market? The most successful executives are able to consider a wide range of possible courses of action for their company. They answer these types of long-range questions by developing concrete plans of action.

Business must operate day by day also. Managers set short-range targets and communicate these goals to subordinates. To increase profits, a business may have to increase production to 35,000 units next month. Similarly, cash inflow from operations may have to be $600,000 during December. Short-range goals like these must fit within the company's long-range strategy.

What features must an accounting system have to best meet management's information needs? What data help managers plan and control business operations? How are decisions made by managers? This chapter and the next several answer these questions. We begin our discussion of management accounting by studying one of a manager's most valuable accounting tools: the budget.

The Budgeting System

A well-designed budgeting system includes the budget, the budget committee, and the budget period.

The Budget

The **budget** is management's quantitative expressions of a plan of action and an aid to coordination and implementation. Budgets include quantities of products that are to be sold and their expected selling prices, the numbers of employees and their pay, and a host of other amounts that are ultimately expressed in dollars. The budget summarizes the planning decisions of the business. A company may use a single budget to control all its operations or a separate budget for each subunit. This choice depends on the plans of the particular company's management. Our discussion will center on a company that uses an overall **master budget** to guide its operations. The master budget includes the major financial statements and supporting schedules.

The Budget Committee

In many small businesses, the budgeting process is rather informal, with the owner and the employees deciding on goals for the future. In most medium-size-to-large organizations the **budget committee** oversees the preparation of the master budget. Because the master budget is the overall financial plan for the entire company, the budget committee includes representatives from all departments. Working together, they develop budget estimates "from the bottom up." Employees at the lowest level provide budget estimates to their supervisors, who make adjustments and forward the budget to middle managers, and so on up the line. For example, the vice-president of sales has each salesperson set a goal for the next period. The vice-president considers the goals of each salesperson and prepares an overall budget for the sales department. With sales personnel at all levels participating in the budget process, they are likely to work harder to achieve the budget than if it is handed down by top management. All other departments likewise collect budget information and forward it to the budget committee.

The committee coordinates the budget for the company as a whole. Without this coordination, the cost-of-goods-sold budget or the operating expense budget may be out of line with the sales budget, and vice versa.

Although top management has the final say in establishing the budget, it is best when many employees contribute to the overall process. An ideal budget results in all employees striving for excellence by trying to meet a clear-cut, coordinated set of goals.

The Budget Period

Budgets may cover any period. Many companies use monthly, weekly, and daily cash budgets to ensure that they have enough cash on hand to meet immediate needs. Sales and expense budgets usually cover the accounting period, which may be a month, a quarter, or a year. Aligning the budget period with the accounting period makes the comparison of budgeted amounts and actual amounts easy. Most long-range budgets cover a five-year period. However, spans of 2, 3, or even 10 years are used.

Benefits of a Budget

The budgeting process offers these advantages:

1. *Provides direction.* The budgeting system forces managers to set realistic goals for the future. Without a formal plan, managers lack direction. This lack of planning filters throughout the company. The budget guides managers and department employees toward the achievement of specific goals. We all work better with a goal in mind.

2. *Motivates employees.* The budget motivates employees at all levels to meet the business's goals. Their work in preparing the budget makes it their personal target. This motivational aspect of budgeting underscores how budgeting affects employee behavior. Budgets can have negative effects on employee morale if used improperly. For example, some top managers simply impose the budget on their employees and hold employees responsible for its achievement. In this case, the budgeting system may demoralize workers and actually result in lower, rather than higher, profits.

3. *Coordinates activities.* The budget coordinates the activities of the entire organization. Coordination is crucial because the budget for one department affects other departments. For example, the company may need to sell 50,000 units to earn its target net income. But the manufacturing plant may be able to produce only 40,000 units. The budget thus helps top managers identify the need to expand the plant by purchasing additional equipment. Or, the company may decide to increase prices in the short run, as a way of moderating demand and taking advantage of the temporary capacity constraint. In turn, managers may identify the need for additional sales personnel, office workers, delivery vehicles, and so on.

4. *Helps performance evaluation.* A budgeting system aids performance evaluation. The comparison of budgeted and actual amounts highlights areas that are performing according to plan, areas that need improvement, or areas that are outperforming the plan and deserve acknowledgment. An actual cost of goods sold that is in excess of the budgeted amount may lead the business to start buying from a new supplier, or it may lead top management to speak to the purchasing manager responsible for paying too high a price for inventory. Without the budget, the top management may not even know the company is spending too much on inventory.

   Exhibit 20-2 diagrams how managers use budgeting. Management planning (see the upper left corner of the exhibit) results in the budget. During the period, the business takes action by engaging in transactions — buying and selling. These transactions produce source documents, accounting records and, in turn, performance reports. The performance reports are evaluated by managers whose feedback helps control the organization. Managers then make new plans. Thus begins a new cycle of management planning and control.

EXHIBIT 20-2 *Management Use of Budgeting and Accounting*

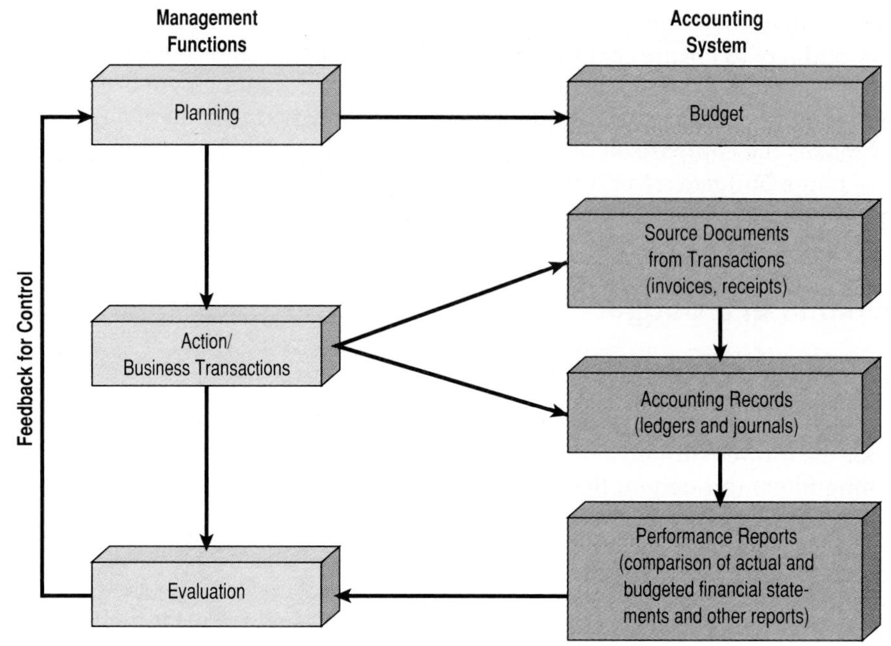

The Performance Report

The comparison of budgeted goals to actual results is a key element in evaluating operations, identifying the need for corrective action, and preparing next period's budget. This point deserves a closer look. The performance report in Exhibit 20-3 serves as the basis for our discussion.

Actual 19X7 sales in Exhibit 20-3 were $550,000, which is $50,000 less than budgeted sales. The low sales level reduced actual net income to half the budgeted amount. Top managers would ask what went wrong. The vice-president of sales would have to explain why sales revenue was so far below the budgeted goal. The vice-president, in turn, would meet with the sales staff to learn why they failed to meet the budget. At least one of two problems exists in this example: (1) the budget was unrealistic, or (2) the business did a poor job of selling during the period. Of course, both of these factors may have contributed to the poor results.

Managers also use performance reports like this one to identify corrective action. The sales department did not perform well, and management must decide what to do about it. Perhaps the sales manager should be replaced. Or the problem may be due to our selling an inferior product. In any event, should budgeted sales be lowered for the next period? The answers to these questions will affect next period's budget. This example illustrates how managers use a budget to plan operations and to control the company in its drive for success.

EXHIBIT 20-3 *Summarized Income Statement Performance Report for 19X7 — Used for Control by Management*

	Actual	Budget	Actual – Budget
Sales revenue	$550,000	$600,000	($50,000)
Total expenses	510,000	520,000	(10,000)
Net income	$40,000	$ 80,000	($40,000)

Whereas both of these examples of using budgets for performance evaluation are negative or punitive in nature, budgets can also be used to isolate exceptional or outstanding performance. When an employee achieves results which favorably exceed the budget, performance reports allow the manager to identify these achievements, and reward or acknowledge the employee. Further, such exceptional results may indicate opportunities for the corporation to increase profitability, if it takes advantage of the situation promptly.

Components of the Master Budget

The master budget includes the operating budget, capital expenditures budget, and financial budget. The **operating budget** sets the target revenues and expenses — and thus net income —for the period. The **capital expenditures budget** presents the company's plan for purchases of property, plant and equipment, and other assets that management uses to produce revenues over the long term. The **financial budget** projects the means of raising money from shareholders and creditors, and plans cash management. This chapter discusses components of the operating budget and financial budget. Chapter 26 covers budgeting for capital expenditures.

We summarize the components of the master budget as follows:

A. Operating budget
    1. Sales or revenue budget
    2. Purchases, cost of goods sold, and inventory budget
    3. Operating expense budget
    4. Budgeted income statement

B. Capital expenditures budget

C. Financial budget
    1. Cash budget: statement of budgeted cash receipts and disbursements
    2. Budgeted balance sheet

The capstone of the operating budget is the budgeted income statement, which shows target revenues, expenses, and net income for the period. The financial budget results in the budgeted balance sheet, which gives budgeted amounts for each asset, liability, and owner equity. The budgeted financial statements look exactly like ordinary statements. The only difference is that they list budgeted rather than actual figures.

Exhibit 20-4 diagrams the various sections of the master budget for a nonmanufacturing company, like Zellers, Loblaws, or a wholesaler of auto parts. In addition to the components of the master budget in the preceding list, the diagram includes ending inventory, which is directly related to sales, purchases, and cost of goods sold. Without a budget for inventory, the company could accidentally end the period with too much or too little inventory, and either event would be unwelcome. Too much inventory is expensive to keep in stock, and too little inventory risks losing a customer who needs the goods immediately.

Sales — the cornerstone of the master budget — is usually budgeted first because inventory levels, purchases, cost of goods sold, and operating expenses depend on sales activity. Sales revenue is the major measure of business activity. After sales and expenses are projected, the budgeted income statement can be prepared.

The capital expenditures budget, income statement, and plans for raising cash and paying debts provide information for the cash budget, which feeds into the budgeted balance sheet. Preparing the budgeted balance sheet is usually the last step in the process. We use Exhibit 20-4 as the framework for the remainder of the chapter.

EXHIBIT 20-4 *Master Budget for a Nonmanufacturing Company*

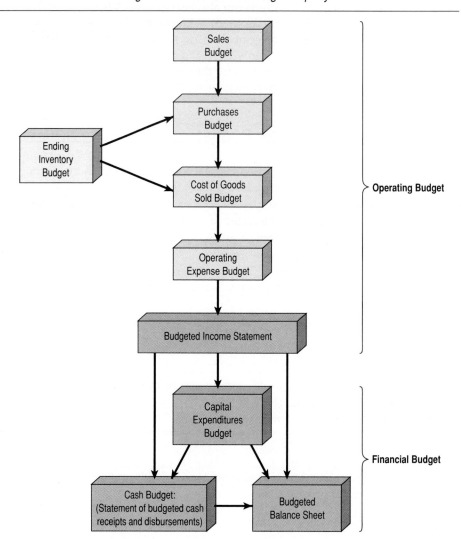

Preparing the Master Budget

To learn how to apply the concepts and methods of budgeting, you should prepare a master budget. The following problem and solutions provide an illustration of the budgeting process.

Facts for Illustration

1. Suppose you manage Whitewater Sporting Goods Ltd. store number 18, which carries a complete line of canoeing, hiking, and other outdoor recreation gear. You know the merchandising aspect of the business, but little about accounting and finance. Top management wants your input in the budgeting process. You are to prepare the master budget for your store for April, May, June, and July, the main selling season for these sporting goods. The division manager and assistant controller (head of the accounting department) of the company will be here from headquarters tomorrow to review the budget with you.

2. Cash collections follow sales because the company sells on account. When extra cash is needed, the company borrows on six-month instalment notes payable.

3. The balance sheet of your store at March 31, 19X5, beginning of the budget period, follows:

Whitewater Sporting Goods Ltd. Store No. 18
Balance Sheet
March 31, 19X5

Assets		Liabilities	
Current assets		Current liabilities	
Cash	$15,000	Accounts payable.............	$ 16,800
Accounts receivable,		Wages and com-	
net	16,000	missions payable	4,250
Inventory..........................	48,000	Total liabilities.......................	21,050
Prepaid insurance............	1,800		
	80,800		
Capital assets		**Owners' Equity**	
Equipment and		Owners' equity	78,950
fixtures	32,000		
Accumulated			
depreciation.................	(12,800)		
	19,200	Total liabilities	
Total assets............................	$100,000	and owners' equity..........	$100,000

---

4. Sales in March were $40,000. Monthly sales are projected by salespersons as follows:

April..	$50,000
May	80,000
June	60,000
July	50,000
August	40,000

Sales are 60 percent cash and 40 percent on credit. All accounts receivable amounts are collected in the month following sale. The $16,000 of accounts receivable at March 31 arose from credit sales made in March (40 percent of $40,000). Uncollectible accounts are insignificant, so you can ignore them.

5. Whitewater wishes to maintain inventory equal to $20,000 plus 80 percent of the budgeted cost of goods sold for the following month. (All these percentages are drawn from the business's past experience.) Cost of goods sold averages 70 percent of sales. These data explain why the inventory on March 31 is $48,000, computed as follows:

March 31
inventory = $20,000 + .80 × (.70 × **April sales of $50,000**)
= $20,000 + (.80 × $35,000)
= $20,000 + $28,000
= $48,000

Whitewater pays for inventory as follows: 50 percent during the month of purchase and 50 percent during the next month. Accounts payable consist of inventory purchases only.

6. Monthly payroll consists of two parts: fixed wages of $2,500 plus sales commissions equal to 15 percent of sales. The company pays half of this amount during the month and half early in the following month. Therefore, at the end of each month, Whitewater reports wages and commissions payable equal to half

the month's payroll. This is why the $4,250 liability appears on the March 31 balance sheet — half the March payroll of $8,500.

$$\text{March payroll} = \text{Fixed wages of \$2,500} + \text{Sales commissions of \$6,000 (.15} \times \text{\$40,000)}$$
$$= \$8,500$$

$$\text{March 31 wages and commissions payable} = .50 \times \$8,500$$
$$= \$4,250$$

7. Other monthly expenses are

Rent expense	$2,000, paid as incurred
Depreciation expense,	
including truck	500
Insurance expense	200, expiration of prepaid amount
Miscellaneous expense	5 % of sales, paid as incurred

8. A used delivery truck will be purchased in April for $3,000 cash.

9. The company wishes to maintain a minimum cash balance of $10,000 at the end of each month. If necessary, the business can borrow the money on notes payable of $1,000 each at an annual interest rate of 12 percent. Management borrows no more money than the amount needed to maintain the $10,000 minimum cash balance. Notes payable require six equal monthly payments consisting of principal plus monthly interest on the entire unpaid principal. Borrowing and all principal and interest payments occur at the end of the month.

10. Income taxes are the responsibility of corporate headquarters, so you can ignore tax for budgeting purposes.

Assume you have studied the company guidelines on how to prepare a budget. The directions instruct you to prepare the following detailed schedules:

Schedule

A   Sales budget
B   Purchases, cost of goods sold, and inventory budget
C   Operating expense budget
D   Budgeted cash collections from customers
E   Budgeted cash disbursements for purchases
F   Budgeted cash disbursements for operating expenses

After compiling the schedules, you must prepare the following statements:

Exhibit

20-5   Budgeted income statement for the four months ended July 31, 19X5
20-6   Statement of budgeted cash receipts and disbursements by month for the four months ended July 31, 19X5
20-7   Budgeted balance sheet at July 31, 19X5

Preparing the Operating Budget

OBJECTIVE 2

Budget the components of the income statement

As you work through the preparation of this budget, keep in mind that you are developing the company's operating and financial plan for the next four months. The steps in this process may seem mechanical, but remember that budgeting stimulates thoughts about pricing, product lines, job assignments, needs for additional equipment, and negotiations of loans with banks. Preparation of the bud-

EXHIBIT 20-5 Budgeted Income Statement

OBJECTIVE 3

Prepare a budgeted income statement

Whitewater Sporting Goods Ltd. Store No. 18
Budgeted Income Statement
Four months ending July 31, 19X5

	Amount	Source
Sales...	$240,000	Schedule A
Cost of goods sold.................................	168,000	Schedule B
Gross margin..	72,000	
Operating expenses		
Wages and commissions................. $46,000		Schedule C
Rent...................................... 8,000		
Depreciation 2,000		
Insurance............................... 800		
Miscellaneous......................... 12,000	68,800	
Income from operations......................	3,200	
Interest expense...................................	225	Exhibit 20-6
Net income...	$ 2,975	

get leads to decisions that affect the future course of the business. The operating budget — consisting of the sales budget, purchases, cost of goods sold, inventory budget, and operating expense budget — results in the budgeted income statement.

Preparing the Budgeted Income Statement   Step 1. Sales — Schedule A is the start of the budget effort. The budgeted sales amount for each product is determined by multiplying its sale price by the predicted unit sales. The overall sales budget is the sum of the budgets for individual products. Trace the April–July total sales, $240,000, to the budgeted income statement in Exhibit 20-5.

Schedule A: Sales Budget
(Fact 4, p. 895)

	April	May	June	July	April–July Total
Cash sales, 60%	$30,000	$48,000	$36,000	$30,000	
Credit sales, 40%	20,000	32,000	24,000	20,000	
Total sales, 100%	$50,000	$80,000	$60,000	$50,000	$240,000

Step 2. After budgeting sales, prepare the purchases, cost of goods sold, and inventory budget, which is Schedule B. This schedule determines cost of goods sold for the budgeted income statement, ending inventory for the budgeted balance sheet, and purchases for the cash budget. The relationship among these items is given by the cost-of-goods-sold computation:

Beginning Inventory + Purchases – Ending Inventory = Cost of Goods Sold

Beginning inventory is known, budgeted cost of goods is a fixed percentage of sales, and budgeted ending inventory is a specified amount. Therefore, you must solve for the budgeted purchases figure. By moving beginning inventory and ending inventory to the right side of the equation, isolate Purchases on the left side.

Purchases = Cost of Goods Sold + Ending Inventory – Beginning Inventory

Since Schedule B is a forecast, you cannot know the actual ending inventory amount. You must include the desired ending inventory figure in the computation of projected purchases.

To solidify your understanding of how this information fits into the master budget, trace the total budgeted cost of goods sold ($168,000) to the income statement in Exhibit 20-5. We will be using the budgeted inventory and purchases amounts later.

Schedule B: Purchases, Cost of Goods Sold, and Inventory Budget
(Fact 5, p. 895)

	April	May	June	July	April–July Total
Cost of goods sold (.70 × sales, from Schedule A).............	$35,000	$56,000	$42,000	$35,000	$168,000
+ Desired ending inventory ($20,000 + .80 × Cost of goods sold for next month).	64,800 *	53,600	48,000	42,400 ***	
= Total needs....................	99,800	109,600	90,000	77,400	
– Beginning inventory.....	(48,000)**	(64,800)	(53,600)	(48,000)	
= Purchases......................	$51,800	$44,800	$36,400	$29,400	

---

* 20,000 + (.80 x $56,000) = $64,800
** Balance at March 31 (Fact 3, p. 895)
*** Assumed for illustrative purposes

Step 3. Some budgeted operating expenses, like sales commissions and delivery expenses, fluctuate and thus vary with changing sales. Other expenses, like rent, depreciation, and insurance, are the same each month (fixed) and do not vary with sales. Schedule C is the operating expense budget.

Trace the April–July totals (wages and commissions of $46,000, rent of $8,000, and so on) to the budgeted income statement in Exhibit 20-5.

Step 4. Steps 1 through 3 provide the information to determine income from operations on the budgeted income statement in Exhibit 20-5. (We explain computation of the interest expense as part of the cash budget.)

Preparing the Financial Budget

The second major section of the master budget is the financial budget, which consists of the budgeted statement of cash receipts and disbursements (cash budget) and the budgeted balance sheet.

Preparing the Cash Budget (Statement of Budgeted Cash Receipts and Disbursements)

The **cash budget**, or **statement of budgeted cash receipts and disbursements**, details how the business intends to go from the beginning cash balance to the desired ending balance. Cash receipts and disbursements depend in part on revenues and expenses, which appear in the budgeted income statement. The cash budget, then, is usually prepared after the budgeted income statement.

The cash budget has the following major parts: cash collections from customers (Schedule D), cash disbursements for purchases (Schedule E), cash disbursements for operating expenses (Schedule F), and capital expenditures.

Schedule C: Operating Expenses Budget
(Facts 6 and 7, pp. 895–896)

	April	May	June	July	April–July Total
Wages, fixed amount...	$ 2,500	$ 2,500	$ 2,500	$ 2,500	
Commission, 15% of sales from Schedule A	7,500	12,000	9,000	7,500	
Total wages and commissions	10,000	14,500	11,500	10,000	$46,000
Rent, fixed amount..	2,000	2,000	2,000	2,000	8,000
Depreciation, fixed amount	500	500	500	500	2,000
Insurance, fixed amount...	200	200	200	200	800
Miscellaneous, 5% of sales	2,500	4,000	3,000	2,500	12,000
Total operating expenses..	$15,200	$21,200	$17,200	$15,200	$68,800

Schedule D: Budgeted Cash Collections from Customers

	April	May	June	July
Cash sales from Schedule A..	$30,000	$48,000	$36,000	$30,000
Collection of last month's credit sales from Schedule A (Fact 4, p. 895)...	16,000*	20,000	32,000	24,000
Total collections..	$46,000	$68,000	$68,000	$54,000

*March 31 accounts receivable

Schedule E: Budgeted Cash Disbursements for Purchases

	April	May	June	July
50% of last month's purchases, from Schedule B.........................	$16,800*	$25,900	$22,400	$18,200
50% of this month's purchases, from Schedule B	25,900	22,400	18,200	14,700
Total disbursements for purchases...	$42,700	$48,300	$40,600	$32,900

*March 31 accounts payable

Schedule F: Budgeted Cash Disbursements for Operating Expenses

	April	May	June	July
Expense amounts from Schedule C				
Wages and commissions				
50% of last month's expenses from Schedule C (Fact 6, pp. 895–896)...	$ 4,250*	$ 5,000	$ 7,250	$ 5,750
50% of this month's expenses from Schedule C	5,000	7,250	5,750	5,000
Total wages and commissions..	9,250	12,250	13,000	10,750
Rent (Fact 7, p. 896)	2,000	2,000	2,000	2,000
Miscellaneous (5% of sales, Schedule C)..................................	2,500	4,000	3,000	2,500
Total disbursements for operating expenses.............................	$13,750	$18,250	$18,000	$15,250

*March 31 wages and commissions payable

EXHIBIT 20-6 *Cash Budget*

Whitewater Sporting Goods Ltd. Store No. 18
Statement of Budgeted Cash Receipts and Disbursements
Four months ending July 31, 19X5

		April	May	June	July
	Beginning cash balance..	$15,000	$10,550	$10,410	$18,235
	Cash receipts, collections from customers				
	(Schedule D)	46,000	68,000	68,000	54,000
	Cash available before financing	$61,000	$78,550	$78,410	$72,235
	Cash disbursements				
	Purchase of inventory (Schedule E).........................	$42,700	$48,300	$40,600	$32,900
	Operating expenses (Schedule F).............................	13,750	18,250	18,000	15,250
	Purchase of truck (Fact 8, pp. 896).........................	3,000	—	—	—
	Total disbursements	59,450	66,550	58,600	48,150
(1)	Ending cash balance before financing...........................	1,550	12,000	19,810	24,085
	Minimum cash balance desired.......................................	10,000	10,000	10,000	10,000
	Cash excess (deficiency)	$(8,450)	$2,000	$9,810	$14,085
	Financing of cash deficiency (See notes b – d below)				
	Borrowing (at end of month)	$9,000			
	Principal payments (at end of month)......................		$(1,500)	$(1,500)	$(1,500)
	Interest expense (at 12% annually)...........................		(90)	(75)	(60)
(2)	Total effects of financing..	9,000	(1,590)	(1,575)	(1,560)
	Ending cash balance (1) + (2)...	$10,550	$10,410	$18,235	$22,525

Notes: a. Insurance expense is the expiration of prepaid insurance, and depreciation is the expensing of the cost of a capital asset. Therefore, these expenses do not require cash outlays in the current accounting period.

b. Borrowing occurs in multiples of $1,000 and only for the amount needed to maintain a minimum cash balance of $10,000.

c. Monthly principal payments: $9,000/6 = $1,500.

d. Interest expense: May $9,000 \times (.12 \times \frac{1}{2}) = \$90$

                June $(\$9,000 - \$1,500) \times (.12 \times \frac{1}{2}) = \$75$

                July $(\$9,000 - \$1,500 - \$1,500) \times (.12 \times \frac{1}{2}) = \$60$

                Total $\$90 + \$75 + \$60 = \$225$

OBJECTIVE 4

Prepare a cash budget

The cash receipts and disbursements data in Schedules D, E, and F and the $3,000 capital expenditure to acquire the truck appear in the cash budget, Exhibit 20-6. Acquisitions of long-term assets like the truck are based on a decision process called capital budgeting. We cover this management tool in Chapter 26.

In preparing the cash budget (Exhibit 20-6), you must first determine the cash available before financing. (This amount is $61,000 for April.) Add total disbursements ($59,450) to the minimum desired cash balance ($10,000) to find the total cash needed during April ($69,450). If cash available exceeds cash needed, an excess occurs. If cash needed is greater, a deficiency results. During April, you budget an $8,450 deficiency. The company then borrows $9,000 on a six-month note payable. (The loan exceeds the deficiency because Whitewater borrows in even $1,000 amounts.) Compute the budgeted cash balance at the end of each month by subtracting total disbursements from the cash available before financing and then adding the total projected effects of financing.[1] Exhibit 20-6 shows that Whitewater expects to end April with $10,550 of cash. The exhibit also shows the budgeted cash balance at the end of May, June, and July.

---

[1] In the case of loan payments, you will be adding a negative amount.

EXHIBIT 20-7 *Budgeted Balance Sheet*

Whitewater Sporting Goods Ltd. Store No. 18
Budgeted Balance Sheet
July 31, 19X5

Assets

Current assets

Cash (Exhibit 20-6)..	$ 22,525	
Accounts receivable, net (.40 x July sales of $50,000; Schedule A)	20,000	
Inventory (Schedule B)...	42,400	
Prepaid insurance (beginning balance of $1,800 – $800 for		
four months' expiration; Fact 7 on p. 896)...	1,000	$ 85,925

Capital assets

Equipment and fixtures (beginning balance of $32,000 + $3,000 truck		
acquisition; Fact 8 on p. 896)	35,000	
Accumulated depreciation (beginning balance of $12,800 + $500		
depreciation for each of four months; Fact 7 on p. 896)....................	(14,800)	20,200
Total assets		$106,125

Liabilities

Current liabilities

Short-term note payable ($9,000 – $4,500 paid back; Exhibit 20-6).....................	$ 4,500	
Accounts payable (.50 x July purchases of $29,400; Schedule B)	14,700	
Wages and commissions payable (.50 x July expense of $10,000;		
Schedule C)...	5,000	
Total liabilities		$ 24,200

Owners' Equity

Owners' equity (beginning balance of $78,950 + $2,975 net income;		
Exhibit 20-5)..		81,925
Total liabilities and owners' equity		$106,125

Interest expense for the four months totals $225 ($90 + $75 + $60). This item is listed on the budgeted income statement in Exhibit 20-5.

Preparing the Budgeted Balance Sheet   The final step in preparing the master budget is to complete the balance sheet. You project each asset, liability, and owner equity account based on the plans outlined in the previous schedules and exhibits. Exhibit 20-7 presents the budgeted balance sheet. If desired, you can prepare separate schedules to show the computations of accounts receivable, capital assets, and so on.

> **OBJECTIVE 5**
> Prepare a budgeted balance sheet

The master budget has now been completed. It consists of the budgeted financial statements and all supporting schedules.

Summary of Budgeting Procedures

The most important budget documents are the budgeted income statement (Exhibit 20-5), budgeted statement of cash receipts and disbursements (Exhibit 20-6), and budgeted balance sheet (Exhibit 20-7). Top management analyzes these statements to ensure that all the budgeted figures are consistent with company goals. As the business strives to reach these goals, management controls operations by comparing actual results with the forecasted performance (as shown in Exhibit 20-3, the performance report).

The Importance of Sales Forecasting _____

The Whitewater Sporting Goods Ltd. illustration began with the sales budget, which is the foundation of a master budget. Managers, under the direction of the top marketing executive, invest ample resources to forecast sales accurately. Factors considered in projecting sales include

1. *Patterns of past sales.* By learning from past sales activity, a company can fine tune its sales budget. This includes breaking sales down by product line, geographical region, and salesperson. The more detailed the budget, the more helpful it is likely to be.

2. *Predictions of marketing personnel.* These people are calling on customers on a regular basis, and can provide the most reliable, current information for forecasting sales. They conduct market research to learn which customers prefer certain products.

3. *Analysis of general and industry economic conditions.* In an economic recession, consumers usually delay expenditures on leisure-time products like Whitewater's sporting goods. What is the outlook for the economy next year?

4. *Strength of competitors.* A business must stay informed about what competitors are doing. For example, an effective advertising campaign by Chrysler Canada can lure customers away from Ford and General Motors, and decrease Ford and GM's profits. An effective budgeting effort must consider the activity of competitors.

5. *Future changes in prices.* Budgeted sales equal the budgeted quantity multiplied by the expected future selling price. Any changes in prices affect the sales budget.

6. *Development of new product lines and phasing out of old product lines.* The budget must include the sales of new products expected to be introduced and eliminate old products that will be phased out. This ensures that the budget is based on an up-to-date product line.

7. *Plans for advertising and sales promotion.* Advertising stimulates sales, so plans for upcoming promotional efforts will affect the budgeted level of sales.

The importance of the sales forecast is not limited to profit-seeking organizations. For example, the revenue forecast is critical to hospitals, churches and synagogues, universities, cities, and provinces. Unless these organizations budget revenues accurately, they risk spending too much and running out of money just like profit-seeking businesses. All types of organizations base their budgets on general economic and industry data plus information that is specific to the entity. An entire industry exists to provide economic forecasting data. All types of organizations subscribe to forecasting newsletters, primarily to aid their budgeting efforts.

Budgeting and Short-Term Financing _____

The cash budget in Exhibit 20-6 illustrates the usual pattern of **short-term, self-liquidating financing**. This term refers to debt incurred to buy inventories that will be sold on credit. Cash collections are used to pay the debt.

This diagram shows the financing plan budgeted in Exhibit 20-6. Whitewater had a temporary need for $9,000. The company borrowed this amount and paid it back from cash generated by operations.

Many companies have seasonal peaks of high sales volume and valleys of low activity. For example, retailers like Eaton's, The Bay, and Woodward's make most of their sales during November and December. June, July, and August are slow months. Companies use the slow months to stock up on inventory for the rush near the end of the year and to remodel stores and make repairs. By increasing a store's attractiveness and efficiency, the company can attract more customers and increase sales.

When monthly sales fluctuate seasonally, companies often borrow on short-term, self-liquidating loans. A cash budget can help managers avoid a cash shortage. By planning ahead, the manager can shop around for the best interest rate on a short-term loan. Then, if a cash shortage looms in some months, the company is prepared. A carefully mapped budget keeps the cash balance well matched to cash needs.

Continuous (Rolling) Budgets _____

A **continuous**, or **rolling**, **budget** systematically adds a month as the month just ended is deleted. This budget keeps managers thinking ahead, with a steady planning horizon. Suppose Whitewater Sporting Goods prepared the following six-month sales budget:

<table>
<tr><td></td><td>March</td><td>April</td><td>May</td><td>June</td><td>July</td><td>August</td></tr>
<tr><td>Budgeted sales............</td><td>$40,000</td><td>$50,000</td><td>$80,000</td><td>$60,000</td><td>$50,000</td><td>$40,000</td></tr>
</table>

> **OBJECTIVE 6**
> Use a continuous budget

The first budget covers March through August. Roll 1 deletes March and adds September; roll 2 then deletes April and adds October; and so on.

<table>
<tr><td>Roll 1</td><td>March</td><td>April</td><td>May</td><td>June</td><td>July</td><td>August</td><td>September</td><td>October</td></tr>
<tr><td>Budgeted sales............</td><td>—</td><td>$50,000</td><td>$80,000</td><td>$60,000</td><td>$50,000</td><td>$40,000</td><td>$25,000</td><td>—</td></tr>
<tr><td>Roll 2</td><td></td><td></td><td></td><td></td><td></td><td></td><td></td><td></td></tr>
<tr><td>Budgeted sales............</td><td>—</td><td>—</td><td>$80,000</td><td>$60,000</td><td>$50,000</td><td>$40,000</td><td>$25,000</td><td>$20,000</td></tr>
</table>

When managers desire, the sales budgets for individual months can be combined into quarterly or semiannual totals.

Budget Models, What-If Questions, and Computer Applications _____

The master budget models the entire organization's objectives, inputs and outputs. When we combine the budget's broad coverage with the speed and ease of computers, we have a powerful tool for management analysis, planning and control.

Many software programs allow preparation of the master budget on an electronic spreadsheet. The manager or the accountant can then ask "what-if" questions by changing any figure. What net income can we expect if we increase advertising by 20 percent? What will the cash balance be if we prepay the full cost of the advertising campaign at the beginning of the next period? When the accountant changes one amount, the computer prepares a new budget that includes all the effects of that change. Computers make possible this nearly instant analysis of changes in the company's forecast. Managers can then study the answers to these questions.

The spreadsheet that displays these changes to "what-if" questions may be linked to increasingly detailed subsets of information. For example, assume that General Motors Canada (GMC) wants to examine "what-if" questions regarding possible car sales for February. The results of this investigation lead to changes in GMC's net sales, required purchases, and projected cash receipts, not just for February but also for one or two subsequent months.

The first draft of a budget is seldom the final draft. Answers to what-if questions can provide revenue, expense, and income data on a wide range of possible sales levels. Managers can then respond to changes in the business with information rather than hunches. Suppose the budget, based on the best possible forecast, shows a poor year ahead. Managers can examine various patterns of sales and net income, and cash receipts and disbursements. They can study ways to cut costs and develop marketing strategies to increase demand for the company's products. The master budget may then be revised. Chapter 24 examines flexible budgets (those based on various levels of activity) in greater detail.

The computer's speed also enables managers to react promptly to new and unexpected situations as they arise. For example, some companies, whose operations depend on continuous supplies of raw materials, use computers to calculate the effect of strikes by suppliers so that adjustments can be made if the supply of a critical raw material is cut off by a strike. Without having to wait for monthly or quarterly financial statements, the company could begin reacting immediately. Computers and user-friendly software give these capabilities to many employees who are not expert computer programmers. Knowing what to expect is a result of a successful budgeting system.

Summary Problem for Your Review

Review the Whitewater Sporting Goods Ltd. illustration in the chapter. Suppose near the end of June you think that July sales might be $40,000 instead of the projected $50,000 in Schedule A, p. 897. You draw up a new budget to learn what effect the change in the sales amount will have on the store.

Required

1. Revise schedules A, B, and C. Prepare a revised budgeted income statement for the four months ended July 31, 19X5.
2. Revise schedules D, E, and F. Prepare a revised cash budget for July and a revised budgeted balance sheet at July 31, 19X5.

Note: You need not repeat the parts of the revised schedules that do not change.

SOLUTION TO REVIEW PROBLEM

Note: Although not required, this solution repeats the budgeted amounts for April, May, and June for completeness. Revised figures appear in bold-face for emphasis.

Requirement 1

Revised Schedule A: Sales Budget

	April	May	June	July	April–July Total
Cash sales, 60%	$30,000	$48,000	$36,000	**$24,000**	
Credit sales, 40%	20,000	32,000	24,000	**16,000**	
Total sales, 100%	$50,000	$80,000	$60,000	**$40,000**	**$230,000**

Revised Schedule B: Purchases, Cost of Goods Sold and Inventory Budget

	April	May	June	July	April–July Total
Cost of goods sold (.70 x sales from Revised Schedule A)	$35,000	$ 56,000	$ 42,000	**$28,000**	**$161,000**
+ Desired ending inventory ($20,000 + .80 × cost of goods sold for next month)	64,800	53,600	**42,400**	42,400	
= Total needs	99,800	109,600	84,400	**70,400**	
– Beginning inventory	(48,000)	(64,800)	(53,600)	**(42,400)**	
= Purchases	$51,800	$44,800	**$30,800**	**$28,000**	

Revised Schedule C: Operating Expenses Budget

	April	May	June	July	April–July Total
Wages, fixed amount	$ 2,500	$ 2,500	$ 2,500	**$ 2,500**	
Commission, 15% of sales from Revised Schedule A	7,500	12,000	9,000	**6,000**	
Total wages and commissions	10,000	14,500	11,500	**8,500**	**$44,500**
Rent, fixed amount	2,000	2,000	2,000	2,000	8,000
Depreciation, fixed amount	500	500	500	500	2,000
Insurance, fixed amount	200	200	200	200	800
Miscellaneous, 5% of sales	2,500	4,000	3,000	**2,000**	**11,500**
Total operating expenses	$15,200	$21,200	$17,200	**$13,200**	**$66,800**

REVISED EXHIBIT 20-5 *Budgeted Income Statement*

Whitewater Sporting Goods Ltd. Store No. 18
Budgeted Income Statement
Four months ending July 31, 19X5

	Amount		Source
Sales..		$230,000	Revised Schedule A
Cost of goods sold..		161,000	Revised Schedule B
Gross margin...		69,000	
Operating expenses			
Wages and commissions	$44,500		Revised Schedule C
Rent	8,000		Revised Schedule C
Depreciation...	2,000		Revised Schedule C
Insurance...	800		Revised Schedule C
Miscellaneous	11,500	66,800	Revised Schedule C
Income from operations		2,200	
Interest expense...		225	Revised Exhibit 20-6
Net income		$ 1,975	

Requirement 2

Revised Schedule D: Budgeted Cash Collections from Customers

	April	May	June	July
Cash sales from Revised Schedule A	$30,000	$48,000	$36,000	$24,000
Collection of last month's credit sales,				
from Revised Schedule A	16,000*	20,000	32,000	24,000
Total collections...	$46,000	$68,000	$68,000	$48,000

*Amounts assumed for illustration

Revised Schedule E: Budgeted Disbursements for Purchases

	April	May	June	July
50% of last month's purchases, from Revised Schedule B........	$16,800*	$25,900	$22,400	$15,400
50% of this month's purchases, from Revised Schedule B........	25,900	22,400	15,400	14,000
Total disbursements for purchases..	$42,700	$48,300	$37,800	$29,400

* Amounts assumed for illustration

Revised Schedule F: Budgeted Disbursements for Operating Expenses

	April	May	June	July
Expense amounts from Revised Schedule C:				
Wages and commissions				
50% of last month's expenses from Revised Schedule C..	$4,250*	5,000	$7,250	$5,750
50% of this month's expenses from Revised Schedule C..	5,000	7,250	5,750	4,250
Total wages and commissions	9,250	12,250	13,000	10,000
Rent	2,000	2,000	2,000	2,000
Miscellaneous	2,500	4,000	3,000	2,000
Total disbursements for operating expenses..........................	$13,750	$18,250	$18,000	$14,000

* March 31 wages and commissions payable

REVISED EXHIBIT 20-6 *Cash Budget*

Whitewater Sporting Goods Ltd. Store No. 18
Statement of Budgeted Cash Receipts and Disbursements
Four months ending July 31, 19X5

	April	May	June	July
Beginning cash balance	$15,000	$10,550	$10,410	**$21,035**
Cash receipts, collections from customers (Revised Schedule D)	46,000	68,000	68,000	**48,000**
Cash available before financing	$61,000	$78,550	$78,410	**$69,035**
Cash disbursements				
Purchases of inventory (Revised Schedule E)	$42,700	$48,300	**$37,800**	**$29,400**
Operating expenses (Revised Schedule F)	13,750	18,250	18,000	**14,000**
Purchase of truck	3,000	—	—	—
Total disbursements	59,450	66,550	**55,800**	**43,400**
(1) Ending cash balance before financing	1,550	12,000	**22,610**	25,635
Minimum cash balance desired	10,000	10,000	10,000	**10,000**
Cash excess (deficiency)	$(8,450)	$2,000	**$12,610**	**$15,635**
Financing of cash deficiency				
Borrowing (at end of month)	$9,000			
Principal payments (at end of month)		$(1,500)	$(1,500)	$(1,500)
Interest expense (at 12% annually)		(90)*	(75)*	**(60)***
(2) Total effects of financing	9,000	(1,590)	(1,575)	**(1,560)**
Ending cash balance (1)+(2)	$10,550	$10,410	$21,035	$24,075

* Interest expense: $90 + $75 + $60 = $225

REVISED EXHIBIT 20-7 *Budgeted Balance Sheet*

Whitewater Sporting Goods Ltd. Store No. 18
Budgeted Balance Sheet
July 31, 19X5

Assets

Current assets
Cash (Revised Exhibit 20-6) ... **$24,075**
Accounts receivable, net (.40 x July sales of $40,000; Revised Schedule A) ... **16,000**
Inventory (Revised Schedule B) ... 42,400
Prepaid insurance ... 1,000 $ 83,475
Capital assets
Equipment and fixtures ... 35,000
Accumulated depreciation ... (14,800)   20,200
Total assets ... $103,675

Liabilities

Current liabilities
Short-term note payable ... $ 4,500
Accounts payable (.50 x July purchases of **$28,000**; Revised Schedule B) ... **14,000**
Wages and commissions payable (.50 x July expense of $8,500; Revised Schedule C) ... 4,250
Total liabilities ... $22,750

Owners' Equity

Owners' equity (beginning balance of $78,950 + **$1,975** net income; Revised Exhibit 20-5) ... 80,925
Total liabilities and owners' equity ... $103,675

Summary

Management accounting helps managers plan and control the operations of their organizations. A major element of the management plan is the *budget*, which expresses the business's goals for earning income and for asset, liability, and owner equity position. The master budget consists of the budgeted financial statements and supporting schedules.

The budget forces managers to set specific goals for the future. Such goals provide direction for the organization and meaning to the work of individual employees. The budget coordinates the various activities of the organization and aids performance evaluation. Comparisons of budgeted and actual amounts reveal areas of the business that need improvement.

Many organizations have a *budget committee*, which includes representatives of all departments, to prepare the budget. The *budget period* usually coincides with the accounting period to ease the comparison of actual and budgeted amounts.

The components of the master budget that cover operations include *sales, purchases, cost of goods sold, inventory,* and *operating expenses*. These budgets are usually prepared in this order and are combined into the *budgeted income statement*. Sales comes first because most expenses, assets, and liabilities depend on sales volume. A second component of the master budget is the *capital expenditures budget*, which includes plans for purchasing long-term capital assets. The third main component is the financial budget, consisting of the *cash budget*, which is a statement of budgeted cash receipts and disbursements, and the *budgeted balance sheet*.

Many companies use *continuous*, or *rolling*, *budgets* that systematically add a future month as the month just ended is deleted. Continuous budgets keep managers thinking ahead with a steady planning horizon.

Computers and electronic spreadsheets are ideally suited for use in budgeting because they allow managers to answer what-if questions. Analyzing data over a wide range of outcomes enables managers to meet the challenges brought about by changes in the business.

Self-Study Questions

Test your understanding of the chapter by marking the best answer for each of the following questions:

1. The budget is *(p. 890)*
   a. A general, not specific, statement of the business's goals
   b. Not used by most successful businesses
   c. A major tool of financial rather than management, accounting
   d. None of the above

2. For the budget to be most effective, it should be prepared *(p. 890)*
   a. From the bottom up, with participation from employees at all levels
   b. From the top down, with managers developing goals based on their own experience
   c. Without reference to results obtained in past periods
   d. None of the above

3. Which of the following is not a benefit of a budgeting system? *(p. 891)*
   a. Coordinates activities
   b. Automatically fires lazy employees
   c. Aids performance evaluation
   d. Provides direction to the business

4. Chewning Corporation's actual revenues are $90,000 and expenses are $50,000. Budgeted revenues were $86,000 and budgeted expenses were $51,000. What is the relationship between actual net income and budgeted net income? *(p. 892)*
   a. Actual exceeds budget by $40,000   c. Actual exceeds budget by $5,000
   b. Budget exceeds actual by $35,000   d. Budget exceeds actual by $5,000

5. The master budget starts with *(p. 893)*
   a. Cash
   b. Owners' equity
   c. Sales
   d. Inventory

6. The operating budget ends with *(p. 893)*
   a. Budgeted sales
   b. The budgeted income statement
   c. The cash budget
   d. The budgeted balance sheet

7. The most complex single part of the master budget is preparation of *(pp. 898–900)*
   a. Budgeted sales
   b. The budgeted income statement
   c. The cash budget
   d. The budgeted balance sheet

8. The master budget usually ends with *(p. 901)*
   a. Budgeted sales
   b. The budgeted income statement
   c. The cash budget
   d. The budgeted balance sheet

9. A continuous (rolling) budget *(p. 903)*
   a. Adds a month and deletes the month just ended
   b. Keeps managers thinking ahead
   c. Maintains a steady planning horizon
   d. All of the above

10. Managers can use a computer along with a master budget to *(p. 903)*
    a. Develop strategies for dealing with a variety of possible situations
    b. Eliminate all the uncertainty of the business environment
    c. Prepare the budget correctly on the first attempt
    d. Set near-perfect goals for the company

Answers to the Self-Study Questions are at the end of the chapter.

Accounting Vocabulary

budget *(p. 890)*
budget committee *(p. 890)*
capital expenditures budget *(p. 893)*
cash budget *(p. 898)*

continuous budget *(p. 903)*
financial budget *(p. 893)*
master budget *(p. 890)*
operating budget *(p. 893)*
rolling budget *(p. 903)*

short-term, self-liquidating financing *(p. 902)*
statement of budgeted cash receipts and disbursements *(p. 898)*

ASSIGNMENT MATERIAL _____

Questions

1. How does management accounting differ from financial accounting?

2. Identify two types of goals set by managers.

3. Briefly discuss three components of a budgeting system.

4. What are four benefits of using a budgeting system?

5. Draw a diagram that shows how managers use a budgeting system.

6. How does a manager use a performance report?

7. List the components of a master budget.

8. A Jaguar dealer sets a goal of selling more Jaguar automobiles than any other dealer in the city. Does this goal represent a budget? Give your reason.

9. Turner Corporation installs a budgeting system in which the president sets all the goals for the company. The vice-president checks up on all 90 employees to

ensure that they are meeting top management's budget goals. What is the weakness in this budgeting system? How can the system be improved?

10. In most successful budgeting systems, who or what group in the organization prepares the budget? What makes this approach successful?

11. Why should the capital expenditures budget be prepared before the cash budget and the budgeted balance sheet?

12. How does a company budget inventory purchases? In your answer, show the relationships among purchases, cost of goods sold, and inventories.

13. What is the first step in preparing the master budget? Why does this step come first?

14. Outline the four steps in preparing an operating budget.

15. Identify the last item (prior to net income) to compute for the budgeted income statement. Where is this item computed initially, and why does it come last?

16. What is another name for the cash budget? Identify six subtotals or totals listed on the cash budget.

17. What is the last document to prepare for the master budget? Why does it come last?

18. Is sales forecasting important only to a profit-seeking business, or is it used by nonprofit organizations like hospitals and colleges? Give your reason.

19. Suppose you are the marketing vice-president of a company. What factors would you consider in forecasting the company's sales for the coming year?

20. Describe how short-term, self-liquidating financing works.

21. Tick-Tock Clocks Ltd. is a chain of specialty shops operating in resort areas. During some periods, the managers of the company's 42 stores budget for the coming quarter, and during other periods, they budget for the coming year. What type of budget should top management use to keep store managers looking ahead with a steady planning horizon? How does this budget work?

22. Why are computers and electronic spreadsheets well suited for budgeting?

Exercises

Exercise 20-1   *Preparing a performance report (L.O. 1)*

During August, Ogden Publishing Limited's actual revenues were $131,000 compared with budgeted revenues of $142,000. August operating expenses were $122,000 and budgeted expenses were $137,000. The company also incurred interest expense, a nonoperating expense, of $5,000, which was not included in the budget because it arose from unexpected borrowing.

Prepare a performance report for Ogden to show the differences between actual income and budgeted income for August. What caused August results to turn out as they did? Comment on results as measured by operating income.

Exercise 20-2   *Budgeting sales, cost of goods sold, and gross profit (L.O. 2)*

Melissa Mueller operates Twin Oaks Gift Shop. She expects cash sales of $3,000 for October and a $500 monthly increase during November and December. Credit card sales of $1,000 during October should be followed by 20 percent increases during November and December. Sales returns can be ignored. Credit card companies like VISA, MasterCard, and American Express charge 5 percent on credit-card sales, so Twin Oaks will net 95 percent. Cost of goods sold averages 60 percent of net sales.

Melissa asks you to prepare a schedule of budgeted sales, cost of goods sold, and gross profit for each month of the last quarter of 19X3. Also show totals for the quarter.

Exercise 20-3 *Budgeting purchases, cost of goods sold, and inventory* **(L.O. 2)**

The sales budget of Lancer International Ltd. for the nine months ended September 30 follows:

| | Quarter Ended | | | 9-Month |
	March 31	June 30	Sept. 30	Total
Cash sales, 30%	$27,000	$ 42,000	$ 31,500	$100,500
Credit sales, 70%	63,000	98,000	73,500	234,500
Total sales, 100%.............................	$90,000	$140,000	$105,000	$335,000

In the past, cost of goods sold has been 65 percent of total sales. The director of marketing, the production manager, and the financial vice-president agree that ending inventory should not go below $20,000 plus 10 percent of cost of goods sold for the following quarter. Lancer expects sales of $100,000 during the fourth quarter. The January 1 inventory was $22,000.

Required

Prepare a purchases, cost of goods sold, and inventory budget for each of the first three quarters of the year. Compute the cost of goods sold for the entire nine-month period. (Use Schedule B, p. 898, as a model.)

Exercise 20-4 *Identifying amounts of purchases, inventory, and cost of goods sold* **(L.O. 2)**

Compute the missing amount for each of the following independent situations:

	A	B	C	D	E
Beginning inventory	$14,000	$?	$ 24,800	$11,100	$?
Purchases..........................	?	86,200	?	45,300	77,900
Available..........................	73,000	118,800	103,100	?	?
Ending inventory	11,000	?	?	13,700	22,600
Cost of goods sold............	$?	$ 87,700	$ 69,300	$?	$70,000

Exercise 20-5 *Budgeting quarterly income for a year* **(L.O. 3)**

Century 21 is a nationwide real estate firm. Suppose a suburban Hamilton office of the firm projects that year 2 quarterly sales will increase by 3 percent in quarter one, 3 percent in quarter two, 5 percent in quarter three, and 5 percent in quarter four. Management expects total operating expenses to be 80 percent of revenues during each of the first two quarters, 82 percent of revenues during the third quarter, and 85 percent during the fourth. The office manager expects to borrow $100,000 on July 1, with quarterly principal payments of $10,000 beginning on September 30 and interest paid at the annual rate of 12 percent. Year 1 last quarter sales were $520,000.

Required

Prepare a budgeted income statement for each of the four quarters of year 2, and for the entire year. Present the year 2 budget as follows:

Quarter 1	Quarter 2	Quarter 3	Quarter 4	Full Year

Exercise 20-6 *Identifying amounts in a cash budget* **(L.O. 4)**

Dulock Sales Limited has completed its cash budget for May and June. The budget is presented with missing amounts identified by a question mark (?). Dulock's plan for eliminating any cash deficiency is to borrow the exact amount needed from its bank. The current annual interest rate is 12 percent. Dulock pays back all borrowed amounts within one month to the extent cash is available without going below the desired minimum balance.

Dulock Sales Limited
Cash Budget
May and June

	May	June
Beginning cash balance..	$10,900	$?
Cash collections from customers..	65,700	74,800
Sale of capital assets		900
Cash available before financing	$88,800	$?
Cash disbursements		
Purchases of inventory	$52,400	$41,100
Operating expenses..	31,900	30,500
Total disbursements	$84,300	$71,600
(1) Ending cash balance before financing.............................	?	?
Minimum cash balance desired...	10,000	10,000
Cash excess (deficiency)	$(5,500)	$?
Financing of cash deficiency		
Borrowing (at end of month)...	$?	
Principal payments (at end of month)............................		$?
Interest expense (at .010 monthly)		?
(2) Total effects of financing..	?	?
Ending cash balance (1) + (2)..	$?	$?
Interest expense: June: ?		

Required

Fill in each amount identified by a question mark.

Exercise 20-7   *Computing cash receipts and disbursements* **(L.O. 4)**

For each of the items a through d, compute the amount of cash receipts or disbursements Laliberté Inc. would budget for December. A solution to one item may depend on the answer to an earlier item.

a. Management expects to sell 4,000 units in November and 4,200 in December. Each unit sells for $6. Cash sales average 30 percent of the total sales, and credit sales make up the rest. Two thirds of credit sales are collected in the month of sale, with the balance collected the following month.

b. Management has budgeted inventory purchases of $30,000 for November and $25,000 for December. Laliberté pays for 50 percent of its inventory at the time of purchase in order to get a 2 percent discount. The business pays the balance the following month, with no further discount.

c. Management expects to sell equipment that cost $14,100 at a gain of $2,000. Accumulated depreciation on this equipment is $6,000.

d. The company pays rent and property taxes of $6,000 each month. Commissions and other selling expenses average 20 percent of sales. Laliberté pays two thirds of these costs in the month incurred, with the balance paid in the following month.

Exercise 20-8   *Preparing a cash budget* **(L.O. 4)**

Phillips Manor, a family-owned furniture store, began October with $5,400 cash. Management forecasts that collections from credit customers will be $9,000 in October and $12,200 in November. The store is scheduled to receive $5,000 cash on a business note receivable in November. Projected cash disbursements include inventory purchases ($10,200 in October and $12,100 in November) and operating expenses ($3,000 each month).

Phillips's bank requires a $7,500 minimum balance in the store's chequing account. At the end of any month when the account balance goes below $7,500, the bank automatically extends credit to the store in multiples of $1,000. Phillips Manor borrows as little as possible and pays back these loans in monthly installments of $1,000 plus 1.5 percent monthly interest on the entire unpaid principal. The first payment occurs at the end of the month following the loan.

Required

Prepare the store's cash budget for October and November.

Exercise 20-9   *Preparing a budgeted balance sheet* **(L.O. 5)**

Use the following information to prepare a budgeted balance sheet for Bargain Book Store Ltd. at July 31, 19X6. Show computations for cash and owner's equity amounts.

a. July 31 inventory balance, $16,000.

b. July payments for inventory, $5,900.

c. July payments of June 30 accounts payable and accrued liabilities, $6,100.

d. July 31 accounts payable balance, $4,900.

e. June 30 furnitures and fixtures balance, $34,800; accumulated depreciation balance, $27,700.

f. July capital expenditures of $3,200 budgeted for cash purchase of furniture.

g. July operating expenses, including income tax, total $4,200, half of which will be paid during July and half accrued at July 31.

h. July depreciation, $300.

i. Cost of goods sold, 50 percent of sales.

j. June 30 owner's equity, $25,700.

k. June 30 cash balance, $10,300.

l. July budgeted sales, $12,400.

m. July 31 accounts receivable balance, one fourth of July sales.

n. July cash receipts, $12,300.

Exercise 20-10   *Preparing a rolling budget for the income statement* **(L.O. 6)**

Maple Dairy Farm Ltd. budgets the following total revenues, total expenses, and net income for the last four months of the year:

	September	October	November	December
Budgeted total revenues.................	$175,000	$160,000	$170,000	$189,000
Budgeted total expenses.................	93,000	87,000	89,000	97,000
Budgeted net income	$ 82,000	$ 73,000	$ 81,000	$ 92,000

Prepare Maple Dairy Farm's rolling monthly income statement budget for the quarters ending on November 30 and December 31.

Problems   *(Group A)*

Problem 20-1A   *Budgeting income and evaluating income with a performance report* **(L.O. 1, 2, 3)**

The Atlantic district office of Galvan Sales Ltd. divides its annual budget into semi-annual periods. The district manager forecast that sales would increase during the first half of the current year by 8.1 percent over the first half of the preceding year. The manager also believed that second-half sales of the current year would exceed second-half sales of the preceding year by 4.5 percent. Cost of goods sold was budgeted at 43 percent of budgeted sales. Total operating expenses, including income taxes, were expected to be 36 percent of revenues during the first six-month period and 34 percent during the second period.

Actual sales, operating expenses, and net income for the four most recent semi-annual periods follow:

	Preceding Year Semiannual Period		Current Year Semiannual Period	
	1	2	1	2
Sales...	$113,000	$145,000	$124,000	$165,000
Cost of goods sold	40,000	63,000	66,000	81,000
Gross margin.................................	73,000	82,000	58,000	84,000
Operating expenses.......................	52,000	49,000	39,000	47,000
Net income (loss)...........................	$ 21,000	$ 33,000	$ 19,000	$ 37,000

Required

1. Prepare a budgeted income statement for each semiannual period of the current year. Round all amounts to the nearest $1,000.

2. Prepare a summarized income statement performance report for the same period. Present the actual and budgeted income statements side by side. Show the differences between them. Round all amounts to the nearest $1,000.

3. Have operations been more or less successful in the current semiannual period compared with the preceding period? What aspects of operations have improved? What aspects have deteriorated?

Problem 20-2A   *Budgeting income for three months* **(L.O. 2, 3)**

The budget committee of Scott Rubin Corporation has assembled the following data. You are the business manager, and you must prepare the budgeted income statements for April, May, and June 19X3.

a. Sales in March were $31,300. You forecast that monthly sales will increase 1.3 percent in April and May, and 1.8 percent in June.

b. The company tries to maintain inventory of $8,000 plus 20 percent of sales budgeted for the following month. Monthly purchases average 55 percent of sales. Actual inventory on March 31 is $12,000. Sales budgeted for July are $30,600.

c. Monthly salaries amount to $3,000. Sales commissions equal 5 percent of sales. Combine salaries and commissions as a single figure.

d. Other monthly expenses are

Rent expense	$2,700, paid as incurred
Depreciation expense.....................	500
Insurance expense	100, expiration of prepaid amount
Miscellaneous expense	3% of sales
Income tax	20% of income from operations

Required

Prepare Scott Rubin's budgeted income statements for April, May, and June. Show cost of goods sold computations. Round all amounts to the nearest $100. For example, budgeted April sales are $31,700 ($31,300 × 1.013), May sales are $32,100 ($31,700 × 1.013), and June sales are $32,700 ($32,100 × 1.018).

Problem 20-3A *Preparing a budgeted income statement* **(L.O. 2, 3)**

Hulme TV Appliances is budgeting net income for the six months ended June 30, 19X4. Fred Hulme, the owner, expects January sales of $50,000 for TVs and $10,000 for VCRs. He is hoping for 1 percent monthly sales growth for TVs and 3 percent for VCRs. Cost of goods sold is 70 percent of sales for TVs and 60 percent for VCRs. Hulme budgets monthly expenses as follows:

Salaries	$14,000 per month
Rent..	2,000 per month
Depreciation.................................	1,000 per month
Insurance	500 per month
Travel..	750 per quarter (in January and April only)
Utilities...	500 per month
Income tax rate	40%

Note: Problem 20-3A is designed to be completed using a computer spreadsheet model, although it can also be solved manually.

Required

Create a spreadsheet model to prepare Hulme's budgeted income statement for the six months ended June 30, 19X4. Show each expense, total operating expenses, income from operations, income tax expense, and net income. Format the statement as follows:

	A	B	C	D	E	F	G	H
				Hulme TV Appliances Ltd.				
1								
2				Budgeted Income Statement				
3			for the six months ended June 30, 19X4					
4								
5		JAN	FEB	MAR	APR	MAY	JUN	TOTAL
6	Sales							
7	TVS							
8	VCRs							
9	Total Sales							
10								
11	COGS							
12	TVs							
13	VCRs							
14	Total COGS							
15								
16	Gross Pft							
17	TVs							
18	VCRs							
19	Total GP							
20								
21	Oper Exp							
22	Salaries							
23	Rent Exp							
24	Deprec							
25	Ins							
26	Travel							
27	Util							
28	Total Oper Exp							
29								
30	Oper Inc							
31	before tax							
32	Inc Tax							
33	Net Inc							

Problem 20-4A   *Preparing a cash budget for three months* **(L.O. 4)**

Sutfin Recreational Vehicles Inc. is considering opening a sales office in a suburb of Halifax during May of the current year. The business estimates the office opening will cost $92,000. To finance start-up, the Bank of Nova Scotia has agreed to loan Sutfin, in multiples of $10,000, the amount needed to keep Sutfin's cash balance above $5,000. The loan begins on the last day of any month in which Sutfin's cash balance goes below $5,000. The company will repay the loan in monthly install-ments of $10,000 each, beginning one month after the loan starts. Sutfin will also pay monthly interest of 1.5 percent on the entire unpaid balance until the loan is fully repaid.

   Management expects Sutfin's operations to generate the following:

	May	June	July
Sales...	$63,000	$71,000	$74,000
Cost of goods sold........................	45,000	51,000	52,000
Cash operating expenses..............	6,000	9,000	9,000

   On May 1, Sutfin expects to have $9,000 cash and $36,000 of inventory. Inventory is expected to decrease by $4,000 each month. Monthly cash receipts average 95 percent of sales with the balance collected the month after the sale. The company's purchases of inventory are paid for immediately.

Required

Prepare Sutfin's cash budgets for the months of May, June, and July.

Problem 20-5A   *Preparing a budgeted balance sheet* **(L.O. 5)**

Pesco Leather Goods, Inc. has applied for a loan. National Bank has requested a budgeted balance sheet at April 30, 19X8. As the controller (chief accounting offic-er) of Pesco, you have assembled the following information:

a. March 31 equipment balance, $35,200; accumulated depreciation, $22,800.

b. April capital expenditures of $41,700 budgeted for cash purchase of equipment.

c. April operating expenses, including income tax, total $13,600, 25 percent of which will be paid in cash and the remainder accrued at April 30.

d. April depreciation, $700.

e. Cost of goods sold, 60 percent of sales.

f. March 31 owner's equity, $74,900.

g. March 31 cash balance, $26,200.

h. April budgeted sales, $70,000, 60 percent of which is for cash sales. Of the re-maining 40 percent, half will be collected in April and half in May.

i. April cash collections on March sales, $31,200.

j. April cash payments of March 31 liabilities, $17,300.

k. March 31 inventory balance, $22,400.

l. April purchases of inventory, $9,000 for cash and $40,600 on credit. Half of the credit purchases will be paid in April and half in May.

Required

Prepare the budgeted balance sheet of Pesco Leather Goods, Inc. at April 30, 19X8. Show separate computations for cash, inventory, and owner's equity balances.

Problem 20-6A *Preparing a rolling budget for the income statement* **(L.O. 6)**

The budgeted income statements of Goetz Limited Ltd. for the six most recent quarters follow:

Goetz Ltd.
Budgeted Income Statements
for the quarters ended September 30, 19X2 through December 31, 19X3

| | 19X2 | | 19X3 | | | |
	Sept. 30	Dec. 31	Mar. 31	June 30	Sept. 30	Dec. 31
Sales...............	$20,000	$70,000	$50,000	$60,000	$30,000	$80,000
Cost of goods sold	8,000	30,000	22,000	23,000	11,000	30,000
Gross margin.....	12,000	40,000	28,000	37,000	19,000	50,000
Operating expenses........	5,000	16,000	12,000	17,000	10,000	22,000
Net income	$ 7,000	$24,000	$16,000	$20,000	$ 9,000	$28,000

Required

1. Combine the quarterly totals necessary to prepare Goetz's rolling budgeted income statement for the last semiannual period in 19X2 and for the four semiannual periods ending in 19X3. (The first semiannual period in 19X3 ends March 31, the second June 30, and so on.)

2. Based on the comparison of the last half of 19X2 with the last half of 19X3, does Goetz management appear to expect increasing or decreasing sales and net income for 19X3?

Problem 20-7A *Preparing all the components of a master budget* **(L.O. 2, 3, 4, 5)**

Noble & Barnes' balance sheet at September 30, 19X4 follows:

Noble & Barnes
Balance Sheet
September 30, 19X4

Assets		**Liabilities**	
Current assets		Current liabilities	
Cash...	$ 11,000	Accounts payable	$ 40,000
Accounts receivable, net	45,000	Salaries and commissions payable	10,000
Inventory	62,000	Total liabilities	50,000
Prepaid insurance	4,000		
	122,000	**Owners' Equity**	
Capital assets		Owners' equity	140,000
Furniture and fixtures	96,000		
Accumulated depreciation	(28,000)		
	68,000	Total liabilities	
Total assets..	$190,000	and owners' equity.................................	$190,000

Additional budget information follows:

a. Sales in September were $90,000. Management projects these monthly sales: October $80,000; November $70,000; December $80,000; and January $60,000.

Sales are half for cash and half on credit. All accounts receivable are collected in the month following sale. Uncollectible accounts are insignificant and can be ignored.

b. For the new budget period management wishes to maintain inventory of $22,000 plus 75 percent of the cost of goods to be sold in the following month. Cost of goods sold averages 65 percent of sales. Noble & Barnes pays for inventory as follows: 20 percent in the month of purchase, and 80 percent in the next month.

c. Payroll is made up of fixed salaries of $1,000 and sales commissions equal to 10 percent of sales. The monthly payroll is accrued at the end of the month and paid early the next month.

d. Other monthly expenses are

Advertising expense...............	$3,600, paid as incurred
Rent expense...........................	1,300, paid as incurred
Depreciation expense	1,000
Insurance expense...................	400, expiration of prepaid amount
Miscellaneous expense...........	2 % of sales, paid as incurred

e. Management has budgeted $26,000 cash for the acquisition of furniture in October.

f. The company is required by its bank to maintain a minimum cash balance of $8,000 at the end of each month. Money can be borrowed in multiples of $1,000. Management borrows no more than what is needed to maintain the $8,000 minimum balance, and pays back all debts less than $5,000 at the end of the next month. Short-term notes payable greater than $5,000 are paid back in three equal monthly principal payments. The monthly interest rate on all notes payable is 1 percent on the entire unpaid principal. Borrowing and all principal and interest payments occur at the end of the month.

g. In September, purchases were $50,000, and salaries and commissions were $10,000.

h. The business is a partnership. The partners, therefore, pay personal income tax on their earnings. The business itself incurs no income tax liability, so income taxes do not enter into the computations.

Required

Prepare Noble & Barnes' master budget for the fourth quarter of 19X4. Include the following statements and schedules:

Statements
Budgeted income statement for the quarter ending December 31, 19X4
Statement of budgeted cash receipts and disbursements for the quarter ending December 31, 19X4
Budgeted balance sheet at December 31, 19X4

Schedules
Sales
Purchases, cost of goods sold, and inventory
Operating expenses
Cash collections from customers
Cash Disbursements for purchases
Cash Disbursements for operating expenses

(Group B)

Problem 20-1B   *Budgeting income and evaluating income with a performance report* **(L.O. 1, 2, 3)**

The Rocky Mountain regional office of McIntosh Products Ltd. divides its annual budget into semiannual periods. The regional manager forecast that sales would increase during the first half of the current year by 2.5 percent over the first half of the preceding year. The manager also believed that second-half sales of the current year would exceed second-half sales of the preceding year by 8 percent. Cost of goods sold was budgeted at 56 percent of budgeted sales. Total operating expenses, including income taxes, were expected to be 30 percent of revenues during the first six-month period and 32 percent during the second period.

Actual sales, operating expenses, and net income for the four most recent semi-annual periods follow:

| | Preceding Year Semiannual Period | | Current Year Semiannual Period | |
	1	2	1	2
Sales	$32,000	$30,000	$34,000	$36,000
Cost of goods sold	19,000	14,000	16,000	17,000
Gross margin	13,000	16,000	18,000	19,000
Operating expenses	10,000	11,000	11,000	13,000
Net income (loss)	$ 3,000	$ 5,000	$ 7,000	$ 6,000

Required

1. Prepare a budgeted income statement for each semiannual period of the current year. Round all amounts to the nearest $1,000.

2. Prepare a summarized income statement performance report for the same period. Present the actual and the budgeted income statement side by side. Show the differences between them. Round all amounts to the nearest $1,000.

3. Identify the aspects of operations that are performing most successfully, and the aspects that are performing least successfully. Comment on the relative success of overall operations.

Problem 20-2B   *Budgeting income for three months* **(L.O. 2, 3)**

Representatives of the various departments of Thessalon Tire Ltd. have assembled the following data. You are the business manager, and you must prepare the budgeted income statements for July, August, and September 19X6.

a. Sales in June were $18,400. You forecast that monthly sales will increase 2 percent in July, and 2 percent in August, and 3 percent in September.

b. Thessalon tries to maintain inventory of $5,000 plus 20 percent of sales budgeted for the following month. Monthly purchases average 65 percent of sales. Actual inventory on June 30 is $8,000. Sales budgeted for October are $20,500.

c. Monthly salaries amount to $1,200. Sales commissions equal 6 percent of sales. Combine salaries and commissions as a single figure on the income statements.

d. Other monthly expenses are

Rent expense	$1,200, paid as incurred
Depreciation expense..............	300
Insurance expense	100, expiration of prepaid amount
Miscellaneous expense	5% of sales
Income tax	20% of income from operations

Required

Prepare Thessalon's budgeted income statements for July, August, and September. Show cost of goods sold computations. Round all amounts to the nearest $100. For example, budgeted July sales are $18,800 ($18,400 × 1.02), August sales are $19,200 ($18,800 × 1.02), and September sales are $19,800 ($19,200 × 1.03).

Problem 20-3B *Preparing a budgeted income statement* **(L.O. 2, 3)**

Advanced Information Systems, Inc. is budgeting gross profit (gross margin) for the six months ended June 30, 19X5. Lynn Bradshaw, the owner, expects January sales of $70,000 for computer hardware and $25,000 for software. She is hoping for 2 percent monthly sales growth for hardware and 4 percent for software. Cost of goods sold is 70 percent of sales for hardware and 50 percent for software. The business budgets expenses as follows:

Salaries.................................	$20,000 per month
Rent.......................................	2,500 per month
Depreciation	2,000 per month
Insurance..............................	1,500 per month
Travel	900 per quarter (in January and April only)
Utilities	650 per month
Income tax rate....................	40%

Note: Problem 20-3B is designed to be completed using a computer spreadsheet model, although it can also be solved manually.

Required

Create a spreadsheet model to prepare the Advanced Information Systems income statement for the six months ended June 30, 19X5. Show each expense, total operating expenses, income from operations, income tax expense, and net income. Format the statement as follows:

	A	B	C	D	E	F	G	H
			Advanced Information Systems, Inc.					
1								
2			Budgeted Income Statement					
3			for the six months ended June 30, 19X4					
4								
5		JAN	FEB	MAR	APR	MAY	JUN	TOTAL
6	Sales							
7	Hardware							
8	Software							
9	Total Sales							
10								
11	COGS							
12	Hardware							
13	Software							
14	Total COGS							
15								
16	Gross Pft							
17	Hardware							
18	Software							
19	Total GP							
20								
21	Oper Exp							
22	Salaries							
23	Rent							
24	Deprec							
25	Ins							
26	Travel							
27	Util							
28	Total Oper Exp							
29								
30	Oper Inc							
31	before tax							
32	Inc Tax							
33	Net Inc							

Problem 20-4B   *Preparing a cash budget for three months* (L.O. 4)

Prairie Development Ltd. is considering opening an office in a suburb of Calgary during September of the current year. The business estimates that the office opening will cost $17,000. To finance start-up, Western Bank has agreed to loan Prairie, in multiples of $1,000, the amount needed to keep Prairie's cash balance above $10,000. The loan begins on the last day of any month in which Prairie's cash balance goes below $10,000. The company will repay the loan in monthly installments of $1,000 each, beginning two months after the loan starts. Prairie will also pay monthly interest of 1 percent on the entire unpaid balance until the loan is repaid.

Management expects Prairie's operations to generate the following:

	August	September	October
Sales	$41,000	$44,000	$52,000
Cost of goods sold...	17,000	21,000	26,000
Cash operating expenses	19,000	22,000	24,000
Collection of note receivable		25,000	

On August 1, Prairie expects to have $7,000 cash and $7,000 of inventory. Inventory is expected to increase by $3,000 each month. Monthly cash receipts average 95 percent of sales, with the balance collected the month after the sale. The company's purchases of inventory are paid for immediately.

Required

Prepare Prairie's cash budgets for the months of August, September, and October.

Problem 20-5B   *Preparing a budgeted balance sheet* (L.O. 5)

Mazeroski, Inc. has applied for a loan. The Toronto-Dominion Bank has requested a budgeted balance sheet at June 30, 19X4. As the controller (chief accounting officer) of Mazeroski, you have assembled the following information:

a. May 31 equipment balance, $60,600; accumulated depreciation, $11,700.

b. June capital expenditures of $15,800 budgeted for cash purchase of equipment.

c. June operating expenses, including income tax, total $38,800, 75 percent of which will be paid in cash and the remainder accrued at June 30.

d. June depreciation, $400.

e. Cost of goods sold, 45 percent of sales.

f. May 31 owners' equity, $97,400.

g. May 31 cash balance, $33,900.

h. June budgeted sales, $50,000, 40 percent of which is for cash. Of the remaining 60 percent, half will be collected in June and half in July.

i. June cash collections on May sales, $14,900.

j. June cash payments of May 31 liabilities, $10,700.

k. May 31 inventory balance, $10,400.

l. June purchases of inventory, $11,000 for cash and $27,400 on credit. Half of the credit purchases will be paid in June and half in July.

Required

Prepare the budgeted balance sheet of Mazeroski, Inc. at June 30, 19X4. Show separate computations for cash, inventory, and owner's equity balances.

Problem 20-6B   *Preparing a rolling budget for the income statement* **(L.O. 6)**

The budgeted income statements of Polonski Ltd. for the six most recent quarters follow:

Polonski Ltd.
Budgeted Income Statements
for the quarters ended September 30, 19X5 through December 31, 19X6

	19X5		19X6			
	Sept. 30	**Dec. 31**	**Mar. 31**	**June 30**	**Sept. 30**	**Dec. 31**
Sales........................	$50,000	$90,000	$60,000	$80,000	$ 40,000	$120,000
Cost of goods sold...................	25,000	50,000	35,000	50,000	25,000	75,000
Gross margin........	25,000	40,000	25,000	30,000	15,000	45,000
Operating expenses	22,000	20,000	22,000	23,000	25,000	24,000
Net income (loss).	$ 3,000	$ 20,000	$ 3,000	$ 7,000	$(10,000)	$ 21,000

Required

1. Combine the quarterly totals necessary to prepare Polonski's rolling budgeted income statement for the last semiannual period in 19X5 and for the four semiannual periods ending in 19X6. (The first semiannual period in 19X6 ends March 31, the second June 30, and so on.)
2. Based on the comparison of the last half of 19X6 with the last half of 19X5, does Polonski management appear to expect increasing or decreasing sales and net income for 19X6?

Problem 20-7B   *Preparing all the components of a master budget* **(L.O. 2, 3, 4, 5)**

Copeland & Holtizer's balance sheet at September 30, 19X4, follows:

Copeland & Holtizer
Balance Sheet
September 30, 19X4

Assets		**Liabilities**	
Current assets		Current liabilities	
Cash	$ 7,000	Accounts payable.................................	$ 32,000
Accounts receivable, net	25,000	Salaries and commissions payable.....	8,000
Inventory..	67,000	Total liabilities	40,000
Prepaid insurance	2,000		
	101,000	**Owners' Equity**	
Capital assets		Owners' equity	90,000
Furniture and fixtures	48,000		
Accumulated depreciation	(19,000)		
	29,000	Total liabilities	
Total assets	$130,000	and owners' equity................................	$130,000

Additional budget information follows:

a. Sales in September were $50,000. Management projects these monthly sales: October $60,000; November $70,000; December $80,000; and January $80,000.
   Sales are half for cash and half on credit. All accounts receivable are collected in the month following sale. Uncollectible accounts are insignificant and can be ignored.

b. Management wishes to maintain inventory of $40,000 plus 75 percent of the cost of goods sold in the following month. Cost of goods sold averages 60 percent of sales. Copeland & Holtizer pays for inventory as follows: 20 percent of each month's purchases in the month of purchase, and the remaining 80 percent in the next month.

c. Payroll is made up of fixed salaries of $3,000 and sales commissions equal to 10 percent of sales. The monthly payroll is accrued at the end of the month and paid early the following month.

d. Other monthly expenses are

Advertising expense............	$1,500, paid as incurred
Rent expense........................	900, paid as incurred
Depreciation expense	600
Insurance expense...............	200, expiration of prepaid amount
Miscellaneous expense.......	2% of sales, paid as incurred

e. Management has budgeted $8,000 cash for the acquisition of furniture in October.

f. The company keeps a minimum cash balance of $5,000 at the end of each month. The company may borrow on short-term notes payable in multiples of $1,000. Management borrows no more than necessary. The company repays the notes in three equal monthly installments that begin one month after the company borrows. The notes also carry monthly interest of 1 percent on the entire unpaid principal. Borrowing and all principal and interest payments occur at the end of the month.

g. In September, purchases were $40,000, and salaries and commissions were $8,000.

h. The business is a partnership. The partners, therefore, pay personal income tax on their earnings. The business itself incurs no income tax liability, so income taxes do not enter into the computations.

Required

Prepare Copeland & Holtizer's master budget for the fourth quarter of 19X4. Include the following statements and schedules:

Statements
Budgeted income statement for the quarter ending December 31, 19X4
Statement of budgeted cash receipts and disbursements for the quarter ending December 31, 19X4
Budgeted balance sheet at December 31, 19X4

Schedules
Sales
Purchases, cost of goods sold, and inventory
Operating expenses
Cash collections from customers
Cash disbursements for purchases
Cash disbursements for operating expenses

Extending Your Knowledge

Decision Problems

1. *Preparing a cash budget to analyze a loan request (L.O. 4)*

Twin Sisters, a women's boutique, is requesting a $40,000 loan to finance the remodeling of its store. The bank requires a statement of budgeted cash receipts and disbursements to support the loan application.

The Twin Sisters cash balance at February 28 is $5,100. During March. the store expects to collect $3,900 from sales made in January and February. Also, in February, the store sold an old display case for $700, and the owners expect to receive that amount during March. During March, the business will pay off accounts payable of $2,100, and a note payable of $6,000 plus $540 interest.

The store expects monthly sales of $9,500 for March, April, and May. Experience indicates that the store will collect 60 percent of sales in the month of sale, 30 percent in the month following sale, and 7 percent in the second month after sale. The remaining 3 percent is uncollectible.

The February 28 inventory is $37,800. Purchases average one half of sales. The owners pay all accounts payable arising from inventory purchases in time to receive a 2 percent discount, 80 percent in the month of purchase, and 20 percent the next month.

Budgeted operating expenses for March are rent (8 percent of sales), advertising ($500), utilities ($330), depreciation ($240), and insurance ($120). Depreciation and insurance are recorded as the assets expire. Half of the advertising expense is paid as incurred, and half is accrued at the end of the month. During March, Twin Sisters will pay advertising of $160 that was accrued at February 28.

In order to make the loan, the bank requires that Twin Sisters' cash balance be at least $2,000 before any effects of financing.

Required

Prepare a cash budget (a statement of budgeted cash receipts and disbursements) for Twin Sisters for March. As the bank loan officer, decide if the store qualifies for the loan.

2. *Projecting cash flow and financial statements to analyze alternatives (L.O. 2, 3, 4, 5)*

Jacky Carleton is a librarian in the business library of Canada Trust. Each autumn, as a hobby, Jacky weaves cotton placemats for sale through a local craft shop. The shop charges 10 percent commission and remits the net proceeds to Jacky at the end of December. The mats sell in the shop for $20 per set of four; the cost of the cotton is $7 per set. Jacky has woven and sold 25 sets each year for the past two years. Each December 31, Jacky has always paid for the cotton and repaid $200 of the principal, along with accrued interest at 9 percent, on the loan she received on September 1, 19X1 for her four-harness loom. This was also the day the loom was purchased.

Jacky's weaving is very professional. She is considering buying an eight-harness loom immediately so she can weave more intricate placemats in linen. She estimates that each set would sell for $50, and the cost of the linen would be $18 per set. She can weave 15 sets in time for the Christmas rush. Jacky's supplier will sell her linen on credit until December 31. The new loom would cost $1,000. The bank has agreed to lend her the money at 12 percent per annum, with $200 principal plus accumulated interest payable each December 31. Jacky plans to keep her original loom. She could make 25 sets of cotton placemats with her newly purchased supply of cotton. The old loom is depreciated at $10 per month; monthly depreciation on the new loom would be $20. The balance sheet for Jacky's weaving at August 31, 19X3 follows:

Jacky Carleton, Weaver
Balance Sheet
August 31, 19X3

Current assets			Current liabilities		
Cash		$ 15	Bank loan payable		$100
Inventory of cotton		175	Accounts payable		74
		190	Interest payable		6
					180
Capital assets					
Loom		500			
Accumulated			Owner's equity		270
depreciation		(240)			
		260	Total liabilities		
Total assets		$450	and owner's equity		$450

Required

Prepare a statement of budgeted cash receipts and disbursements for the four months ended December 31, 19X3 for the two alternatives: weaving the placemats in cotton, and weaving the placemats in linen. For each alternative, prepare a budgeted income statement for the four months ended December 31, 19X3, and a budgeted balance sheet at December 31, 19X3. Which alternative would you recommend for Jacky? Give your reason.

Ethical Issue

Maxim Gorky, Inc. practices top-down budgeting. Top managers set targets for sales managers, who then develop goals for individual salespersons. Grace Faile, manager for the western district, uses her contacts and interpersonal skills to raise money for the Liberal party. Randall Van Houten, president of Maxim Gorky, is a prominent Conservative. He suspects that Faile is using too much time for fund-raising and shirking her duty to the company. For 1994, Van Houten sets Faile's sales goal 40 percent above actual amounts for 1993. The increases expected of other sales managers average 25 percent. Van Houten justifies Faile's sales budget on the grounds that the western district has experienced the greatest growth, and that Faile is extremely talented.

Required

1. What is the preferred model for establishing a budget — top-down or bottom up? Give your reason.
2. Is Van Houten's treatment of Faile ethical? Explain.

Financial Statement Problem

Preparing a budget income statement and comparing the budget to actual (L.O. 1, 3)

Suppose Schneider Corporation managers had based their fiscal 1991 budget on these figures for the income statement:

	Increase (Decrease) over 1990
a. Sales	2%
b. Cost of products sold	2
c. Selling, marketing, and administrative	3
d. Depreciation and amortization	1

Use the company's actual data in Appendix C to prepare the budgeted income statement for fiscal 1991. Follow the Schneider format, showing accounts in thousands rounded to the nearest $1,000. Compare the actual and budgeted figures as shown in Exhibit 20-3 to report the difference for each item through earnings from operations.

Answers to Self-Study Questions

1. d
2. a
3. b
4. c Actual: $90,000 – $50,000 = $40,000
   Budget: 86,000 – 51,000 = 35,000
   Actual over budget: $5,000
5. c
6. b
7. c
8. d
9. d
10. a

Chapter 21

Cost-Volume-Profit Relationships and the Contribution Margin Approach to Decision-Making

Global competition in the 1990s suggests that to survive, a business must be *big and efficient*. Why is "bigness" a major competitive advantage? Consider the experience of Dorel Industries Inc. of Montreal, Quebec.

Prior to 1987, Dorel was a medium-sized private furniture manufacturing company with sales, almost exclusively in Canada, of $36 million (net income of $2.3 million). Leo Schwartz, the company president, stated, "We knew we had to get bigger to survive." Over the next three years, Dorel purchased two American furniture manufacturing companies. Sales soared to $157 million in 1990, and for the first nine months of 1991 were $130 million (net income of $5.3 million).

What were some of the secrets that Dorel used to grow during a period when, in Canada, 65 furniture operations closed? First, it drastically improved the efficiency of the American factories by automation. Second, it focused on volume sales to major retail chains. Third, it introduced new products to its product line. Fourth, it controlled its costs. Fifth, it developed very close working relationships with its customers.

Restating the above strategy in cost-volume-profit (CVP) terminology, Dorel did the following. Its first step cut variable cost per unit. The second and third steps, which focused on volume, increased its total contribution margin. The fourth ensured that fixed costs did not get too high: this allowed Dorel to stay well above its break-even point. The fifth is not a CVP notion—it is just good old-fashioned common sense.

In our day-to-day conversations we call this strategy "economies of scale." After reading this chapter, you will know the mechanics of this proven and extremely successful business practice.

Source: Michael Salter, "No Kidding," *Report on Business Magazine* (March 1992), pp. 29–32.

LEARNING OBJECTIVES

After studying this chapter, you should be able to:

1 Identify different cost behavior patterns

2 Use a contribution margin income statement to make business decisions

3 Compute break-even sales

4 Compute the sales level needed to earn target operating income

5 Graph a set of cost-volume-profit relationships

6 Compute a margin of safety

7 Separate a mixed cost into its variable and fixed components

---

How much additional income does Ford Motor Co. of Canada Ltd. earn when it sells 500 more Sables? How much in additional expense does the sale of these 500 cars cost Ford? How many Sables must Ford sell for the Ford division to break even — earn zero profit?

Many questions in business — on the number of cars sold, the number of passengers transported by an airline, and so on —boil down to this general question: What effects does a change in volume have on profits? To answer these questions, managers study the links among cost, volume, and profit.

Cost-volume-profit (CVP) analysis helps managers predict the outcome of their decisions by expressing the relationships among a business's costs, volume, and profit or loss. It is an important part of the budgeting system. We begin our discussion of this valuable decision-making tool by looking at costs.

Types of Costs

A **cost driver** is any factor whose change makes a difference in a related total cost. There are many possible cost drivers. The most prominent driver is volume, which is often expressed in physical units sold or produced, or in total sales dollars. For example, the more T-shirts a company produces (that is, the greater the T-shirt volume) the greater the costs the company incurs. Non-volume factors also act as cost drivers. An example is weight, which may affect freight costs. To emphasize basic concepts in this chapter, we focus on volume as the cost driver.

Cost behavior describes how costs change (indeed, if they change) in response to a shift in a cost driver. We examine three basic types of costs: variable, fixed, and mixed. A **variable cost** (**variable expense**) is a cost that changes in total in direct proportion to changes in volume. For example, sales commissions are variable costs; the higher the sales, the higher the sales commissions. Variable costs also include cost of goods sold and delivery expense. Each of these costs rises or falls directly with any increase or decrease in sales volume.

Exhibit 21-1 shows the graphs of three different variable costs. The first graph presents the cost behavior of a product that costs $2 an item. The sloped line indicates the 3,000 T-shirts cost $6,000 (3,000 × $2). We see that 4,500 T-shirts cost $9,000 (4,500 × $2).

The higher the cost of an item, the steeper the graph of its variable cost. For example, the second graph in Exhibit 21-1 is based on each item costing $3. Study this graph to confirm that 2,000 T-shirts cost $6,000 (2,000 × $3) and 4,000 T-shirts cost $12,000 (4,000 × $3). The third variable cost graph, showing the cost behavior of designer T-shirts that cost $10 each, is steeper yet.

A variable cost graph always passes through the origin (where the cost and volume axes intersect) because at zero volume, the variable cost is zero. As volume increases, variable cost increases in a straight line that leads out from the origin. The steepness of the graph's slope depends on the variable cost per unit. A higher variable unit cost results in a steeper slope. A lower variable unit cost has a lower slope.

OBJECTIVE 1

Identify different cost behavior patterns

EXHIBIT 21-1 *Variable Cost Pattern*

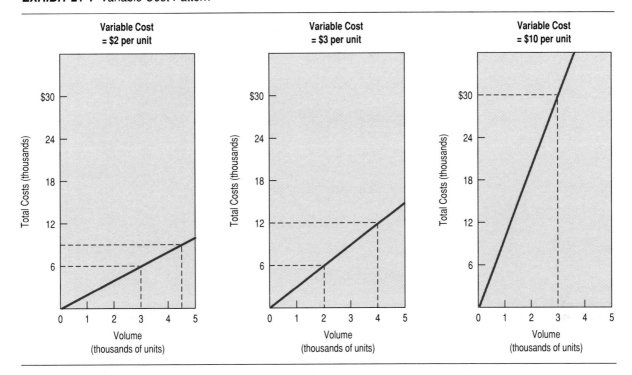

A **fixed cost (fixed expense)** is a cost that does not change in total despite changes in volume. For example, office rent does not usually change with the volume of business. A company must still pay its monthly rent regardless of whether sales volume rises, falls, or stays steady. Other examples of fixed costs are depreciation, property taxes, and many executive salaries. These costs occur even if the company makes no sales, for this is the nature of a fixed cost. Exhibit 21-2 graphs a fixed cost, which is always a horizontal line intersecting the cost axis at the level of the fixed cost. In the graph, fixed cost is $12,000, not changing with any shift in the volume of activity.

EXHIBIT 21-2 *Fixed Cost Pattern*

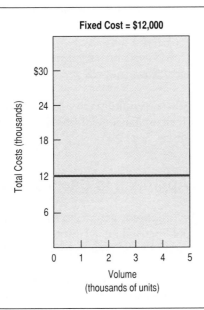

EXHIBIT 21-3 *Mixed Cost Pattern*

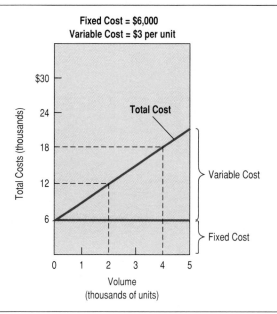

A **mixed cost (mixed expense)** is part variable and part fixed. It is also called a semivariable cost. Consider a utility expense like electricity, for example. The company must pay a minimum charge regardless of how much electricity it uses. In our illustrations, this fixed cost is $6,000. In addition, the company must pay a variable cost, which works out to be $3 for every product it sells. Exhibit 21-3 shows this mixed cost graph.

In a mixed cost graph, total cost is the sum of the fixed cost plus the variable cost. At sales volume of 2,000 units, total cost is $12,000 [fixed cost of $6,000 + variable cost of $6,000 (2,000 × $3)]. At volume of 4,000 units, total cost is $18,000 [fixed cost of $6,000 + variable cost of $12,000 (4,000 × $3)]. All graphs of mixed costs show the same pattern. They intersect the cost axis at the fixed cost point, and the slope of the graph is the variable cost per unit.

Synonyms abound in accounting. In cost-volume-profit analysis the following synonyms are widely used:

sales and *revenue*
variable cost and *variable expense*
fixed cost and *fixed expense*
income from operations and *operating income*
net income and *net profit*

Because you will encounter these synonyms in actual practice, we will use them freely in this chapter. To underscore basic relationships, income tax is assumed to be included among the expenses.

Contribution Margin Approach to Decision-Making _____

An income statement can be prepared using two fundamentally different methods. The early part of this book focused on accounting from the perspective of external users of the financial statements. That emphasis leads to the conventional income statement.

The present focus on management's use of accounting information calls for a different format for the income statement. In the management focus, the nature of an expense is important. Whether a cost is variable or fixed affects management decisions. Managers, then, want an income statement format that identifies the different types of costs. The contribution margin income statement provides this information.

The **contribution margin income statement** separates expenses into variable costs and fixed costs and highlights the **contribution margin,** which is the excess of revenue less variable expenses. Exhibit 21-4 presents a contribution margin income statement alongside a conventional income statement for comparison.

Income from operations is the same on both income statements. However, the contribution margin of $9,000 differs from the gross margin of $16,000. The primary categories of expenses on the contribution margin statement are variable expenses and fixed expenses. By contrast, the conventional income statement contains no such distinctions. Instead, its primary categories of expenses are cost of goods sold and operating expenses.

The contribution margin receives its name because the excess of revenues over variable expenses "contributes" to the payment of fixed expenses. The amount of revenues left over "contributes" to profit. Management's goal, of course, is to make the contribution margin as large as possible.

EXHIBIT 21-4 *Contribution Margin Income Statement*

Reynolds Company Conventional Income Statement Month ended December 31, 19XX				Reynolds Company Contribution Margin Income Statement Month ended December 31, 19XX			
Sales revenue............................		$40,000		Sales revenue........................			$40,000
Cost of goods sold		24,000		**Variable** expenses			
Gross margin		16,000		Cost of goods sold............	$24,000		
Operating expenses				Selling	4,000		
Selling....................................	$6,000			General and administrative	3,000	31,000	
General and administrative	4,000	10,000		**Contribution margin**			**9,000**
Income from operations........		$ 6,000		**Fixed** expenses			
				Selling		2,000	
				General and administrative		1,000	3,000
				Income from operations			$ 6,000

Suppose that Reynolds Company managers are trying to predict the impact on operating income if sales increase by $4,000 (10 percent), from $40,000 to $44,000. Management, in drawing up the company budget, must know the impact of this possible sales increase on income from operations. If sales increase by 10 percent, variable expenses can be expected to increase by the same percentage. Fixed expenses will remain at $3,000.

We compute the income from operations resulting from the sales increase as follows:

> **OBJECTIVE 2**
>
> Use a contribution margin income statement to make business decisions

Increase in sales revenue	$4,000
Increase in expenses	
Fixed expenses..	-0-
Variable expenses	
$\dfrac{\text{Increase in sales}}{\text{Current sales}} \times$ Current variable expenses	
$\dfrac{\$4,000}{\$40,000} \quad\times\qquad \$31,000$	3,100
Increase in contribution margin	**900**
Income from operations before sales increase...	6,000
Income from operations after sales increase..	$6,900

Management can use this information to decide whether to expand operations. If the $900 increase in contribution margin is considered adequate, Reynolds will expand the business. If $900 is considered inadequate, then Reynolds will come up with another plan.

Important points about the analysis are that (1) fixed expenses do not change, and (2) variable expenses increase by 10 percent ($4,000/$40,000 = .10), and so variable expenses and the contribution margin also increase by 10 percent.

Similar analysis using the conventional income statement is not possible. Managers cannot use the conventional income statement to accurately predict the change in income from an increase in sales because this statement does not show which expenses are variable and which are fixed.

Relevant Range

A **relevant range** is the band of volume in which a specific relationship between cost and volume is valid. A fixed cost is fixed only in relation to a given relevant range (usually large) and a given time span (usually a particular budget period). Exhibit 21-5 shows a fixed cost level of $50,000 for the volume range of 0 to 10,000 units. Between 10,000 and 20,000 units, fixed expenses may be $80,000, and they will increase to $100,000 for volume above 20,000 units.

Companies use the relevant range concept in budgeting their costs. Suppose the business in Exhibit 21-5 expects sales volume of 12,000 during the year. For this period the relevant range is between 10,000 and 20,000 units, and mangers would budget fixed expenses of $80,000. If actual sales for the year exceed 20,000 units, the company will consider hiring additional employees and perhaps open a new store, increasing rent expense. Fixed expenses will increase as the relevant range shifts to a new band of volume.

Fixed costs change from year to year, and so does the relevant range. Expecting sales of only 8,000 units next year, the business would budget fixed expenses in a

EXHIBIT 21-5 *Relevant Range*

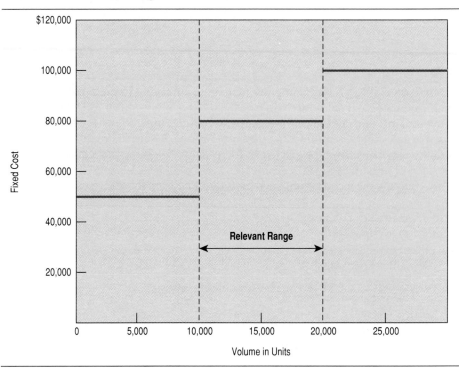

lower relevant range. The company may have to shut down a sales office, lay off employees, and eliminate other fixed expenses.

The relevant range concept also applies to variable costs. Some variable expenses may behave differently at different levels of volume. For example, utility expenses for water and electricity often cost less per unit as usage increases. Also, a company may pay higher sales commission rates for higher levels of sales to encourage extra selling effort. Therefore, businesses should consider cost behavior (how both fixed and variable expenses change) over the full range of sales volumes that are likely to occur during the budget period.

Cost behavior is one of the most challenging aspects of budgeting. After managers set the business's sales goal for the next period, accountants estimate costs. The behavior of various costs affects the expense budget. If budgeted expenses are too high, top managers may revise budgets for sales or expenses before setting the profit goal for the period.

In cost-volume-profit analysis, which we discuss next, we begin by classifying each cost as either variable or fixed. Later in this chapter, we show how to separate a mixed cost into its variable and fixed components.

Cost-Volume-Profit Analysis

The easiest way to learn cost-volume-profit analysis is with an example. Suppose Francine Deslauriers is considering renting a booth at a county fair. Francine plans to sell travel posters for $3.50 each. She can purchase the posters for $2.10 each and return all unsold items for a full refund. Rent for the booth will cost $700. Using this information, let us answer six questions about Francine's business.

Question 1: What is Francine's Break-Even Sales Level?

The study of cost-volume-profit analysis is often called **break-even analysis**. Why? CVP analysis allows us to compute an amount in unit sales or dollar sales at which revenue equals expenses. This sales level is called the **break-even point**. In other words, we may calculate the sales volume at which the business breaks even. Revenue must reach the break-even point to cover costs. Sales below the break-even point mean a loss. Sales above break-even bring a profit. CVP, or break-even, analysis answers the questions, How many units must the business sell to cover expenses? and How much in sales must we reach before we earn a profit? The break-even point is often only incidental to managers because their focus is on the sales level needed to earn a target operating income. However, the break-even point is a useful place to start the analysis of CVP relationships.

Two popular methods in cost-volume-profit analysis are the equation approach and the contribution margin approach. The focus in CVP analysis is often on operating income (income from operations) rather than on net income. Operating income is easier to predict because it omits extraordinary gains and losses and other special items that affect net income.

Equation Approach   In the equation approach, we start by dividing total expenses into variable expenses and fixed expenses.

For Francine Deslauriers, the variable cost is her cost of goods sold. This expense will equal the number of posters sold multiplied by her $2.10 cost to purchase each item. Her fixed cost is the $700 rent expense. A large company would have numerous variable expenses and fixed expenses. Such a business would combine all variable expenses into a single total and compute a single total for fixed expenses.

> **OBJECTIVE 3**
>
> Compute break-even sales

Our next step is to express income in equation form:

Sales – Variable expenses – Fixed expenses = Operating income

We find it useful to rearrange the equation to place the variables on the left-hand side and the dollar amounts on the right:

Sales – Variable expenses = Fixed expenses + Operating income

At the break-even point, income equals expenses, so operating income is zero. Sales equals the unit selling price multiplied by the number of units sold. Variable expenses equals variable cost per unit times the number of units sold. We substitute these terms into the equation and enter the dollar amounts that we have:

Sales	**–**	**Variable expenses**	**= Fixed expenses + Operating income**

$$\left(\begin{array}{c}\text{Unit}\\\text{sale}\\\text{price}\end{array} \times \text{Units sold}\right) - \left(\begin{array}{c}\text{Unit}\\\text{variable}\\\text{cost}\end{array} \times \text{Units sold}\right) = \text{Fixed expenses} + \text{Operating income}$$

($3.50 × Units sold)	–	($2.10 × Units sold)	= $700	+	$0
	($3.50	–	$2.10) × Units sold	= $700	+	$0
			$1.40 × Units sold	= $700		
			Units sold	= $700/$1.40		
		Break-even sales in units	= 500 units		

Francine must sell 500 units to break even. Her break-even sales in dollars is the 500 units times their selling price of $3.50. Break-even dollar sales are $1,750 (500 units × $3.50).

Another form of the equation approach determines dollar sales first and unit sales second. We divide the variable expense per unit, $2.10, by the selling price, $3.50, to determine the ratio of the variable expense to the selling price:

$$\frac{\text{Variable expense}}{\text{Selling price}} = \frac{\$2.10}{\$3.50} = .60$$

We use this ratio in the equation, as follows:

Sales –	Variable expenses	=	Fixed expenses	+	Operating income
Sales –	(.60 × Sales)	=	$700	+	$0
Sales –	(.60 × Sales)	=	$700		
	.40 × Sales	=	$700		
	Sales	=	$700/.40		
Break-even sales in dollars		=	$1,750		
Break-even sales in units		=	500 ($1,750/$3.50)		

Contribution Margin Approach   A second way to do CVP analysis is the contribution margin approach. Each unit sold has a contribution margin, which is the excess of the sale price over variable expenses. The contribution margin can be expressed per unit, as a percentage or a ratio. Sales revenue "contributes" this excess, so to speak, to the recovery of fixed costs, with any remaining excess going to operating income, as follows for Francine Deslaurier's business:

	Per Unit	Percent	Ratio
Sale price..	$ 3.50	100%	1.00
Variable expense..............................	– 2.10	–60	–.60
Contribution margin.........................	$ 1.40	40%	.40

In percentage terms, sales of 100 percent minus the variable expense percentage equals the **contribution margin percentage**. Likewise, 100 percent minus the contribution margin percentage equals the variable expense percentage. These relationships can be diagrammed:

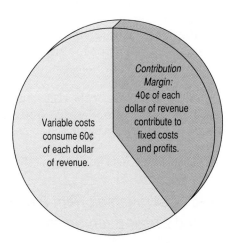

Breakdown of $1 of Revenue

In our illustration, the contribution margin per unit is $1.40 ($3.50 – $2.10). To compute break-even sales in units sold, divide fixed expenses by the contribution margin per unit:

$$\text{Break-even sales in units} = \frac{\text{Fixed expenses}}{\text{Contribution margin per unit}}$$

$$= \frac{\$700}{\$1.40}$$

$$= 500 \text{ units}$$

We may use percentages in the contribution margin approach. In our example, the contribution margin percentage is $1.40/$3.50, or 40 percent. Earlier we subtracted the variable cost percentage (60 percent) from sales (100 percent) to compute the 40 percent contribution margin percentage. The contribution margin percentage equals the contribution margin divided by the sale price.

We may use the sale price and variable cost of a single item, or we may use the total sales figure and the total variable cost amount of the entire product line in our computations. For example, consider the figures that arise from Francine's selling 500 items. Total sales equals $1,750 ($3.50 × 500), and total contribution margin is $700 ($1.40 × 500). We see that $700/$1,750 equals .40, or 40 percent. Break-even sales in dollars can be computed as follows by the contribution margin approach:

$$\text{Break-even sales in dollars} = \frac{\text{Fixed expenses}}{\text{Contribution margin ratio}}$$

$$= \frac{\$700}{.40}$$

$$= \$1,750$$

If unit costs rise, then the amount needed to reach break-even sales increases. Why? A higher unit cost lowers the contribution margin. In contrast, a lower unit cost means a higher contribution margin, which leads to lower break-even sales.

If sales increase, so does operating income. To find the increase in operating income, we can multiply the increase in sales by the contribution margin ratio. For example, Francine's contribution margin ratio is .40. If sales increase by $1,000, for example, then operating income grows by $400.

The business press often refers to break-even sales or break-even revenues. For example, a news story might report that "the Big Three auto makers have slashed their sales break-even point in North America from 12.2 million cars and trucks to only 9.1 million this year." The companies could accomplish this by decreasing fixed expenses, which is the numerator of the break-even formula. As the numerator decreases, the break-even amount decreases too. Similarly, increasing the contribution margin per unit (the denominator in the formula) will also decrease the break-even amount. For example, a reduction in variable expenses like tires or radiators will increase the contribution margin per automobile, and so reduce the break-even amount.

Should you use the equation approach or the contribution margin approach? Use either, depending on your personal preference. You should know both approaches, however, because certain decision situations may give the information in one form or the other — but not both.

We return to questions about Francine's business.

Question 2: If a Fixed Cost (such as Rent Expense) is Changed, what would Break-Even Sales be?

Suppose the rental on the booth were $1,050 instead of $700. What is Francine's break-even point in units sold and dollar sales?

Use the formula discussed in the contribution margin approach.

$$\text{Break-even sales in units} = \frac{\text{Fixed expenses}}{\text{Contribution margin per unit}}$$

$$= \frac{\$1,050}{\$1.40}$$

$$= 750 \text{ units}$$

$$\text{Break-even sales in dollars} = \frac{\text{Fixed expenses}}{\text{Contribution margin ratio}}$$

$$= \frac{\$1,050}{.40}$$

$$= \$2,625$$

The $1,050 in fixed expenses is an increase of $350, or 50 percent, in excess of $700. Note that the break-even point also rises by 50 percent, from 500 to 750 units. This match in percentage between the increase in fixed expenses and the increase in the break-even point always exists (if other factors are held constant). Francine must sell more posters to cover the higher fixed costs. Similarly, a decrease in fixed expenses means that she can sell less and still cover these costs.

Question 3: If the Sale Price is Changed, what would Break-Even Sales be?

Suppose the sale price per poster is $3.85 rather than $3.50. Variable expense per unit remains at $2.10, and fixed expenses stay at $700. What are Francine's revised break-even sales in units and in dollars? The unit contribution margin becomes $1.75 ($3.85 – $2.10), and the new contribution margin ratio is .4545 ($1.75/$3.85).

Compute break-even in units and in dollars as follows:

$$\text{Break-even sales in units} = \frac{\text{Fixed expenses}}{\text{Contribution margin per unit}}$$

$$= \frac{\$700}{\$1.75}$$

$$= 400 \text{ units}$$

$$\text{Break-even sales in dollars} = \frac{\text{Fixed expenses}}{\text{Contribution margin ratio}}$$

$$= \frac{\$700}{.4545}$$

$$= \$1,540$$

Note that an increase in sale price reduces break-even sales, in units and in dollars. This occurs because the contribution margin per unit increases. Consequently, it takes fewer sales at the higher price to break even. Conversely, a reduction in sale price would decrease the contribution margin and force Francine to increase sales just to break even.

Question 4: If a Variable Cost is Changed, what would Break-Even Sales be?

Suppose that variable cost per unit is $2.38 instead of $2.10. The unit sale price remains $3.50, and fixed costs stay at $700. Compute break-even sales in units and in dollars.

The new unit contribution margin is $1.12 ($3.50 – $2.38), and the new contribution margin ratio is .32 ($1.12/$3.50). Break-even sales are

$$\text{Break-even sales in units} = \frac{\text{Fixed expenses}}{\text{Contribution margin per unit}}$$

$$= \frac{\$700}{\$1.12}$$

$$= 625 \text{ units}$$

$$\text{Break-even sales in dollars} = \frac{\text{Fixed expenses}}{\text{Contribution margin ratio}}$$

$$= \frac{\$700}{.32}$$

$$= \$2,187.50$$

An increase in variable cost per unit decreases the contribution margin and means that Francine must increase sales in units and in dollars to break even. A decrease in variable cost per unit would lower the break-even point.

Question 5: How many Units must be Sold to Earn a Target Operating Income?

Suppose Francine would be content with operating income of $490 for a week's work in the booth. Assuming a unit sale price of $3.50, variable expense of $2.10 per unit and fixed expenses of $700, how many posters must Francine sell to earn a profit of $490?

Until now, we have concentrated on break-even sales, the point where operating income is zero. How should we consider a target operating income greater than zero? The contribution margin must be sufficient to cover the fixed expenses plus the target operating income. Our contribution margin approach is basically unchanged. However, the numerator now contains both fixed expenses and the target operating income.

OBJECTIVE 4

Compute the sales level needed to earn a target operating income

$$\text{Target sales in units} = \frac{\text{Fixed expenses} + \text{Target operating income}}{\text{Contribution margin per unit}}$$

$$= \frac{\$700 + \$490}{\$1.40}$$

$$= \frac{\$1,190}{\$1.40}$$

$$= 850 \text{ units}$$

$$\text{Target sales in dollars} = \frac{\text{Fixed expenses} + \text{Target operating income}}{\text{Contribution margin ratio}}$$

$$= \frac{\$700 + \$490}{.40}$$

$$= \frac{\$1,190}{.40}$$

$$= \$2,975$$

The minimum level needed to earn operating income of $490 is 850 units, or $2,975 (850 × $3.50).

Question 6:   What Operating Income is Expected at Various Sales Levels?

OBJECTIVE 5

Graph a set of cost-volume-profit relationships

A convenient way to answer this question is to graph the cost-volume-profit relationships, as shown in Exhibit 21-6.

To set up the graph, we place units on the horizontal axis and dollars on the vertical axis. We label each axis appropriately. (We have chosen to place labels every 100 units and every $500. These labels offer enough detail for ease in

EXHIBIT 21-6 *Cost-Volume-Profit Graph*

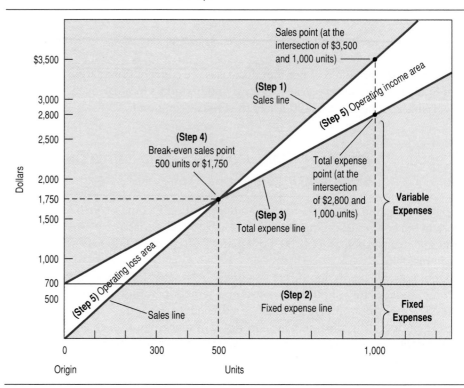

understanding the graph but do not clutter it. Labels on the graphs depend on the data in the problem. The labels should be helpful but not crowd the information.) We use Francine Deslaurier's data (as originally given) and follow five steps:

Step 1. Choose a relevant sales volume, such as 1,000 units. Plot the point for sales dollars at that volume: 1,000 units × $3.50 per unit = sales of $3,500. Draw the sales line from the origin through the $3,500 point.

Step 2. Draw the fixed expense line, which intersects the dollar amount axis at $700 and runs across the graph horizontally.

Step 3. Compute variable expense at a relevant sales volume, such as 1,000 units: 1,000 units × $2.10 per unit = variable expense of $2,100. Add variable expense to fixed expense: $2,100 + $700 = $2,800. Plot the total expense point ($2,800) for 1,000 units. Then draw a line through this point from $700 fixed expenses intercept on the dollar amount axis. This is the total expense line.

Step 4. Identify the break-even point. The break-even point is the spot where the sales line intersects the total expense line. The equations we used earlier told us that Francine's break-even point was 500 units, or $1,750 in sales. The graph gives us the same information visually.

Step 5. Mark the operating income and operating loss area on the graph. To the left of the break-even point, expenses exceed sales. Consider unit sales of 300, which provide dollar sales of $1,050 (300 × $3.50). Total expenses are $1,330 [(300 × $2.10) + $700]. Therefore, the graph point for sales of 300 units lies in the operating loss area. The vertical distance between the total expense line and sales line equals the operating loss. For sales of 300 units, the loss is $280 (sales of $1,050 minus total expenses of $1,330).

To the right of the break-even point, Francine earns a profit. The vertical distance between the sales line and total expense line equals the amount of operating income.

We can tell from the graph whether operating loss, break-even, or operating income results from a given sales figure. We can also see the amount of any operating loss or operating income. By contrast, the equation approach indicates income or loss for a single sales amount. Many computer programs display graphs for CVP analysis. The CVP graph is a valuable budgeting tool, because it can show expected operating income or operating loss for all sales levels from zero units to the company's upper limit.

Summary Problem for Your Review

Grady Nutt is considering opening a booth at the county fair. Grady's rent expense will be $600. He plans to sell souvenirs, which cost $.95 each, at an average selling price of $1.75.

Required

1. Use the contribution margin approach to compute Grady's break-even sales in units and in dollars. Round the contribution margin ratio to three decimal places.

2. How many units must he sell to earn operating income of $720? What are dollar sales at this level? Round to the nearest dollar.

3. Prepare a graphic solution to the break-even problem, showing operating income and operating loss areas from 0 to 2,000 units. Mark the break-even sales level and sales level needed to earn operating income of $720.

SOLUTION TO SUMMARY PROBLEM

Requirement 1

The unit contribution is $.80 ($1.75 − $.95). The contribution margin ratio is .457 ($.80/$1.75).

$$\text{Break-even sales in units} = \frac{\text{Fixed expenses}}{\text{Contribution margin per unit}} = \frac{\$600}{\$.80} = \textbf{750 units}$$

$$\text{Break-even sales in dollars} = \frac{\text{Fixed expenses}}{\text{Contribution margin ratio}} = \frac{\$600}{.457} = \textbf{\$1,313}$$

Requirement 2

$$\text{Target sales in units} = \frac{\text{Fixed expenses + Operating income}}{\text{Contribution margin per unit}}$$

$$= \frac{\$600 + \$720}{\$.80} = \frac{\$1,320}{\$.80} = \textbf{1,650 units}$$

$$\text{Target sales in dollars} = \textbf{\$2,888 (1,650 units} \times \textbf{\$1.75)}$$

Requirement 3

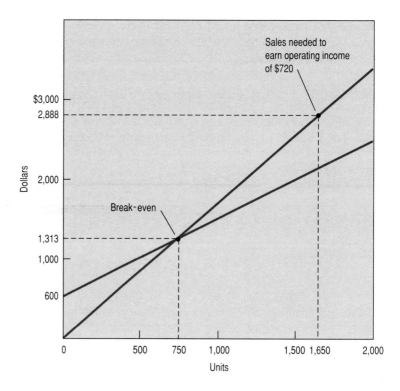

Margin of Safety

The **margin of safety** is the excess of expected sales over break-even sales. In other words, the margin of safety is the drop in sales dollars that the company can absorb before incurring an operating loss. A high margin of safety serves as a cushion. A low margin of safety is a warning. Managers use the margin of safety to evaluate current operations or to measure the risk of a new business plan. The lower the margin, the higher the risk becomes. The higher the margin, the lower the risk will be.

Suppose the break-even point is 375 units, and the company expects to sell 825 units during the period. Assuming a sale price of $3.50 per unit, we compute the margin of safety as follows:

Margin of safety in units = Expected sales in units – Break-even sales in units

$$= 825 – 375 = 450$$

Margin of safety in dollars = Margin of safety in units × Sale price per unit

$$= 450 \text{ units} \times \$3.50 = \$1,575$$

> **OBJECTIVE 6**
> Compute a margin of safety

Sales can drop by 450 units, or $1,575, before the company incurs a loss.

For any level of sales, managers can compute the margin of safety as a percentage. We divide the margin of safety in units (450) by sales in units (825), which equals 55 percent. We reach the same percentage by dividing the margin of safety in dollars ($1,575) by sales in dollars (825 × $3.50 = $2,888).

Assumptions Underlying CVP Analysis

Cost-volume-profit analysis is based on the following assumptions:

1. The cost-volume-profit relationships are linear over a wide range of production and sales. Linear relationships can be graphed as straight lines (like all the lines in Exhibit 21-6).
2. Expenses can be classified as either variable or fixed (we discuss mixed costs later in this chapter).
3. Sale prices, unit variable costs, and total fixed expenses will be unchanged during the period under consideration.
4. Volume is the sole cost driver. The influences of other possible cost drivers (such as weight or size) are held constant or regarded as insignificant.
5. The relevant range of volume is specified.
6. The sales mix of products will be unchanged during the period under consideration. **Sales mix** is the combination of products that make up total sales. For example, the sales mix of a furniture store may be 70 percent household furniture and 30 percent office furniture. We discuss sales mix in the next section.

When these conditions are met, CVP analysis is precise. Most actual business conditions do not perfectly correspond to these assumptions, and the resulting analysis becomes an approximation. The next two sections discuss how to deal with these real-world situations.

Sales Mix

Our illustrations thus far have focused on a single product, travel posters. Most companies sell more than one product, so the sales mix must be considered in figuring CVP relationships. The sales mix has an important effect on profits. For example, the business earns more income selling high-margin products than by selling an equal number of low-margin items.

Management's discussion of income statements often refers to sales mix. For example, an annual report of Deere and Company, a manufacturer of farm equipment, stated that profits decreased because of "a less favorable mix of products sold." What is a "less favorable mix of products"? It is the selling of items with relatively low contribution margins.

We may perform CVP analysis for a company that sells more than one product by using the same equations that we have discussed in analyzing a company selling a single product. However, we must first express the number of units in terms of a single product.

Let us return to the Francine Deslauriers example. Suppose Francine plans to sell two types of posters. Recall that the basic poster costs $2,10 and sells for $3.50. The second, larger, poster costs $3.92 and will sell for $6.00.

An ongoing business uses its experience to compute its sales mix. Francine, however, is starting a new venture. Suppose she estimates that she will sell 500 large posters and 400 regular posters. To compute break-even sales in units, Francine arranges the data as follows:

	Regular Posters	Large Posters	Total
Sale price per unit	$3.50	$6.00	
Variable expense per unit	2.10	3.92	
Contribution margin per unit	$1.40	$2.08	
Estimated sales in units	× 400	× 500	900
Estimated contribution margin	$560 +	$1,040 =	$1,600
Weighted-average contribution margin per unit ($1,600/900 units) — rounded to three decimal places			$1.778

$$\text{Break-even sales in total units} = \frac{\text{Fixed expenses}}{\text{Weighted-average contribution margin per unit}} = \frac{\$700}{\$1.778} = 394 \text{ units}$$

Break-even sales of regular posters $\left(394 \times \dfrac{400}{900}\right)$ .... 175 units

Break-even sales of large posters $\left(394 \times \dfrac{500}{900}\right)$ .... 219 units

The overall break-even point in dollar sales in $1,927: 175 regular posters (175 × $3.50 = $613) plus 219 large posters (219 × $6 = $1,314). At break-even, Francine's operating income can be computed:

	Regular	Large	Total
Sales			
Regular (175 units × $3.50)	$613		
Large (219 units × $6.00)		$1,314	$1,927
Variable expenses			
Regular (175 units × $2.10)	368		
Large (219 units × $3.92)		859	1,227
Contribution margin	$245	$ 455	$ 700
Fixed expenses			700
Operating income			$ -0-

Let us review our approach. First, we computed the weighted-average contribution margin per unit. This figure expresses both types of posters in terms of a single hypothetical product that has a contribution margin of $1.778. From here on, the contribution margin approach follows the usual pattern. Divide fixed expenses by contribution margin per unit to determine break-even sales in total units. The last step is to separate total units (394) into regular posters (175) and large posters (219).

After performing a CVP analysis, prepare an income statement as a check on your analysis. If the CVP analysis focuses on breaking-even as in the preceding example, the income statement should show operating income of zero. If the CVP analysis shows the sales level needed to earn a target operating income, the income statement should report that income amount.

If Francine's sales mix changes, planned operating income will differ from these estimates. For example, if she sells a higher proportion of large posters, she stands a chance of earning more money because the large posters generate a higher contribution margin.

Management's discussion of results often refers to the sales mix. For example, an annual report of Dover Industries Limited stated that

> . . . the grain division which buys and sells Ontario grown corn, soybeans, and winter wheat operates four country elevators and a mixed feed plant in the Chatham area in southwestern Ontario. Results were lower than expected during 1988, a result of lower yields in the farm community reflecting the drought conditions during the growing season. . . . Our subsidiary company in Halifax achieved new levels of profitability in 1988 as a result of increased sales to wholesale bakeries and the food service trade in Atlantic Canada. Family flour sales also advanced as Topsail all-purpose flour won wider acceptance in Newfoundland and private label sales continued to make market gains. Export sales declined in 1988 due to the opening of a new flour mill in Iceland and stronger competition from the U.S. and the E.E.C. [European Economic Community] in other international markets.

CVP sales-mix analysis enters the budgeting system. Suppose a company's profits have decreased. An analysis of the sales mix in the past may indicate that this decrease resulted from concentrating on low-margin products. This information can be used to budget a campaign to try to sell products with a higher contribution margin.

Separating a Mixed Cost into Its Variable and Fixed Components

An assumption of CVP analysis is that each cost is either variable or fixed. As mentioned previously, some expenses are mixed, combining variable expenses and fixed expenses. We cited utility expense as an example of a mixed cost. Similarly, businesses often pay sales personnel a set monthly salary (a fixed expense) plus a sales commission (a variable expense) based on their sales. The salesperson's overall compensation is a mixed cost to the employer. Mixed expenses, also called semivariable costs, must be separated into their variable and fixed components for CVP analysis.

A number of methods exist for separating mixed expenses into variable and fixed expenses. The more sophisticated methods use statistical computations that are covered in more advanced accounting courses and statistics courses. To introduce you to the concept of separating mixed costs, we present the high-low method.

Assume Camrose Drug Store keeps few accounting records. The available records show total monthly revenues and expenses only. The manager wants to separate the expense of making home service calls into fixed and variable components. See Exhibit 21-7.

To use the **high-low method**, pick the highest and the lowest monthly expense figures. Do the same for revenues. For both expenses and revenues, subtract the lower amount from the higher amount. Camrose Drug's records show:

	Total Expenses	Revenues
High	$18,000	$25,000
Low	15,000	20,000
Change	$ 3,000	$ 5,000

OBJECTIVE 7

Separate a mixed cost into its variable and fixed components

EXHIBIT 21-7 *CVP Graph for High-Low Method*

$$\text{Variable expense percentage} = \frac{\text{Change in total expenses}}{\text{Change in revenues}} = \frac{\$18,000 - \$15,000}{\$25,000 - \$20,000} = \frac{\$3,000}{\$5,000} = .60 \text{ of revenues}$$

Fixed expenses	=	Total expense	–	Variable expenses		
At high point	:	$18,000	–	($25,000 × .60)	=	$3,000
At low point	:	$15,000	–	($20,000 × .60)	=	$3,000

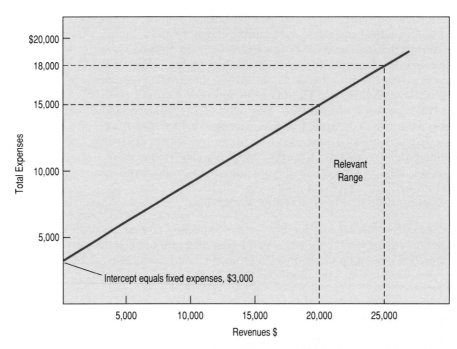

Exhibit 21-7 graphs the CVP relationships for the relevant range, which is between revenues of $20,000 and $25,000.

Divide the difference in total expenses (in our example, $3,000) by the difference in revenues ($5,000). The result is the ratio of variable expenses to revenues. Multiply this ratio ($3,000/$5,000 = .60) by the *high* revenue amount to determine variable expenses:

Variable expenses	=	.60 of revenues
	=	$25,000. × 60
	=	$15,000

By subtracting variable expenses from total expenses at the high level of volume, we arrive at fixed expenses:

Fixed expenses	=	Total expenses – Variable expenses
	=	$18,000 – $15,000
	=	$3,000

Alternatively, we can multiply the .60 ratio by the lower revenue amount ($20,000) to compute variable expenses ($12,000) at that revenue level. Subtract variable expenses from the corresponding total expense amount ($15,000) to compute fixed expenses:

Fixed expenses = **Total expenses – Variable expenses**

=	$15,000	– ($20,000 × .60)
=	$15,000	– $12,000
=	$ 3,000	

Camrose Drug's cost behavior can be described as fixed monthly expenses of $3,000 plus variable monthly expenses that average 60 percent of revenues. These data can be used for analyzing the store's CVP relationships, for example, to prepare a cost budget. Because budget estimates are usually based on historical data from the past, the method can be applied to actual past costs in order to estimate budgeted amounts. Exhibit 21-7 summarizes these computations.

Computer Spreadsheet Analysis of CVP Relationships

Computer spreadsheets are ideally suited for cost-volume-profit analysis because computers can be programmed to show income for any number of sales levels. Spreadsheet programs answer as many "what-if" questions as managers wish to ask: What will variable expenses be if sales rise by a certain amount? By a certain number of units? What if sales fall? If we cut fixed expenses, how many units of each product must we sell to reach a certain level of profits? Computer spreadsheet programs allow managers to analyze the results of any one change or the results of many changes in the business's figures.

Suppose Handel Limited wishes to expand its operations by opening two new stores. The business has received two bids from outside contractors for the construction job. The first bid is $100,000 and the second bid is $140,000. Variable expenses fluctuate between 40 percent and 50 percent of its sales. Fixed costs are expected to be from $280,000 to $420,000. Managers need to know the sales level that the business must reach to earn operating income of $100,000, operating income of $150,000, and operating income of $200,000. A computer spreadsheet program provides the answers to these questions, as shown in Exhibit 21-8, which gives management the information it needs to make an informed decision.

The person who writes the spreadsheet program uses a single formula based on the CVP relationships. The computer places the varying input amounts in the

EXHIBIT 21-8 *Spreadsheet Analysis of CVP Relationships*

D8: [W13] ^$716,667					READY
	A	B	C	D	E
1		Sales Required to Earn Annual Operating Income of			
2					
3			$100,000	$150,000	$200,000
4	Fixed	Variable	--------	--------	--------
5	Expense	Expense			
6	-------	--------			
7					
8	$280,000	40% of Sales	$633,333	$716,667	$800,000
9		45% of Sales	690,909	781,818	872,727
10		50% of Sales	760,000	860,000	960,000
11					
12					
13	$350,000	40% of Sales	750,000	833,333	916,667
14		45% of Sales	818,818	909,091	1,000,000
15		50% of Sales	900,000	1,000,000	1,100,000
16					
17					
18	$200,000	40% of Sales	866,667	950,000	1,033,333
19		45% of Sales	945,455	1,036,364	1,127,273
20		50% of Sales	1,040,000	1,140,000	1,240,000
17-Jul-92 11:29 AM					NUM

formula and computes the 27 amounts that appear in the exhibit. The computer handles this job in seconds and figures the amounts without computational error.

Managers can insert new figures for fixed expenses, variable expenses, operating income — whatever they wish to change — in order to evaluate the financial results of the various situations. Managers use the computer output, which covers the wide range of cost, volume, and profit patterns, to plan their best course of action. As discussed in the preceding chapter, the spreadsheet is a valuable budgeting tool.

Summary Problem for Your Review

Part A   Chambers Company sells its product for $8. Management expects October sales to be between 12,000 units and 20,000 units. The business will incur expenses of $58,000 in selling 12,000 units and expenses of $90,000 in selling 20,000 units.

Required

1. Use the high-low method to separate total expenses into variable and fixed components.
2. Use both the equation approach and the contribution margin approach to compute the company's break-even monthly sales in units and in dollars.
3. Compute the monthly sales level needed to earn operating income of $14,000. Use either the equation approach or the contribution margin approach.

Part B   Chambers's sales reach 18,000 units during October. Cost of goods sold makes up 60 percent of variable expenses. Operating expenses are the other 40 percent of variable expenses and all of fixed expenses.

Required

1. Prepare a contribution margin income statement for Chambers for the month of October.
2. Compute income from operations if sales decrease by 10 percent.

SOLUTION TO REVIEW PROBLEM

Part A Requirement 1

	Total Expenses	Sales	
High..	$90,000	$160,000	(20,000 × $8)
Low	58,000	96,000	(12,000 × $8)
Change...	$32,000	$ 64,000	

$$\text{Variable expense percentage} = \frac{\text{Change in total expenses}}{\text{Change in sales}} = \frac{\$32,000}{\$64,000} = .50 \text{ of sales}$$

Fixed expenses = Total expenses – Variable expenses

At high point   : $90,000   –   ($160,000 × .50)   = $10,000

At low point   : $58,000   –   ($96,000 x .50)   = $10,000

Requirement 2

Equation approach

$$\text{Sales} - \text{Variable expenses} = \text{Fixed expenses} + \text{Operating income}$$

$$\begin{pmatrix} \text{Unit} \\ \text{sale} \times \text{Units sold} \\ \text{price} \end{pmatrix} - \begin{pmatrix} \text{Unit} \\ \text{variable} \times \text{Units sold} \\ \text{cost} \end{pmatrix} = \text{Fixed expenses} + \text{Operating income}$$

($8 × Units sold) −	($8 × .50) × Units sold	= $10,000	+ $0
	($8 − $4) × Units sold	= $10,000	+ $0
	$4 × Units sold	= $10,000	
	Units sold	= $10,000/$4	
	Break-even sales in units	= 2,500 units	
	Break-even sales in dollars =	2,500 units × $8 = $20,000	

Contribution margin approach

$$\text{Break-even sales in units} = \frac{\text{Fixed expenses} + \text{Target operating income}}{\text{Contribution margin per unit}}$$

$$= \frac{(\$10,000 + 0)}{(\$8 - \$4)}$$

$$= \frac{\$10,000}{\$4}$$

$$= 2{,}500 \text{ units}$$

Break-even sales in dollars = 2,500 units × $8 = $20,000

Requirement 3

Equation approach

$$\begin{pmatrix} \text{Unit} \\ \text{sale} \times \text{Units sold} \\ \text{price} \end{pmatrix} - \begin{pmatrix} \text{Unit} \\ \text{variable} \times \text{Units sold} \\ \text{cost} \end{pmatrix} = \text{Fixed expenses} + \begin{matrix} \text{Target} \\ \text{operating income} \end{matrix}$$

($8 × Units sold) −	($8 × .50) × Units sold	= $10,000	+ $14,000
	($8 − $4) × Units sold	= $10,000	+ $14,000
	$4 × Units sold	= $24,000	
	Units sold	= $24,000/$4	
	Target sales in units	= 6,000 units	
	Target sales in dollars	= 6,000 units × $8 = $48,000	

Contribution margin approach

$$\text{Target sales in units} = \frac{\text{Fixed expenses} + \text{Target operating income}}{\text{Contribution margin per unit}}$$

$$= \frac{(\$10,000 + \$14,000)}{(\$8 - \$4)}$$

$$= \frac{\$24,000}{\$4}$$

$$= 6{,}000 \text{ units}$$

Target sales in dollars = 6,000 units × $8 = $48,000

Part B
Requirement 1

Chambers Company
Contribution Margin Income Statement
Month of October 19XX

Sales revenue (18,000 × $8)		$144,000
Variable expenses		
Cost of goods sold ($144,000 × .50 × .60)	$43,200	
Operating expenses ($144,000 × .50 × .40)	28,800	72,000
Contribution margin...		72,000
Fixed expenses		
Operating expenses		10,000
Income from operations		$62,000

Requirement 2

Decrease in sales revenue ($144,000 × .10)	$14,400
Decrease in expenses	
Fixed expenses...	-0-
Variable expenses ($72,000 × .10)..	7,200
Decrease in contribution margin	(7,200)
Income from operations before sales decrease	62,000
Income from operations after sales decrease	$54,800

Summary

Cost-volume-profit (CVP) analysis examines the relationships among a company's expenses, revenues, and income. These relationships depend on cost behavior. We classify costs as fixed, variable, or mixed.

Two popular ways to use cost-volume-profit analysis are the *equation approach* and *contribution margin approach*. The contribution margin is the excess of the sale price over variable expenses. The contribution margin ratio is the contribution margin divided by the sale price.

CVP analysis yields an amount in unit sales or in dollar sales at which operating income equals expenses, which is the *break-even point*. Management can also project target sales using CVP analysis. Graphic displays of CVP relationships present information over a wide range of sales levels, not just at the break-even point. CVP analysis is widely used in budgeting.

The *margin of safety* is the excess of actual or expected sales over the sales figure at break-even. The larger the margin, the lower the risk of a given plan.

CVP analysis has certain limitations. For example, we must restrict analysis to the span of volume over which fixed costs remain unchanged, which we call the *relevant range*. Also, mixed costs must be separated into fixed costs and variable costs. We can use the *high-low method* to achieve this separation.

The contribution margin *income statement* reports variable expenses and fixed expenses separately. This format allows management to analyze costs. Computer spreadsheet programs can be programmed to measure CVP relationships across a wide range of conditions.

Self-Study Questions

Test your understanding of the chapter by marking the best answer for each of the following questions:

1. Cost-volume-profit analysis is most directly useful to *(p. 928)*
   a. Managers for predicting the outcome of their decisions
   b. Investors for deciding how much to pay for a company's stock
   c. Lenders for analyzing a loan request
   d. Tax authorities for setting income tax rates

2. The graph of a mixed cost *(p. 930)*
   a. Passes through the origin and slopes upward
   b. Is horizontal from the point marking the level of fixed costs
   c. Has a steeper slope than the graph of a fixed cost or a variable cost
   d. Slopes upward from the point marking the level of fixed costs

3. Refer to Exhibit 21-4, p. 931. What will income from operations be if sales increase by 25 percent? *(pp. 931–32)*
   a. $7,500   c. $10,000
   b. $8,250   d. $12,750

4. Refer to Exhibit 21-5, p. 932. If sales are 21,000 units, the business can expect fixed expenses of *(pp. 932–33)*
   a. $50,000
   b. $80,000
   c. $100,000
   d. Cannot be determined from the information given.

5. At the break-even point *(p. 933)*
   a. Sales equal fixed expenses
   b. Sales equal variable expenses
   c. Sales equal total expenses
   d. Sales exactly equal operating income

6. Variable expenses consume 70 percent of sales, and fixed expenses total $420,000. The break-even point in dollars is *(p. 934)*
   a. $140,000   c. $1,260,000
   b. $600,000   d. $1,400,000

7. What happens to the break-even point if both variable expenses and fixed expenses increase? *(p. 936)*
   a. Break-even sales increase.
   b. Break-even sales decrease.
   c. Break-even sales are unchanged because the two changes offset each other.
   d. The effect on break-even cannot be determined from the information given.

8. William Thomas Corporation's monthly sales have averaged $480,000 for the past year. The monthly break-even point is $400,000. The company's margin of safety percentage is *(p. 941)*
   a. 16⅔%   c. 62½%
   b. 20%   d. 100%

9. Raj Mujadeen sells handmade Oriental rugs for $1,000 each and machine-made rugs for $300 each. Customers buy five times as many machine-made rugs as handmade rugs. Variable expenses consume 80 percent of sales, and monthly fixed expenses total $2,000. How many of each type of rug must Raj sell to earn monthly operating income of $3,000? *(pp. 941–43)*
   a. 8 handmade and 40 machine-made
   b. 10 handmade and 50 machine-made
   c. 12 handmade and 60 machine-made
   d. 20 handmade and 100 machine-made

10. Separating mixed costs into fixed and variable components is useful for
    (pp. 943–45)
    a. Budgeting costs
    b. Analyzing cost-volume-profit relationships
    c. Computing break-even sales
    d. All of the above

Answers to the Self-Study Questions are at the end of the chapter.

Accounting Vocabulary

break-even analysis *(p. 933)*
break-even point *(p. 933)*
contribution margin *(p. 931)*
contribution margin income statement *(p. 931)*
contribution margin percentage *(p. 935)*
cost behavior *(p. 928)*
cost driver *(p. 928)*
cost-volume-profit (CVP) analysis *(p. 928)*
fixed cost *(p. 929)*
fixed expense *(p. 929)*
high-low method *(p. 943)*
margin of safety *(p. 940)*
mixed cost *(p. 930)*
mixed expense *(p. 930)*
relevant range *(p. 932)*
sales mix *(p. 941)*
variable cost *(p. 928)*
variable expense *(p. 928)*

ASSIGNMENT MATERIAL

Questions

1. How is cost-volume-profit analysis used in budgeting?
2. Define the three types of cost behavior patterns.
3. Draw graphs of the three types of costs.
4. What are six questions cost-volume-profit analysis can answer?
5. How does a contribution margin income statement differ from a conventional income statement? Which income statement is more useful for predicting the income effect of a change in sales? Why?
6. Why is the concept of the relevant range important to cost-volume-profit analysis?
7. Draw a graph of fixed expenses from 0 to 50,000 units. The relevant range lies between 20,000 and 35,000 units, where fixed expenses are $300,000. Below the relevant range, fixed expenses are $200,000. Above the relevant range, fixed expenses are $400,000.
8. What is the break-even point? What is its significance to a business?
9. Give the contribution margin formulas for break-even sales in units and in dollars.
10. How does an increase in fixed expenses affect the break-even point? How does a decrease in fixed expenses affect break-even sales? Give the reason for each answer.
11. How does an increase in variable expenses affect the break-even point? How does a decrease in variable expenses affect break-even sales? Give the reason for each answer.
12. How does an increase in selling price affect the break-even point? How does a decrease in selling price affect break-even sales? Give the reason for each answer.
13. Briefly outline two ways to compute the target sales in dollars needed to earn a given operating income.

14. Give the contribution margin formula for target sales in units needed to earn a given operating income. Do the same for target sales in dollars.

15. Identify the steps in the preparation of a cost-volume-profit graph.

16. What advantages does a CVP graph have over the equation approach and the contribution margin approach?

17. How does the margin of safety serve as a measure of risk?

18. Give the assumptions underlying cost-volume-profit analysis.

19. Briefly describe how to perform CVP analysis when a company sells more than one product.

20. McMillan Corporation's expenses are mixed. Management wishes to know its break-even point and seeks your advice. How can you separate total expenses into variable and fixed components?

21. Why are computer spreadsheets useful for CVP analysis?

Exercises

Exercise 21-1   *Graphing cost behaviors (L.O. 1)*

Graph each of the following cost behavior patterns over a relevant range from 0 to 10,000 units:

a. Fixed expenses of $25,000.

b. Mixed expenses made up of fixed costs of $10,000 and variable costs of $3 per unit.

c. Variable expenses of $5 per unit.

Exercise 21-2   *Preparing a contribution margin income statement (L.O. 2, 3)*

Sauve Limited's April income statement follows:

Sauve Limited
Income Statement
April 19XX

Sales revenue...		$637,000
Cost of goods sold..		448,000
Gross margin..		189,000
Operating expenses		
Selling...	$72,000	
General and administrative (including income tax)..............	42,000	114,000
Income from operations		$ 75,000

Sauve accounting records indicate that cost of goods sold is a variable expense, and that selling expense is 20 percent fixed and 80 percent variable. General and administrative expense is half fixed and half variable.

Required

Prepare Sauve's contribution margin income statement for April. Compute the expected increase in operating income to the nearest $1,000 if sales increase by $100,000. Round decimals to three places.

Exercise 21-3   *Using a contribution margin income statement* **(L.O. 2, 3)**

For its top managers, Sun Refining Corp. formats its income statement as follows:

Sun Refining Corp. Contribution Margin Income Statement Three months ended March 31, 19X3	
Sales revenue	$385,000
Variable expenses	154,000
Contribution margin	231,000
Fixed expenses	196,000
Income from operations	$ 35,000

Sun's relevant range is between sales of $310,000 and $430,000. Prepare contribution margin income statements at those volume levels. Also compute break-even sales in dollars.

Exercise 21-4   *Computing break-even sales by the contribution margin approach* **(L.O. 3)**

Bent Tree Associates has fixed expenses of $50,000 and variable expenses of $3 per unit of its product, which it sells for $5.50 per unit.

Required

1. Compute the company's contribution margin per unit and its contribution margin ratio to six decimal places.
2. Determine the break-even point in units and in dollars, using the contribution margin approach.

Exercise 21-5   *Computing break-even sales under different CVP relationships* **(L.O. 3)**

For several years, Chin's Chinese Restaurant has offered a lunch special for $4.50. Monthly fixed expenses have been $4,500. The variable cost of a meal has been $1.50. Rudy Chin, the owner, believes that by remodeling the restaurant and upgrading the food services, he can increase the price of lunch special to $5.25. Monthly fixed expenses would increase to $6,300, and the variable expenses would increase to $1.75 per meal.

Required

Use the equation approach to compute Chin's monthly break-even sales in dollars before and after remodeling.

Exercise 21-6   *Computing break-even sales and operating income or loss under different conditions* **(L.O. 3, 4)**

Transco Truck Lines delivers freight through New Brunswick, Nova Scotia, and Prince Edward Island. The company has monthly fixed expenses of $420,000 and a contribution margin of 70 percent of revenues.

Required

1. Compute Transco's monthly break-even sales in dollars. Use the contribution margin approach.
2. Compute Transco's monthly operating income or operating loss if revenues are $500,000 and if they are $700,000.

Exercise 21-7   *Computing break-even sales and sales needed to earn a given operating income; sales-mix considerations* **(L.O. 3, 4)**

a. Dale's Auto Supply has fixed monthly expenses of $3,900 and a contribution margin ratio of 30 percent. What must monthly sales be for the business to break even? To earn operating income of $3,300?

b. Barb's Boutique sells two product lines, one with a contribution margin ratio of 50 percent and the other with a contribution margin ratio of 60 percent. Each product line makes up one half of sales. If monthly fixed expenses are $3,850, what must monthly sales be for the business to break even? To earn operating income of $4,950?

Exercise 21-8   *Cost-volume-profit analysis with a sales mix* **(L.O. 3, 4)**

Three college friends open an off-campus shop named Big Bear T-Shirts. They plan to sell a standard T-shirt for $6 and a fancier version for $7.50. The $6 shirt costs them $3, and the $7.50 shirt costs them $3.50. The friends expect to sell two fancy T-shirts for each standard T-shirt. Their monthly fixed expenses are $1,870. How many of each type of T-shirt must they sell monthly to break even? To earn $1,210? Round decimals to three places.

Exercise 21-9   *Graphing cost-volume-profit relationships* **(L.O. 5)**

Suppose that the Skydome, the home field for the Toronto Blue Jays baseball team, earns total revenue that averages $9 for every ticket sold. Assume that annual fixed expenses are $8 million and that variable expenses are $1 per ticket.

Required

Prepare the Skydome's cost-volume-profit graph under these assumptions. Show the break-even point in dollars and in tickets. Label fixed expenses, variable expenses, operating loss area, and operating income area on the graph.

Exercise 21-10   *Analyzing a cost-volume-profit graph* **(L.O. 5)**

The top managers of Bronson Stoker, Inc. are planning the budget for 19X6. The accountant who prepared the accompanying cost-volume-profit graph forgot to label the lines.

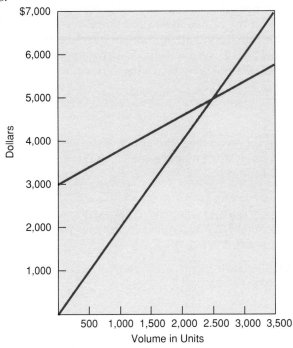

Required

Answer the following questions asked by the managers:

1. What do the lines mean?
2. Where is the operating income area? The operating loss area?
3. What is break-even sales in units and in dollars?
4. What will operating income (or operating loss) be if sales are 1,700 units?
5. What sales level in dollars is needed to earn operating income of $1,000?

Exercise 21-11 *Computing a margin of safety (L.O. 6)*

A Becker's convenience store has a monthly operating profit goal of $5,000. Variable expenses are 60 percent of sales, and fixed monthly expenses are $7,000. Compute the monthly margin of safety in dollars if the store achieves its profit goal. Express the margin of safety for the Becker's store as a percent of target sales.

Exercise 21-12 *Analyzing cost behavior by the high-low method (L.O. 2, 7)*

Hillcrest Hospital is struggling to break even. Its management has decided to install a new accounting system. Management wishes to know the behavior of the hospital's costs. The lowest and highest expected monthly revenues are $450,000 and $900,000. Corresponding total expenses are $530,000 and $800,000.

Required

Separate total expenses into variable and fixed components. Express the hospital's cost behavior as follows: Total monthly expenses = Fixed expenses + Variable expenses as a percent of revenues. Compute Hillcrest Hospital's break-even monthly revenues in dollars. Follow the equation approach.

Problems

(Group A)

Problem 21-1A *Explaining the effects of different cost behavior patterns on the break-even point and on likely profits (L.O. 1)*

Saffron Restaurant Supply is opening early next year. The owner is considering two plans for obtaining the capital assets and employee labor needed for operations. Plan 1 calls for purchasing all equipment outright and paying employees straight salaries. Under plan 2, Saffron would lease equipment month by month, and pay employees low salaries but give them a big part of their pay in commissions on sales.

Required

Discuss the effects of the two plans on variable expenses, fixed expenses, break-even sales, and likely profits for a new business in the start-up stage. Indicate which plan you favor for Saffron.

Problem 21-2A *Analyzing cost behavior; computing break-even sales and operating income under different CVP relationships; preparing a contribution margin income statement (L.O. 1, 2, 3, 7)*

Canadian Shield Manufacturing Ltd. accounting records summarize the fiscal year ended February 28, 19X3:

Quarter ended	Sales	Total expenses
May 31, 19X2	$230,500	$210,000
Aug. 31, 19X2	185,000	186,500
Nov. 30, 19X2	199,500	187,000
Feb. 28, 19X3	265,000	218,500

Required

1. Categorize total expenses as fixed, variable, or mixed. Give your reasoning.

2. Use the high-low method to separate total quarterly expenses into fixed and variable components. Multiply quarterly fixed expenses by 4 to compute annual fixed expenses.

3. Compute break-even sales in dollars for the year. Use the contribution margin approach.

4. Prepare Canadian Shield's contribution margin income statement at the break-even point for the year ended February 28, 19X3. Cost of goods sold is 83 percent of total variable expenses. The remainder of variable expenses is 11 percent selling and 6 percent general. Fixed expenses are 40 percent selling and 60 percent general.

5. Compute income from operations if sales increase by $150,000 above the break-even point.

Problem 21-3A   *Contribution margin and break-even analysis* **(L.O. 2, 3)**

The accounting records of four different companies yield the following information:

	A	B	C	D
Target sales....................................	$560,000	$280,000	$248,000	$____
Variable expenses..........................			132,000	130,000
Fixed expenses..............................	312,000	120,000		
Income (loss) from operations....	$____	$____	$ 7,000	$160,000
Units sold	112,000	11,000		8,000
Unit contribution margin.............		$12	$4	$40
Contribution margin ratio	.30			

Required

Fill in the blanks for each company. Show your work and round contribution margin ratios to three decimal places. By just looking over the data, which company do you think has the lowest break-even point? Which company actually does have the lowest break-even point? What causes the low break-even point?

Problem 21-4A   *Computing break-even revenue and the revenue needed to earn a target operating income; preparing a contribution margin income statement* **(L.O. 2, 3, 4)**

Seaway Limited sails a schooner in the Toronto harbor. The average cruise has 90 tourists on board. Each person pays $75 for a day sail along the shoreline. The ship sails 100 days each year.

The schooner has a crew of 12. Each member earns an average of $85 per cruise. The crew is paid only when the ship sails. Other variable expenses are for refreshments, which average $14 per passenger per cruise. Fixed annual expenses total $115,800.

Required

1. Compute revenue and variable expenses for each cruise.
2. Use the equation approach to compute the number of cruises needed annually to break even.
3. Use the contribution margin approach to compute the number of cruises needed annually to earn $200,000. Is this profit goal realistic? Give your reason.
4. Prepare Seaway's contribution margin income statement for 100 cruises each year. Report only two categories of expenses: variable and fixed.

Problem 21-5A   *CVP analysis under different conditions* **(L.O. 2, 3, 4)**

Suppose Dalhousie Ballpoint Pen Limited imprints pens with company names. The company has fixed expenses of $480,000 each month plus variable expense of $2 per box of pens. For each box of pens sold, Dalhousie earns revenue of $3.20.

Required

1. Use the equation approach to compute the number of boxes of pens Dalhousie must sell each month to break even.
2. Use the contribution margin approach to compute the dollar amount of monthly revenue Dalhousie needs in order to earn $60,000 in operating income.
3. Prepare Dalhousie's contribution margin income statement for June for sales of 450,000 boxes of pens. Cost of goods sold is 70 percent of variable expenses. Operating expenses make up the rest of variable and all of fixed expenses.
4. The company is considering an expansion that will increase fixed expenses by 40 percent and variable expenses by 10 percent. Compute the new break-even point in units and in dollars. Use either the equation approach or the contribution margin approach. Compute the contribution margin ratio to four decimal places.

Problem 21-6A   *Using a contribution margin income statement for break-even analysis; sales mix, margin of safety, and changes in the CVP relationship* **(L.O. 2, 3, 6)**

The contribution margin income statement of Robinette Men's Store for November 19X5 is as follows:

Robinette Men's Store
Contribution Margin Income Statement
November 19X5

Sales revenue...		$60,000
Variable expenses		
Cost of goods sold...	$22,000	
Selling..	13,000	
General and administrative	7,000	42,000
Contribution margin		18,000
Fixed expenses		
Selling..	11,000	
General and administrative	1,000	12,000
Income from operations		$ 6,000

Robinette sells two ties for every belt. The ties sell for $7, with variable expense of $4.90 per unit. The belts sell for $6, with variable unit cost of $4.20.

Required

1. Determine Robinette's monthly break-even point in the numbers of ties and belts. Prove the correctness of your computation by preparing a summary contribution income statement at break-even. You need to show only two categories of expenses: variable and fixed.

2. Compute Robinette's margin of safety in dollars.

3. Suppose Robinette increases monthly sales by 15 percent above $60,000. Compute income from operations.

4. Robinette may expand the store and increase monthly fixed expenses by $4,800. Use the contribution margin approach to determine the new break-even sales in dollars.

Problem 21-7A   *Computing break-even sales and sales needed to earn a given operating income; graphing cost-volume-profit relationships*   **(L.O. 3, 4, 5)**

Bon Voyage Travel is opening an office in New Bedford. Fixed monthly expenses are office rent ($3,400), depreciation of office furniture ($190), utilities ($140), a special telephone line ($390), a connection with the airlines' computerized reservation service ($480), and the salary of a travel agent ($1,800). Variable expenses are utilities (2 percent of sales), incentive compensation of the employee (7 percent of sales), advertising (6 percent of sales), supplies and postage (1 percent of sales), and a usage fee for the telephone line and computerized reservation service (4 percent of sales). The business is a partnership, so it pays no business income tax.

Required

1. Use the contribution margin approach to compute the travel agency's break-even sales in dollars. If the average fee from the airline is $400 per plane ticket, how many units does it take to break even?

2. Use the equation approach to compute dollar sales needed to earn monthly operating income of $3,500.

3. Graph the travel agency's cost-volume-profit relationships. Assume an average fee of $400 per plane ticket. Show the break-even point, fixed expenses, variable expenses, operating loss area, operating income area, and the sales in units and dollars where monthly operating income of $3,500 is earned. The graph should range from 0 to 40 units.

4. Assume that the average fee increases to $600. Use the contribution margin approach to compute the new break-even point in units. What is the effect of the fee increase on the break-even point?

(Group B)

Problem 21-1B   *Explaining the contribution margin approach and the margin of safety to decision-makers*   **(L.O. 2, 6)**

Huntington Clothiers is managed as traditionally as the button-down shirts that have made it famous. Arch Huntington founded the business in 1952 and has directed operations "by the seat of his pants" ever since. Approaching retirement, he must turn the business over to his son, Ralph. Recently Mr. Huntington and Ralph had this conversation:

> Ralph: Dad, I am convinced that we can increase sales by advertising. With our contribution margin, I think we can spend $500 monthly on advertising and increase monthly sales by $6,000. Net income should increase by $3,100.

Mr. Huntington: You know how I feel about advertising. We've never needed it in the past. Why now?

Ralph: Two new shops have opened near us this year, and those guys are getting lots of business. I've noticed our profit margin slipping as the year has unfolded. Our margin of safety is at its lowest point ever.

Mr. Huntington: Profit margin I understand, but what is the contribution margin that you mentioned? And what is this margin of safety?

Required

Explain for Mr. Huntington the contribution margin approach to decision-making. Show how Ralph computed the $3,100. Treat advertising as a fixed cost. Also, describe what Ralph means by the margin of safety, and explain why the business's situation is critical.

Problem 21-2B *Analyzing cost behavior; computing break-even sales and operating income under different CVP relationships; preparing a contribution margin income statement* **(L.O. 1, 2, 3, 7)**

Galindo Baking Limited accounting records summarize the fiscal year ended November 30, 19X2:

Quarter ended	Sales	Total expenses
Feb. 28, 19X2	$161,000	$115,000
May 31, 19X2	138,000	109,000
Aug. 31, 19X2	111,000	93,000
Nov. 30, 19X2	119,000	101,000

Required

1. Categorize total expenses as fixed, variable, or mixed. Give your reasoning.
2. Use the high-low method to separate total quarterly expenses into fixed and variable components. Multiply quarterly fixed expenses by 4 to compute annual fixed expenses.
3. Compute break-even sales in dollars for the year. Use the contribution margin approach.
4. Prepare Galindo's contribution margin income statement at the break-even point for the year ended November 30, 19X2. Cost of goods sold is 69 percent of total variable expenses. The remainder of variable expenses is 20 percent selling and 11 percent general. Fixed expenses are evenly divided between selling and general.
5. Compute income from operations if sales increase by $30,000 above the break-even point.

Problem 21-3B *Contribution margin and break-even analysis* **(L.O. 2, 3)**

The accounting records of four different companies yield the following information:

	A	B	C	D
Target sales.......................................	$	$290,000	$	$500,000
Variable expenses..........................	100,000	120,000	104,000	
Fixed expenses..............................	80,000	138,000		
Income (loss) from operations....	$	$	$ 35,000	$ 60,000
Units sold	5,000			100,000
Unit contribution margin............		$100	$6	$2
Contribution margin ratio	.200		.600	

Required

Fill in the blanks for each company. Show your work, and round contribution margin ratios to three decimal places. By just looking over the data, which company do you think has the lowest break-even point? Which company actually does have the lowest break-even point? What causes the low break-even point?

Problem 21-4B   *Computing break-even revenue and the revenue needed to earn a target operating income; preparing a contribution margin income statement   (L.O. 2, 3, 4)*

The Bluenose is a schooner that sails along the eastern seaboard during spring and fall. During summer the ship leaves from Halifax. The average cruise has 45 tourists on board, and each person pays $50 for a day sail. The ship sails 80 days each year.

   The Bluenose has a crew of 8. Each member earns an average of $100 per cruise. The crew is paid only when the ship sails. The other variable expenses are for refreshments, which average $12 per passenger per cruise. Fixed annual expenses total $51,000.

Required

1. Compute revenue and variable expenses for each cruise.

2. Use the equation approach to compute the number of cruises the Bluenose must take each year to break even.

3. Use the contribution margin approach to compute the number of cruises needed each year to earn $70,000. Is this profit goal realistic? Give your reason.

4. Prepare the Bluenose's contribution margin income statement for 80 cruises for the year. Report only two categories of expenses: variable and fixed.

Problem 21-5B   *CVP analysis under different conditions   (L.O. 2, 3, 4)*

Suppose London Clip-Quick Ltd. imprints ballpoint pens with company logos. The company has fixed expenses of $331,500 each month plus variable expenses of $1.60 per box of pens. For each box of pens sold, the company earns revenue of $2.90.

Required

1. Use the equation approach to compute the number of boxes of pens London must sell each month to break even.

2. Use the contribution margin approach to compute the dollar amount of monthly sales London needs in order to earn $25,500 in operating income. Round the contribution margin ratio to six decimal places.

3. Prepare London's contribution margin income statement for August for sales of 240,000 boxes of pens. Cost of goods sold is 80 percent of variable expenses. Operating expenses make up the rest of variable expenses and all of fixed expenses.

4. The company is considering an expansion that will increase fixed expenses by 30 percent and variable expenses by 10 cents per box of pens. Compute the new break-even point in units and in dollars? Use either the equation approach or the contribution margin approach. (Round the contribution margin ratio to six decimal places.)

Problem 21-6B   *Using a contribution margin income statement for break-even analysis; sales mix, margin of safety, and changes in the CVP relationship   (L.O. 2, 3, 6)*

The contribution margin income statement of Mario's Pizza for 19X6 is as follows:

Mario's Pizza
Contribution Margin Income Statement
19X6

Sales revenue..		$160,000
Variable expenses		
Cost of goods sold...	$32,000	
Selling	25,000	
General and administrative...............................	3,000	60,000
Contribution margin		100,000
Fixed expenses		
Selling...	27,000	
General and administrative...............................	9,000	36,000
Income from operations..		$ 64,000

Mario's sells three small pizzas for every large pizza. A small pizza sells for $10, with variable expense of $4.25. A large pizza sells for $20, with variable expense of $6.

Required

1. Determine Mario's break-even point in the numbers of small pizzas and large pizzas. Prove the correctness of your computation by preparing a summary contribution margin income statement at break-even. You need to show only two categories of expenses: variable and fixed.

2. Compute Mario's margin of safety in dollars.

3. If Mario can increase sales by 15 percent above $160,000, what will income from operations be?

4. Mario's hopes to decrease fixed expenses by $10,000 to scale back operations. Use the contribution margin approach to determine the new break-even sales in dollars.

Problem 21-7B *Computing break-even sales and sales needed to earn a given operating income; graphing cost-volume-profit relationships* **(L.O. 3, 4, 5)**

Air & Sea Travel is opening an office in the Okanagan Valley. Fixed monthly expenses are office rent ($3,000), depreciation of office furniture ($200), utilities ($110), a special telephone line ($520), a connection with the airlines' computerized reservation service ($380), and the salary of a travel agent ($1,400). Variable expenses are utilities (2 percent of sales), incentive compensation for the employee (4 percent of sales), advertising (4 percent of sales), supplies and postage (1 percent of sales), and a usage fee for the telephone line and computerized reservation service (4 percent of sales). The business is a proprietorship, so it pays no business income tax.

Required

1. Use the contribution margin approach to compute Air & Sea's break-even fee revenue in dollars. If the average fee is $350 per plane ticket, how many units does it take to break even?

2. Use the equation approach to compute fee revenue needed to earn monthly operating income of $4,000.

3. Graph the travel agency's cost-volume-profit relationships. Assume an average fee is $300 per plane ticket. Show the break-even point, fixed expenses, variable expenses, operating loss area, operating income area, and the fee revenue in

units and dollars where monthly operating income of $4,000 is earned. The graph should range from 0 to 50 units.

4. Assume that the average fee increases to $440. Use the contribution margin approach to compute the new break-even point in units. What is the effect of the fee increase on the break-even point?

Extending Your Knowledge

Decision Problems

1. Using cost-volume-profit analysis to make business decisions (L.O. 1, 3, 4)

William and Roberta Higgins live in Calgary, Alberta. Their daughter, Celine, is now six months old, and Roberta is considering going back to work. Roberta's mother lives in Calgary and would be delighted to babysit her new granddaughter.

Two years ago, William and Roberta spent their vacation in Thailand. Both of them enjoyed Thai food. Roberta is a professional chef and was impressed with the cooking methods and the spices used. Calgary has no Thai restaurant, and the Higgins are contemplating opening one. Roberta would supervise the cooking, and William would leave his current job with an oil company to be the maître d'. The restaurant would serve dinner Tuesday through Saturday, 6 p.m. to midnight.

Calgary is one of the fastest growing cities in Canada. International companies have established offices in the city, and services, including retailers of high-quality merchandise, have quickly expanded. People eat dinner out two or three nights a week. Business entertaining is also frequent.

William has noticed a restaurant for lease a short drive from the Higgins' home. The seating capacity is seven tables, each of which can seat four. Tables could be moved together for a large party. Roberta is planning two seatings per evening.

William and Roberta have drawn up the following estimates:

Average revenue, including drinks and dessert..................	$ 40 per meal
Average cost of the food, including preparation.................	12 per meal
Chef and dishwasher's salaries..	50,000 per year
Rent (premises, equipment)...	3,000 per month
Cleaning (linen and premises)	500 per month
Replacement of dishes, cutlery, glasses...............................	300 per month
Utilities, advertising, telephone..	1,400 per month

Required

Compute break-even revenue for the restaurant. Also compute the amount of revenue needed to earn net income of $80,000 for the year. Is this target net income realistic? Give your reason.

2. Using a contribution margin income statement to make business decisions (L.O. 2, 3)

Biltrite Toys Limited markets three lines of toys. Each line is manufactured by a different company, and each line has a different set of cost-volume-profit relationships.

	Newborns	Toddlers	Preschoolers
Sales	$330,000	$150,000	$270,000
Variable expenses	64,000	75,000	108,000
Contribution margin	266,000	75,000	162,000
Fixed expenses	188,000	120,000	126,000
Income (loss) from operations	$ 78,000	$(45,000)	$ 36,000

Average sale prices are $2 for newborns' toys, $3 for toddlers' toys and $5 for preschoolers' toys.

Required

1. Which product line is the least profitable?
2. Compute break-even sales in units for the company as a whole. Carry the weighted average contribution margin per unit to four decimal places.
3. Prepare a contribution margin income statement for each product line at the break-even point.
4. Prepare a contribution margin income statement assuming that sales of toddler toys are eliminated altogether.
5. Would it be wise to drop the toddler toy line? What would explain the overall operating loss that would result if the company did drop the toddler toy line?

Ethical Issue

In recent years, professional sports teams have shifted from paying stars straight salaries to paying them lower salaries but adding a bonus that depends on team revenues. In this way, a star is motivated to play harder. The more the team wins, the greater the team revenues, as more and more fans flock to the stadium and television companies increase payments for the rights to broadcast the games. If the star has a bad year, the team may lose more and revenue could drop, which would lower the star's compensation. By shifting player compensation from straight salary to a bonus based on team revenues, these player contracts increase the team's percentage of variable costs and decreases its percentage of fixed costs.

Required

1. Why would team-owners favor these contracts?
2. Are team-owners taking advantage of stars? Are these contracts ethical?

Financial Statement Problem

CVP relationships for an actual company (L.O. 2, 3, 4)

Schneider's income statement in Appendix C can be summarized as follows for fiscal year 1991 (amounts in thousands):

	1991
Sales	$630,966
Operating costs	614,980
Operating earnings	$ 15,986

Assume that managers are budgeting for fiscal 1992. Assume also that 96 percent of cost of products, selling, marketing, and administrative expense is variable. Further, assume fixed costs will equal 1991 levels in 1992.

Required

1. Compute break-even gross sales in dollars. Use the contribution margin approach.
2. Suppose managers' operating earnings goal for fiscal 1992 is $18 million. Compute the target sales needed to achieve this goal. Is this target a reasonable goal for 1992? Explain your conclusion.

Answers to Self-Study Questions

1. a
2. d
3. b Increase in contribution margin ($9,000 × .25)............................. $2,250
    Income from operations before sales increase............................   6,000
    Income from operations after sales increase............................... $8,250
4. c
5. c
6. d Sales − .70 Sales = $420,000; .30 Sales = $420,000;
    Break-even sales = $420,000/.30 = $1,400,000
7. a
8. a Margin of safety in dollars = $80,000 ($480,000 − $400,000)
    Margin of safety as a percentage = 16⅔% ($80,000/$480,000)
9. b

	Handmade	Machine-Made	Total
Sale price per unit...	$1,000	$300	
Variable expense per unit (80%)	800	240	
Contribution margin per unit	$ 200	$ 60	
Estimated sales in units...	× 1	× 5	6
Estimated contribution margin..	$ 200 +	$300 =	$ 500
Weighted-average contribution margin per unit ($500/6 units)...			$83.333

$$\frac{\text{Target sales}}{\text{in total units}} = \frac{\text{Fixed expenses} + \text{Target operating income}}{\text{Weighted-average contribution margin per unit}} = \frac{\$2,000 + \$3,000}{\$83.333} = 60 \text{ units}$$

Target sales of handmade rugs (60 units × ⅙).. 10 units
Target sales of machine-made rugs (60 units × ⅚)................................ 50 units

10. a or d

Chapter 22

Manufacturing Accounting and Job Order Costing

How much of the value of all 1989 Honda Civics was produced in North America and how much came from elsewhere? If it was over 50 percent manufactured in North America it would be exempt of a 2.5 percent duty; if not, Honda Canada would be liable to pay an import duty of $23 million to U.S. Customs. Ask the company and it says 69 percent; ask a U.S. Customs auditor and the answer is 45 percent; ask American university researchers and they say 42 percent! Who is right? Is there a single, correct answer?

The Honda problem revolves around whether various overhead costs, in particular non-mortgage interest cost, are a part of the cost of the car or not. Are insurance, property taxes, employee training costs and management costs incurred in North America part of the "cost" of the Honda? What is the "cost" of a part made overseas by the parent company? Should the cost include a profit (resulting in a higher foreign cost percentage) or is the profit only realized when the car is sold (thereby lowering foreign cost percentage)?

The answer to this riddle is typical of many management accounting problems, which, unlike financial accounting issues, do not have rules or GAAP to refer to. Lawyers, accountants, and engineers debated the problem for some time. Eventually, the issue was referred to the Canada-U.S. Free Trade Agreement panel, which on June 9, 1992 unanimously decided that non-mortgage interest is part of the cost of the Honda. But it is still far from certain that the car is indeed over 50 percent North-American-made.

As you read this chapter, consider how the implementation of a manufacturing accounting system quickly becomes a difficult matter when applied to typical and realistic situations such as this Honda scenario.

Sources: John Daly, "Bumpy Road Ahead," *Maclean's* (February 17, 1992), pp. 32, 34. Nancy Wood, "Estranged Partners," *Maclean's* (March 16, 1992), pp. 34-35.

LEARNING OBJECTIVES

After studying this chapter, you should be able to

1 Prepare the financial statements of a manufacturing company

2 Compute cost of goods manufactured

3 Use job order costing information

4 Account for materials in a job order costing system

5 Account for labor in a job order costing system

6 Account for factory overhead in a job order costing system

This chapter shifts gears to focus on an important sector of business: manufacturing. Previous chapters dealt with merchandisers that acquired their inventory through purchases. This chapter and the next show how manufacturers account for the cost of the goods they produce. Consider the distinction between a sporting goods store and the manufacturer of athletic shoes.

The Sportster specializes in athletic shoes. Like all merchandisers, The Sportster buys its inventory ready for resale to customers. Determining the cost of the shoes is relatively easy. Cost is the price that the merchandiser pays for the goods plus the freight and insurance charges incurred in transporting them to the store.

How do we account for the companies — Nike, Reebok, Adidas, and others — that make the shoes The Sportster sells? Manufacturers use their labor force and factory assets to shape raw materials into finished products. Their manufacturing processes begin with materials — cloth, rubber, plastics and related items. These materials are cut, glued, stitched and formed into athletic shoes. The process of converting these materials into finished products makes it more difficult to measure a manufacturer's inventory cost than that of a merchandiser.

In this and the next chapter we turn our attention to manufacturers, with emphasis on their cost accounting systems. The first part of this chapter introduces manufacturing accounting. The second part discusses a particular system for controlling and determining a manufacturer's costs — job order costing.

Manufacturing and the Value Chain

Before proceeding, let us regard manufacturing in perspective. Consider a company like Apple Computer. Many people would describe Apple (or IBM or Hewlett-Packard) as a manufacturing company. More accurately, Apple may be described as a company that does manufacturing. Why? Because manufacturing is only one of its major business functions. Indeed, Apple's marketing costs exceed its manufacturing costs. Companies that do manufacturing also do many other things, as illustrated by the value chain shown below.

In talking about the value chain, managers sometimes use the image of a river to describe the flow of value. Research, development, and product design are

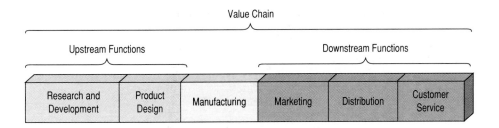

"upstream." That is, they occur prior to manufacturing. Similarly, marketing, distribution, and customer service are "downstream" in the sense that they follow manufacturing.

Considered in relationship to one another, the two upstream functions, manufacturing, and the three downstream functions form a chain. A **value chain** is the sequence of all business functions in which value is added to a firm's products or services.

Modern companies are concerned about the value chain taken as a whole. They aim to control the total costs of the entire chain. For example, companies may willingly spend more in manufacturing to enhance product quality and therefore reduce the customer service costs of honoring product warranties later on. Even though the manufacturing costs are higher then, the total costs of the product, as measured by the entire value chain, may be lower.

Traditionally, cost accounting has been associated with manufacturing. Why? Because manufacturers must determine the costs of the products they make, and accountants can measure these costs. Nevertheless, the basic concepts of how to plan and control costs and how to compute the costs of products and services are applicable to the entire value chain.

Many companies commonly regarded as manufacturers do little if any manufacturing themselves. Instead, they subcontract manufacturing to suppliers. Examples are shoe companies like Nike or Reebok. Almost all their shoes are manufactured by low-wage factories in places like Taiwan and South Korea. Nike and Reebok are intermediaries between the manufacturer and the consumer. Nike's and Reebok's principal functions are product design and marketing.

Objectives of a Cost System

Companies that do manufacturing have developed cost accounting systems to serve more than one purpose simultaneously:

> Cost control: to help plan and control the manufacturing function
> Product costing: to compute manufacturing product costs for financial statements
> Product costing: to compute manufacturing product costs for pricing and product-mix decisions. The full cost of a product extends beyond manufacturing and encompasses all the upstream and downstream business functions in the value chain.

Exhibit 22-1 illustrates the dual objectives of cost control and product costing for a shoe manufacturer like Nike, Inc.

An important focus of cost accounting is the control of cost. Businesses achieve cost control through the evaluation of management performance. Managers strive for the maximum output of finished products at the minimum total cost to the company — not only of manufacturing but of all the functions in the value chain. The company's actual product cost and output provide the information the company needs to measure manufacturing performance — how well a manager succeeds in controlling costs while manufacturing goods.

Product costing (determining the cost to the manufacturer of each of its products) is a primary objective in cost accounting. The manufacturer must know its product costs in order to measure inventory values (and so the cost of goods sold) and profitability (revenues minus expenses, which include the cost of goods sold).

Product costs for the entire value chain frequently help managers decide on pricing: How much does the manufacturer charge the merchandiser for its goods? The answer depends in large part on how much it costs to manufacture and market these goods. Also, managers must determine which products to emphasize. For example, Nike managers may learn that the company is losing money on

EXHIBIT 22-1 *Dual Objectives of a Manufacturing Cost Accounting System*

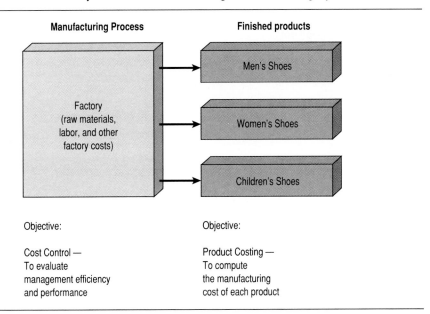

children's shoes, and this information may lead the company to drop that product line. This decision depends on accurate product cost data for each product.

Our discussion in this chapter centres on product costing. Chapter 24 focuses on cost control. We will now take a closer look at manufacturing inventory.

Manufacturing Accounts _____

Inventory Accounts: Materials, Work in Process and Finished Goods

Inventory considerations differ between merchandiser and manufacturer. Merchandisers need only one category of inventory for the finished goods they buy and sell. By contrast, manufacturers have three inventory accounts, as we discuss in a moment. Exhibit 22-2 compares the inventory accounts of a manufacturing company and a merchandising company. Note that the two types of business have identical balance sheets except for the inventory accounts.

The **Materials Inventory**, also called **Raw Materials Inventory**, account holds the cost of materials on hand and intended for use in the manufacturing process. A shoe manufacturer's materials include leather, glue, plastics, cloth and thread. Raw materials for Sydney Steel include iron ore, coal and chemicals. Materials, kept in vats, bins or other storage areas, are collectively called *stores*.

The **Work in Process Inventory** account gives the cost of the goods that are in the manufacturing process and not yet complete. For a shoe manufacturer, partially completed shoes make up its work in process inventory. For a petroleum refiner, work in process is the crude oil being distilled into gasoline, different grades of oils and other products. Work in process inventory is also called *work in progress* and *goods in process*.

The cost of completed goods that have not yet been sold makes up the **Finished Goods Inventory** account. Manufacturers store finished goods in warehouses, tanks or whatever storage facility is appropriate to the particular type of inventory. Finished goods are what the manufacturer sells to a merchandising business. For example, Procter and Gamble manufactures Tide soap and Crest toothpaste,

> **OBJECTIVE 1**
>
> Prepare the financial statements of a manufacturing company

EXHIBIT 22-2   *Inventory Accounts of a Manufacturing Firm and a Merchandising Firm*

Manufacturing Firm			Merchandising Firm		
Current assets			Current assets		
Cash		$ X,XXX	Cash		$ X,XXX
Short-term			Short-term		
investments		X,XXX	investments		X,XXX
Receivables		X,XXX	Receivables		X,XXX
Inventories			**Inventories**		**13,000**
Materials	**$1,000**		Prepaid expenses		X,XXX
Work in					
process	**4,000**				
Finished goods	**8,000**				
Total inventories		**13,000**			
Prepaid expenses..		X,XXX			
Total current			Total current		
assets		$XX,XXX	assets		$XX,XXX

which it sells to such stores as Safeway, Loblaws and Provigo. The Finished Goods account of a manufacturer, then, becomes the Inventory account of a merchandiser.

Materials, work in process and finished goods are assets to the manufacturer and so are reported as current assets on the balance sheet, as Exhibit 22-2 shows. Our goal is to take the information in these inventory accounts to compute the cost of goods manufactured.

Cost of Goods Manufactured

You know the merchandiser's computation of cost of goods sold: beginning inventory + purchases – ending inventory = cost of goods sold. All of a merchandiser's inventory is finished goods. The merchandiser has no materials or work in process inventory. A manufacturer, however, produces its own inventory. **Cost of goods manufactured** is the manufacturer's counterpart to the merchandiser's Purchases account. Therefore, cost of goods manufactured represents the cost of finished goods that the business has produced. Exhibit 22-3 shows that Cost of Goods Manufactured takes the place of Purchases in computing cost of goods sold. Otherwise, a manufacturer's income statement is identical to the income statement of a merchandiser.

Purchases, for a merchandiser, is simply the total cost of all goods bought during the current period for resale. Cost of goods manufactured is more complex. Before we illustrate how to compute this amount, we must introduce some new terms.

Definitions of Key Manufacturing Terms

Direct Materials   To be considered **direct materials**, materials must meet two requirements: (1) the materials must become a physical part of the finished product, and (2) the cost of the materials must be separately and conveniently traceable through the manufacturing process to finished goods. Consider again the athletic-shoe manufacturer. The leather uppers, rubber and plastic soles, and laces are among the direct materials. We can trace them *directly* to the finished shoe. Also, we can follow their costs from the purchase of raw materials through work in process to finished goods.

EXHIBIT 22-3 *Cost of Goods Manufactured on the Income Statement*

Manufacturing Firm		Merchandising Firm	
Sales revenue..................	$XX,XXX	Sales revenue	$XX,XXX
Cost of goods sold		Cost of goods sold	
Beginning finished		Beginning	
goods inventory ...	6,000	inventory	6,000
Cost of goods		**Purchases**	42,000
manufactured.......	42,000	Goods available	
Goods available		for sale....................	48,000
for sale	48,000	Ending inventory	(8,000)
Ending finished		Cost of goods sold....	40,000
goods inventory ...	(8,000)	Gross margin..................	X,XXX
Cost of goods sold	40,000	Operating expenses	
Gross margin	X,XXX	Marketing	X,XXX
Operating expenses		General	X,XXX
Marketing	X,XXX	Total operating	
General......................	X,XXX	expenses	X,XXX
Total operating		Net income....................	$ X,XXX
expenses	X,XXX		
Net income......................	$ X,XXX		

Direct Labor   **Direct labor** is the compensation of the employees who physically convert materials into the company's products. For a shoe manufacturer, direct labor includes the wages of the machine operators and the persons who actually assemble the shoes. For General Motors of Canada Ltd., direct labor is the pay of employees who work on production lines manufacturing automobiles. The efforts of these persons can be traced directly to finished goods.

Factory Overhead   **Factory overhead** includes all manufacturing costs other than direct materials and direct labor. Examples include indirect materials, indirect labor and other costs such as factory utilities, repairs, maintenance, rent, insurance, and property taxes and depreciation on the factory building and equipment. Factory overhead is also called *manufacturing overhead* and, more accurately, *indirect manufacturing cost.*

Indirect Materials   The glue and the thread used in the athletic shoes are also materials that become physical parts of the finished product. However, compared to the cost of the leather uppers and rubber soles, glue and thread costs are minor. Measuring the cost of these low-priced materials is difficult for a single pair of shoes. How would a supervisor figure the cost of a brush full of glue? Of the thread used in a shoe? And how useful would this detailed information be? We call the material whose cost cannot conveniently be traced directly to particular finished products **indirect material**. Indirect materials are accounted for as part of factory overhead cost.

Indirect Labor   Other factory labor costs are classified as **indirect labor**. These costs are difficult to trace to specific products. Examples include the pay of forklift operators, janitors and plant guards. Forklift operators move a wide variety of materials and finished goods around the factory. Plant guards provide security for the entire building. Indirect labor, like indirect materials, is a part of factory overhead.

> **OBJECTIVE 2**
> Compute cost of goods manufactured

    Two of the major cost elements are sometimes combined in cost terminology as follows. **Prime costs** consist of direct materials plus direct labor. **Conversion costs** consist of direct labor plus factory overhead.

EXHIBIT 22-4 *Statement of Cost of Goods Manufactured*

Shoes Unlimited			
Statement of Cost of Goods Manufactured			
year ended December 31, 19X3			
Beginning work in process inventory.....			$ 5,000
Add: Direct materials used:			
Beginning inventory..............................	$ 9,000		
Purchases of materials...........................	27,000		
Available for use.....................................	36,000		
Ending inventory	(22,000)		
Direct materials used...............................		$14,000	
Direct labor..		19,000	
Factory overhead			
Indirect materials	$ 1,500		
Indirect labor...	3,500		
Depreciation — factory building	2,000		
Depreciation — factory equipment......	1,000		
Utilities..	2,500		
Insurance	1,000		
Property tax...	500	12,000	
Total manufacturing costs			
incurred during the year......................			45,000
Total manufacturing costs			
to account for...			50,000
Less: Ending work in process			
inventory...			(4,000)
Cost of goods manufactured			$46,000

Prime costs $\left\{\begin{array}{l}\text{Direct materials}\\\text{Direct labor}\\\text{Factory overhead}\end{array}\right.$ $\left.\begin{array}{l}\\\\\end{array}\right\}$ Conversion costs

Exhibit 22-4 shows the computation of cost of goods manufactured. This statement of cost of goods manufactured is an internal statement, prepared by cost accountants for the business's managers.

Computation of cost of goods manufactured starts with the work in process inventory ($5,000) at the beginning of the period. These goods become complete in the manufacturing process during the current period, so their cost becomes part of cost of goods manufactured. To this amount we add the three components of manufacturing cost: direct materials used ($14,000), direct labor ($19,000) and factory overhead cost ($12,000). Exhibit 22-4 looks closely at direct materials used. Direct labor is simply the total direct labor cost incurred during the period. Factory overhead is the sum of various costs. Direct materials used, direct labor and factory overhead total $45,000, which is the **total manufacturing cost** incurred during the period. We subtract ending work in process inventory (because cost of goods manufactured refers to the cost of finished goods manufactured) to get $46,000.

Exhibit 22-5 diagrams the flow of costs through a manufacturing system. It reveals a similar computational format at all three stages: direct materials, work in process and finished goods. The cost of direct materials used is beginning direct materials plus purchases minus the ending balance. Observe that the final amount at each stage flows into the next stage. Thus, the cost of direct materials used

EXHIBIT 22-5   *Flow of Costs through a Manufacturing Company: Three Similar Computations*

Direct Materials	Work in Process	Finished Goods

Beginning inventory
+ Purchases
	Beginning inventory
	+ Direct materials used
	  Direct labor
	  Factory overhead
		Beginning inventory
		+ Cost of goods
		  manufactured

= Direct materials
  available for use
− Ending inventory
	= Subtotal
	
	− Ending inventory
		= Goods available for
		  sale
		− Ending inventory

= Direct materials
  used
	= Cost of goods
	  manufactured
		= Cost of goods sold

The authors are indebted to Judith Cassidy for this presentation.

becomes part of cost of goods manufactured, which in turn is included in cost of goods sold. Trace the direct materials and work in process portions of the exhibit in Exhibit 22-4, which gives more details for computing costs of goods manufactured.

Inventoriable Costs and Period Costs

The rules of financial accounting have a major influence on accounting for manufacturing costs. For example, the manufacturing costs are **inventoriable costs**, which are all costs of a product regarded as an asset for financial reporting under generally accepted accounting principles. Inventoriable costs become expenses (in the form of cost of goods sold) only when the units in inventory are sold. Of course, the sales may occur in the same accounting period as manufactured or in a subsequent period. Manufacturing costs are regarded as inventoriable because direct materials, direct labor, and factory overhead costs are necessary to obtain the physical products in inventory.

All costs other than manufacturing costs are regarded as immediate expenses. These costs are often called **period costs** because they are expensed in the period in which they are incurred. They are never traced through the inventory accounts. Examples are research, marketing, and distribution expenses.

The distinction between inventoriable costs and period costs is illustrated as follows:

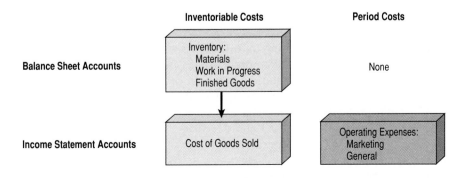

The boxes also help distinguish between companies that do manufacturing and those that do not. For example, a retailer or wholesaler buys goods for resale without changing their basic form. The *only* inventoriable cost is the cost of merchandise.

All labor, depreciation, insurance, utilities, and other operating costs are period costs. In contrast, any of these costs that are related to the manufacturing effort are inventoriable for companies that do manufacturing.

Note that a manufacturing company may classify some labor, depreciation, utilities, and other operating costs as inventoriable costs and some as period costs. All such costs identified with the manufacturing function are inventoriable costs. Those costs identified with marketing or other functions in the value chain are period costs.

Various Meanings of Product Costs

Accountants frequently use the term *product costs* to describe those costs allocated to units of product. **Product cost** is a general term that denotes different costs allocated to products for different purposes. As Exhibit 22-6 shows, accountants should use *manufacturing product costs* to denote *inventoriable costs*.

The term *full product costs* denotes a set of complete product costs encompassing the entire value chain. For decisions regarding choices and pricing of products, managers want the cost of products to include all (or nearly all) the costs of the entire business.

EXHIBIT 22-6   *Different Meanings of the Term "Product Costs" and Their Relations to the Value Chain*

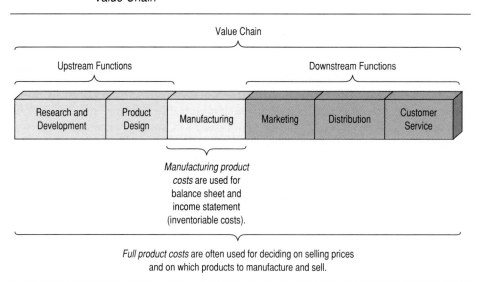

Perpetual and Periodic Inventory Systems _____

Chapter 9 compared the accounting for inventories under the periodic system and the perpetual system. Most manufacturers use the perpetual system because they need a continuous record of materials, work in process and finished goods on hand. The perpetual records help managers control operations and also provide the data for interim financial statements. Physical counts of inventories are taken at least annually to check the accuracy of the records.

Manufacturers that use a periodic inventory system follow the general accounting procedures that merchandisers use, as discussed in Chapter 9. In this chapter we concentrate on the perpetual system because it is more commonly used by manufacturers.

Summary Questions for Your Review

1. What inventory accounts does a manufacturer have that a merchandising entity does not need?

2. What is the manufacturer's counterpart to a merchandiser's Purchases account?

3. Show how to compute cost of goods manufactured. Use the following amounts: direct materials used ($24,000), direct labor ($9,000), factory overhead ($17,000), and work in process, beginning ($5,000) and ending ($4,000).

4. Diagram the flow of costs through a manufacturing company.

5. Identify the following as either an inventoriable cost or a period cost:
   a. Depreciation on factory equipment
   b. Depreciation on salespersons' automobiles
   c. Insurance on factory building
   d. Factory manager's salary
   e. Marketing manager's salary

ANSWERS TO REVIEW QUESTIONS

1. Materials Inventory, Work in Process Inventory and Finished Goods Inventory

2. Cost of goods manufactured

3. Cost of goods manufactured

Beginning work in process inventory		$ 5,000
Add: Direct materials used	$24,000	
Add: Direct labor	9,000	
Add: Factory overhead	17,000	
Total manufacturing costs incurred during the period		50,000
Total manufacturing costs to account for		55,000
Less: Ending work in process inventory		(4,000)
Cost of goods manufactured		$51,000

4. Flow of costs through a manufacturing company:

Direct Materials	**Work in Process**	**Finished Goods**
Beginning inventory + Purchases	Beginning inventory + Direct materials used Direct labor Factory overhead	Beginning inventory + Cost of goods manufactured
= Direct materials available for use − Ending inventory	= Subtotal − Ending inventory	= Goods available for sale − Ending inventory
= Direct materials used	= Cost of goods manufactured	= Cost of goods sold

5. a. Inventoriable cost
   b. Period cost
   c. Inventoriable cost
   d. Inventoriable cost
   e. Period cost

Job Order Costing _____

There are two main types of accounting systems for product costing: *job order costing* and *process costing*. This chapter discusses job order costing, and the next chapter covers process costing. Because these chapters deal primarily with inventory costs, our discussions emphasize inventoriable costs, not period costs. Manufacturers account for and control period costs the same way that merchandisers do.

Job order costing is an accounting system used by companies that manufacture products (1) as individual units or (2) in distinct batches that receive varying degrees of attention and skill. Industries using job order costing include aircraft, furniture, construction and machinery. Their inventory items are unique or few of a kind, differing from the identical products that roll off a production line, such as tubes of toothpaste, boxes of cereal and rolls of carpet. Mass-produced inventories are accounted for by the process costing system, discussed in Chapter 23.

The essential feature of job order costing (often shortened to job costing) is the allocation of costs to a specific job. (The job may be a production order, work order, project, or batch.) The job may consist of a single unit, like a bridge built by a construction contractor, or a group of similar units in a distinct batch, like 10 recliner chairs built by a furniture manufacturer. We illustrate job order costing for a manufacturing situation, but the system applies to other types of business, such as an auto-repair shop (the job is one automobile needing repair), a research organization (the job is a research project), and a public accounting firm (the job is a tax return).

In a job cost system, the job is the focus, so the manufacturer accumulates materials, labor and overhead costs by job. Cost control is the key to earning a profit on each job. If cost is too high, profit is reduced or eliminated. Managers monitor each job to help ensure that its cost stays within the budgeted limits.

Job Costing Illustrated

OBJECTIVE 3

Use job order costing information

Consider the Leclerc Furniture Limited, which has a job order costing system with the following inventories on December 31, 19X4:

Materials inventory (many kinds)	$20,000
Work in process inventory (5 jobs)	29,000
Finished goods inventory (unsold units from 2 jobs)	12,000

The following is a summary of relevant transactions for the year 19X5:

1.	Materials purchased on account	$320,000
2.	Direct materials requisitioned for manufacturing	285,000
	Indirect materials requisitioned for manufacturing	40,000
3.	Factory wages incurred	335,000
4.	Direct labor on jobs	250,000
	Indirect labor to support factory activities	85,000
5.	Factory overhead (depreciation on plant and equipment)	50,000
6.	Factory overhead (factory utilities)	20,000
7.	Factory overhead (factory insurance)	5,000
8.	Factory overhead (property taxes — factory)	10,000
9.	Factory overhead applied to jobs	200,000
10.	Cost of goods completed and transferred to finished goods inventory	740,000
11.	Sales on account	996,000
	Cost of goods sold	734,000

The accounting for these transactions will now be explained, step by step.

Job Cost Record

The bulk of the work in cost accounting is a detailed recording and summarization of source documents such as requisitions, time tickets and invoices. The document used to accumulate and control cost in a job order system is a **job cost record**. This cost record lists the materials, labor and overhead costs charged to the job. It is the basic internal document used by management to control costs in this system. Exhibit 22-7 illustrates a job cost record. It includes sections for direct materials, direct labor and overhead costs.

This cost record shows that for Job 293, the direct materials cost $500, direct labor cost $400 and factory overhead cost $480, for a total of $1,380. Each chair cost the manufacturer $138 ($1,380/10). Managers would use this information by comparing these actual costs to budgeted amounts. Suppose the direct materials budget for this job was $470. The $500 actual cost of direct materials exceeds budget, so managers would determine the reason for the cost overrun and seek to improve future performance. The remainder of the chapter discusses how to account for the direct materials, direct labor and factor overhead costs.

The job cost record in Exhibit 22-7 is the basic record for product costing. A file of current job cost records is the subsidiary ledger for the general ledger account, Work in Process Inventory. As each job begins, a job cost record is prepared. As units are worked on, costs are applied to the products. When the job is completed, its cost is transferred to Finished Goods Inventory. We now illustrate these accounting procedures.

EXHIBIT 22-7   *Job Cost Record*

	Job Cost Record						

Job No. ___293___

Customer Name and Address ___Eaton's Mississauga___
Job Description ___10 recliner chairs___

Date Promised 7-31		Date Started 7-24		Date Completed 7-29			
	Direct Materials		Direct Labor		Factory Overhead Costs		
Date	Requisition Numbers	Amount	Time Ticket Numbers	Amount	Date	Rate	Amount
19X5 7-24	334	$ 90	236,251,258	$150	7-29	120% of Direct labor	$480
25	338	180	264,269,273,291	200			
28	347	230	305	50		Overall Cost Summary	
					Direct materials......... $ 500		
					Direct labor............ 400		
					Factory overhead........ 480		
Totals		$500		$400	Total Job Cost $1,380		

Accounting for Materials in a Job Cost System

Manufacturing companies that use job order costing tend to have relatively low inventories. Only when they receive an order do they acquire the added materials needed to fill the order, produce the goods and deliver the merchandise. Suppose Leclerc, our furniture manufacturer, receives an order for 10 recliner chairs. The

> **OBJECTIVE 4**
>
> Account for materials in a job order costing system

EXHIBIT 22-8   *Materials Ledger Record*

Materials Ledger Record											
Item No. B-220					Description Lumber/Recliner chairs						
	Received				**Used**				**Balance**		
Date	Rec. Report No.	Units	Price	Total Price	Mat. Req. No.	Units	Price	Total Price	Units	Price	Total Price
19X5 7-20									30	$9.00	$270
7-23	678	20	$9.00	$180					50	9.00	450
7-24					334	10	$9.00	$90	40	9.00	360

company may need to buy additional lumber, so Leclerc sends a *purchase order* to a lumber supplier.

In practice, general ledger entries are made monthly. To offer a sweeping overview, however, we use a summary entry for the entire year 19X5. Our first entry is for purchase of materials (data from p. 974):

1. Materials Inventory	320,000	
Accounts Payable		320,000

Leclerc receives the lumber and stores it. Control over materials in storage is established with a subsidiary materials ledger. This ledger holds perpetual inventory records, which list the quantity and the cost of manufacturing materials received and used. They show the cost of materials on hand at all times. Exhibit 22-8 shows a materials ledger record for the lumber (only) that goes into the manufacture of chairs.

Materials received are logged in by receiving report number (abbreviated as *Rec. Report No.* in Exhibit 22-8). Materials used in the product are recorded by materials requisition number (*Mat. Req. No.*). Management can use these underlying data to follow the flow of materials through the production process and so control operations on a day-to-day basis.

The general ledger has a Materials Inventory account. This account is supported by a subsidiary ledger, the materials ledger, that includes a separate record for each raw material. Exhibit 22-9 illustrates the general ledger account and the materials ledger for Leclerc. The balance of Materials Inventory in the general ledger equals the sum of the balances in the materials ledger.

After materials are purchased and stored, the manufacturing process is set in motion by a document called a **materials requisition**, the formal title for a request prepared by manufacturing personnel. In effect, they ask that the lumber be moved from storage to the factory so work can begin. Exhibit 22-10 illustrates a materials requisition for the lumber needed to manufacture the 10 recliner chairs that make up Job 293. (See the job description in Exhibit 22-7 and the "Used" section in Exhibit 22-8.) The details in materials requisitions are posted to job cost records.

Direct and Indirect Materials   To introduce the main points of manufacturing accounting, the first half of this chapter omitted some of the detailed procedures. One such step is the way to account for direct materials separately from indirect materials.

EXHIBIT 22-9   *Materials Inventory Accounts*

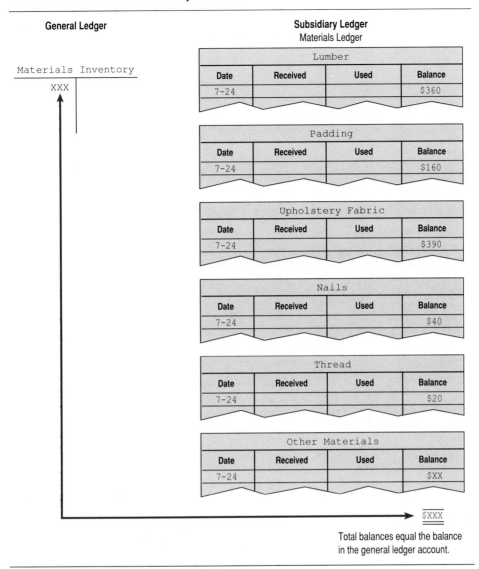

Total balances equal the balance
in the general ledger account.

Recall that the cost of indirect materials is part of Factory Overhead. The flow of materials costs is diagrammed as follows (data from p. 974):

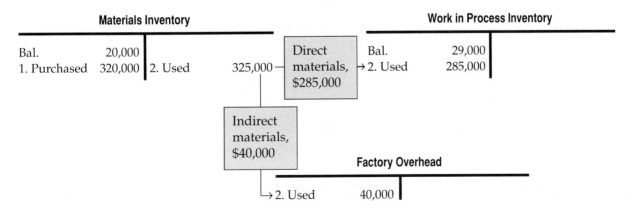

Materials Inventory is debited for the cost of all materials purchased, direct and indirect. Observe that the Materials Inventory account in Exhibit 22-9 includes the cost of direct materials (lumber, padding, and upholstery fabric) and the cost of

Exhibit 22-10 Materials Requisition

Materials Requisition No. 334

Date 7-24-X5   Job No. 293

Item No.	Item	Quantity	Unit Price	Amount
B-220	Lumber/Recliner chairs	10	$9.00	$90

---

indirect materials (nails and thread). When either type of materials is used in production, Materials Inventory is credited. For direct materials, the debit is made directly to Work in Process Inventory. For indirect materials, the debit is made to Factory Overhead. (Recall that factory overhead includes all manufacturing costs other than direct materials and direct labor.)

Of course, the furniture manufacturer will work on many jobs over the course of the accounting period. At regular intervals (commonly a month but for our illustration a year), accountants collect the data from the materials requisitions to make a single journal entry, like the following 19X5 entry for Leclerc:

2. Work in Process Inventory	285,000	
Factory Overhead	40,000	
Materials Inventory		325,000

As Exhibit 22-10 indicates, $90 of the direct materials relates to Job 293. The Leclerc computer would enter the $90 on the job cost record.

Job Cost Record

Job No. 293

Customer Name and Address   Eaton's Mississauga

Job Description   10 recliner chairs

Date Promised	7-31	Date Started	7-24	Date Completed	

Date	Direct Materials		Direct Labor		Factory Overhead Costs		
	Requisition Numbers	Amount	Time Ticket Numbers	Amount	Date	Rate	Amount
19X5							
7-24	334	$ 90					

Overall Cost Summary

Direct materials. . . . .$

Direct labor. . . . .

Factory overhead. . . . .

| Totals | | | | | Total Job Cost . . . . $ | | |

Accounting for Labor in a Job Cost System

Control over labor cost in a job cost system is established through time tickets and payroll registers, as discussed in Chapter 11. Exhibit 22-11 illustrates a time ticket used in a job cost system. Managers use its data to charge labor cost to a particular job.

The **labor time ticket** identifies the employee, the hours spent on a particular job and the labor cost charged to the job. Time tickets are accumulated by job to determine the labor cost to be allocated to each job.

The company's entry for 19X5 for all factory wages for all jobs is

OBJECTIVE 5
Account for labor in a job order costing system

3. Factory Wages...   335,000
        Wages Payable   335,000

This entry records the actual labor cost incurred. The separation of direct labor and indirect labor is accomplished as shown in the accompanying diagram.

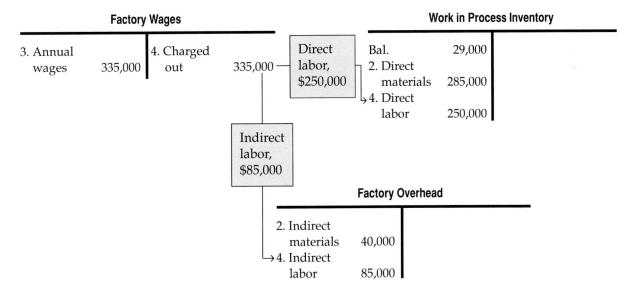

Direct and Indirect Labor   After the factory wages have been recorded, direct labor is debited directly to Work in Process Inventory. Indirect labor passes through the Factory Overhead account en route to Work in Process Inventory. The transfer

EXHIBIT 22-11 *Labor Time Ticket*

Labor Time Ticket	No. 251
EMPLOYEE Jay Barlow	Date 7-24

JOB   293

Time:	Rate $8.00
Started 1:00	Cost of labor
Stopped 8:30	charged to job $60.00
Elapsed 7:30	

Employee   *Jay Barlow*

Supervisor   *G. Dean Chichs*

of labor cost to production results in a credit to the Factory Wages account. The following entry allocates wages to Work in Process Inventory and Factory Overhead:

4. Work in Process Inventory 250,000
    Factory Overhead 85,000
        Factory Wages 335,000

This entry brings the balance in Factory Wages to zero, its transferred balance now allocated between Work in Process Inventory (direct labor) and Factory Overhead (indirect labor).

Assume that $150 of the direct labor cost relates to Job 293. The Leclerc computer would enter Job 293's direct labor on the job cost record. The $150 amount in the accompanying job cost record includes Jay Barlow's wages of $60 (ticket 251, Exhibit 22-11) and the labor costs entered onto time tickets 236 and 258.

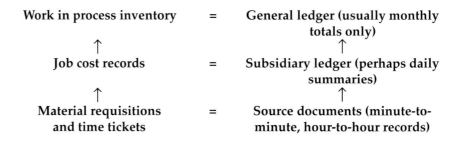

Job Cost Record

Job No. ___293___

Customer Name and Address ___Eaton's Mississauga___
Job Description ___10 recliner chairs___

Date Promised	7-31		Date Started	7-24		Date Completed		

	Direct Materials		Direct Labor		Factory Overhead Costs		
Date	Requisition Numbers	Amount	Time Ticket Numbers	Amount	Date	Rate	Amount
19X5 7-24	334	$ 90	236,251,258	$150			

Overall Cost Summary
Direct materials. . . . .$
Direct labor. . . . .
Factory overhead. . . . .

| Totals | | | | | Total Job Cost . . . . $ | |

The Work in Process Inventory account now contains the cost of direct materials and direct labor charged to Job 293 — and the costs of many other jobs as well. Work in Process Inventory serves as a control account, with the job cost records giving the supporting details for each job. The balance in Work in Process Inventory should equal the total of the individual job costs, in the same manner illustrated for Materials Inventory in Exhibit 22-9. The job cost records thus serve as a subsidiary ledger for the general ledger balance in Work in Process Inventory.

We summarize the accounting for materials and labor just illustrated:

Work in process inventory　=　**General ledger (usually monthly totals only)**

↑　　　　　　　　　　↑

Job cost records　=　**Subsidiary ledger (perhaps daily summaries)**

↑　　　　　　　　　　↑

Material requisitions and time tickets　=　**Source documents (minute-to-minute, hour-to-hour records)**

We see that accounting data are most condensed in the general ledger and most detailed in the source documents.

In practice, the daily accounting duties are carried out using source documents and subsidiary ledgers. Copies of the source documents are independently summarized and usually journalized and posted to the general ledger only once a month.

Accounting for Factory Overhead in a Job Cost System

Materials requisitions and labor time tickets make it easy to identify direct materials and direct labor with a specific job. Factory overhead, on the other hand, includes a variety of costs that cannot be linked to a particular job. How do we allocate overhead cost to jobs?

Overhead costs are recorded as incurred. The following entries — depreciation on plant and equipment, factory utilities, insurance and property taxes — are typical. Note that all these overhead costs are debited to a single account —Factory Overhead in the general ledger. The account titles in parentheses in the following entries indicate the subsidiary accounts that are debited in an overhead subsidiary ledger. Budgeting these individual items and then keeping track of their actual amounts helps managers control overhead costs.

5. Factory Overhead (Depreciation — Plant and Equipment)..	50,000	
Accumulated Depreciation — Plant and Equipment...		50,000
6. Factory Overhead (Factory Utilities)...........................	20,000	
Cash..		20,000
7. Factory Overhead (Factory Insurance).......................	5,000	
Prepaid Insurance — Factory.................................		5,000
8. Factory Overhead (Property Taxes — Factory)..........	10,000	
Property Tax Payable..		10,000

The Factory Overhead account now contains all the overhead costs of the period:

Factory Overhead

2. Indirect materials	40,000
4. Indirect labor	85,000
5. Depreciation — plant and equipment	50,000
6. Factory utilities	20,000
7. Factory insurance	5,000
8. Property taxes — factory	10,000
Total actual overhead cost	210,000

It would be virtually impossible to say that a specific amount of overhead (for example, the property taxes on the factory) was incurred on any particular job. Yet factory overhead costs certainly add to the costs of producing goods. We now discuss how accountants apply overhead in job costing.

The Budgeted Rate in Applying Overhead

Management wants to tie overhead cost to the costs of manufacturing the business's different products. After all, indirect materials, indirect labor and all the other individual accounts that make up factory overhead contribute to product costs. And if product costs are to help management in product pricing, income determination, and inventory valuation, they must be timely as well as accurate.

The most accurate application of overhead could be made only at the end of the year, after actual results are determined. However, this timing would be too late. Managers want product-cost information throughout the year, not only at the end of the period. To meet these needs, accountants usually budget overhead application rates, that is, they compute a rate in advance of production. The usual steps in applying factory overhead using an annual averaging process follow:

1. Select a **cost application base**, which is a common denominator linking costs among all products. This application base should be the best available measure of the cause-and-effect relationship between overhead costs and production volume. In many companies direct labor costs generally rise and fall proportionately with changes in production volume, and direct labor dollars are often chosen as the cost application base. In companies with highly automated production processes, labor is less important, and the cost allocation base is often machine hours.

2. Prepare a budget for the planning period, ordinarily a year. The two key items are (a) budgeted total overhead, and (b) budgeted total volume of the cost application base, which is direct labor cost in our Leclerc illustration.

3. Compute the **budgeted factory overhead** rate by dividing the total budgeted overhead by the cost application base.

4. Obtain the actual application base data (such as direct labor cost or machine hours) as the year unfolds.

5. Apply the budgeted overhead to the jobs by multiplying the budgeted rate times the actual application base data for each job.

6. At the end of the year, account for any differences between the amount of overhead actually incurred and the amount of overhead applied to products.

The Leclerc forecast is based on a volume of activity expressed in direct labor cost. Assume detailed forecasts predict total overhead of $212,000 for the next year at an anticipated $265,000 direct-labor-cost level of activity. The budgeted factory overhead rate is computed as follows:

$$\text{Budgeted factory overhead rate} = \frac{\text{Total budgeted overhead}}{\text{Total budgeted direct labor cost}} = \frac{\$212,000}{\$265,000} = .80 \text{ or } 80\%$$

The 80 percent rate would be used for applying overhead cost to jobs.

To *apply overhead* means to debit Work in Process Inventory for the cost of overhead and to credit the Factory Overhead account. The overhead application rate is used to compute the amount of overhead to apply to a specific job. In our example, for each dollar of direct labor debited to Work in Process Inventory, 80 cents in overhead cost is also debited to that account. If the actual direct labor cost of a job is $800 (see Step 4), 80 percent of that amount, or $640, is debited to Work in Process Inventory as factory overhead (see Step 5 above).

The budgeted factory overhead rate is applied to all jobs uniformly throughout the year. After the direct materials and direct labor costs have been applied to a job, the overhead is applied, as shown in the accompanying record for Job 293. Recall that total direct labor cost for the job is $400. With an overhead application rate of 80 percent of direct labor, the amount of overhead to charge to Job 293 is $320 ($400 × .80).

The job cost record for Job 293 is complete. It provides the detailed subsidiary ledger support for the debits to the general ledger account, Work in Process Inventory.

Job Cost Record

Job No. _____293_____

Customer Name and Address ___Eaton's Mississauga___

Job Description ___10 recliner chairs___

Date Promised	7-31	Date Started	7-24	Date Completed	7-29

Date	Direct Materials		Direct Labor		Factory Overhead Costs		
	Requisition Numbers	Amount	Time Ticket Numbers	Amount	Date	Rate	Amount
19X5							
7-24	334	$ 90	236,251,258	$150	7-29	120% of	
25	338	180	264,269,273,291	200		Direct labor	$480
28	347	230	305	50			
					Overall Cost Summary		
					Direct materials.........$ 500		
					Direct labor............. 400		
					Factory overhead........ 480		
Totals		$500		$400	Total Job Cost......... $1,380		

Of course, similar applications of overhead have been made for other jobs in 19X5. The total overhead applied to all jobs worked on during 19X5 was 80 percent of $250,000 direct labor, .80 × $250,000 = $200,000. The journal entry to apply overhead to production is

9. Work in Process Inventory	200,000	
Factory Overhead		200,000

Trace this application of Factory Overhead to Work in Process Inventory:

Factory Overhead					Work in Process Inventory	
2.	40,000	9. Applied	200,000		Bal.	29,000
4.	85,000				2.	285,000
5.	50,000				4.	250,000
6.	20,000				9.	200,000
7.	5,000					
8.	10,000					
Actual costs	210,000					
Bal.	10,000					

Factory Overhead Applied → 9.

An additional detail exists in accounting for overhead cost. First, however, we need to discuss accounting for finished goods and the sale of inventory.

Accounting for Finished Goods, Sales and Cost of Goods Sold

As each job is completed, its cost is transferred from Work in Process Inventory to Finished Goods Inventory. The completion date is written on the job cost record, which is compared to the budget and filed away. Then, sales of finished goods are recorded as they occur.

A summary entry for goods completed in 19X5 follows:

10. Finished Goods Inventory	740,000	
Work in Process Inventory		740,000

In turn, familiar entries would be made for sales and cost of goods sold.

11.	Accounts Receivable	996,000	
	Sales Revenue		996,000
	Cost of Goods Sold..	734,000	
	Finished Goods Inventory		734,000

The second entry is needed to maintain the perpetual inventory record. (Only the first entry is needed as sales are made in a periodic inventory system).

The key accounts for product costs now show:

Work in Process Inventory					Finished Goods Inventory				Cost of Goods Sold	
Bal.	29,000	10.	740,000	Bal.	12,000	11.	734,000 →	11.	734,000	
2.	285,000			10.	740,000					
4.	250,000			Bal.	18,000					
9.	200,000									
Bal.	24,000									

Disposing of Overapplied and Underapplied Overhead

The application of factory overhead cost to production will usually not bring to zero the balance in the Factory Overhead account. This account is debited for *actual cost* and credited for *estimated amounts* — equal to the budgeted factory overhead rate multiplied by the actual direct labor cost.

The total debits to Factory Overhead for the year may not equal the total credits to the account. A *debit* balance remaining in the Factory Overhead account is called **underapplied overhead**. In our illustration, actual overhead ($210,000 debited to the account) exceeded the amount applied to jobs ($200,000 credited to the account) during the period, which resulted in $10,000 in underapplied overhead. Conversely, a *credit* balance, called **overapplied overhead**, results when applied overhead exceeds the actual amount. Accountants usually ignore over- and underapplied overhead during the year and dispose of it at year end. The entry to close the Factory Overhead account adjusts the records to account for the actual overhead cost incurred during the year. The more accurate the budgeted overhead rate, the less the difference between actual and applied amounts of factory overhead for the year.

If the amount of over- or underapplied overhead is *significant*, it often is allocated to Work in Process, Finished Goods and Cost of Goods Sold based on their relative balances before the allocation. Suppose 15 percent of the year's production is still in process, 25 percent is finished but unsold, and the remaining 60 percent has been sold. If *overapplied* overhead at the end of the period is $50,000 — a significant amount in relation to total factory overhead, cost of goods sold, or another appropriate benchmark — the Factory Overhead Account will have a $50,000 credit balance. The entry to dispose of this credit balance debits Factory Overhead as follows:

Dec.	31	Factory Overhead...	50,000	
		Work in Process Inventory ($50,000 × .15)...		7,500
		Finished Goods Inventory ($50,000 × .25) ...		12,500
		Cost of Goods Sold ($50,000 × .60)................		30,000

This entry removes the $50,000 credit balance from Factory Overhead. It also adjusts Work in Process, Finished Goods and Cost of Goods Sold to actual costs.

If the over- or underapplied amount is *insignificant*, it can be closed to Cost of Goods Sold without seriously affecting the financial statements. This is an application of the materiality concept. Suppose actual overhead cost exceeded the amount of overhead applied to jobs. In our illustration the year's production resulted in the following summary activity in the Factory Overhead account:

Factory Overhead

Actual	210,000	Applied	200,000
Balance — Underapplied	10,000		

The $10,000 is minor relative to the $210,000 of actual overhead cost for the year. Moreover, the Cost of Goods Sold balance ($734,000) dwarfs the Work in Process Inventory and Finished Goods Inventory balances ($24,000 and $18,000, respectively). This means that an allocation of $10,000 to the three accounts would have tiny effects on the balances in ending work in process and finished goods. Therefore, we may close this underapplied overhead to Cost of Goods Sold as follows:

Dec. 31	Cost of Goods Sold	10,000	
(Entry 12)	Factory Overhead		10,000

Posting this entry brings the Factory Overhead account to a zero balance and completes the job order cost accounting example.

Overview of Illustration

Exhibit 22-12 provides an overview of the Leclerc job order costing illustration. The key Inventory accounts and Cost of Goods Sold are displayed at the top. Accounts for Factory Wages and Factory Overhead also are shown. The relationship of subsidiary material records to Materials Inventory and that of subsidiary job cost records to Work in Process Inventory are also illustrated.

As Exhibit 22-12 makes clear, the ending balance sheet accounts would be

Materials Inventory	$15,000
Work in Process Inventory	24,000
Finished Goods Inventory	18,000

The condensed income statement for 19X5 would report the following through gross margin:

Sales	$996,000
Cost of goods sold	734,000
Gross margin (or gross profit).......................................	$262,000

As mentioned previously, the remainder of the manufacturer's income statement (operating expenses, other revenue and expense and net income) is the same as for a merchandising entity.

Computers and Manufacturing Accounting _____

Managers need a tremendous amount of information to plan manufacturing operations and to keep costs under control. A company manufacturing hundreds of items may have a materials subledger running to perhaps thousands of accounts. Little wonder then that so many manufacturers have turned to computerized accounting.

Also, during periods of high customer demand, a manufacturer will focus on meeting production schedules, and important accounting controls may be relaxed. As peak production season winds down, managers may find it difficult to bring the

EXHIBIT 22-12 Job Order Costing, General Flow of Costs (in thousands)

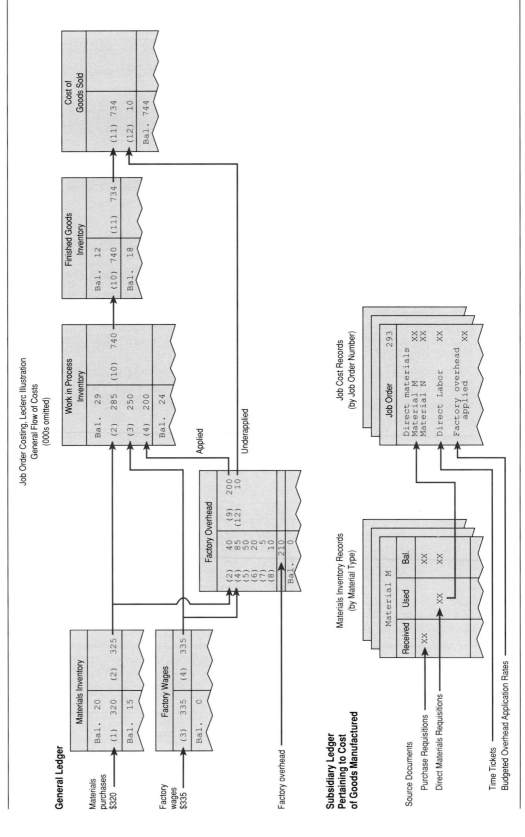

accounting information up to date. A computerized system is easier to keep current throughout the entire year.

Computer software for manufacturers may integrate all facets of cost accounting, from materials purchases to overhead application. Assume management wants to manufacture a range of products within a certain time frame. The computer can access engineering specifications for the product, calculate materials and time requirements, coordinate deadlines with limited production capacity, and issue a series of purchase orders and work orders consistent with management plans.

A computerized accounting package can generate a broad variety of management reports. These reports are available at critical points in the production process, giving management the opportunity to monitor progress and make improvements on the spot.

Collecting certain data for a computerized system is straightforward. For example, a number of computer terminals may be set up on the production floor. At various stages in the manufacturing process, an employee inserts his or her magnetically imprinted identification card into the terminal. The system thus captures direct labor time and cost without detailed labor records.

Summary Problem for Your Review

Hillis Limited had the following inventories at the end of 19X4:

Materials	$20,000
Work in Process	17,000
Finished Goods	11,000

During January 19X5, Hillis completed the following transactions:

1. Purchased materials on account, $31,000.
2. Requisitioned (placed into production) direct materials, $39,000.
3. Factory payroll incurred, $40,000.
4. Allocated factory labor as follows: direct labor, 90 percent; and indirect labor, 10 percent.
5. Requisitioned (placed into production) indirect materials, $3,000.
6. Incurred other factory overhead, $13,000 (credit Accounts Payable).
7. Applied factory overhead to product as 50 percent of direct labor.
8. Completed production, $99,000.
9. Sold goods on account, $172,000; cost of goods sold, $91,400.
10. Closed ending balance of Factory Overhead to Cost of Goods Sold.

Required

1. Record these transactions in the general journal.
2. Determine the ending balances in the three inventory accounts and Cost of Goods Sold.

SOLUTION TO REVIEW PROBLEM

Requirement 1   Journal entries

1.	Materials Inventory...	31,000	
	Accounts Payable		31,000
2.	Work in Process Inventory...................................	39,000	
	Materials Inventory...		39,000
3.	Factory Wages..	40,000	
	Wages Payable		40,000
4.	Work in Process Inventory ($40,000 × .90)...........	36,000	
	Factory Overhead ($40,000 × .10)........................	4,000	
	Factory Wages..		40,000
5.	Factory Overhead..	3,000	
	Materials Inventory...		3,000
6.	Factory Overhead..	13,000	
	Accounts Payable		13,000
7.	Work in Process Inventory ($36,000 × .50)...........	18,000	
	Factory Overhead..		18,000
8.	Finished Goods Inventory	99,000	
	Work in Process Inventory................................		99,000
9.	Accounts Receivable	172,000	
	Sales Revenue		172,000
	Cost of Goods Sold...	91,400	
	Finished Goods Inventory		91,400
10.	Cost of Goods Sold...	2,000	
	Factory Overhead..		2,000

Balance in Factory Overhead for entry 10 is

Factory Overhead

(4)	4,000	(7)	18,000
(5)	3,000		
(6)	13,000		
Bal.	2,000		

Requirement 2   Ending balances

Materials Inventory

Bal.	20,000	(2)	39,000
(1)	31,000	(5)	3,000
Bal.	9,000		

Work in Process Inventory

Bal.	17,000	(8)	99,000
(2)	39,000		
(4)	36,000		
(7)	18,000		
Bal.	11,000		

Finished Goods Inventory

Bal.	11,000	(9)	91,400
(8)	99,000		
Bal.	18,600		

Cost of Goods Sold

(9)	91,400		
(10)	2,000		
Bal.	93,400		

Summary

Manufacturing companies use cost accounting systems to help plan and control the manufacturing function and to compute manufacturing product costs for the financial statements and for pricing and product mix decisions. They use separate inventory accounts for raw materials, work in process and finished goods. The *Materials Inventory* account carries the cost of direct and indirect materials that are held for use in production. The *Work in Process Inventory* account shows the cost of goods that are still in the manufacturing process and not yet complete. *Finished Goods Inventory* represents completed goods that have not yet been sold. This account corresponds to the single inventory account of a merchandising business.

A manufacturer obtains inventory for resale by producing the goods. The manufacturer's *Cost of Goods Manufactured* account replaces the purchases account of a merchandiser. Otherwise, a manufacturer's income statement resembles the income statement of a merchandiser.

Direct materials include all the important materials used to make the product. *Direct labor* is the cost of employing people who physically produce the company's product. These two costs are traced directly to finished goods. *Factory overhead* covers all other manufacturing costs, including *indirect materials* and *indirect labor*.

Manufacturers keep inventory costs separate from all the other costs of running the business. *Inventoriable costs* are those identified with inventory. *Period costs* are accounted for as operating expenses and are never traced through the inventory accounts.

In a *job order costing system*, designed to account for products manufactured as individual units or in batches, costs are accumulated for specific jobs. A *job cost record* lists the materials, labor and overhead costs of completing the job. In a job cost system this document is the basic internal management device for accumulating and controlling costs. It serves as the subsidiary record for Work in Process Inventory. The cost of materials is traced via materials ledger cards. Labor costs are traced by time tickets.

The Factory Overhead account, which includes many different costs, is debited for actual costs incurred. Overhead cost is applied to product at a budgeted rate usually stated as a percentage of direct labor cost. At the end of the period, any *underapplied* or *overapplied overhead* is closed.

Self-Study Questions

Test your understanding of the chapter by marking the best answer for each of the following questions:

1. Which of the following is an inventory account of a manufacturer but not of a merchandiser? *(pp. 967–68)*
   a. Cost of goods manufactured
   b. Merchandise inventory
   c. Work in process
   d. Direct labor

2. Cost of goods manufactured is used to compute *(p. 968)*
   a. Cost of goods sold
   b. Factory overhead applied
   c. Direct materials used
   d. Finished goods inventory

3. Beginning work in process inventory is $35,000; manufacturing costs for the period total $140,000; and ending work in process inventory is $20,000. What is the cost of goods manufactured? *(pp. 969–70)*
   a. $125,000
   b. $155,000
   c. $175,000
   d. $195,000

4. Which of the following is a period cost? *(p. 971)*
   a. Materials inventory
   b. Direct labor
   c. Factory overhead
   d. Selling expense

5. Job order costing would be an appropriate system to account for the manu-facture of *(p. 974)*
   a. Aircraft
   b. Matches
   c. Zippers
   d. Cardboard boxes

6. What purpose does a job cost record serve? *(p. 975)*
   a. Lists total materials, labor and overhead costs charged to a job
   b. Is management's basic internal document that helps to control cost in a job cost system
   c. Both of the above
   d. Neither of the above

7. Using direct materials in production and charging direct labor costs to a job result in a debit to *(pp. 978–80)*
   a. Direct materials and direct labor
   b. Work in process inventory
   c. Finished goods inventory
   d. Materials inventory and factory wages

8. Which documents serve as a subsidiary ledger for the general ledger balance in Work in Process Inventory? *(pp. 975, 980)*
   a. Job cost records
   b. Materials requisitions
   c. Labor time tickets
   d. Materials ledger accounts

9. Why is direct labor often used as a basis for applying overhead cost to jobs? *(p. 982)*
   a. Overhead is very similar to direct labor
   b. Overhead includes direct labor
   c. Overhead occurs before direct labor is charged to a job
   d. Overhead occurs in relation to the incurrence of direct labor cost

10. At the end of the period, after overhead has been applied to all jobs, Factory Overhead has a credit balance of $900. We would say that overhead has been *(p. 984)*
    a. Misstated
    b. Incorrectly applied
    c. Overapplied
    d. Underapplied

Answers to the Self-Study Questions are at the end of the chapter.

Accounting Vocabulary

budgeted factory
  overhead rate *(p. 982)*
conversion costs *(p. 969)*
cost application base
  (p. 982)
cost of goods
  manufactured *(p. 968)*
direct labor *(p. 969)*
direct material *(p. 968)*
factory overhead *(p. 969)*
finished goods
  inventory *(p. 967)*
indirect labor *(p. 969)*

indirect materials
  (p. 969)
inventoriable cost *(p. 971)*
job cost record *(p. 975)*
job order costing *(p. 974)*
labor time ticket
  (p. 979)
materials inventory
  (p. 967)
materials requisition
  (p. 976)
overapplied overhead
  (p. 984)

period cost *(p. 971)*
prime costs *(p. 969)*
product cost *(p. 972)*
raw materials inventory
  (p. 967)
total manufacturing cost
  (p. 970)
underapplied overhead
  (p. 984)
value chain *(p. 966)*
work in process
  inventory *(p. 967)*

ASSIGNMENT MATERIAL _____

Questions

1. How do manufacturing companies differ from merchandisers? What inventory accounts does a manufacturer use that a merchandiser does not need?

2. Identify the various business functions in the value chain of a manufacturing company. Separate the upstream functions from the downstream functions. To which functions is cost accounting relevant?

3. What are the purposes of the cost accounting systems of a manufacturer?

4. What is the manufacturer's counterpart to the Purchases account of a merchandiser?

5. Distinguish direct materials from indirect materials and direct labor from indirect labor. Direct materials and direct labor are debited directly to what inventory account when placed in production? What account do indirect materials and indirect labor pass through en route to this inventory account?

6. Give examples of direct material and indirect material for a home builder.

7. Identify six or more components of factory overhead. Is overhead an asset or an expense account to a manufacturer?

8. Outline the flow of inventory costs through a manufacturing company's accounting system.

9. Distinguish between inventoriable costs and period costs. Which represents an asset, and which is used to account for expenses?

10. What costs should managers consider in deciding on the selling price of a product: inventoriable costs or full product costs? Give your reason.

11. Name two benefits of a perpetual inventory system.

12. What do the terms "charged to a job" and "applied to jobs" mean? What account is debited when a cost is applied to a job?

13. What is the essential nature of a job order costing system? How can companies that use a job cost system operate with low levels of inventories?

14. What document is used to control costs in a job cost system? Identify the three categories of costs listed on this document.

15. Name three documents or records used to account for raw materials, control them and move them through the production process. Give the function served by each document.

16. Use T-accounts to outline how the costs of materials and labor are transferred to Work in Process Inventory. Include both direct and indirect materials and direct and indirect labor.

17. What document is used to charge labor cost to specific jobs? Briefly describe how the document is used.

18. Is factory overhead cost applied to jobs by a precise identification of the overhead cost of each job or by an estimation process? Briefly discuss the process.

19. Is Factory Overhead debited for actual overhead cost or the amount of overhead applied to product? Which amount is credited to Factory Overhead?

20. How can factory overhead be underapplied? How can it be overapplied?

21. Insignificant amounts of over- or underapplied overhead are closed to what account? Significant amounts are closed to what three accounts?

22. Which of the following accounts have their balances brought to zero at the end of the period? Which keep their ending balances to start the next period— Materials Inventory, Factory Overhead, Finished Goods Inventory, Factory Wages?

23. What three categories of manufacturing costs are listed on a statement of cost of goods manufactured?

24. Summarize the computation of cost of goods manufactured. You can use your own dollar amounts.

Exercises

Exercise 22-1 *Reporting current assets of a manufacturer (L.O. 1)*

Consider the following selected accounts of Frostex Foods:

Cost of goods sold	101,000	Prepaid expenses	5,000
Direct labor	47,000	Marketing expense	39,000
Direct materials	25,000	Work in process inventory	42,000
Accounts receivable	73,000	Factory overhead	26,000
Cash	9,000	Finished goods inventory	68,000
Cost of goods manufactured	94,000	Materials inventory	21,000

Required

Show how Frostex would report current assets on the balance sheet. Not all accounts are used.

Exercise 22-2 *Computing cost of goods manufactured (L.O. 2)*

Compute cost of goods manufactured for K Inc. from the following account balances:

	Beginning of Year	End of Year
Materials inventory	$22,000	$26,000
Work in process inventory	36,000	30,000
Finished goods inventory	18,000	23,000
Purchases of raw materials		75,000
Direct labor		82,000
Indirect labor		15,000
Factory insurance		9,000
Depreciation — factory building and equipment		11,000
Repairs and maintenance — factory		4,000
Marketing expenses		63,000
General and administrative expenses		29,000
Income tax expense		30,000

Exercise 22-3 *Preparing a manufacturer's income statement (L.O. 1, 2)*

Prepare an income statement for the company, K Inc., in Exercise 22-2, assuming it sold 27,000 units of its product at a price of $14 during the current year.

Exercise 22-4 *Computing cost of goods manufactured and cost of goods sold (L.O. 2)*

Compute cost of goods manufactured and cost of goods sold for the following situation:

Direct materials used	$53,000
Ending finished goods inventory	34,000
Depreciation of factory equipment	11,000
Factory repairs and maintenance	16,000
Beginning work in process inventory	19,000
Direct labor	59,000
Indirect labor	23,000
Indirect materials	13,000
Miscellaneous factory overhead	4,000
Property tax on factory building	3,000

Marketing expenses	37,000
Beginning finished goods inventory	27,000
Factory utilities	17,000
Ending work in process inventory...............................	26,000
Depreciation of factory building	9,000
Nonfactory administrative expenses............................	43,000

Exercise 22-5   *Computing gross margin for a manufacturer* **(L.O. 2)**

Supply the missing amounts from the following computation of gross margin:

Sales revenue			$483,000
Cost of goods sold			
Beginning finished goods			
inventory..		$ 91,000	
Cost of goods			
manufactured			
Beginning work in			
process inventory......................		$ 57,000	
Direct materials used....................	$84,000		
Direct labor	X		
Factory overhead	51,000		
Total manufacturing costs			
incurred during the period......		231,000	
Total manufacturing costs			
to account for............................		X	
Ending work in process			
inventory.....................................		(40,000)	
Cost of goods			
manufactured		X	
Goods available for sale		X	
Ending finished goods			
inventory..		(107,000)	
Cost of goods sold...............................			X
Gross margin			$ X

Exercise 22-6   *Analyzing job cost data* **(L.O. 3)**

Bancroft Publishing Limited job cost records yielded the following information:

Job No.	Dates Started	Dates Finished	Dates Sold	Total Cost of Job at July 31
1	June 19	July 14	July 15	$ 1,700
2	June 29	July 21	July 26	17,000
3	July 3	Aug. 11	Aug. 13	6,500
4	July 7	July 29	Aug. 1	6,200
5	July 9	July 30	Aug. 2	2,700
6	July 22	Aug. 11	Aug. 13	1,300
7	July 23	July 27	July 29	1,300

Compute Bancroft's cost of (a) work in process inventory at July 31, (b) finished goods inventory at July 31, and (c) cost of goods sold for July.

Exercise 22-7 *Journalizing manufacturing transactions* **(L.O. 4, 5, 6)**

Record the following transactions in the general journal:

a. Purchased materials on account, $11,100.

b. Paid factory wages, $14,000.

c. Used in production: direct materials, $9,000; and indirect materials, $2,000.

d. Applied factory labor to jobs: direct labor, 80 percent; and indirect labor, 20 percent.

e. Recorded factory overhead: depreciation, $13,000; insurance, $1,700; and property tax, $4,200 (credit Property Tax Payable).

f. Applied factory overhead to jobs, 150% percent of direct labor.

g. Completed production, $27,000.

h. Sold inventory on account, $22,000; and cost of goods sold, $14,000.

i. Paid marketing expenses, $2,000.

Exercise 22-8 *Identifying manufacturing transactions* **(L.O. 4, 5, 6)**

Describe the transactions indicated by the letters in the following manufacturing accounts:

Materials Inventory		Work in Process Inventory		Finished Goods Inventory	
(a)	(b)	(b)	(h)	(h)	(i)
	(e)	(d)	(j)		(j)
		(g)			

Factory Wages		Factory Overhead		Cost of Goods Sold	
(c)	(d)	(d)	(g)	(i)	(j)
		(e)			
		(f)			
		(j)			

Exercise 22-9 *Using the Work in Process Inventory account* **(L.O. 4, 5, 6)**

August production generated the following activity in the Work in Process Inventory account of Bronstadt Manufacturing Ltd.:

Work in Process Inventory

August 1 Bal.	10,000
Direct materials used	23,000
Direct labor charged to jobs	31,000
Factory overhead applied to jobs	11,000

Completed production, not yet recorded, consists of Jobs B-78, G-65 and Y-11, with total costs of $14,000, $19,000 and $33,000, respectively.

Required

1. Compute the cost of work in process at August 31.

2. Journalize completed production for August.

3. Journalize the credit sale of Job G-65 for $41,000. Also make the cost-of-goods-sold entry.

Exercise 22-10   *Accounting for overhead cost* **(L.O. 6)**

Selected cost data for Henderson & Tipton Ltd. are presented below:

Budgeted factory overhead cost for the year	$105,000
Budgeted direct labor cost for the year	84,000
Actual factory overhead cost for the year	100,600
Actual direct labor cost for the year	80,000

Required

1. Compute the budgeted factory overhead rate.
2. Journalize the application of overhead cost for the year.
3. By what amount is factory overhead over- or underapplied? Is this amount significant or insignificant?
4. Based on your answer to question 3, journalize disposition of the overhead balance.

Problems   *(Group A)*

Problem 22-1A   *Completing a manufacturer's income statement* **(L.O. 1, 2)**

Certain item descriptions and amounts are missing from the income statement of Rocky Mountain Construction Inc.

Rocky Mountain Construction Inc.
Income Statement
for the month ended March 31, 19X6

Sales revenue				$231,000
Cost of goods sold				
Beginning _____ inventory		$ X		
Cost of goods _____				
Beginning _____ inventory		$ X		
Direct _____				
Beginning materials inventory	$ 34,000			
Purchases of materials	70,000			
Materials available for use	$ X			
Ending materials inventory	(26,000)			
Direct _____		$ X		
Direct _____		83,000		
_____		19,000		
Total _____ costs _____		X		
Total _____ costs _____		X		
Ending _____ inventory		(49,000)		
Cost of goods _____			163,000	
Goods available for sale			192,000	
Ending _____ inventory			(54,000)	
Cost of goods _____				$ X
Gross margin				93,000
Operating expenses				
Marketing			23,000	
General			26,000	
Total operating expense				X
Income before income tax				X
Income tax expense (30%)				X
Net income $				$ X

Required

Supply the missing item descriptions (_____) and the missing amounts (X).

Problem 22-2A   *Analyzing job cost data (L.O. 3)*

Atchison and Truro Fabricating Limited job cost records yielded the following information. The company has a perpetual inventory system.

Job No.	Dates Started	Dates Finished	Dates Sold	Total Cost of Job at March 31	Total Manufacturing Cost Added in April
1	Feb. 26	Mar. 7	Mar. 9	$2,200	
2	Feb. 3	Mar. 12	Mar. 13	1,100	
3	Mar. 29	Mar. 31	Apr. 3	300	
4	Mar. 31	Apr. 1	Apr. 1	400	$ 400
5	Mar. 17	Apr. 24	Apr. 27	1,400	2,200
6	Apr. 8	Apr. 12	Apr. 14		700
7	Apr. 23	May 6	May 9		1,200
8	Apr. 30	May 22	May 26		600

Required

1. Compute Atchison and Truro's cost of (a) work in process inventory at March 31 and April 30, (b) finished goods inventory at March 31 and April 30, and (c) cost of goods sold for March and April.

2. Make summary journal entries to record the transfer of completed units from work in process to finished goods for March and April.

3. Record the sale of Job 5 for $7,000.

Problem 22-3A   *Computing manufacturing cost amounts for the financial statements*
(L.O. 2, 4, 5, 6)

Assume Levi Strauss & Company Canada Ltd. accounting records include the following cost information on jobs for the manufacture of a line of jeans. During the most recent year Levi Strauss incurred total manufacturing cost of $163.2 million on materials, labor and factory overhead, of which $28.2 million represented direct materials used. Beginning balances for the year were materials inventory, $3.4 million; work in process inventory, $2.6 million; and finished goods inventory, $7.4 million. The company applies overhead to work in process (and finished goods) based on the relationship between overhead and direct labor costs. At year end the inventory accounts showed these balances (millions):

	Materials	Direct Labor	Factory Overhead
Materials inventory	$0.9	$-0-	$-0-
Work in process inventory	1.5	2.0	2.5
Finished goods inventory................	2.4	3.2	4.0

Required

1. Prepare Levi Strauss's statement of cost of goods manufactured for the line of jeans.

2. Compute cost of goods sold for the product.

3. Record the transfer from Work in Process Inventory to Finished Goods Inventory and the transfer from Finished Goods Inventory to Cost of Goods Sold during the year.

Problem 22-4A   *Accounting for manufacturing transactions*   **(L.O. 3, 4, 5, 6)**

Monarch Homes Ltd. builds prefabricated houses in a factory. The company uses a perpetual inventory system and a job cost system in which each house represents a job. The following transactions and events were completed during May:

a. Purchases of materials on account, $204,900.

b. Requisitions of direct materials and direct labor used in manufacturing:

	Direct Materials	Direct Labor
House #613	$26,100	$11,600
House #614	41,700	22,500
House #615	31,000	14,700
House #616	54,000	23,800
House #617	43,900	20,700
House #618	32,800	14,600

c. Depreciation of factory equipment used on different houses, $14,300.

d. Other overhead costs incurred on houses #613 – #618:

Factory wages	$21,600
Equipment rentals paid	6,000
Liability insurance expired	3,900

e. Applied overhead to jobs at the budgeted overhead rate of 30 percent of direct labor.

f. Houses completed: #613, #615, #616.

g. Houses sold: #615 for $59,900; and #616 for $103,900.

Required

1. Record the foregoing transactions and events in the general journal.

2. Open T-accounts for Work in Process Inventory and Finished Goods Inventory. Post the appropriate entries to these accounts, identifying the entry by letter. Determine the ending account balances assuming the beginning balances were zero.

3. List the costs of unfinished houses, and show that this total amount equals the ending balance in the Work in Process Inventory account.

4. List the costs of completed houses that have not yet been sold, and show that this total amount equals the ending balance in the Finished Goods Inventory account.

Problem 22-5A   *Preparing and using a job cost record*   **(L.O. 4, 5, 6)**

Montreal Belt Corporation produces conveyor belts used by other companies in their manufacturing processes. Montreal has a job cost system and a perpetual inventory system.

On September 22 Montreal received an order for 50 industrial-grade belts from Ogden Jones Corporation at a price of $56 each. The job, assigned number 449, was promised for October 15. After purchasing the materials, Montreal began production on September 30 and incurred the following costs in completing the order:

Date	Materials Requisition No.	Description	Amount
9-30	593	20 kg. rubber @ $9	$180
10-2	598	30 metres polyester fabric @ $7	210
10-3	622	12 metres steel cord @ $12	144

Date	Time Ticket No.	Description	Amount
9-30	1754	8 hours @ $9	$ 72
10-3	1805	31 hours @ $8	248

Montreal charges overhead to jobs based on the relationship between estimated overhead ($375,000) and estimated direct labor ($250,000). The job was completed on October 3 and shipped to Ogden Jones on October 5.

Required

1. Prepare a job cost record similar to Exhibit 22-7.

2. Journalize in summary form the requisition of direct materials and the application of direct labor and factory overhead to Job 449.

3. Journalize completion of the job and sale of the goods.

Problem 22-6A   *Comprehensive accounting treatment of manufacturing transactions*
   (L.O. 1, 3, 4, 5, 6)

James Bay Limited manufacturers specialized parts used in the generation of power. Initially, the company manufactured the parts for its own use, but it gradually began selling them to other public utilities as well. The trial balance of James Bay's manufacturing operation on January 1 of the current year follows:

James Bay Limited — Manufacturing Operations
Trial Balance
January 1, 19XX

Cash...	$ 32,740	
Accounts receivable..	65,860	
Inventories		
Materials..	18,910	
Work in process..	43,350	
Finished goods..	78,550	
Capital assets...	342,860	
Accumulated depreciation...		$145,960
Accounts payable..		88,650
Wages payable...		5,700
Common stock..		200,000
Retained earnings		141,960
Sales revenue		—
Cost of goods sold...	—	
Factory wages..	—	
Factory overhead...	—	
Marketing and general expenses	—	
	$582,270	$582,270

January 1 balances in the subsidiary ledgers:

Materials ledger: Steel, $4,730; Petrochemicals, $5,280; Electronic parts, $7,800; Indirect materials, $1,100;
Work in process ledger: Job 86, $43,350; and
Finished goods ledger: Transformers, $35,770; Transmissions lines, $21,910; Switches, $20,870.

January transactions are summarized as follows:

a. Materials purchased on credit: Steel, $12,660; Petrochemicals, $19,570; Electronic parts, $28,360; Indirect materials, $6,130.

b. Materials used in production (requisitioned):
Job 86: Steel, $1,580, Petrochemicals, $3,400.
Job 87: Steel, $10,580, Petrochemicals, $9,870; Electronic parts, $4,690.
Job 88: Steel, $2,930, Petrochemicals, $7,680; Electronic parts, $29,920.
Indirect materials, $4,760.

c. Factory wages incurred during January, $51,730, of which $49,560 was paid. Wages payable at December 31 were paid during January, $5,700.

d. Labor time tickets for the month: Job 86, $3,650; Job 87, $19,880; Job 88, $16,560; Indirect labor, $11,640.

e. Factory overhead incurred on account, $27,660.

f. Depreciation recorded on factory plant and equipment, $6,710.

g. Payments on account, $79,330.

h. Factory overhead applied at the budgeted rate of 125 percent of direct labor.

i. Jobs completed during the month: Job 86, one transformer at total cost of $56,360; Job 87, 620 switches at total cost of $68,876.

j. Marketing and general expenses paid, $21,660.

k. Credit sales on account: All of Job 86 for $91,490 (cost $56,360); Job 87, 480 switches for $88,030 (cost, $53,323).

l. Collections on account, $177,880.

Required

1. Open T-accounts for the general ledger, the materials ledger, the work in process ledger and the finished goods ledger. Insert each account balance as given, and use the reference Bal.

2. Record the January transactions directly in the accounts, using the letters as references. James Bay Limited has a perpetual inventory system.

3. Prepare a trial balance at January 31 of the current year.

4. Prepare a multiple-step income statement through income from operations for January of the current year, assuming any balance in Factory Overhead is insignificant. Take amounts directly from the trial balance, and report cost of goods sold as a single amount.

Problem 22-7A *Using a manufacturing system to account for overhead cost (L.O. 4, 5, 6)*

Selected accounts of Kwang & Foster, a partnership, follow:

Accounts Receivable

| Aug. 1 | Balance | 122,400 | Aug. 31 | Collections | 365,900 |
| Aug. 31 | Sales | (1) | | | |

Materials Inventory

Aug. 1	Balance	31,500	Aug. 31	Requisitions		(2)
Aug. 31	Purchases	54,600				

Work in Process Inventory

Aug. 1	Balance	73,200	Aug. 31	Jobs completed		(5)
Aug. 31	Direct materials	(3)				
	Direct labor	104,000				
	Factory overhead	(4)				

Finished Goods Inventory

Aug. 1	Balance	59,500	Aug. 31	Jobs sold		(7)
Aug. 31	Jobs completed	(6)				

Factory Overhead

Aug. 1	Balance	800	Aug. 31	Applied at rate of		
Aug. 31	Costs incurred:			80% of direct		
	indirect materials			labor cost		(8)
	of $31,400, indirect					
	labor, etc.					
	Total amount	81,900				

Cost of Goods Sold

Aug. 31	Jobs sold	(9)	

Sales Revenue

		Aug. 31	Sales	(10)

Selected balances at August 31 are

Accounts receivable	$103,700
Materials inventory...	28,400
Work in process inventory	43,700
Finished goods inventory	72,900

Required

1. Determine the amounts of the numbered items in the accounts.
2. a. Was factory overhead under- or overapplied at August 1?
   b. What is the August 31 balance in Factory Overhead? Is factory overhead under- or overapplied at August 31?
   c. Assume August 31 is the end of the company's fiscal year. Give the year-end entry to close the Factory Overhead account, depending on whether the August 31 balance is significant or insignificant. You must make this judgment.

(Group B)

Problem 22-1B   *Completing a manufacturer's income statement (L.O. 1, 2)*

Certain item descriptions and amounts are missing from the income statement of Lakewood Manufacturing Corp.

Lakewood Manufacturing Corp.
Income Statement
for the year ended June 30, 19X9

Sales revenue			$ X
Cost of goods sold			
Beginning _____ inventory.....................		$101,000	
Cost of goods _____			
Beginning _____ inventory..............	$ 28,000		
Direct _____			
Beginning materials inventory.......	$ X		
Purchases of materials....................	62,000		
Available for use............................	79,000		
Ending materials inventory...........	(23,000)		
Direct _____	$ X		
Direct _____	X		
_____	38,000		
Total _____ costs _____	166,000		
Total _____ costs _____	X		
Ending _____ inventory...................	(31,000)		
Cost of goods _____	163,000		
Goods available for sale...........................	X		
Ending _____ inventory.........................	($ X)		
Cost of goods _____		168,000	
Gross margin..		234,000	
Operating expenses			
Marketing..		99,000	
General		X	
Total operating expense		144,000	
Income before income tax		X	
Income tax expense (40%).............................		$ X	
Net income..		$ X	

Required

Supply the missing item descriptions (_____) and the missing amounts (X).

Problem 22-2B   *Analyzing job cost data* **(L.O. 3)**

Burleson and Schmidt Manufacturing Limited job cost records yielded the following information. The company has a perpetual inventory system.

Job No.	Dates Started	Finished	Sold	Total Cost of Job at June 30	Total Manufacturing Cost Added in July
1	May 26	June 7	June 9	$ 700	
2	June 3	June 12	June 13	1,700	
3	June 3	June 30	July 1	2,400	
4	June 17	July 24	July 27	100	$ 500
5	June 29	July 29	Aug. 3	400	1,600
6	July 8	July 12	July 14		800
7	July 23	Aug. 6	Aug. 9		300
8	July 30	Aug. 22	Aug. 26		2,900

Required

1. Compute Burleson and Schmidt's cost of (a) work in process inventory at June 30 and July 31, (b) finished goods inventory at June 30 and July 31, and (c) cost of goods sold for June and July.

2. Make summary journal entries to record the transfer of completed units from work in process to finished goods for June and July.

3. Record the sale of Job 4 for $850.

Problem 22-3B *Computing manufacturing cost amounts for the financial statements (L.O. 2, 4, 5, 6)*

Stride-Rite Shoe Corp. makes the Sperry Top-Sider deck shoe. Assume Stride-Rite accounting records include the following cost information on jobs for the manufacture of the basic brown leather Top-Sider.

During the most recent year Stride-Rite incurred total manufacturing cost of $21.4 million on materials, labor and factory overhead, of which $4.6 million represented overhead applied. Beginning balances for the year were materials inventory, $500,000; work in process inventory, $700,000; and finished goods inventory, $400,000. The company applies overhead to work in process (and finished goods) based on the relationship between overhead and direct labor costs. At year end the inventory account showed these balances:

	Materials	Direct Labor	Factory Overhead
Materials inventory	$600,000	$ -0-	$ -0-
Work in process inventory......	300,000	450,000	150,000
Finished goods inventory	100,000	150,000	50,000

Required

1. Prepare Stride-Rite's statement of cost of goods manufactured for the brown leather Top-Sider shoe.

2. Compute cost of goods sold for the Top-Sider product.

3. Compute the cost of materials purchased during the year.

Problem 22-4B *Accounting for manufacturing transactions (L.O. 3, 4, 5, 6)*

Olympic and Yukon Ltd., located in Calgary, Alberta, is one of the largest home builders in Canada. Assume Olympic and Yukon uses a perpetual inventory system and a job cost system in which each house represents a job. Because it constructs houses on-site rather than in a factory, the company uses accounts titled Construction Wages (not Factory Wages), Overhead (not Factory Overhead), and Supervisory Salaries for indirect labor. The following transactions and events were completed during August:

a. Purchases of materials on account, $385,600.

b. Requisitions of direct materials and direct labor used in manufacturing:

	Direct Materials	Direct Labor
House #302	$36,800	$19,100
House #303	39,100	17,400
House #304	45,600	20,500
House #305	22,400	11,000
House #306	63,900	33,700
House #307	52,800	27,500

c. Depreciation of equipment used in construction, $5,800.

d. Other overhead costs incurred on houses #302 – #307:

Supervisory salaries..	$17,000
Equipment rentals paid..	7,300
Liability insurance expired..	5,100

e. Applied overhead to jobs at the budgeted overhead rate of 30% of direct labor excluding supervision.

f. Houses completed: #302, #304, #305, #307.

g. Houses sold: #305 for $41,500; and #307 for $115,000.

Required

1. Record the foregoing transactions and events in the general journal.

2. Open T-accounts for Work in Process Inventory and Finished Goods Inventory. Post the appropriate entries to these accounts, identifying the entry by letter. Determine the ending account balances assuming the beginning balances were zero.

3. List the costs of unfinished houses, and show that this total amount equals the ending balance in the Work in Process Inventory account.

4. List the costs of completed houses that have not yet been sold, and show that this total amount equals the ending balance in the Finished Goods Inventory account.

Problem 22-5B   *Preparing and using a job cost record (L.O. 4, 5, 6)*

Maxell Magnetic Tape Company of Canada Ltd. manufactures cassettes for use in reproducing sound. Maxell has a job cost system and a perpetual inventory system.

On November 2, Maxell began production of 10,000 cassettes, assigned job number 378, to be sold to music stores for $1.25 each. The company incurred the following costs in completing the job:

Date	Materials Requisition No.	Description	Amount
11-2	36	31 kg. polypropylene @ $8	$248
11-2	37	68 kg. magnetic filament @ $13	884
11-3	42	7 kg. bucylic acid @ $48	336

Date	Time Ticket No.	Description	Amount
11-2	556	12 hours @ $10	$120
11-3	557	24.5 hours @ $8	196

Maxell charges overhead to jobs based on the relationship between estimated overhead ($560,000) and estimated direct labor ($448,000). The job was completed on November 3 and shipped to music stores when ordered.

Required

1. Prepare a job cost record similar to Exhibit 22-7.

2. Journalize in summary form the requisition of direct materials and the application of direct labor and factory overhead to Job 378.

3. Journalize completion of the job and sale of 500 cassettes.

Problem 22-6B *Comprehensive accounting treatment of manufacturing transactions*
(L.O. 1, 3, 4, 5, 6)

Pacific Telecommunications Inc. manufactures specialized parts used in its business. Initially, the company manufactured the parts for its own use, but it gradually began selling them to other companies as well. Pacific's trial balance on April 1, the beginning of the current fiscal year, follows:

Pacific Telecommunications Inc. Trial Balance April 1, 19XX		
Cash	$ 19,160	
Accounts receivable	74,290	
Inventories		
Materials	6,780	
Work in process	35,880	
Finished goods	18,960	
Capital assets	244,570	
Accumulated depreciation		$103,680
Accounts payable		26,770
Wages payable		3,670
Common stock		120,000
Retained earnings		145,520
Sales revenue		—
Cost of goods sold	—	
Factory wages	—	
Factory overhead	—	
Marketing and general expenses	—	
	$399,640	$399,640

April 1 balances in the subsidiary ledgers:

Materials ledger: Steel, $1,580; Plastics, $2,810; Electronic parts, $1,960; Indirect materials, $430.
Work in process ledger: Job 145, $35,880.
Finished goods ledger: Transformers, $5,310; Transmissions lines, $4,780; Switches, $8,870.

April transactions are summarized as follows:

a. Materials purchased on credit: Steel, $5,540; Plastics, $9,690; Electronic parts, $15,830; Indirect materials, $3,590.

b. Materials used in production (requisitioned):
Job 145: Steel, $340, Plastics, $1,770.
Job 146: Steel, $3,570, Plastics, $5,720; Electronic parts, $3,980.
Job 147: Steel, $1,970, Plastics, $3,610; Electronic parts, $3,730.
Indirect materials, $2,380.

c. Factory wages incurred during April, $31,930, of which $30,520 was paid. Wages payable at March 31 were paid during April, $3,670.

d. Labor time tickets for the month: Job 145, $3,000; Job 146, $12,050; Job 147, $9,940; Indirect labor, $6,940.

e. Factory overhead incurred on account, $4,630.

f. Depreciation recorded on factory plant and equipment, $3,450.

g. Payments on account, $36,040.

h. Factory overhead applied at the budgeted rate of 72 percent of direct labor.

i. Jobs completed during the month: Job 145, two transformers at total cost of $43,090; Job 146, 200 switches at total cost of $33,755.

j. Marketing and general expenses paid, $27,470.

k. Credit sales on account: All of Job 145 for $97,640 (cost $43,090); Job 146, 120 switches for $35,100 (cost, $20,253).

l. Collections on account, $127,470.

Required

1. Open T-accounts for the general ledger, materials ledger, work in process ledger and finished goods ledger. Insert each account balance as given, and use the reference Bal.

2. Record the April transactions directly in the accounts, using the letters as references. Pacific has a perpetual inventory system.

3. Prepare a trial balance at April 30 of the current year.

4. Prepare a multiple-step income statement through income from operations for April of the current year, assuming any balance in Factory Overhead is insignificant. Take amounts directly from the trial balance, and report cost of goods sold as a single amount.

Problem 22-7B   *Using a manufacturing system to account for overhead cost* **(L.O. 4, 5, 6)**

Selected accounts of Weimar & Mercure, a partnership follow:

Accounts Receivable

Nov. 1	Balance	28,900	Nov. 30	Collections	254,600
Nov. 30	Sales	(1)			

Materials Inventory

Nov. 1	Balance	8,400	Nov. 30	Requisitions	(2)
Nov. 30	Purchases	41,700			

Work in Process Inventory

Nov. 1	Balance	24,600	Nov. 30	Jobs completed	(5)
Nov. 30	Direct materials	(3)			
	Direct labor	68,000			
	Factory overhead	(4)			

Finished Goods Inventory

Nov. 1	Balance	101,200	Nov. 30	Jobs sold	(7)
Nov. 30	Jobs completed	(6)			

Factory Overhead

Nov. 30	Costs incurred: indirect materials of $9,000, indirect labor, etc.		Nov. 1	Balance	1,100
			Nov. 30	Applied at rate of 110% of direct labor cost	(8)
	Total amount	75,200			

Cost of Goods Sold

Nov. 30 Jobs sold	(9)	

Sales Revenue

	Nov. 30 Sales	(10)

Selected balances at Nov. 30 are

Accounts receivable	$31,400
Materials inventory	10,100
Work in process inventory	21,900
Finished goods inventory	89,800

Required

1. Determine the amounts of the numbered items in the accounts.

2. a. Was factory overhead under- or overapplied at November 1?
   b. What is the November 30 balance in Factory Overhead? Is factory overhead under- or overapplied at November 30?
   c. Assume November 30 is the end of the company's fiscal year. Give the year-end entry to close the Factory Overhead account depending on whether the November 30 balance is significant or insignificant. You must make this judgment.

Extending Your Knowledge

Decision Problems

1. Costing and pricing for identical orders (L.O. 3, 4, 5, 6)

Davison Chocolate Ltd. is located in Halifax, Nova Scotia. The company prepares gift boxes of chocolates as favors for private parties and corporate promotions. Each order contains a selection of chocolates determined by the customer, and the box is designed according to the customer's specifications.

One of Davison's largest customers is the Andrews and Meredith law firm. This organization sends chocolates to its clients each Christmas and also provides them at firm gatherings. The law firm's managing partner, Peter Andrews, placed the client gift order in September for 500 boxes of cream-filled dark chocolates. However, Andrews and Meredith did not organize its December staff party until the last week of November. This order for an additional 100 boxes is identical to the ones which will be distributed to the clients.

The cost per box for the original 500-box order was estimated as follows:

Chocolate, filling, wrappers, box	$14.00
Employee time to fill and wrap the box (10 min.)	1.00
Factory overhead	.50
Total manufacturing cost	$15.50

Because Andrews and Meredith is such a good customer, Joan Davison, the president of Davison Chocolate Ltd., priced the order at $18.00 per box.

In the past few months Davison Chocolate Ltd. has experienced price increases for both dark chocolate and employee time. All other costs have remained the same. The cost per box for the second order is estimated to be

Chocolate, filling, wrappers, box...	$15.00
Employee time to fill and wrap the box (10 min.)..........................	1.10
Factory overhead	.55
Total manufacturing cost	$16.65

Required

1. Do you agree with the cost analysis for the second order? Explain your answer.
2. Should the two orders be accounted for as one job or two in Davison Chocolate Ltd.'s system?
3. What selling price per box should Joan Davison set for the second order? What are the advantages and disadvantages of this price?

2. Using cost data to price a new product (L.O. 4, 5, 6)

Northern Telecom Ltd. is experimenting with a new process for manufacturing special telephone equipment in an attempt to lower the cost and sale price of its products. The goal is to capture a larger share of the telephone equipment market. The new process uses laser technology that decreases the amount of raw material needed to make a telephone. The current manufacturing process requires the following inputs per 1,000 telephones:

Direct materials
Material A	20 kg. @	$ 11
Material B......................................	130 kg. @	9
Material C......................................	8 kg. @	106

Direct labor
Fabricating	80 hr. @	$ 10
Assembling	20 hr. @	12
Testing...	50 hr. @	13

Factory overhead @ 150% of direct labor cost

The new technology would decrease the amounts of material A by 20 percent and of material C by 40 percent. It would also require three kilos of material D, which costs $22 per kilo. Fabricating and testing would require 10 percent less time, but purchase of the laser machine would increase overhead to 175 percent of direct labor cost.

Northern Telecom sells its products for 60 percent above cost but would need to increase this margin to 65 percent for telephone equipment manufactured by the new process to compensate for the lower selling price. Market analysis shows that customer demand for telephones is extremely sensitive to price. Northern Telecom personnel believe any sale price reduction more than 50 cents per telephone will increase sales volume enough to warrant using the new production process.

Required

Compute the current selling price of a telephone and the price of a telephone using the laser technology to decide whether to proceed with the new process. Make a recommendation to the company.

Ethical Issue

Southern Ontario has the greatest concentration of furniture manufacturers in Canada. These companies dominate furniture sales in central Canada. To break into this market, Leclerc Furniture Limited is considering several options. Under one plan, Leclerc would charge no overhead cost to products destined for the central-Canada market. This would enable Leclerc to offer its furniture at lower prices than its competitors charge.

Required

1. Is Leclerc's pricing strategy ethical? Discuss.
2. Can Leclerc expect to follow this strategy indefinitely? Give your reason.

Answers to Self-Study Questions

1. c
2. a
3. b   ($35,000 + $140,000 − $20,000 = $155,000)
4. d
5. a
6. c
7. b
8. a
9. d
10. c

Chapter 23

Process Costing, Activity-Based Costing, and Joint Products

The Fleming Company, managed by Jim Fleming, mass-produces furniture in Halifax, Nova Scotia. Assume its main customers are Eaton's and The Bay. Like many other businesses, its competitive advantage depends on producing an affordable product. Jim Fleming is shaking his head over the cost report he has just received — another set of what he believes are nonsense figures. The data show that stained-and-lacquered tables bear four times the overhead that painted tables do. He knows that stained-and-lacquered dining tables sell for $80 each and a painted table goes for $20, but the allocation of overhead does not seem reasonable. Fleming charges into the accounting department. "Why is it that a lacquered table bears four times the overhead cost that a painted table bears?" he asks.

"Simple," replies Andrea Domini, the cost accountant. "Production of a lacquered table requires one hour of direct labor. A painted table takes 15 minutes. We allocate overhead based on direct labor hours."

Fleming returns to his office, muttering, "I don't care what she says. A better table does not consume four times as much overhead as a cheaper one. There must be a better way to determine the cost of making furniture."

This situation illustrates how cost accounting procedures can fail to serve their intended purpose. The chapter section on activity-based costing describes how to address this problem.

Job order costing and process costing are the two major accounting systems for determining the costs of products. Chapter 22 discussed job order costing. This chapter explains process costing. It also covers the related subjects of activity-based costing and accounting for joint products and by-products.

LEARNING OBJECTIVES

After studying this chapter, you should be able to

1 Distinguish process costing from job order costing

2 Compute equivalent units of production

3 Apply total cost to units completed and units in ending work in process inventory

4 Record process costing transactions

5 Account for process costing in a second department

6 Account for an activity-based costing system

7 Allocate cost to joint products and byproducts

Process Costing: An Overview

The major difference between job order product costing described in the preceding chapter and process product costing is the type of products that are the objects of costing. Job order costing and process costing are the ends of a spectrum.

Exhibit 23-1 compares job order costing and process costing. **Process costing** is a system for assigning costs to goods that are mass-produced in a continuous sequence of steps called *processes*. Companies in manufacturing industries (chemicals, petroleum, cosmetics, food and beverages, for example) use process costing systems. Each of several departments is responsible for one specific process, although a single department may perform more than one process

In the manufacturing process, the physical form of the product often changes as it passes from one process to another (and so from one department to another). For example, corn flake cereal starts as raw corn. The corn is cleaned and cooked before being packaged as corn flakes and shipped for sale to consumers. A company that produces corn flakes (like Kellogg's or General Mills) may have one department for cleaning, one for cooking, one for packaging and one for shipping

A mass-production manufacturing process produces large numbers of identical units (boxes of cereal, gallons of paint, and cases of Coca-Cola). In contrast, a job system produces custom goods. In a process system the flow of goods through the factory is continuous and repetitive. Job cost records are not used. Instead, cost is accumulated in each department for a week or a month. At the end of the period, total manufacturing cost is the sum of the costs added in the processing departments. Unit cost is computed by dividing total manufacturing cost by the number of units produced. For example, if it cost $600,000 to produce 150,000 units during July, unit cost is $4.00 ($600,000/150,000 units).

Consider a manufacturing company that produces its goods in three steps. The business mixes materials to produce ceramic blocks, shapes the blocks into figurines and heats the figures for hardness. The company has a Mixing Department, a Shaping Department and a Heating Department. To account for the costs that make up the finished products, accountants use three work in process inventory

EXHIBIT 23-1   *Comparison of Process Costing and Job Order Costing*

Job-Order Costing: Examples include aircraft, construction, furniture, auditing, repairing, and jewelry

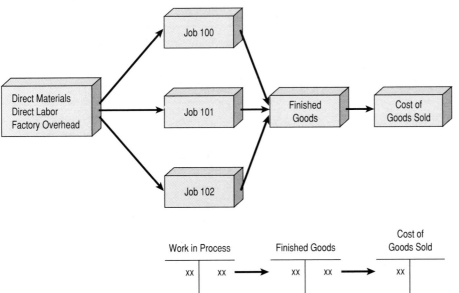

Process Costing: Examples include flour, glass, paint, paper, and silicon wafers

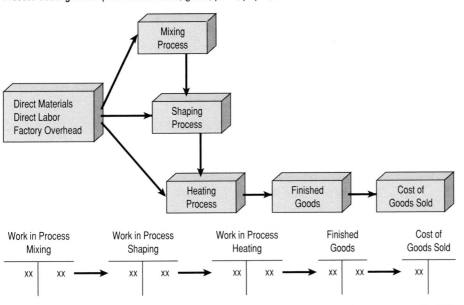

accounts) one for mixing, one for shaping, and one for heating. Exhibit 23-1 shows the flow of costs in this three-step process.

Note in the exhibit that mixing costs accumulate in the Work in Process Inventory — Mixing account. After mixing is completed, the blocks are transferred to the Shaping Department, and so are the costs. When shaping has been completed, product costs flow to Work in Process — Heating and then on to Finished Goods Inventory. When the figurines are sold, the cost of the inventory is transferred into Cost of Goods Sold. For comparison, the exhibit also diagrams the flow of costs through a job order costing system, which has only one Work in Process account.

Exhibit 23-2 uses dollar amounts to illustrate costs flowing through a process system. Each Work in Process account lists direct materials, direct labor, and factory overhead.

EXHIBIT 23-2   *Flow of Costs through a Process Costing System (amounts in thousands)*

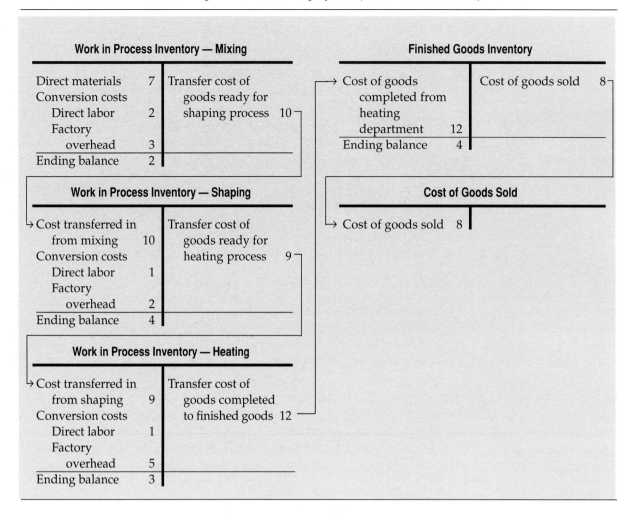

You will notice that each of the Work in Process accounts has a nonzero ending balance. Why? Because the manufacturing process is ongoing. No department ever sits idle. At any time, the Mixing Department will be carrying on its function while the Shaping Department and the Heating Department are handling their tasks. Before the Mixing Department ships off the most recent batch of ceramic blocks, it has already begun preparing the next batch. In Exhibit 23-2, we see that the Mixing Department has forwarded goods costing $10,000 to the Shaping Department. At the start of the next period, the Mixing Department is working on goods costing $2,000, which are left over from the preceding period.

Likewise, as the Shaping Department is completing one batch of figurines, it may be starting to shape a second batch. Since any department at any time will be engaged in the manufacturing process, its Work in Process Inventory account will carry a nonzero balance.

Recording Costs

The journal entries for a process cost accounting system are like those for a job order costing system. That is, direct materials, direct labor and factory overhead are recorded as follows (all amounts are in thousands and assumed for illustrative purposes):

To purchase materials and incur labor and factory overhead:

Materials Inventory...	11	
Accounts Payable		11
Factory Wages...	3	
Wages Payable		3
Factory Overhead...	5	
Accumulated Depreciation		1
Property Tax Payable		1
Accounts Payable, and so on		3

To requisition materials, assign labor cost and assign factory overhead cost to the Mixing Department (these entries are posted to Work in Process — Mixing in Exhibit 23-2):

Work in Process Inventory — Mixing	7	
Materials Inventory...		7
Work in Process Inventory — Mixing	2	
Factory Wages		2
Work in Process Inventory — Mixing	3	
Factory Overhead		3

The following entry transfers cost from one processing department to the next:

To transfer cost from the Mixing Department to the Shaping Department:

Work in Process Inventory — Shaping	10	
Work in Process Inventory — Mixing		10

Remaining entries for adding cost in the Shaping Department, transferring costs on to finished goods and accounting for cost of goods sold follow:

To record the additional labor and overhead cost of the Shaping Department (these entries affect the Work in Process Inventory —Shaping account in Exhibit 23-2):

Work in Process Inventory — Shaping	1	
Factory Wages		1
Work in Process Inventory — Shaping	2	
Factory Overhead		2

Entries for the Heating Department parallel those for the Shaping Department.

To transfer cost of goods completed from the Heating Department to Finished Goods:

Finished Goods Inventory	12	
Work in Process Inventory — Heating		12

To account for the cost of goods sold:

Cost of Goods Sold..	8	
Finished Goods Inventory...		8

Unlike a job order costing system, a process costing system is likely to have a separate work in process account for each processing department. In a job order system the work in process account is supported by job cost records for the various jobs.

Conversion Costs

Conversion costs are all manufacturing costs other than direct materials costs. The preceding chapter provided the usual major distinctions among manufacturing costs: the threefold category of direct materials, direct labor, and indirect manufacturing costs (factory overhead). This time-honored threefold category still dominates practice, but not as much as it once did. Why? Because many companies, particularly those using process costing and automation, have seen direct labor costs become less and less important in relation to total manufacturing costs. A twofold category is often used:

> **Direct materials**
> **Conversion costs**

In many companies direct labor has vanished as a major cost category. It has become merely an element of conversion costs. This reduces accounting expense by eliminating the elaborate tracking of labor cost.

Tracing the Flow of Costs

In process costing, the accounting task is to trace the flow of costs through the production process. This task has two parts. First, we must account for the cost of goods that have been completed in one department and sent to the second department. Second, we must account for the cost of incomplete units, which remain within a department.

Let us look at a sports company that manufactures swimming masks. This company's Shaping Department shapes the body of the swim masks. The direct material is the plastic that is formed into the masks. The partially completed masks then move to the Finishing Department, where the clear faceplate is inserted in the body and sealed in place.

Assume that during October, the Shaping Department incurs the following costs in processing 50,000 masks:

Direct materials.......................................		$140,000
Conversion costs		
Direct labor..	$21,250	
Factory overhead	46,750	68,000
Cost to account for		$208,000

If the shaping process is complete for all 50,000 masks, the cost to be transferred to Work in Process Inventory — Finishing is the full $208,000. The unit cost is $4.16 ($208,000/50,000 units). But suppose that shaping is complete for only 40,000 units. At October 31, the Shaping Department still has 10,000 masks in process. How do we compute unit cost when the total cost applies to finished units and unfinished units? Accountants answer this question by using the concept of *equivalent units of production*.

Equivalent Units of Production

OBJECTIVE 2

Compute equivalent units of production

Equivalent units of production, often simply called **equivalent units**, is a measure of the number of complete units that *could* have been manufactured from start to finish using the costs incurred during the period.

Let us assume that the 10,000 unfinished units still in the Shaping Department are one quarter complete. The number of equivalent units equals the number of partially complete units times the percentage of completion: 10,000 units × 25%

complete = 2,500 units. The number 2,500 tells us how many whole units are represented by the partially complete units. We add the 2,500 units to the number of finished units (40,000) to arrive at the period's equivalent units of production regarding conversion costs: 42,500.

The idea of equivalent units is not confined to manufacturing situations. It is a basic common denominator for measuring activities, output and workload. For example, colleges and universities measure student enrolments in "full-time equivalents." Suppose a full-time class load is 12 hours per term. Assume, 1,000 students are taking a full load and an additional 1,000 students are taking an average of 6 hours in classes. This school has a full-time equivalent enrolment of 1,500 students [1,000 + (1,000 × ⁶⁄₁₂)].

Steps in Process Cost Accounting

Using the data from the swimming mask example, we will discuss the five-step application of process costing.

Step 1: *Summarize the Flow of Production in Physical Units*

The left part of Exhibit 23-3 tabulates the movement of swimming masks into and out of the Shaping Department. We assume for clarity that work began October 1, so the Work in Process account had no balance at September 30.

EXHIBIT 23-3   *Step 1: Flow of Production in Physical Units*
Step 2: Equivalent Units of Production

Shaping Department
for the month ended October 31, 19XX

Flow of Production	Step 1 Flow of Physical Units	Step 2 Direct Materials	Step 2 Conversion Costs
Units to account for			
Work in process, Sept. 30	—		
Started production during October	50,000		
Total physical units to account for	50,000		
Units accounted for			
Completed and transferred out during October	40,000	40,000	40,000
Work in process, Oct. 31	10,000	10,000	2,500*
Total physical units accounted for	50,000		
Equivalent units of production		50,000	42,500*

*10,000 units each 25% complete = 2,500 equivalent units

Step 2: *Compute Output in Terms of Equivalent Units of Production*

Cost accountants compute equivalent units separately for the two types of costs incurred in manufacturing: direct materials and conversion costs. The Shaping Department has 10,000 units unfinished at October 31. We assume that all direct materials have been added (the chemicals have been added to begin shaping the bodies of the swimming masks), but that three quarters of the conversion costs (direct labor and factory overhead) remain to be applied. Thus all 50,000 units are finished in terms of direct material. We must compute equivalent units for the conversion costs. Since 25 percent of conversion costs have already been added, we multiply the 10,000 unfinished units by .25, which gives us 2,500 units. Added to the 40,000 finished units, the equivalent units for conversion costs come to 42,500.

Exhibit 23-3 combines the data for Step 1 and Step 2. Note that the number of equivalent units for direct materials and conversion costs are different. This is often the case.

Step 3: Summarize Total Costs to Account for

Exhibit 23-4 summarizes the total costs to account for in the Shaping Department (cost data are assumed). These costs are the total debits in Work in Process Inventory — Shaping, including any beginning balance. The Shaping Department has 50,000 units and $208,000 of cost to account for.

EXHIBIT 23-4 *Step 3: Summary of Total Costs to Account for*

Shaping Department
for the month ended October 31, 19XX

Work in Process — Shaping

	Physical Units	Dollars		Physical Units	Dollars
Inventory, Sept. 30	-0-	$ -0-	Transferred out	40,000	$?
Production started	50,000		Ending inventory	10,000	?
Direct materials		140,000	Total accounted for	50,000	
Conversion costs					
Direct labor		21,250			
Factory overhead		46,750			
Total to account for	50,000	$208,000			

Step 4: Compute Equivalent-Unit Costs

In Step 2 we computed the number of equivalent units for direct materials (50,000) and conversion costs (42,500). Because their equivalent units differ, a separate cost per unit must be computed for materials cost and for conversion costs. Exhibit 23-4 provides the data. The direct materials cost is $140,000. Conversion costs are $68,000, the sum of direct labor ($21,250) and factory overhead ($46,750).

We now have all the data needed to apply process costing in this example. We divide the direct materials cost by the equivalent units for direct materials: $140,000/50,000 = $2.80. The $2.80 is the unit price for direct materials. We compute unit price for conversion cost in a similar manner: $68,000/42,500 = $1.60. Exhibit 23-5 shows the computation of unit costs.

OBJECTIVE 3

Apply total cost to units completed and units in ending work in process inventory

Step 5: Apply Total Cost to Units Completed and to Units in Ending Work in Process Inventory

Exhibit 23-6 shows how the unit costs computed in Step 4 are applied to units completed and to units in ending work in process. With Step 5, we account for the cost of the shaping process during the period.

EXHIBIT 23-5 *Step 4: Computation of Unit Costs*

	Shaping Department for the month ended October 31, 19XX		
	Direct Materials	**Conversion Costs**	**Total**
Work in process, September 30	$ -0-	$ -0-	$ -0-
Costs added during October	$140,000	$ 68,000	$208,000
Divide by equivalent units of production....	÷50,000	÷42,500	
Cost per equivalent unit	$ 2.80	+ $ 1.60	= $ 4.40

The 40,000 units completed and transferred out of the Shaping Department bear a unit cost of $4.40 (direct materials of $2.80 + conversion cost of $1.60). The 10,000 units still in process at the end of the period have 10,000 equivalent units of direct materials (at $2.80 per unit) and 2,500 equivalent units of conversion cost (at $1.60 per unit). Observe that the sum of these two unit costs ($2.80 and $1.60) is the same as total unit cost of the completed units ($4.40), from Step 4. Also, total cost accounted for ($208,000) must agree with the total from Step 3.

October production in the Shaping Department would be recorded thus:

To requisition materials and apply labor and overhead cost to the Shaping Department (Exhibit 23-4)

<table>
<tr><td>Work in Process Inventory — Shaping ....</td><td>140,000</td><td></td></tr>
<tr><td>   Materials Inventory ....</td><td></td><td>140,000</td></tr>
<tr><td>Work in Process Inventory — Shaping ....</td><td>21,250</td><td></td></tr>
<tr><td>   Factory Wages...</td><td></td><td>21,250</td></tr>
<tr><td>Work in Process Inventory — Shaping ....</td><td>46,750</td><td></td></tr>
<tr><td>   Factory Overhead...</td><td></td><td>46,750</td></tr>
</table>

The entry to transfer the cost of completed units from the Shaping Department to the Finishing Department is given following Exhibit 23-6.

> **OBJECTIVE 4**
> Record process costing transactions

EXHIBIT 23-6 *Step 5: Application of Total Cost to Units Completed and to Units in Ending Work in Process Inventory*

	Shaping Department for the month ended October 31, 19XX		
	Direct Materials	**Conversion Costs**	**Total**
Units completed and transferred out (40,000)	40,000 × $4.40		= $176,000
Units in ending work in process inventory (10,000)			
Direct materials	10,000 × $2.80		= 28,000
Conversion costs		2,500 × $1.60 =	4,000
Total cost of work in process			32,000
Total cost accounted for...			$208,000

| Work in Process Inventory — Finishing.................................. | 176,000 | |
| Work in Process Inventory — Shaping .... | | 176,000 |

After these entries are posted, the Work in Process Inventory — Shaping account appears as follows:

Work in Process Inventory — Shaping

Balance, Sept. 30	—	Transferred to Finishing	176,000
Direct materials	140,000		
Direct labor	21,250		
Factory overhead	46,750		
Balance, Oct. 31	32,000		

With Shaping Department costs accounted for, we proceed to the Finishing Department. First, however, let us reinforce what you have learned with a Summary Problem for Your Review.

Summary Problem for Your Review

Identify the missing amounts X and Y in the following production cost report prepared by Jacobs-Webster, Ltd. for May:

Assembly Department
Production Cost Report
for the month ended May 31, 19XX

	Physical Units	Total Costs
Work in process, Apr. 30	—	$ —
Started in production during May	20,000	43,200*
Total to account for	20,000	$ 43,200
Completed and transferred to Finishing Department during May	16,000	$ X
Work in process, May 31 (25% complete as to direct materials, 55% complete as to conversion cost).................	4,000	Y
Total accounted for	20,000	$43,200*

* Includes direct materials of $6,800 and conversion costs of $36,400.

SOLUTION TO REVIEW PROBLEM

Step 1: Flow of Production in Physical Units
Step 2: Equivalent Units of Production

Assembly Department
for the month ended May 31, 19XX

Flow of Production	Step 1 Flow of Physical Units	Step 2 Equivalent Units of Production Direct Materials	Conversion Costs
Units to account for			
Work in process, Apr. 30	—		
Started production during May	20,000		
Total physical units to account for	20,000		
Units accounted for			
Completed and transferred out during May	16,000	16,000	16,000
Work in process, May 31	4,000	1,000*	2,200*
Total physical units accounted for	20,000		
Equivalent units of production		17,000	18,200*

*Direct materials: 4,000 units each 25% complete = 1,000 equivalent units
Conversion costs: 4,000 units each 55% complete = 2,200 equivalent units

Step 3: Summary of Total Costs to Account for

Assembly Department
for the month ended May 31, 19XX

Work in Process — Assembly

	Physical Units	Dollars
Inventory, Apr. 30	-0-	$ -0-
Production started	20,000	
Direct materials		6,800
Conversion costs		36,400
Total to account for	20,000	$43,200

Step 4: Computation of Equivalent-Unit Costs

Assembly Department
for the month ended May 31, 19XX

	Direct Materials	Conversion Costs	Total
Work in process, Apr. 30	$ -0-	$ -0-	$ -0-
Costs added during May	6,800	36,400	43,200
Divide by equivalent units of production	÷17,000	÷18,200	
Cost per equivalent unit	$ .40 +	$ 2.00 =	$ 2.40

Step 5: Allocation of Total Cost to Units Completed and Units in Ending Work in Process Inventory

Assembly Department
for the month ended May 31, 19XX

	Direct Materials	Conversion Costs	Total
X Units completed and transferred out (16,000).......................	16,000 × $2.40		= $38,400
Units in ending work in process inventory (4,000)			
Direct materials...	1,000 × $.40		= 400
Conversion costs		2,200 × $2.00	= 4,400
Y Total cost of work in process			4,800
Total cost accounted for..			$43,200

Process Costing Extended to a Second Department _____

OBJECTIVE 5

Account for process costing in a second department

Most manufacturing systems include multiple processing steps. In this section, we introduce a second processing department to complete the picture of process costing. We continue with the manufacture of swim masks. The Finishing Department adds the faceplate and sealant to the shaped swim masks. The faceplate is the direct material added in the finishing process. It is important to keep in mind that *direct materials* in the Finishing Department refers to the faceplates added *in that department* and not to the materials (the chemicals) added in the previous Shaping Department. Likewise, *conversion cost* in the Finishing Department refers to all manufacturing costs (other than direct materials) of that department only.

We assume 5,000 units were in process in the Finishing Department on October 1. These units were 60 percent complete as to Finishing Department conversion costs, but 0 percent complete as to direct materials because the faceplates are added near the end of the finishing process. These facts, used throughout discussion of the accounting for the Finishing Department, are summarized in Exhibit 23-7. (Refer to Exhibit 23-6, p. 1017).

EXHIBIT 23-7 *Finishing Department Facts for October*

Units		
Work in process, Sept. 30 (0% complete as to direct materials, 60% complete as to conversion costs)...................		5,000 units
Transferred in from Shaping Department during October...		40,000
Completed during October		38,000
Work in process, Oct. 31, (0% complete as to direct materials, 30% complete as to conversion costs)..................		7,000
Costs		
Work in process, Sept. 30		$ 24,000
Transferred in from Shaping Department during October...		176,000
Direct materials added during October..........................		19,000
Conversion costs added during October		
Direct labor	$ 3,710	
Factory overhead	11,130	14,840

Equivalent Units in a Second Department

The major accounting task in dealing with a second department is the computation of equivalent units. Exhibit 23-8 summarizes the flow of physical units (Step 1) in order to compute the equivalent units of production (Step 2) for the Finishing Department. Note that there are three categories of equivalent units. In addition to equivalent units for *direct materials* and *conversion costs* added in the Finishing Department, we must also compute equivalent units for those units that were *transferred* in from the preceding department. Whenever there is a second department, it will always have units and costs transferred in from the preceding department. In our illustration, 40,000 units were transferred into the Finishing Department during October. Of these transferred-in units, 33,000 units were completed and 7,000 units remained in ending inventory. For transferred-in costs, equivalent units include the full total (33,000 + 7,000 = 40,000).

Equivalent units of *direct materials* have three components: beginning work-in-process inventory, units transferred in and completed during the month, and ending work-in-process inventory. Exhibit 23-7 indicates that beginning inventory contained 5,000 units that were 0 percent complete as to direct materials. The first-in, first-out (FIFO) method is employed in Exhibit 23-7 in accounting for work in process inventories. Under FIFO, the computation of equivalent units is confined to the work done during the current period, October in this example. Therefore, the $24,000 beginning balance is kept separate from the costs added during the current period. The $24,000 is not included in the computation of the unit costs of equivalent units for the work done in October. The major advantage of the FIFO method is that the efficiency of performance in October can be judged independently from the performance in September. In brief, the work done during the current period is key information for planning and control purposes as well as for FIFO inventory valuation.[1]

Under the FIFO cost method, beginning inventory is completed first. During October, the Finishing Department added the faceplates (100 percent of the direct materials that the Finishing Department adds) to complete these 5,000 units. The 33,000 units that were transferred in and completed are automatically part of equivalent units. Ending inventory is 0 percent complete as to direct materials (faceplates have not yet been added). Consequently, ending inventory accounts for no equivalent units. Altogether, equivalent production for direct materials is 38,000 units (5,000 units from beginning inventory + 33,000 units transferred in during the month).

Equivalent units of *conversion costs* also have three components: beginning work-in-process inventory, units transferred in and completed during the month, and ending work-in-process inventory. The Finishing Department's beginning inventory of 5,000 units was 60 percent complete as to conversion costs when the last period ended. During October, the Finishing Department completed these 5,000 units by adding the remaining 40 percent of conversion costs. For beginning inventory, equivalent production is 2,000 units (5,000 × .40). Units transferred in and completed during the month (33,000 units) are the second component of equivalent production. Ending inventory is the third component. At October 31, the inventory of 7,000 units still in process in the Finishing Department is 30 percent complete as to conversion costs, so equivalent production includes 2,100 units (7,000 × .30). Altogether, equivalent production for conversion costs totals 37,100 units (2,000 + 33,000 + 2,100). Exhibit 23-8 summarizes the equivalent unit computations for the Finishing Department.

---

[1] Other methods, such as weighted-average cost, can also be used. They are explored in cost accounting textbooks.

EXHIBIT 23-8   *Step 1: Flow of Production in Physical Units*
Step 2: Equivalent Units of Production

| | Step 1 | Step 2 | | |
| | Flow of | Equivalent Units of Production | | |
Flow of Production	Physical Units	Transferred In	Direct Materials	Conversion Costs
Units to account for				
Work in process, Sept. 30..	5,000			
Transferred in during October..	40,000			
Total physical units to account for	45,000			
Units accounted for				
Completed and transferred out during October				
From beginning inventory	5,000	—	5,000*	2,000*
Transferred in and completed during October				
(38,000 – 5,000)	33,000	33,000	33,000	33,000
Work in process, Oct. 31	7,000	7,000	— **	2,100**
Total physical units accounted for	45,000			
Equivalent units of production..		40,000	38,000	37,100

*   Direct materials: 5,000 units each 100% completed in Finishing Department during October = 5,000 equivalent units
    Conversion costs: 5,000 units each 40% completed in Finishing Department during October = 2,000 equivalent units
** Direct materials: 7,000 units each 0% completed in Finishing Department during October = 0 equivalent units
    Conversion costs: 7,000 units each 30% completed in Finishing Department during October = 2,100 equivalent units

Finishing Department for the month ended October 31, 19XX

Equivalent-Unit Costs in a Second Department

The October costs of the Finishing Department are accumulated as shown in Exhibit 23-9. The exhibit shows how equivalent units are used to compute the unit costs in the Finishing Department process.

EXHIBIT 23-9 *Steps 3 and 4: Computation of Total Costs to Account for and of Equivalent-Unit Costs*

	Transferred-In Costs	Direct Materials	Conversion Costs	Total
Work in process, Sept. 30 (from Exhibit 23-7)	Work done before October			$ 24,000
Costs added during October (from Exhibit 23-7)...........	$176,000	$ 19,000	$ 14,840	209,840
Divide by equivalent units (from Exhibit 23-8)	÷40,000	÷38,000	÷37,100	
Cost per equivalent unit..	$4.40	$.50	$.40	
Total Cost to account for				$233,840

Finishing Department for the month ended October 31, 19XX

Application of Total Cost in a Second Department

Exhibit 23-10 shows how to apply total cost of the Finishing Department to units completed and transferred to finished goods and to units still in process at the end of the period.

EXHIBIT 23-10   *Steps 5: Application of Total Cost to Units Completed and Units in Ending Work in Process Inventory*

	Transferred-In Costs	Direct Materials	Conversion Costs	Total
Finishing Department **for the month ended October 31, 19XX**				
Units completed and transferred out to Finished Goods Inventory				
From work in process, Sept. 30..				$ 24,000
Costs added during October				
Direct materials	—	5,000 × $.50		2,500
Conversion costs	—		2,000 × $.40	800
Total completed from Sept. 30 inventory...................				27,300
Units transferred in and completed during				
October...	33,000 × ($4.40 + $.50 + $.40)			174,900
Total costs transferred out.................................				$202,200
Work in process, Oct. 31				
Transferred-in costs..	7,000 × $4.40			$ 30,800
Direct materials..		—		—
Conversion costs...			2,100 × $.40	840
Total work in process, Oct. 31				31,640
Total cost accounted for..................................				$233,840

The entries for the Shaping Department were recorded on p. 1018. The following entries record Finishing Department activity during October:

To transfer in cost of completed units from the Shaping Department (repeat of the last entry in the Shaping Department, p. 1018):

Work in Process Inventory — Finishing....................................	176,000	
Work in Process Inventory — Shaping		176,000

To requisition materials and apply labor and overhead cost to the Finishing Department (amounts from Exhibit 23-7):

Work in Process Inventory — Finishing....................................	19,000	
Materials Inventory		19,000
Work in Process Inventory — Finishing....................................	3,710	
Factory Wages..		3,710
Work in Process Inventory — Finishing....................................	11,130	
Factory Overhead..		11,130

The entry to transfer the cost of completed units from the Finishing Department to finished goods is based on the dollar amount taken from Exhibit 23-10 and listed on the production cost report in Exhibit 23-11.

Finished Goods Inventory...	202,200	
Work in Process Inventory — Finishing		202,200

After posting, the key accounts appear as follows. Observe the accumulation of costs as debits to Work in Process and the transfer of costs from one account to the next.

Work in Process Inventory — Shaping

(Exhibit 23-4)		(Exhibit 23-6)	
Balance, Sept. 30	—	Transferred to Finishing	176,000
Direct materials	140,000		
Direct labor	21,250		
Factory overhead	46,750		
Balance, Oct. 31	32,000		

Work in Process Inventory — Finishing

(Exhibit 23-7)		(Exhibit 23-10)	
Balance, Sept. 30	24,000	Transferred to Finished Goods	202,200
Transferred from Shaping	176,000		
Direct materials	19,000		
Direct labor	3,710		
Factory overhead	11,130		
Balance, Oct. 31	31,640		

Finished Goods Inventory

Balance, Sept. 30	—		
Transferred from Finishing	202,200		

Production Cost Report

A **production cost report** summarizes the activity in a processing department for the period. Exhibit 23-11 is a production cost report for the Finishing Department for October. It shows the department's beginning inventory (5,000 units; cost $24,000), the number of units and the cost transferred in during the month (40,000 units; cost $176,000), and the costs added. These amounts make up the totals to account for. The production report also shows the units completed (38,000), and the costs transferred out of the department ($202,200), and the ending inventory (7,000 units; cost $31,640).

These reports vary from company to company, depending on the level of detail desired by the managers. If managers want more detail, some or all of the additional information in Exhibits 23-8, 23-9 and 23-10 can be included. For example, Exhibit 23-12 provides more detail than Exhibit 23-11.

How is the production report used for decision-making? Managers compare direct materials and conversion costs (particularly the unit costs in Exhibit 23-12) with budgeted amounts for the department. If these costs are too high, corrective action is taken. If costs are below budget, the employees responsible may receive incentive awards.

Managers also compare the number of units produced with budgeted production. Production that is too low can be investigated and corrected. If production in excess of budget is welcomed, such performance may lead to various rewards for responsible employees.

Activity-Based Costing

The description of cost systems in this chapter and the preceding chapter has focused on *product* costing. To maximize long-term profitability, systems should also serve the planning and control purpose. Many managers plan and control business

EXHIBIT 23-11   *Production Cost Report*

Finishing Department
Production Cost Report
for the month ended October 31, 19XX

	Physical Units	Total Costs
Work in process, Sept. 30...	5,000	$ 24,000
Transferred in from Shaping Department during October	40,000	176,000
Cost added in Finishing Department during October		
Direct materials	—	19,000
Conversion costs ($3,710 + $11,130)...............................	—	14,840
Total to account for	45,000	$233,840
Completed and transferred to finished goods		
during October...	38,000	$202,200
Work in process, October 31	7,000	31,640
Total accounted for..	45,000	$233,840

EXHIBIT 23-12   *Production Cost Report (Expanded)*

Finishing Department
Production Cost Report (Expanded)
For the Month Ended October 31, 19XX

		Transferred-in Costs	Direct Materials	Conversion Costs	Total
	Work in process, Sept. 30.....................................				$ 24,000
	Cost added during October.................................	$176,000	$ 19,000	$ 14,840	209,840
(Step 3)	Total costs to account for..................................				$233,840
	Equivalent units for work during October				
	(Steps 1 and 2 in Exhibit 23-8).....................................	÷40,000	÷38,000	÷37,100	
(Step 4)	Cost per equivalent unit.....................................	$ 4.40	$ .50	$ .40	
(Step 5)	Application of total costs				
	From work in process, Sept. 30				$ 24,000
	Costs added during October......................................		5,000 × $.50	2,000 × $.40	
			= $2,500	= $800	3,300
	Total completed from Sept. 30 inventory				27,300
	Units transferred in and completed during October.	33,000 × ($4.40 + $.50 + $.40)			174,900
					202,200
	Work in process, Oct. 31				
	Transferred-in costs..	7,000 × $4.40			30,800
	Direct materials..		—		—
	Conversion costs..			2,100 × $.40	840
	Total work in process, Oct. 31				31,640
	Total costs accounted for				$233,840

functions by personal observation and with budget and cost systems. These functions are often divided into departments, as described in the first part of the chapter.

This section describes an emerging new approach to cost accounting. A **cost object** can be anything for which it is worthwhile to compile costs, such as an activity (spray-painting), a department (finishing), or a product (a table). **Activity-based**

costing (ABC), also called *activity-based accounting*, is a system that focuses on *activities* as the fundamental cost objects and uses the cost of these activities as building blocks for compiling the costs of products and other cost objects. ABC is generic. It can be used in conjunction with a job order costing system or a process costing system that is divided into departments.

If dividing companywide functions into departments helps managers, wouldn't dividing departments into activities further sharpen managers' focus? Exhibit 23-13, Panel A, shows the different functions in a furniture manufacturer's value chain. Panel B divides the manufacturing function into departments, and Panel C lists common activities in a Finishing Department. Note that costs are accumulated for each activity separately. The activity costs are then applied to products as the products move through production. For example, a table's finishing calls for polishing, and the cost of that activity (the polishing) is added to the table. If the table is to be sold as a less-expensive model, the company may not finish it. In this case, the table bears no cost for finishing. Inspection cost and packaging cost are likewise added to the cost of the table as appropriate. The product cost of a dining table is "built up" from the cost of the specific activities undertaken to manufacture it.

Exhibit 23-13 shows how cost objects become even more finely granulated, from a particular business function such as manufacturing to departments, including painting and finishing, to activities such as polishing and inspecting. But how do the refinements of ABC translate into better decisions?

EXHIBIT 23-13   *Overview of Business Functions, Departments, and Activities*

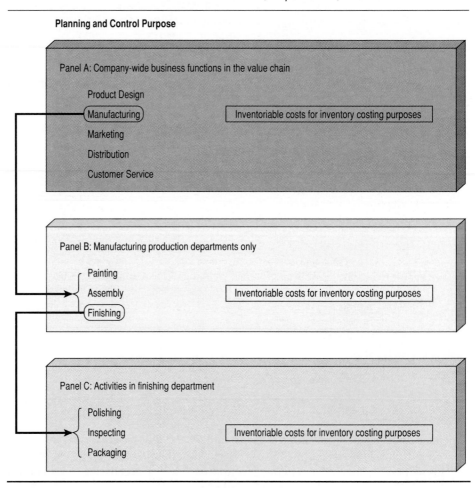

Demand for Activity-Based Costing

The chapter-opening situation illustrates manager frustration with a time-honored cost accounting practice — allocating all overhead cost to products based on a single application base such as direct labor. In recent years many managers, such as Jim Fleming in the chapter-opening vignette, and accountants have experienced frustration with their cost accounting systems. Some companies have installed ABC systems, and their number is growing. There are several reasons why managers demand ABC.

1. Activities in various departments may be combined with activities in other departments. For example, quality control activities occur in several departments. In our illustration, it would be the sum of the inspection costs in the Painting Department, the Assembling Department, and the Finishing Department. Only if detailed records are kept by activities can the total company cost of quality control (or any other activity) be used by managers. Focusing on cost by product can obscure the costs of the various manufacturing activities. More than ever, managers focus attention on activities rather than on products. Fundamentally, people manage activities, not products. If the activities are managed well, costs will fall and the resulting products will be more competitive.

2. Managers often lack faith in product costs generated by traditional cost accounting systems. Allocating overhead cost to production based on a single cost driver can result in an unrealistic product cost. Recall that a cost driver is any factor whose change causes a change in a related total cost. For example, Jim Fleming's stained-and-lacquered tables include overhead cost of $16 compared with overhead cost of $4 for a painted model. But a more expensive table should not necessarily bear four times as much overhead cost. After all, a stained table requires only slightly more inspection time and takes no more packaging materials than does a painted model. There are more reasonable ways to allocate these costs to products than by direct labor hours. ABC shifts the focus of managers and accountants to the activities that manufacture the tables. For example, inspection cost could be allocated on the basis of inspection time. Also, the only difference in packaging is the label on the box, so each table should bear an equal amount of packaging cost. It is unlikely that the materials for a lacquered table cost four times what the materials for a painted table cost. This reasoning is behind Jim Fleming's dissatisfaction with the company's cost allocation system.

A key feature of ABC is allocation of activity costs based on multiple cost drivers. Each cost driver is selected for its relationship to the activity. The more precise relationships yield more realistic product costs than under traditional systems that use a single allocation base for conversion costs. Better cost figures help managers make wiser decisions.

Developments in information technology make activity-based costing possible. Optical scanning, bar coding, and robotics have reduced the cost of processing the information demanded by ABC. Before these techniques became available, it was convenient to use direct labor hours or direct labor dollars as the sole basis for allocating overhead cost. Now it is relatively inexpensive to obtain more precise cost allocations for multiple cost drivers.

Product Costing in an Activity-Based System _____

Product cost build-up in an ABC system follows the pattern of other cost systems, with one exception. Conversion costs are applied to products based on various manufacturing activities rather than on a single measure, such as direct labor hours in traditional systems. Suppose Du Quesnay's, Inc., uses ABC, and the direct material of its wrought-iron lawn chairs costs $4 per unit. Each chair includes eight parts and required fifteen minutes of machine time. Du Quesnay's conversion costs,

OBJECTIVE 6

Account for an activity-based costing system

organized by manufacturing activities, and the associated cost drivers and unit application rates follow. Note the procession of analysis:

1. Identify activities.
2. Identify the cost of the activity.
3. Identify the cost drivers for each activity.
4. Choose the primary cost driver as the application base for each activity.

Manufacturing Activity	Cost of Activity		Cost Driver Chosen as Application Base		Conversion Cost Per Unit of Application Base
1. Material Handling	$ 800	÷	Number of parts (8,000)	=	$ .10
2. Machining	5,000	÷	Machine hours (250)	=	20.00
3. Assembling	4,800	÷	Number of parts (8,000)	=	.60
4. Inspecting	1,400	÷	Number of finished units (1,000)	=	1.40

Each chair's manufacturing cost is $16.00, computed as follows:

Direct materials...	$ 4.00
Conversion costs	
Material handling (8 parts × $.10)...................	.80
Machining (¼ machine hour × $20.00)............	5.00
Assembling (8 parts × $.60)	4.80
Inspecting (1 finished unit × $1.40)	1.40
Total manufacturing cost per unit.......................	$16.00

The detailed breakdown of conversion costs by activity pinpoints opportunities for cost control. For example, machining costs of $5.00 per unit may be too high. Managers could take action to bring machining cost down. In a traditional costing system this information may not be available, and cost may escalate without managers' attention.

Managers are also concerned about full product cost, which includes the costs of upstream activities and downstream activities in the value chain. Recall that upstream activities precede manufacturing and downstream activities follow. Du Quesnay's full product cost per chair is $26.60, computed as follows:

Upstream activities	
Product design (assumed)..	$ 1.40
Total manufacturing cost per unit (as before)...	16.00
Downstream activities	
Marketing, distribution, and customer service (assumed)..................	9.20
Full product cost per unit...	$26.60

Internal decisions, such as cost control and product pricing, will focus on the components of full product cost. However, the external financial statements will report chairs at $16 each because that is their manufacturing (inventoriable) cost. The costs of upstream and downstream activities are expensed as incurred.

Activity-Based Costing and Management Decisions ———

A major feature of activity-based costing is the use of several cost application bases instead of just one or two. In particular, people who favor ABC warn that the use of a single application base may result in unrealistic product costs and lead to unwise decisions. The following illustration is exaggerated to emphasize the underlying ABC concepts.

Quality Instrument Limited manufactures two products, space missile instruments (20 per month) and testing instruments (400 per month). The company has had the same cost accounting system since its founding in 1971. A single plantwide rate based on machine hours of running time has been used for applying all conversion costs to production. Direct materials cost and machine hours are the same for the two products, so their total manufacturing costs are equal. In the following tabulation of total cost per unit, focus on conversion cost:

| | Conversion Costs per Unit | | | Direct Materials | |
Product	Machine Hours Per Unit	Application Rate Per Machine Hour	Total Cost	Cost Per Unit	Total Manufacturing Cost Per Unit
Space missile instrument	5 ×	$120	= $600	$200	$800
Testing instrument	5 ×	120	= 600	200	800

In recent years the cost of each machine setup has soared to $42,000 as precision requirements have tightened. The use of a single cost application rate that is based on machine hours of running time ignores the role of setup cost. To better gauge the cost of each product, management decides to use two activities, machine setups and machine running time, for applying conversion cost to products. Each product requires one machine setup. When machine setup cost is subtracted from total manufacturing cost, the application rate for machine running time decreases to $80 per hour from the previous level of $120. The ABC computations of product cost differ significantly from the earlier figures:

| | Conversion Costs | | | | | | Direct Materials | |
Product	Machine Setups	Running of Machines Units	Running of Machines Hours	Running of Machines Rate	Total Cost	Per Unit	Cost Per Unit	Total Manufacturing Cost Per Unit
Space missile instrument............	$42,000 +	(20 ×	5 ×	$80)	= $ 50,000	$2,500*	$200	$2,700
Testing instrument............	42,000 +	(400 ×	5 ×	80)	= 202,000	505**	200	705

* $ 50,000/20 units = $2,500
** $202,000/400 units = $505

Compare the total manufacturing cost per unit under the two methods of allocating conversion costs:

| | Total Manufacturing Cost per Unit | |
Product	Using Plantwide Rate	Using ABC Rate
Space missile instrument	$800	$2,700
Testing instrument	800	705

Activity-based costing is likely to give managers better information for decision-making. ABC identifies the various activities and cost drivers that cause certain costs and uses those relationships to apply costs more precisely. For example, use of a single cost application base ignores the high cost of machine setups. Manufacture of each group of instruments requires one setup costing $42,000, but that information is ignored in the traditional approach. Consequently, the same amount of conversion cost ($600) is allocated to each space missile instrument and each testing instrument. The accounting records indicate that each product's manufacturing cost is $800. A product pricing decision based on these cost figures can be disastrous. Suppose the marketing department prices each space missile instrument and each testing instrument at $1,500. Managers believe each sale will yield a $700 profit ($1,500 – $800). However, the company will lose $1,200 ($2,700 – $1,500) on the sale of each space missile instrument.

The ABC cost amounts lead to an entirely different conclusion. Each space missile instrument is allocated $2,500 of conversion costs, and the accounting records indicate that total cost is $2,700. Company managers are more likely to price the products realistically.

Another decision is whether Quality Instrument Limited should make these products or buy them from an outside supplier. Suppose an outside company offers to supply each product for $1,000. Using a single cost application base, Quality managers would reject the offer. They would think they could make each instrument for $800. Using ABC, they would accept the outside offer for space missile instruments. The purchase price of $800 is much lower than Quality's manufacturing cost of $2,700.

All of the above decisions may be influenced by other factors. For example, managers should consider whether certain costs are fixed or variable. Nevertheless, the figures produced by ABC consistently provide more accurate costs than those produced by a single cost-application base.

Joint Product Cost

OBJECTIVE 7

Allocate cost to joint products and byproducts

A manufacturing process that produces more than one product simultaneously is called a joint process. **Joint products** are goods that are specifically identified as individual products only after a juncture in the production process called the **split-off point**. To be called a joint product, the item must have a sales value that is significant in relation to the other item produced. For example, refining crude oil produces gasoline and natural gas as joint products. Exhibit 23-14 diagrams this joint process.

Many industries have manufacturing processes that create joint products. Soap making, for example, produces lanolin and other oils for cosmetics, in addition to soap. Refining copper also produces ammonia, which has many uses.

How do we assign costs to individual products that are manufactured by a joint process? After the split-off point, costs are easily assigned. For example, after gasoline and natural gas are separated in the refining process, further costs can be separately identified with the two products. But what costs incurred *before* split-off are assigned to the individual joint products? For example, how should we allocate the cost of exploring and drilling for oil to final products (gasoline and natural gas)? These *joint processing costs* may be allocated using the *relative sales value* method.

Assume the joint cost of processing 65,000 litres of gasoline and liquid natural gas is $72,000. Exhibit 23-15 shows how to allocate this joint cost to the two products.

The relative sales value of each joint product is computed by dividing its individual sales value by the total sales value. In the exhibit, the gasoline sales value makes up two thirds of the total and liquid natural gas makes up one third. Multiplying joint cost of $72,000 by these fractions gives the two products' individual costs of $48,000 and $24,000. Any cost of processing gasoline after split-off is added to $48,000 to determine the total cost of the gasoline. The cost of liquid natural gas is computed similarly.

EXHIBIT 23-14   *Joint Products*

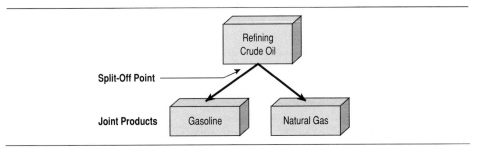

EXHIBIT 23-15   *Allocation of Joint Cost to Joint Products*

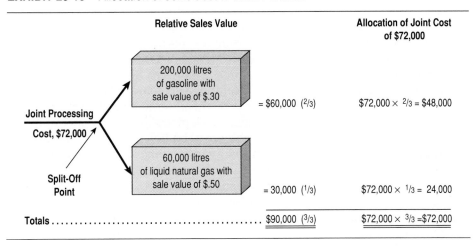

Byproduct Cost

The difference between a joint product and a byproduct depends on the relative sales values of the products. **Byproducts** are those outputs of joint processes with minor sale value in comparison to the main products. Sawdust is a byproduct of a lumber company. Meat packing yields pet food as a byproduct.

Accounting for the cost of byproducts is straightforward. Byproducts are assigned an accounting value called **net realizable value**, which is their sales value less the cost of selling them. Suppose a lumber company's Work in Process — Milling account has a balance of $229,000. This amount includes the estimated sales value of the byproduct sawdust, $5,600. It will cost the company $600 to sell the sawdust, so the net realizable value of the sawdust is $5,000 ($5,600 – $600). The entry to record the net realizable value of the sawdust is

Byproducts Inventory................................	5,000	
Work in Process — Milling		5,000

Sale of the byproduct is accounted for in the usual manner. Because its cost is embedded in the cost of the main product, the accounting value of the byproduct is subtracted from the main product's cost. In this illustration, the cost assigned to lumber is $224,000 ($229,000 – $5,000).

Just-in-Time (JIT) Production Systems

Stockpiles of idle inventory (raw materials, work in process, and finished goods) tie up cash, so businesses strive to keep the level of unused inventory to a minimum. **Just-in-time (JIT) production** is a system in which each component on a production line is produced immediately as needed by the next step. The goal is to eliminate waste and reduce investment in inventories.

To see how a JIT system works, consider the manufacture of cardboard by a company such as MacMillan Bloedel. The company may stockpile lumber and chemicals for production. Raw materials are placed in production, labor and overhead are expended, and the work in process moves through various stages to finished goods. If a bottleneck occurs — say, a machine breaks down — then a significant amount of work in process may build up. The bottleneck creates a waste because work stops until the machine is fixed. Upon completion, the finished goods may sit around for days or weeks awaiting sale. This creates waste because idle inventory accumulates storage cost but no revenue.

JIT systems are based on a "demand-pull" philosophy. At Hewlett-Packard Company, for example, workers follow the slogan "Never build nothing, nowhere, for nobody, unless they ask you for it." NCR, a manufacturer of printers, also applies the JIT philosophy to its operations. How does this philosophy affect production? Ideally, the company maintains no inventories — no raw materials, no work in process beyond what is in production, and no finished goods. How is this accomplished?

Manufacturing is activated by the receipt of a customer order. Receiving the order, the manufacturer purchases the raw materials for immediate delivery. Upon arrival, materials are placed in production, which proceeds without interruption to the completion of finished goods. The absence of bottlenecks (that is, there are no interruptions) keeps work in process inventory from sitting idle. Finished goods are minimal because goods are sold before manufacture.

JIT systems depend on careful planning and control of manufacturing operations as well as cooperation and trust between suppliers, producers, and end-users. They require reliable suppliers who meet the manufacturer's demands without fail. Of course, this is not always possible, and JIT systems are designed to compensate for disruptions in production. Workers are trained more broadly than in non-JIT plants. For example, production employees not only rivet parts as they move down the line, they also inspect goods for defects and have the authority to stop the production line if necessary.

Delaying production until after a customer has ordered goods may mean frequent equipment setups. Production-line employees in JIT systems do more setup work than in traditional systems that use separate departments to modify equipment. In JIT systems production employees also perform routine maintenance on equipment between production runs. By cross-training employees, maintenance cost can be reduced. There is evidence that employee morale increases with the added responsibility.

Computers are a major element of many JIT systems. Computers are ideal for synchronizing raw material orders, production scheduling, inventory costing, and customer billing. Robotic assembly lines are programmed and operated by computers. The goal is a steady stream of high-quality products delivered to the customer at relatively low cost.

JIT systems work well for the manufacturer. For the supplier of the raw materials, they can create nightmares. To deliver materials with split-second precision, the supplier also needs reliable sources. To achieve this reliability the supplier may have to stockpile the material, which shifts some of the cost burden for storing material from the manufacturer to the supplier. In another arrangement, the manufacturer eliminates the need for outside suppliers by producing the raw material itself.

JIT production systems simplify cost accounting. A number of accounts can be eliminated, including Raw Material Inventory, the various Work in Process Inventory accounts, and Finished Goods Inventory. During production, costs are accumulated in a single account titled Raw-and-in-Process Inventory. Upon completion, the goods are delivered to the customer. The final journal entry debits Cost of Goods Sold and credits Raw-and-in-Process Inventory. Details of these accounting systems are described in cost accounting textbooks.

Summary Problem for Your Review

This problem extends the Summary Problem for Your Review on p. 1018 to a second processing department. Jacobs-Webster Ltd. had the following activity in its Finishing Department during May:

Finishing Department Facts for May

Units
   Work in process, Apr. 30 (20% complete as to direct materials,
      70% complete as to conversion costs) .... 4,000 units
   Transferred in from Assembly Department during May 16,000
   Completed during May 15,000
   Work in process, May 31, (36% complete as to direct materials,
      80% complete as to conversion costs) 5,000
Costs
   Work in process, Apr. 30 .... $18,000
   Transferred in from Assembly Department during May 38,400
   Direct materials added during May 6,400
   Conversion costs added during May 24,300

Required

Show the allocation of total cost to units completed and units in ending work in process inventory in the Finishing Department during May.

SOLUTION TO REVIEW PROBLEM

Step 1: Flow of Production in Physical Units
Step 2: Equivalent Units of Production

Finishing Department
for the month ended May 31, 19XX

	Step 1	Step 2		
		Equivalent Units of Production		
	Flow of			
	Physical	*Transferred*	*Direct*	*Conversion*
Flow of Production	Units	*In*	*Materials*	*Costs*
Units to account for				
Work in process, Apr. 30	4,000			
Transferred in during May	16,000			
Total physical units				
to account for	20,000			
Units accounted for				
Completed and transferred				
out during May				
From beginning inventory	4,000	—	3,200*	1,200*
Transferred in and				
completed during May				
(16,000 – 5,000)	11,000	11,000	11,000	11,000
Work in process, May 31	5,000	5,000	1,800**	4,000**

Total physical units accounted for	20,000		
Equivalent units of production.........................		16,000	16,000	16,200

*   Direct materials: 4,000 units each 80% completed = 3,200 equivalent units
   Conversion costs: 4,000 units each 30% completed = 1,200 equivalent units
** Direct materials: 5,000 units each 36% completed = 1,800 equivalent units
   Conversion costs: 5,000 units each 80% completed = 4,000 equivalent units

Steps 3 and 4: Computation of Unit Costs

Finishing Department
for the month ended May 31, 19XX

	Transferred-In Costs	Direct Materials	Conversion Costs	Total
Work in process, Apr. 30........................	Work done before May			$18,000
Costs added during May......................	$ 38,400	$ 6,400	$ 24,300	69,100
Divide by equivalent units...................	÷16,000	÷16,000	÷16,200	
Cost per equivalent unit.......................	$ 2.40	$ .40	$ 1.50	
Total cost to account for........................				$87,100

Step 5: Application of Total Cost to Units Completed and Units in Ending Work in Process Inventory

Finishing Department
for the month ended October 31, 19XX

	Transferred-In Costs	Direct Materials	Conversion Costs	Total
Units completed and transferred out to Finished Goods Inventory				
From work in process, Apr. 30				$18,000
Costs added during May				
Direct materials................	—	3,200 × $.40		1,280
Conversion costs..............	—		1,200 × $1.50	1,800
Total completed from Apr. 30 inventory.............				21,080
Units transferred in and completed during May	11,000 × ($2.40 + $.40 + $1.50)			47,300
Total costs transferred out				$68,380
Work in process, May 31				
Transferred-in costs	5,000 × $2.40			$12,000
Direct materials..........................		1,800 × $.40		720
Conversion costs........................			4,000 × $1.50	6,000
Total work in process, May 31				18,720
Total cost accounted for				$87,100

Summary

Processing costing is a system for assigning costs to products that are mass-produced in continuous fashion through a sequence of production steps. In a process costing system costs are accumulated by processes (departments) and flow from one department to another until the product is completed.

The main accounting problem in process costing is determining the cost of the work in process transferred from one department to the next. This complication arises because the goods in process may be in various stages of completion. Cost accountants compute the number of *equivalent units* of production that could have been manufactured from start to finish with the costs that were incurred in each department during the period. Cost divided by the number of equivalent units equals unit cost. This unit cost, multiplied by the number of units transferred out of the department, determines the cost entering the next department. Equivalent-unit cost, multiplied by the number of units remaining in Work in Process Inventory, measures the department's ending inventory. Companies summarize the activity in each processing department for the period on a production cost report.

Activity-based costing (ABC) is a system that focuses on activities as the fundamental cost objects and uses the costs of these activities as building blocks for compiling the costs of products and other cost objects. Activity-based costing is general in the sense that it can be part of job order costing, process costing, or some hybrid costing system.

Joint products are those items with significant value that are not identified as specific products until after a split-off point in the production process. Cost is allocated to joint products based on their relative sales values. *Byproducts* are insignificant relative to the main item produced. The value assigned to a byproduct is its *net realizable value* (expected sale price less the cost of selling the byproduct).

Just-in-time production systems minimize inventory quantities to reduce cost. They rely on dependable suppliers to deliver materials just as they are needed. Inventory is sold before manufacturing begins.

Self-Study Questions

Test your understanding of the chapter by marking the best answer to each of the following questions:

1. For which of the following products is a process costing system most appropriate? (p. 1010)
   a. Breakfast cereal
   b. Automobiles
   c. Houses
   d. Furniture

2. A key difference between job order costing and process costing is that (p. 1011)
   a. Costs are assigned to direct materials in job costing and to indirect materials in process costing.
   b. Job costing uses a single work in process account and process costing uses a separate work in process account for each department.
   c. Job order costing, but not process costing, uses conversion costs.
   d. Factory overhead is used in process costing but not in job order costing.

3. During August, the Assembly Department of Fisk Manufacturing Co. Ltd. completed and transferred 20,000 intercom units to the Finishing Department. The Assembly Department's August 31 inventory included 6,000 units, 90 percent complete as to direct materials and 75 percent complete as to conversion costs. August equivalent units of the Assembly Department total (pp. 1014–15)
   a. 20,000
   b. 24,500
   c. 25,400
   d. 25,400 as to direct materials and 24,500 as to conversion costs

4. The concept of equivalent units is useful for *(p. 1016)*
    a. Measuring the cost of direct materials and conversion costs incurred in a processing department
    b. Measuring the unit costs of direct materials and conversion costs to compute the cost of goods transferred from one processing department to the next
    c. Separating the cost of a manufacturing process from the cost of a manufacturing operation
    d. Dividing ending inventory between finished goods and work in process

5. The entry to record the transfer of goods from the Heating Department to the Drying Department is *(p. 1018)*
    a. Finished Goods XXX
        Work in Process — Drying XXX
    b. Work in Process — Heating... XXX
        Work in Process — Drying XXX
    c. Work in Process — Heating... XXX
        Finished Goods — Drying...................................... XXX
    d. Work in Process — Drying XXX
        Work in Process — Heating.................................... XXX

6. The costs to account for in a second processing department include those associated with *(p. 1020)*
    a. Beginning work in process and goods transferred in during the period
    b. Beginning work in process and costs added during the period
    c. Beginning work in process, goods transferred in and costs added during the period.
    d. Beginning work in process and ending work in process

7. Refer to the production cost report in Exhibit 23-11, p. 1025. The unit cost of goods completed and transferred to finished goods during October was *(p. 1030)*
    a. $4.40   c. $4.90
    b. $4.80   d. $5.32

8. Activity-based costing is *(pp. 1025–26)*
    a. A hybrid system that can be used with a job cost system or a process cost system
    b. Closer to a job cost system than to a process cost system
    c. Closer to a process cost system than to a job cost system

9. The joint cost of manufacturing Products A and B is $160,000. Product A can be sold for $240,000 and Product B for $80,000. The costs of Products A and B are *(p. 1030)*
    a. $240,000 and $80,000
    b. $160,000 and $80,000
    c. $120,000 and $40,000
    d. Cannot be determined from the information given

10. The accounting value assigned to byproducts is called *(p. 1031)*
    a. Sales value   c. Net realizable value
    b. Net value   d. Selling cost

Answers to the Self-Study Questions are at the end of the chapter.

Accounting Vocabulary

activity-based costing ABC *(p. 1025)*
byproduct *(p. 1031)*
conversion costs *(p. 1014)*
cost object *(p. 1025)*
equivalent units *(p. 1014)*

joint product *(p. 1030)*
Just-in-time (JIT) production *(p. 1031)*
net realizable value *(p. 1031)*

process costing *(p. 1010)*
production cost report *(p. 1024)*
split-off point *(p. 1030)*

ASSIGNMENT MATERIAL ————————————

Questions

1. Distinguish a process cost accounting system from a job order system.

2. Which type of costing system — job order or process costing —would be better suited to account for manufacture of each of the following products: (a) chemicals, (b) automobiles, (c) lumber, (d) hand-held calculators, or (e) custom lampshades?

3. Why does a process costing system use multiple work in process accounts but a job order system use only one such account?

4. Give the entries (accounts only) to record the following: (a) purchase of materials; (b) incurrence of labor; (c) overhead cost; (d) requisition of materials and application of labor and overhead to Work in Process Inventory — Department 1 (combine in one entry); (e) transfer of cost of work in process inventory from Department 1 to Department 2; (f) transfer of cost of completed units to finished goods; (g) cost of goods sold.

5. What is an equivalent unit of production? Give an example of equivalent units.

6. Montague Manufacturing Limited completed and transferred 35,000 units of its product to a second department during the period. At the end of the period, another 10,000 units were in work in process inventory, 20 percent complete. How many equivalent units did Montague produce during the period?

7. Outline the five steps to account for a process costing system.

8. How are equivalent units used in Exhibits 23-5 and 23-6?

9. Why might a company have different numbers of equivalent units for direct materials and conversion costs?

10. What information does a production cost report give? Why does the format of the report differ from company to company?

11. What is the major accounting challenge in a process costing system that has more than one processing department? Why is this such a challenge?

12. Compute the equivalent units of production for Department 2 during July:

    Units
    Work in process, June 30 (10% complete as to direct
       materials, 40% complete as to conversion costs)............. 1,000 units
    Transferred in from Department 1 during July.................... 25,000
    Completed during July... 22,000
    Work in process, July 31 (20% complete as to direct
       materials, 70% complete as to conversion costs)............. 4,000

13. Briefly describe an activity-based costing system, indicating the advantages it offers over traditional cost accounting systems.

14. "Executives should decide which of the following three basic cost accounting systems is best for their company: job order costing, process costing, or activity-based costing." Do you agree? Explain.

15. Distinguish joint products from byproducts.

16. How is the cost of a joint product determined?

17. How is an accounting value assigned to a byproduct? Give the entry to record the value of a byproduct.

Exercises

Exercise 23-1 *Diagramming flows through a process costing system* **(L.O. 1)**

Mueller & Chabot, Inc. manufactures furniture in a three-stage process that includes milling, assembling, and finishing, in that order. Direct materials are added in the milling and finishing departments, and direct labor and overhead are applied in all three departments. The company's general ledger includes the following accounts:

Work in Process Inventory — Finishing	Factory Wages
Raw Materials Inventory	Work in Process Inventory — Milling
Finished Goods Inventory	
Factory Overhead	Work in Process Inventory — Assembling
Cost of Goods Sold	

Required

Outline the flow of costs through the company's accounts. Include a T-account for each account title given.

Exercise 23-2 *Computing equivalent units in a single department* **(L.O. 2)**

Insert the missing values:

		Equivalent Units of Production	
Flow of Production	**Flow of Physical Units**	**Direct Materials**	**Conversion Costs**
Units to account for			
Work in process, Nov. 30...	12,000		
Started production during December....................	X		
Total physical units to account for..........................	67,000		
Units accounted for			
Completed and transferred out during December			
From beginning inventory.................................	12,000	X*	X*
Started and completed during December ...	47,000	X	X
Work in process, Dec. 31	X	X**	X**
Total physical units accounted for....................	67,000		
Equivalent units of production..............................		X	X

*   Direct materials: 40 percent completed during December
    Conversion costs: 50 percent completed during December
** Direct materials: 20 percent completed during December
    Conversion costs: 30 percent completed during December

Exercise 23-3   *Computing equivalent units and applying cost to completed units and work in process* **(L.O. 2, 3)**

Leslie Production Limited experienced the following activity in its Finishing Department during December:

Units

Work in process, Nov. 30 (70% complete as to direct materials, 80% complete as to conversion costs)......	8,000 units
Transferred in from Heating Department during December	31,000 units
Completed during December	26,000
Work in process, Dec. 31 (60% complete as to direct materials, 80% complete as to conversion costs)	13,000

Costs

Work in process, Nov. 30...	$ 59,000
Transferred in from Heating Department during December..	108,500
Direct materials added during December...........................	82,500
Conversion costs added during December	102,000

Required

1. Compute the number of equivalent units produced by the Finishing Department during December.
2. Compute unit costs, and apply total cost to (a) units completed and transferred to finished goods and (b) units in December 31 work in process inventory.

Exercise 23-4   *Transferring costs between processing departments* **(L.O. 2, 3, 4)**

The Mixing Department of a chemical company began February with no work in process inventory. During the month, production that cost $37,500 (direct materials, $9,500 and conversion costs, $28,000) was started on 21,000 units. A total of 17,000 units were completed and transferred to the Heating Department. The ending work in process inventory was 50 percent complete as to direct materials and 75 percent complete as to conversion costs.

Required

1. Journalize the transfer of cost from the Mixing Department to the Heating Department.
2. What is the balance in Work in Process — Mixing on February 28?
3. Account for the total cost incurred during February.

Exercise 23-5   *Computing processing costs and journalizing cost transfers* **(L.O. 2, 4)**

The following information was taken from the ledger of Thompson Polyvinyl Products Inc. Ending inventory is 70 percent complete as to direct materials but only 40 percent complete as to conversion costs.

Work in Process — Forming

	Physical Units	Dollars		Physical Units	Dollars
Inventory, Nov. 30	-0-	$ -0-	Transferred to Painting	72,000	?
Production started	80,000		Ending inventory	8,000	
Direct materials		271,600	Total accounted for	80,000	
Conversion costs		225,600			
Total to account for	80,000	$497,200			

Required

Journalize the transfer of cost to the Painting Department.

Exercise 23-6   *Computing equivalent units in two departments (L.O. 2, 5)*

Selected production and cost data of Gulig Enterprises Inc. follow for May 19X5.

	Flow of Physical Units	
Flow of Production	Sanding Department	Finishing Department
Units to account for		
Work in process, Apr. 30...	20,000	6,000
Transferred in during May...	70,000	70,000
Total physical units to account for	90,000	76,000
Units accounted for		
Completed and transferred out during May		
From beginning inventory	20,000*	6,000***
Transferred in and completed during May	55,000	65,000
Work in process, May 31...	15,000**	5,000****
Total physical units accounted for	90,000	76,000

*	Direct materials: 20 percent completed during May
	Conversion costs: 30 percent completed during May
**	Direct materials: 50 percent completed during May
	Conversion costs: 40 percent completed during May
***	Direct materials: ⅔ completed during May
	Conversion costs: 40 percent completed during May
****	Direct materials: 50 percent completed during May
	Conversion costs: 60 percent completed during May

Required

Compute equivalent units for goods transferred in, direct materials and conversion costs for each department.

Exercise 23-7   *Journalizing process costing transactions (L.O. 4)*

Record the following selected process cost accounting transactions in the general journal:

a. Purchase of raw materials on account, $4,200.

b. Requisition of direct materials to Processing Department 1, $1,800.

c. Payment of factory labor, $11,000.

d. Incurrence of factory overhead costs: depreciation, $600; insurance, $500; utilities paid, $900.

e. Application of conversion costs to Processing Department 1: direct labor, $1,900; factory overhead, $2,850.

f. Transfer of cost from Processing Department 1 to Department 2, $5,300.

g. Application of conversion costs to Processing Department 2: direct labor, $700; factory overhead, $1,050.

h. Transfer of cost from Processing Department 2 to finished goods, $5,200.

Exercise 23-8   *Using a production cost report* **(L.O. 4)**

Cost accountants for Wucker, Inc. prepared the following production cost report for February:

	Physical Units	Total Costs
Finishing Department		
Production Cost Report		
for the month ended February 28, 19XX		
Work in process, Jan. 31	14,000	$ 82,000
Transferred in from Grinding Department during February	90,000	392,000
Cost added in Finishing Department during February		
Direct materials	—	58,000
Conversion costs		
Direct labor	—	84,000
Factory overhead	—	83,000
Total to account for	104,000	$699,000
Completed and transferred to finished goods during February	95,000	$650,000
Work in process, Feb. 28	9,000	49,000
Total accounted for	104,000	$699,000

Required

Journalize all February activity in the Finishing Department.

Exercise 23-9   *Product build-up in an activity-based costing system* **(L.O. 6)**

Amarillo Motor Corp. uses activity-based costing to account for its manufacturing process. The direct materials in each electric motor cost $36. Each motor includes 60 parts, and finishing requires five minutes of direct labor time. The manufacture of 1,000 motors requires three machine setups. Conversion costs, listed by manufacturing activity, the related cost drivers, and unit application rates follow:

Manufacturing Activity	Cost Driver Chosen as Application Base	Conversion Cost Per Unit of Application Base
1. Material handling	Number of parts	$ .20
2. Machine setup	Number of setups	400.00
3. Insertion of parts	Number of parts	.50
4. Finishing	Direct labor hours	18.00

Required

1. Compute the total manufacturing cost of each electric motor.

2. Suppose an alternative costing plan would apply conversion costs to electric motors based on direct labor hours. Overall manufacture of each machine requires two direct labor hours. Compute conversion cost per unit under both costing plans. Which plan is preferable? What decisions could be affected by your choice?

Exercise 23-10 *Determining the cost of joint products and byproducts (L.O. 7)*

Part A. Pineville Paper Mill Ltd. manufacturers cardboard and linerboard by a joint process that costs $300,000 on average each month. Cardboard sells for $32 per tonne and linerboard for $12 per tonne. Each month the manufacturing process generates 5,000 tonnes of cardboard and 20,000 tonnes of linerboard. Use the relative sales value method to determine the cost of each tonne of the two products.

Part B. Herald Chair Ltd. makes recliner chairs. The manufacturing process leaves byproducts including scrap wood and upholstery remnants with resale value averaging $1 per chair. Five percent of this amount is consumed by the cost of disposing of byproducts. Herald manufactures 10,000 chairs per year. Make the general journal entry to record the byproduct inventory.

Problems   *(Group A)*

Problem 23-1A *Computing equivalent units and applying cost to completed units and work in process; no beginning inventory or cost transferred in (L.O. 2, 3)*

Matuzak Multigraph Corporation produce component parts that are used in hand-held calculators. One part, a diode generator, is manufactured in a single processing department. No diode generators were in process on May 31, and Matuzak started production on 12,000 units during June. Completed production for June totaled 9,900 units. The June 30 work in process was 20 percent complete as to direct materials and 30 percent complete as to conversion costs. Direct materials costing $6,192 were placed in production during June, and direct labor of $5,100 and factory overhead of $2,271 were applied to the manufacture of diode generators.

Required

1. Compute the number of equivalent units of production and the unit costs for June.

2. Show the application of total cost to (a) units completed and transferred to finished goods and (b) units still in process at June 30.

3. Prepare a T-account for Work in Process Inventory to show its activity during June, including the June 30 balance.

Problem 23-2A *Computing equivalent units, applying cost to completed units and work in process, and journalizing transactions; no beginning inventory or cost transferred in* **(L.O. 2, 3, 4)**

Piet Wool Corp. produces wool fabric by a three-stage process: cleaning, spinning and weaving, in that order. Costs incurred in the Cleaning Department during September are summarized as follows:

Work in Process Inventory — Cleaning

Direct materials	70,400
Direct labor	2,580
Factory overhead	8,700

September activity in the Cleaning Department included completion of 17,000 kilograms of wool, which were transferred to the Spinning Department. Also, work on 3,000 kilograms began, which on September 30 was 20 percent complete with respect to direct materials and 60 percent complete with respect to conversion costs.

Required

1. Compute the equivalent units of production and unit costs in the Cleaning Department for September.
2. Prove that the sum of (a) cost of goods transferred out of the Cleaning Department and (b) ending Work in Process Inventory — Cleaning equals the total cost accumulated in the department during September.
3. Journalize all transactions affecting the company's cleaning process during September, including those already posted.

Problem 23-3A *Computing equivalent units for a second department with beginning inventory; applying cost to completed units and work in process* **(L.O. 2, 3, 5)**

Maremont Fabricator Corporation manufactures auto bumpers in a two-stage process that includes shaping and plating. Steel alloy is the basic raw material of the shaping process. The steel is molded according to the design specifications of the automobile manufacturers (Toyota, Ford and General Motors). The Plating Department then adds a finish plate of chrome to give the new bumper a shiny appearance.

At March 31, before recording the transfer of cost from the Plating Department to Finished Goods Inventory, the Maremont general ledger included the following account:

Work in Process Inventory — Plating

Feb. 28 Balance	24,600
Transferred in from Shaping	30,000
Direct materials	27,060
Direct labor	17,100
Factory overhead	37,620

Work in process of the Plating Department on February 28 consisted of 600 bumpers that were 50 percent complete as to direct materials and conversion costs. During March, 3,000 bumpers were transferred in from the Shaping Department. The Plating Department transferred 2,200 bumpers to finished goods in March, and 1,400 bumpers were still in process on March 31. This ending inventory was 40 percent complete as to direct materials and 70 percent complete as to conversion costs.

Required

1. Compute the equivalent units of production, unit costs and total cost to account for in the Plating Department for March.
2. Show the application of total Plating Department cost for March to (a) cost of goods transferred out of the Plating Department and (b) cost of ending Work in Process Inventory — Plating on March 31.

Problem 23-4A *Preparing a production cost report and recording transactions based on the report's information* **(L.O. 4)**

Required

1. Prepare the March production cost report for the Plating Department in Problem 23-3A.
2. Journalize all transactions affecting the Plating Department during March, including those entries that have already been posted.

Problem 23-5A *Computing equivalent units for a second department with beginning inventory and applying cost to completed units and work in process* **(L.O. 2, 3, 5)**

The manufacture of hand tools, such as pliers and screwdrivers, occurs in four departments and also includes two additional operations. Consider screwdrivers with plastic handles. Manufacture of the handles includes mixing and heating the raw materials, shaping the mix by pouring it into molds and drying. Production of the screwdrivers is then completed in two operations: assembling the handles and shanks, and packaging for shipment to retail outlets such as Canadian Tire, Pro Hardware and Aikenhead hardware stores.

Process costing information for the Drying Department of Frontenac Tool Manufacturing Ltd. for a period follows. No direct materials are required.

Units

Work in process, beginning (63% complete as to conversion costs)	7,000 units
Transferred in from the Molding Department during the period	32,000
Completed during the period	16,000
Work in process, ending (20% complete as to conversion costs)	23,000

Costs

Work in process, beginning	$ 1,190
Transferred in from the Molding Department during the period	3,840
Conversion costs added during the period	1,295

The cost of direct materials in the assembling and packaging phases includes the cost of the plastic handles transferred out of the Drying Department plus the cost of the metal shanks, which is $1,493. The assembling and packaging operations are entirely automated. Assembling occurs at the rate of 4,000 units per hour and packaging at 2,000 per hour. Conversion cost is allocated to the assembling operation at the predetermined rate of $25.00 per machine hour and to packaging at the rate of $27.50 per machine hour. There is only one work order for the screwdrivers.

Required

1. Compute the number of equivalent units (screwdrivers) produced by the Drying-Processing Department during the period.

2. Show the application of total cost to (a) units completed and transferred to finished goods and (b) units in ending work in process inventory.

3. Compute the total manufacturing cost of the screwdrivers completed and transferred to finished goods. Also compute the unit cost of each complete screwdriver to the nearest cent.

Problem 23-6A   *Computing equivalent units for a second department with beginning inventory, applying cost to completed units and work in process, and accounting for byproducts and joint products* **(L.O. 2, 3, 4, 5, 7)**

Frito-Lay, Inc. manufactures convenience foods including potato chips and corn chips. Production of corn chips occurs in five steps: cleaning, mixing, cooking, drying and packaging. Suppose the accounting records of a Frito-Lay plant yielded the following information for corn chips in its Packaging Department during a weekly period:

Cases

Work in process, beginning (40% complete as to direct materials, 0% complete as to conversion costs)	3,000 cases
Transferred in from the Drying Department during the week	18,000
Completed during the week	15,000
Work in process, ending (5% complete as to direct materials, 0% complete as to conversion costs)	6,000

Costs

Work in process, beginning	$ 6,280
Transferred in from the Drying Department during the week	$13,500
Direct materials added during the week	6,750
Conversion costs added during the week	15,000

Required

1. Compute the number of equivalent cases of corn chips produced by the Packaging Department during the week.

2. Show the application of total cost in the Packaging Department to (a) cases completed and transferred to finished goods and (b) cases in ending work in process inventory.

3. Inventory ruined during packaging can be sold as a byproduct. Its sale price is 3 percent, and the cost of selling the byproduct is 1 percent of the total cost to be transferred to finished goods. Record the byproduct inventory.

4. After 300 cases of the byproduct inventory (in requirement 3) are removed, the finished goods inventory consists of 20,700 cases. Of this finished goods inventory, 12,300 cases are Frito corn chips, sold at $5.40 per case, and 8,400 cases are

Doritos, sold at $5.70 per case. Use the relative sales value method to compute the costs per case (to the nearest cent) of these two joint products. Round relative sales value to the nearest percent.

Problem 23-7A   *Product costing in an activity-based system* **(L.O. 6)**

Texas Instruments factory assembles and tests printed-circuit (PC) boards. Using assumed numbers, consider the following data regarding PC Board XR1, which is used in certain computers:

Direct materials...	$65.00
Conversion costs applied	?
Total manufacturing product cost....................................	?

The activities that apply to building the PC boards follow:

Manufacturing Activity	Cost Driver	Conversion Costs Applied for Each Activity
1. Start station	Number of raw PC boards	1 × .90 = $ .90
2. Dip insertion	Number of dip insertions	20 × .25 = ?
3. Manual insertion	Number of manual insertions	12 × ? = 7.20
4. Wave solder	Number of boards soldered	1 × 3.50 = 3.50
5. Backload	Number of backload insertions	? × .70 = 4.90
6. Test	Standard time each board is in test activity	.25 × .80 = ?
7. Defect analysis	Standard time for defect analysis and repair	.16 × ? = 8.00
Total		$?

Required

1. Fill in the blanks in both the opening schedule and the list of activities.
2. How is direct labor identified with products under this product costing system?
3. Why might managers favor this activity-based accounting system instead of the older system, which applied conversion costs based on direct labor?

Problem 23-8A   *Product costing in an activity-based system* **(L.O. 6)**

Blume Furniture Limited manufactures rocking chairs in its two plants in Quebec. The company uses activity-based costing, and its activities and related data follow:

Manufacturing Activity	Budgeted Conversion Costs for 19X8	Cost Driver Chosen as Application Base	Conversion Cost per Unit of Application Base
Material handling	$ 200,000	Number of parts	$ 0.25
Cutting	880,000	Number of parts	1.10
Assembling	3,000,000	Direct labor hours	15.00
Painting	70,000	Number of painted units	2.00

Two styles of chairs were produced in March, the standard chair and an unpainted chair, which had fewer parts and required no painting. Their quantities, direct material costs, and other data follow:

Product	Units Produced	Direct Material Costs	Number of Parts	Assembling Direct Labor Hours
Standard chair	5,000	$90,000	100,000	7,500
Unpainted chair	1,000	15,000	15,000	1,200

Required

1. Compute the total manufacturing costs and unit costs of the standard chairs and the unpainted chairs.

2. Suppose upstream activities, such as product design, were analyzed and applied to the standard chairs at $3 each and the unpainted chairs at $2 each. Moreover, similar analyses were conducted of downstream activities, such as distribution, marketing, and customer service. The downstream costs applied were $21 per standard chair and $16 per unpainted chair. Compute the full product cost per unit.

3. Which costs are used for reporting in the external financial statements? Which costs are used for management decision-making? Explain the difference.

(Group B)

Problem 23-1B   *Computing equivalent units and applying cost to completed units and work in process; no beginning inventory or cost transferred in (L.O. 2, 3)*

Bristol Printing, Inc. is an engraving company in Kingston, Ontario that engraves and prints specialty books for publishers all over Canada. Production occurs in three processes: engraving, printing and binding. The Engraving Department was empty on May 31. In mid-June Bristol started production on 65,000 books. Of this number, 52,600 books were engraved during June. The June 30 work in process in the Engraving Department was 20 percent complete as to direct materials and 50 percent complete as to conversion costs. Direct materials costing $137,700 were placed in production in the Engraving Department during June, and direct labor of $43,140 and factory overhead of $62,700 were applied in this department.

Required

1. Compute the number of equivalent units of production and unit costs in the Engraving Department for June.

2. Show the application of total cost in the Engraving Department to (a) units completed and transferred to Printing during June and (b) units still in process at June 30.

3. Prepare a T-account for Work in Process Inventory — Engraving to show its activity during June, including the June 30 balance.

Problem 23-2B   *Computing equivalent units, applying cost to completed units and work in process, and journalizing transactions; no beginning inventory or cost transferred in (L.O. 2, 3, 4)*

Waco Newsprint, Inc. manufactures newsprint (the paper stock on which newspapers are printed) by a four-stage process that includes mixing, cooking, rolling and cutting. In the Mixing Department, wood pulp and chemicals, the basic raw materials, are blended. The resulting mix is heated in the Cooking Department in much the same way food is prepared. Then the cooked mix is rolled to produce sheets. The final process, cutting, divides the sheets into large rolled units for shipment to newspaper companies.

Cost accumulation in the Mixing Department during August is summarized in the following account:

Work in Process Inventory — Mixing

Direct materials	24,700
Direct labor	7,400
Factory overhead	13,500

August activity in the Mixing Department consisted of completion of the mixing process for 1,800 rolls of newsprint plus partial completion of 300 additional rolls. These in-process units were 33⅓ percent complete with respect to direct materials and conversion costs.

Required

1. Compute the equivalent units of production and unit costs in the Mixing Department for August.

2. Prove that the sum of (a) cost of goods transferred out of the Mixing Department and (b) ending Work in Process Inventory — Mixing equals the total cost accumulated in the department during August.

3. Journalize all transactions affecting the company's mixing process during August, including those already posted.

Problem 23-3B   *Computing equivalent units for a second department with beginning inventory; applying cost to completed units and work in process (L.O. 2, 3, 5)*

Dominion Mills, Inc. manufactures broadloom carpet in seven processes: spinning, dyeing, plying, spooling, tufting, latexing and shearing.

First, fluff nylon purchased from a company such as DuPont or Monsanto is spun into yarn that is dyed the desired color. Then two or more threads of the yarn are joined together, or plied, for added strength. The plied yarn is spooled for use in the actual carpet making. Tufting is the process by which yarn is added to burlap backing. After the backing is latexed to hold it together and make it skid resistant, the carpet is sheared to give it an even appearance and feel.

At March 31, before recording the transfer of cost from department to department, the Dominion Mills general ledger included the following account for one of its lines of carpet:

Work in Process Inventory — Dyeing

Feb. 28 Balance	10,900
Transferred in from Spinning	21,280
Direct materials	12,390
Direct labor	7,207
Factory overhead	42,900

Work in process inventory of the Dyeing Department on February 28 consisted of 75 rolls that were 60 percent complete as to direct materials and conversion costs. During March 560 rolls were transferred in from the Spinning Department. The

Dyeing Department completed 500 rolls of the carpet in March, and 135 rolls were still in process on March 31. This ending inventory was 100 percent complete as to direct materials and 80 percent complete as to conversion costs.

Required

1. Compute the equivalent units of production, unit costs, and total cost to account for in the Dyeing Department for March.
2. Show the application of total Dyeing Department cost for March to (a) cost of goods transferred from Dyeing to Plying and (b) cost of ending Work in Process Inventory — Dyeing on March 31.

Problem 23-4B   *Preparing a production cost report and recording transactions based on the information in the report* **(L.O. 4)**

Required

1. Prepare the March production cost report for the Dyeing Department in Problem 23-3B.
2. Journalize all transactions affecting the Dyeing Department during March, including those entries that have already been posted.

Problem 23-5B   *Computing equivalent units for a second department with beginning inventory and applying cost to completed units and work in process* **(L.O. 2, 3, 5)**

The manufacture of lawn mowers includes two processes: forming the blade housing from steel and assembling the parts of the mower. Two operations, lubricating the moving parts and testing the completed mowers, complete their manufacture. The completed mowers are transferred to finished goods prior to shipment to Sears, Woodward's, The Bay and other department stores.

Process costing information for the Assembling Department of Rocco Garden Machines Limited for a period follows. No direct materials are required.

Units	
Work in process, beginning (60% complete as to conversion costs)	2,000 units
Transferred in from the Forming Department during the period	9,000
Completed during the period	6,000
Work in process, ending (70% complete as to conversion costs)	5,000
Costs	
Work in process, beginning	$ 92,000
Transferred in from the Forming Department during the period	333,000
Conversion costs added during the period	66,400

The cost of direct materials in the lubricating and testing phases is the cost of the mowers transferred out of the Assembling Department. The lubricating operation is entirely automated and takes 30 seconds per mower. Testing each completed mower requires an average of five minutes of a technician's time. Conversion costs are $30 per machine hour for lubricating and $50 per person hour for testing. There is only one work order for the mowers in each production run.

Required

1. Compute the number of equivalent units (mowers) produced by the Assembling Department during the period.

2. Show the application of total cost to (a) units completed and transferred to finished goods and (b) units in ending work in process inventory.

3. Compute the total manufacturing cost of the mowers completed and transferred to finished goods. Also compute the unit cost of each complete mower (to the nearest cent).

Problem 23-6B *Computing equivalent units for a second department with beginning inventory, applying cost to completed units and work in process, and accounting for byproducts and joint products* **(L.O. 2, 3, 4, 5, 7)**

Many products are developed from crude oil, including aviation fuel, gasoline, asphalt and the wax used to make wax paper and automobile wax. This problem focuses on the wax products.

Wax is removed from crude oil by two basic processes, heating and cooling. Heating separates the lighter components, such as aviation fuel and gasoline, from the heavier components. The heavier residue is cooled, passed through a brine solution and filtered to obtain wax. Therefore, the manufacture of wax consists of heating, cooling, mixing and filtering processes, in that order.

Suppose the accounting records of an Imperial Oil Limited refinery yielded the following information about its Wax Filtering Department for a weekly period:

Litres

Work in process, beginning (80% complete as to direct materials, 20% complete as to conversion costs)	8,000 litres
Transferred in from the Mixing Department during the week	62,000
Completed during the week	50,000
Work in process, ending (67% complete as to direct materials, 81% complete as to conversion costs)	20,000

Costs

Work in process, beginning	$17,040
Transferred in from the Mixing Department during the week	99,200
Direct materials added during the week	12,200
Conversion costs added during the week	18,900

Required

1. Compute the number of equivalent litres of wax produced during the week by the Wax Filtering Department. Calculate cost per equivalent to three decimal places.

2. Show the application of total cost in the Wax Filtering Department to (a) litres completed and transferred to finished goods and (b) litres in ending work in process inventory.

3. Assume a lower grade of wax is removed as a byproduct from the wax filtering process. Its sale price is 2 percent, and the cost of selling the byproduct is ¼ percent (.0025), of the total cost to be transferred to finished goods. Record the byproduct inventory.

4. After 4,000 litres of the byproduct inventory (in requirement 3) is removed, the finished goods inventory consists of 46,000 litres of wax. The company will sell 15,000 litres at $2.06 per gallon to a wax paper manufacturer and 31,000 litres at $5.91 per litre to an automobile wax producer. Use the relative sales value method to compute the costs per litre (to the nearest cent) of these two joint products. Round relative sales value to the nearest percent.

Problem 23-7B   *Product costing in an activity-based system* (L.O. 6)

A National Semiconductor Ltd. factory assembles and tests printed-circuit (PC) boards. Using assumed numbers, consider the following data regarding PC Board J47, which is used in certain computers:

Direct materials..	$71.00
Conversion costs applied	?
Total manufacturing product cost............................	$?

The activities that apply to building the PC boards follow:

Manufacturing Activity	Cost Driver	Conversion Costs Applied for Each Activity			
1. Start station	No. of raw PC boards	1	×	$1.30	= $1.30
2. Dip insertion	No. of dip insertions	?	×	.60	= 6.00
3. Manual insertion	No. of manual insertions	11	×	.80	= ?
4. Wave Solder	No. of boards soldered	1	×	1.50	= 1.50
5. Backload	No. of backload insertions	6	×	?	= 4.20
6. Test	Standard time each board is in test activity	.20	×	.90	= ?
7. Defect analysis	Standard time for defect analysis and repair	.10	×	?	= 7.00
Total					$?

Required

1. Fill in the blanks in both the opening schedule and the list of activities.

2. How is direct labor identified with products under this product costing system?

3. Why might managers favor this activity-based accounting system instead of the older system, which applied conversion costs based on direct labor?

Problem 23-8B   *Product costing in an activity-based system* (L.O. 6)

Janelli, Inc., manufactures bookcases and uses an activity-based costing system. Janelli's activity areas and related data follow:

Manufacturing Activity Area	Budgeted Conversion Costs for 19X0	Cost Driver Chosen as Application Base	Conversion Cost per Unit of Application Base
Material handling	$ 100,000	Number of parts	$ 0.10
Cutting	1,000,000	Number of parts	1.30
Assembly	3,000,000	Direct labor hours	18.00
Painting	60,000	Number of painted units	3.00

Two styles of bookcases were produced in March, the standard bookcase and an unpainted bookcase, which had fewer shelves and required no painting. The quantities, direct material costs, and other data follow:

Product	Units Produced	Direct Material Costs	Number of Parts	Assembling Direct Labor Hours
Standard bookcase	2,000	$24,000	30,000	3,000
Unpainted bookcase	3,000	27,000	36,000	2,800

Required

1. Compute the total manufacturing costs and unit costs of the standard bookcases and the unpainted bookcases.

2. Suppose upstream activities, such as product design, were analyzed and applied to the standard bookcases at $4 each and the unpainted bookcases at $3 each. Moreover, similar analyses were conducted of downstream activities, such as distribution, marketing, and customer service. The downstream costs applied were $18 per standard bookcase and $15 per unpainted bookcase. Compute the full product cost per unit.

3. Which costs are used for reporting in the external financial statements? Which costs are used for management decision-making? Explain the difference.

Extending Your Knowledge

Decision Problems

1. *Preparing a production cost report and identifying decisions that would be based on the information (L.O. 5)*

Yorkton Manufacturing Corp. makes automobile parts. The following cost data for the company's Finishing Department are available for October.

Flow of Production	Flow of Physical Units	Equivalent Units of Production		
		Transferred In	*Direct Materials*	*Conversion Costs*
Units to account for				
Beginning work in process inventory	12,000			
Transferred in during October	28,000			
Total units to account for	40,000			
Units accounted for				
Completed and transferred out to finished goods during October				
From beginning inventory	12,000	—	7,200	6,000
Transferred in from Molding and completed during October (36,000 – 12,000)	24,000	24,000	24,000	24,000
Work in process, Oct. 31	4,000	4,000	800	1,200
Total physical units accounted for	40,000			
Equivalent units of production		28,000	32,000	31,200

Unit Costs	Transferred-In Costs	Direct Materials	Conversion Costs	Total
Work in process, Sept. 30	Work done before October			$ 59,000
Costs added during October	$ 64,400	$ 35,200	$ 49,920	149,520
Divide by equivalent units	÷28,000	÷32,000	÷31,200	
Cost per equivalent unit	$ 2.30	$ 1.10	$ 1.60	
Total cost to account for				$208,520

Allocation of total cost	Transferred-In Costs	Direct Materials	Conversion Costs	Total
Units completed and transferred out to finished goods				
From work in process, Sept. 30				$ 59,000
Costs added during October				
Direct materials	—	7,200 × $1.10		7,920
Conversion costs	—		6,000 × $1.60	9,600
Total completed from Sept. 30 inventory				76,520
Units transferred in from Molding and completed during October	24,000 × ($2.30 + $1.10 + $1.60)			120,000
Total costs transferred out				$196,520
Work in process, Oct. 31				
Transferred-in costs	4,000 × $2.30			$ 9,200
Direct materials		800 × $1.10		880
Conversion costs			1,200 × $1.60	1,920
Total work in process, Oct. 31				12,000
Total cost accounted for				$208,520

Required

1. Prepare a production cost report for the Finishing Department for the month of October.

2. Discuss specific decisions that would be based on the information in the report.

2. *Process costing in the same department for two consecutive months* (L.O. 2, 3)

Waterford Pottery Ltd. makes ceramic bowls. The bowls are made, fired and dried in the Forming Department. Then they are transferred to the Finishing Department to be painted and shipped to retail outlets. No bowls are broken at any point in the procedure. The following information is available for the Forming Department for January and February 19X5:

Forming Department

Units

Work in process, Jan. 1 (50% complete as to direct materials, 25% complete as to conversion)	100 bowls
Production started during January	800
Work in process, Jan. 31 (40% complete as to direct materials, 20% complete as to conversion)	300
Production started during February	900

Work in process, Feb. 28 (70% complete as to direct materials, 50% complete as to conversion)		600
Costs		
Work in process, Jan. 1		$ 200
Costs added during January		
Direct materials		1,005
Conversion costs		635
Costs added during February		
Direct materials		1,440
Conversion costs		840

Required

1. Compute the equivalent units of production, unit costs and total cost to account for in the Forming Department for January. Show the application of total Forming Department cost for January to (a) cost of goods transferred from Forming to Finishing and (b) cost of ending Work in Process Inventory — Forming at January 31, 19X5.

2. Compute the equivalent units of production, equivalent-unit costs and total cost to account for in the Forming Department for February. Show the application of total Forming Department cost for February to (a) cost of goods transferred from Forming to Finishing and (b) cost of ending Work in Process Inventory — Forming at February 28, 19X5.

3. Prepare the January and February (individually by month) production cost reports for the Forming Department.

Ethical Issue

Hutch Manufacturing produces component parts for laser optic equipment. Customers include civilian companies and the Canadian government. Under most government contracts Hutch receives reimbursement for its manufacturing costs plus a specified profit margin. For most civilian contracts Hutch bids a fixed price and either earns a profit or incurs a loss, depending on how well the company controls costs. For both government and civilian jobs, top Hutch managers allocate to the government contracts any overhead whose proper allocation to a particular product is less than certain.

Required

1. Is Hutch's overhead allocation practice ethical? Give your reason.
2. Who benefits and who is harmed by the Hutch practice?

Answers to Self-Study Questions

1. a
2. b
3. d   Direct materials: 20,000 + (6,000 × .90)=25,400
     Conversion costs: 20,000 + (6,000 × .75)=24,500

4. b
5. d
6. c
7. d $202,200/38,000=$5.32
8. a
9. c   A: [$240,000/($240,000 + $80,000)] × $160,000 = $120,000
          B: [$80,000/($240,000 + $80,000)] × $160,000 = $40,000
10. c

Chapter 24

Flexible Budgets
and Standard Costs

Lee Nicholas, the manufacturing supervisor of Kayak Manufacturing Limited, was concerned for his job. The results from the most recent month of operations showed unfavorable variances in the manufacturing area. This was not good news.

The company's standard cost system was just in its third month of operations so the system was not yet in use throughout the company. Implementation of the standard cost system had been spurred by the downturn in sales brought about by the economic recession. In short, Kayak Manufacturing Limited intended that the standard cost system would help control costs. Nicholas was certain that his department had worked more efficiently than in previous months. However, the recent period's performance represented the third straight month of dismal results, according to the standard control system.

As you read this chapter, consider what might explain the negative variances, and what Nicholas should do to ensure the system affords fair and objective evaluation of his hard work.

LEARNING OBJECTIVES

After studying this chapter, you should be able to

1 Prepare a flexible budget for the income statement

2 Prepare an income statement performance report

3 Compute direct materials cost variances

4 Compute direct labor cost variances

5 Compute production overhead cost variances

6 Record transactions at standard cost

7 Prepare a standard cost income statement for management

Chapter 20 introduced management accounting by emphasizing that budgets are the main tool for planning and control. Chapter 21 showed how to budget profit levels by analyzing cost-volume-profit relationships. Chapters 22 and 23 explored accounting for manufacturing companies. In this chapter we now explore budgeting in more depth. The first half of the chapter covers flexible budgets, and the second half discusses standard costs, which are an outgrowth of the flexible budget. We begin by reviewing the cost behaviour patterns and the relevant range, which were introduced in Chapter 21.

Cost Behavior Patterns

Accountants define *cost* as resources given up to achieve a specific objective. For now, consider costs as dollars paid for goods and services. Examples are the costs of materials, factory wages, sales commissions, utilities and interest expense. Distinctions among these categories of costs are important in many accounting situations. In budgeting, however, they can be treated similarly.

Cost behavior is the movement of a cost in response to a measure of volume such as sales. Two extreme types of cost behavior are variable and fixed. Variable costs are those whose total amount changes in direct proportion with changes in volume or activity. Fixed costs are costs whose total amount does not change during a given time period over a wide range of volume. Examples include depreciation, property taxes, insurance and executive salaries.

Throughout this chapter, we assume that each cost is either variable or fixed or that it can be divided into variable and fixed portions. A mixed cost has both variable and fixed components. The compensation of a salesperson who is paid a flat monthly salary plus a commission based on his or her sales is a mixed cost. Water expense computed as a fixed monthly amount plus a unit cost per 100 litres used is also a mixed cost.

Note that the "variable" and "fixed" characteristics of a cost relate to its total amount, not its *per-unit* amount. A variable cost is variable with respect to its *total* amount. A fixed cost is fixed with respect to its total amount. The behavior of variable and fixed costs with respect to per-unit sales is different, as the following table shows.

| | If Volume Increases (Decreases) | |
Type of Cost	Total Cost	Cost Per Unit
Variable cost		
(Example: sales commission)	Increases (decreases)	No change
Fixed cost		
(Example: monthly rent)	No change	Decreases (increases)

Illustrations will clarify the difference between the total and the unit amounts of variable cost and fixed cost. Suppose a sales clerk in the shoe department of a Woodward's store is paid a sales commission of $2 per pair of shoes sold, which is a variable cost. Weekly sales of 200 pairs generates total sales commission expense of $400. Unit selling cost (the commission) remains $2 per pair of shoes.

Now consider the fixed monthly rent of a cookie store in a shopping mall. Total monthly rent expense of $2,000 does not change in response to changes in volume. If the store sells 20,000 cookies each month, the rent cost per unit is $.10 ($2,000 rent/20,000 cookies). But if the store sells 40,000 cookies monthly, the unit cost of rent is only $.05 ($2,000/40,000). In either case, the total monthly rent is fixed at $2,000.

Relevant Range

The definition of a fixed cost has two underlying assumptions:

1. The total cost will not change for a given time period, which is the *budget period*. Fixed costs may change from budget year to budget year because of changes in salary levels, number of workers, rent levels and property tax levels. But fixed costs are not expected to change within a given budget period.
2. The total cost will not change over a wide range of volume, which is the *relevant range*.

Fixed costs are based on an expected band of volume. For example, a toy manufacturer may have monthly fixed costs of $200,000 when it is producing 16,000 to 24,000 units per month. However, after the Christmas rush, sales fall below 16,000 units and fixed costs decrease to $175,000. So "fixed" is a useful concept, but "fixed" does not mean forever or under all operating conditions. Instead, it relates to a relevant range of activity, as shown by the following graph of cost behavior:

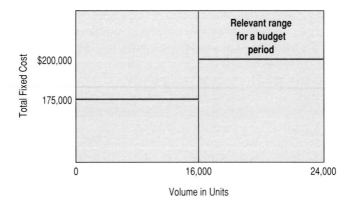

Having reviewed the necessary concepts and terms, let us turn to flexible budgets and their role in management decision-making.

Flexible Budgets

The master budget in Chapter 20 is a **static budget**, which is prepared for only one level of volume. It is not altered after it is drawn up, regardless of changes in volume, cost drivers, or other conditions during the budget period. Consider a master budget based on a single target sales volume of 200,000 units. Assume actual volume turns out to be 180,000 units. The comparison of actual and budgeted results, which is an example of a **performance report**, follows (amounts assumed):

	Actual Results	Static (Master) Budget	Variance
Units sold	180,000	200,000	20,000 U
Sales	$540,000	$600,000	$60,000 U
Expenses..................................	500,000	525,000	25,000 F
Operating income	$40,000	$75,000	$35,000 U

Variance is the difference between an actual amount and the corresponding budgeted amount. Throughout U = unfavorable variance and F = favorable variance.

This performance report is difficult to analyze because the budget is based on 200,000 units, but only 180,000 units were sold. Note the $25,000 expense variance. Why did it occur? Because of efficient cost control? Because of a lower sales volume? We are unsure. This performance report, based on a static budget, simply does not provide enough detail to answer these important management questions.

For a detailed analysis of performance, managers often use a **flexible budget**, which is a set of budgets covering a range of volume rather than a single level of volume. Flexible budgets are also called *variable budgets* because they present budgeted amounts for different levels of volume. Managers find flexible budgets helpful for studying the behaviour of expenses as volume fluctuates. Microcomputers and electronic spreadsheets have placed this budgeting tool at the disposal of most middle and top managers in Canada.

Exhibit 24-1 shows a condensed flexible budget for Bellmead Pools & Supply, Inc., which installs swimming pools. Throughout this illustration we assume that all pools are sold and installed in the same month. Therefore, we use the terms pool sales and pool installations interchangeably.

In this example, the total variable cost of installing a $12,000 swimming pool is $8,000. A more detailed budget would list the individual variable costs, such as direct materials and direct labor. It might also detail various fixed expenses, including depreciation on equipment, insurance and administrative overhead. Total monthly fixed expenses are $20,000.

Flexible budgets are useful both before and after a budget period. As a planning tool, they can help managers identify the level of volume that will serve as the business's target level of activity for the coming period. As a control device, they help managers analyze actual results.

EXHIBIT 24-1   *Flexible Budget*

> **OBJECTIVE 1**
>
> Prepare a flexible budget for the income statement

Bellmead Pools & Supply, Inc.
Flexible Budget
each month of the period April – August 19X5

	Budget Formula per Unit	Various Levels of Volume		
Units	—	6	8	10
Sales...	$12,000	$72,000	$96,000	$120,000
Variable expenses........................	8,000	48,000	64,000	80,000
Fixed expenses	(See note)	20,000	20,000	20,000
Total expenses		68,000	84,000	100,000
Operating income (loss).............		$ 4,000	$12,000	$ 20,000

Note: Fixed expenses are given as a total amount rather than as a cost per unit.

The **budget formula**, the heart of the flexible budget, shows how to compute the budget amounts:

Revenues   **– Variable expenses**   **– Fixed expenses = Operating income (loss)**

$$\left(\begin{array}{c}\textbf{Number of units sold} \\ \times\,\textbf{Unit sale price}\end{array}\right) - \left(\begin{array}{c}\textbf{Number of units sold} \\ \times\,\textbf{Variable cost per unit}\end{array}\right) - \textbf{Fixed expenses} = \textbf{Operating income (loss)}$$

In this illustration, Bellmead Pools' cost behavior is fixed expenses of $20,000 per month plus variable expenses of $8,000 per pool sold and installed. Exhibit 24-1 shows the expected results for three operating levels. Other volume levels could be added for 7, 9 or any other number of pools per month, as the situation warrants. Keep in mind that a flexible budget relates to a specific relevant range only. Expenses are unlikely to behave according to a set formula outside some volume range. For example, a volume of 15 pools per month may not fall within the relevant range. In such cases, managers must develop a new budget formula.

Graphing the Budget Expense Formula _____

Another budgeting tool is a graph of the expense formula. With such a graph, the accountant can provide a budget customized to any volume level. The graph in Exhibit 24-2 shows total expenses for Bellmead Pools & Supply for all volume levels from 0 to 11 pools sold per month. Let us assume this span of volume is the relevant range. Also, we assume that management based the master budget (the static budget) on a projected sales volume of 8 pools per month.

The graph displays an overall picture of the direct materials, direct labor and all other expenses that must be planned at various volume levels. When the company plans to build 8 pools, the total expense level ($84,000) for this volume is highlighted (as Exhibit 24-2 shows).

EXHIBIT 24-2   *Bellmead Pools & Supply, Inc.: Graph of Monthly Flexible Expense Budget*

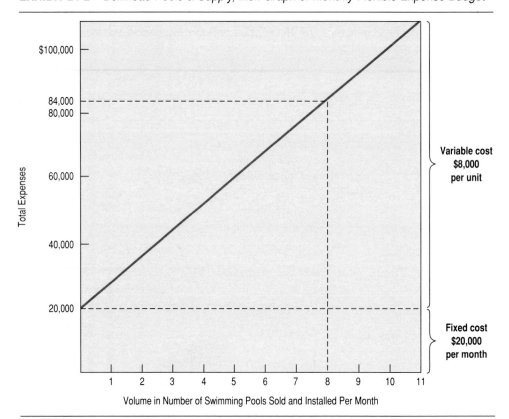

EXHIBIT 24-3   *Bellmead Pools & Supply, Inc.: Graph of Actual and Budgeted Monthly Total Expenses*

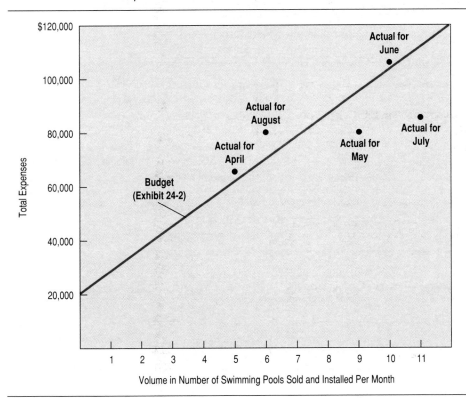

A budget graph also helps analyze actual results. Exhibit 24-3 is the graph of actual versus budgeted results for the peak season of 19X5. The graph shows that actual expenses exceeded budgeted expenses during April, June, and August. Actual expenses were less than budget for May and July. Overall, the budget and actual figures are close.

Analyzing the Results _____

Managers usually have a cycle of planning and control. They (1) prepare a master budget, (2) transact business to achieve their goals, and (3) compare actual results to the master budget. The flexible budget helps managers analyze variances from planned results, which fall into two major categories: sales volume variances and flexible budget variances.

1. **Sales volume variances** are those differences between the amounts in the flexible budget and the corresponding amounts in the static (master) budget. For example, assume Bellmead Pools & Supply set a goal of selling 8 pools each month during April–August, 19X5 and budgeted accordingly. During June the company installs 10 pools. Exhibit 24-4, column 4, shows that the sales volume variance is the difference between the flexible budget for actual volume achieved (column 3) and the static (master) budget (column 5).

2. **Flexible budget variances** are differences between actual results and the flexible budget. This category of variances is based on the actual sales level achieved. For example, Bellmead Pools & Supply budgeted total expenses of $100,000 for the sale of 10 pools. In June the company sells and installs 10 pools, but total expenses exceed budget. This can be seen in Exhibit 24-3, where total expenses for June lie above the budget line. Exhibit 24-4 shows how to compute a flexible budget variance: actual results (column 1) minus the flexible budget for actual volume achieved (column 3).

EXHIBIT 24-4   Income Statement Performance Report

	(1)	(2) (1) - (3)	(3)	(4) (3) - (5)	(5)
	Actual Results at Actual Prices	Flexible Budget Variances	Flexible Budget for Actual Volume Achieved*	Sales Volume Variances	Static (Master) Budget*
Units Sold.................	10	-0-	10	2 F	8
Sales	$120,000	$ -0-	$120,000	$24,000 F	$96,000
Variable expenses.....	83,000	3,000 U	80,000	16,000 U	64,000
Fixed expenses	22,000	2,000 U	20,000	-0-	20,000
Total expenses	105,000	5,000 U	100,000	16,000 U	84,000
Operating income	$ 15,000	$5,000 U	$ 20,000	$ 8,000 F	$12,000

Bellmead Pools & Supply, Inc.
Income Statement Performance Report
for the month ended June 30, 19X5

Flexible budget variance, $5,000 U   Sales volume variance, $8,000 F

Total variance from static budget, $3,000 F

U = unfavorable variance; F = favorable variance
*Amounts from Exhibit 24-1

We have seen that mere comparison of a *static (master)* budget with *actual* results does not explain much, because the actual sales level may differ from the level that was used in preparing the master budget. But a flexible budget does provide the information needed to understand why actual revenues, expenses and income differ from budgeted amounts. Exhibit 24-4 is an income statement performance report based on a flexible budget. Study it carefully, especially the two variance columns.

In Exhibit 24-4, column 3 information is taken from Exhibit 24-1. For the flexible budget amounts, we match units sold to actual sales in units, which in this case is 10. Use of a flexible budget allows us to analyze results over a range of activity levels within the scope of the relevant range. Had actual sales been 6 units, we could have made the comparison based on 6 units by drawing the necessary data from Exhibit 24-1.

OBJECTIVE 2

Prepare an income statement performance report

Exhibit 24-4 shows that actual operating income ($15,000 in column 1) exceeded the static (master) budget amount ($12,000 in column 5) by $3,000. This difference is explained by an $8,000 favorable sales volume variance (column 4) and a $5,000 unfavorable flexible budget variance (column 2). Stated differently, strong sales caused actual income to exceed budget by $8,000. However, the company failed to control expenses as well as expected, resulting in an unfavorable flexible budget variance of $5,000.

How would the owners of the company use this information? Perhaps they would reward the sales staff, and they would certainly determine why expenses were too high. Our analysis of the performance report shows the unfavorable $5,000 variance, but it does not identify why expenses exceeded budget, nor does it identify the cure. Those answers depend on the specific situation. For example, Bellmead's higher-than-expected expenses might have resulted from an increase in the cost of gunite, the concrete derivative used to construct swimming pools. Such an increase might be unavoidable. However, the expense level might have resulted from wasting materials or mismanaging employees. If so, the owner would take corrective action. Variance information can direct a manager to areas of the business deserving praise or needing improvement.

Managers can of course analyze expenses in a more detailed manner — by listing each expense separately. Also, the flexible budget variances can be analyzed further, as the next major section of the chapter explains. First, however, test your understanding of the coverage thus far by working the summary problem for review.

Summary Problem for Your Review

Exhibit 24-4 indicates that Bellmead Pools & Supply, Inc. installed 10 swimming pools during June. Suppose June installations were 7 pools instead of 10. Suppose further that the price of each pool was $12,500 instead of the budgeted $12,000. Actual variable expenses were $57,400 and actual fixed expenses were $19,000.

Required

1. Given these new assumptions, prepare a revised income statement performance report like Exhibit 24-4.

2. Show that the flexible budget variances and the sales volume variances in operating income account for the difference between actual operating income and the static (master) budgeted income.

3. As the company owner, what specific employees would you praise or criticize after you analyze this performance report?

SOLUTION TO REVIEW PROBLEM

Requirement 1

Bellmead Pools & Supply, Inc.
Income Statement Performance Report — Revised
For the Month Ended June 30, 19X5

	(1) Actual Results at Actual Prices	(2) (1) – (3) Flexible Budget Variances	(3) Flexible Budget for Actual Volume Achieved	(4) (3) – (5) Sales Volume Variances	(5) Static (Master) Budget
Units Sold..................	7	-0-	7	1 U	8
Sales	$87,500	$3,500 F	$84,000	$12,000 U	$96,000
Variable expenses.....	57,400	1,400 U	56,000	8,000 F	64,000
Fixed expenses	19,000	1,000 F	20,000	-0-	20,000
Total expenses	76,400	400 U	76,000	8,000 F	84,000
Operating income	$11,100	$3,100 F	$ 8,000	$ 4,000 U	$12,000

Flexible budget variance, $3,100 F   Sales volume variance, $4,000 U

Total variance from static budget, $900 U

U = unfavorable variance; F = favorable variance

Requirement 2

Static (master) budgeted operating income..................	$12,000
Actual operating income at actual prices......................	11,100
Total difference to account for..	$ 900 U ←
Sales volume variance..	$ 4,000 U
Flexible budget variance...	3,100 F
Total variance	$ 900 U ←

Requirement 3

After investigation, management may praise the salespersons who sold pools more expensive than the budgeted sale price of $12,000 and the employees responsible for cutting fixed cost by $1,000.

Management may criticize the sales staff for not meeting the goal of selling 8 pools during the month. Also, construction or purchasing personnel were responsible for spending $1,400 more in variable costs than budget to construct the 7 pools. Of course, just as they are acknowledged for outstanding achievement, managers must shoulder some of the blame when things do not go well. They control the use of company resources hour by hour and day by day. These performance report figures summarize the overall effects of control efforts.

Standard Costing _____

A **standard cost** is a carefully predetermined cost that is usually expressed on a per-unit basis. It is a target cost, a cost that should be attained. Standard costs are budgeted costs for a single unit of output. **Standard cost systems** help to build budgets, gauge performance, obtain product costs and save bookkeeping costs. Such systems help managers analyze the relationships between what should have occurred (standard costs) and what did occur (actual costs). In the chapter-opening vignette, Lee Nicholas is worried because actual manufacturing costs have exceeded the standard costs used to judge his performance.

Standard costs are used by a wide variety of organizations and in conjunction with any kind of product costing: job order, process, or a hybrid system such as ABC costing. A construction company that builds tract houses uses a job cost system to accumulate the cost of each house. To measure performance, the company may compare actual cost for each house to the standard cost. Companies like Canada Packers Inc. use a process cost system for many of the meats they manufacture. To remain competitive, Canada Packers Inc. helps control costs by developing standard costs. Standard costing provides a concrete goal for manufacturing personnel. They strive to produce the product at standard cost or less. The difference between profits and losses often depends on controlling each activity that affects product cost.

Variances between actual and standard costs are divided into price and efficiency effects for direct materials and direct labor. A price variance measures how well a business keeps the unit prices of materials and labor within standards. An *efficiency variance* measures whether the quantity of materials or labor used to make a product is within the budget. By pinpointing price and efficiency effects, standard costing helps managers find ways of reducing costs. This is the purpose of the standard cost system of Kayak Manufacturing Company in the opening vignette. It also identifies those employees who deserve praise for controlling costs. Over which type of variance (price or efficiency) would Lee Nicholas seem to have more control? The efficiency variance, because Nicholas manages the plant, which uses materials. Kayak Manufacturing probably has a purchasing department that is responsible for the prices paid for materials.

At first glance, standard cost systems might appear to be more costly to operate than other systems. Obviously, a startup investment is necessary to develop the standards. But the ongoing data-processing costs can be less than so-called actual cost systems. For example, it is more economical simply to carry all inventories at standard unit prices. In this way, the system avoids the extra data-collection costs and possible confusion of making cost-flow assumptions such as first-in, first-out or last-in, first-out.

This section of the chapter explains how standard costing divides flexible budget variances (explained in the first half of the chapter) into price and efficiency effects. We continue using the Bellmead Pools & Supply, Inc., example.

Relationship between Standard Costs and Flexible Budgets

What standard of performance should be used? *Currently attainable standards* are the most popular. They are standards that can be achieved but with difficulty. Standard costs are set low enough that employees view their fulfilment as possible, though perhaps not probable. When standards are challenging but attainable, managers and staff will accept unfavorable variance as being fair, and acknowledge favorable variance as a measure of their diligence. A standard that is accepted by employees as reasonable has significant positive motivational force.

Does a standard cost differ from a budgeted cost? No, if the standards are attainable. However, the term *standard cost* usually refers to a unit cost, whereas *budgeted cost* refers to a total cost. For example, suppose the budgeted variable expenses in Exhibit 24-4 included direct materials as follows:

	Budget Formula Per Unit	Flexible Budget for Various Levels of Volume		
Swimming pools installed.........	1	6	8	10
Direct materials...........................	$2,000	$12,000	$16,000	$20,000

The standard cost of direct materials is $2,000 *per unit.* Budgeted cost is the total cost for the installation of all pools sold during the period. For 8 pools, budgeted cost is $16,000. For 10 pools, budgeted cost is $2,000. But standard cost of direct materials remains $2,000 per unit regardless of changes in total outlays because of differences in sales volume. *Think of a standard variable cost as a budget for a single unit.*

Illustration of Standard Costing

Let us return to our Bellmead Pools example. Recall that 10 swimming pools were sold and installed during June, and that the static (master) budget had been prepared for 8 pools per month. Exhibit 24-5 provides the cost data to be used throughout our discussion of standard costing applications.

To focus on the main point of standard costing, we assume the standard cost system applies to materials, labor and production overhead, but not to selling and administrative expenses. We also assume purchases of direct materials equals materials used.

Direct Material and Direct Labor Variances

Flexible budget variances for direct material and direct labor are often subdivided into price and efficiency variances.

EXHIBIT 24-5   *Facts for Illustration of Standard Costing*

Bellmead Pools & Supply, Inc.
Facts for Illustration of Standard Costing
Month of June

Panel A — Comparison of Actual Results with Flexible Budget:
Installed 10 Swimming Pools

	Actual Results at Actual Prices	Flexible Budget	Flexible Budget Variances
Variable expenses			
Direct materials...............................	$ 23,100 [a]	$ 20,000 [c]	$3,100 U
Direct labor...	41,800 [b]	42,000 [c]	200 F
Variable production overhead	9,000	8,000 [d]	1,000 U
Selling and administrative expenses	9,100	10,000	900 F
Total variable expenses..............	83,000	80,000	3,000 U
Fixed expenses			
Fixed production overhead............	12,300	12,000 [e]	300 U
Selling and administrative expenses	9,700	8,000	1,700 U
Total fixed expenses..................	22,000	20,000	2,000 U
Total expenses..	$105,000	$100,000	$5,000 U

a $23,100 = 11,969 cubic metres at actual price of $1.93 per cubic metre.
b $41,800 = 3,800 hours at actual price of $11.00 per hour.
c   See Panel B.
d   Variable production overhead was budgeted at $2.00 per direct hour:
    $8,000 = 4,000 direct labor hours (10 pools × 400 direct labor hours) × $2.00.
e   Fixed production overhead was budgeted at $12,000 per month.

Panel B — Standards for Direct Material and Direct Labor Flexible Budget:
10 Swimming Pools

	(1) Standard Inputs Budgeted for 10 Finished Units (Swimming Pools Installed)	(2) Standard Price per Unit of Input	(1) x (2) Flexible Budget for 10 Finished Units of Output
Direct materials.........	1,000 cubic metres per pool × 10 pools = 10,000 cubic metres	$ 2.00	$20,000
Direct labor................	400 hours per pool × 10 pools = 4,000 hours	10.50	42,000

The **price variance** is the difference between actual unit prices of inputs and their standard unit prices, multiplied by the number of *actual inputs used*:

$$\text{Price variance} = \begin{array}{c}\textbf{Difference between}\\\textbf{actual and budgeted}\\\textbf{unit prices of inputs}\end{array} \times \textbf{Actual inputs used}$$

The **efficiency variance**, also called the **usage variance** and the **quantity variance**, is the difference between the quantity of inputs actually used and the quantity that should have been used (the flexible budget) for the actual output achieved, multiplied by the *standard unit price*:

$$
\textbf{Efficiency variance} \;=\; \left(\begin{array}{c}\textbf{Inputs}\\ \textbf{actually}\\ \textbf{used}\end{array}\;-\;\begin{array}{c}\textbf{Inputs that should}\\ \textbf{have been used}\\ \textbf{for actual output}\end{array}\right)\;\times\;\begin{array}{c}\textbf{Standard}\\ \textbf{unit price}\\ \textbf{of input}\end{array}
$$

Price variances are computed not only for their own sake but also to give managers a sharper focus on efficiency. In this way, efficiency can be measured by holding unit prices constant. Thus managers' judgments about efficiency are unaffected by price changes. Efficiency variances have an important underlying assumption: All unit prices are *standard* prices.

Direct Materials Variances   The relevant data for computing Bellmead Pools' direct materials variances are

	Actual Cost	Flexible Budget Standard Cost	Flexible Budget Variance
Cubic metres.........................	11,969	10,000	
Unit price..............................	× $1.93	× $2.00	
Total......................................	$23,100	$20,000	$3,100 U

Managers seek to gain further insight by dividing this flexible budget variance into price and efficiency variances.

$$
\textbf{Price variance} \;=\; \begin{array}{c}\textbf{Difference between}\\ \textbf{actual and budgeted}\\ \textbf{unit prices of inputs}\end{array}\;\times\;\textbf{Actual inputs used}
$$

$$
\begin{aligned}
\textbf{Price variance} &=\quad (\$1.93 - \$2.00)\quad \times 11{,}969\ \textbf{cubic metres}\\
&=\qquad\qquad \$838\ \textbf{F}
\end{aligned}
$$

$$
\textbf{Efficiency variance} \;=\; \left(\begin{array}{c}\textbf{Actual}\\ \textbf{inputs}\\ \textbf{used}\end{array}\;-\;\begin{array}{c}\textbf{Inputs that should}\\ \textbf{have been used}\\ \textbf{for actual output}\end{array}\right)\;\times\;\begin{array}{c}\textbf{Standard}\\ \textbf{unit price}\\ \textbf{of input}\end{array}
$$

$$
\begin{aligned}
\textbf{Efficiency variance} &=\left(\begin{array}{c}\textbf{11,969}\\ \textbf{cubic metres}\end{array}-\begin{array}{c}\textbf{10,000}\\ \textbf{cubic metres}\end{array}\right)\times\begin{array}{c}\textbf{\$2.00 per}\\ \textbf{cubic metre}\end{array}\\
&=\quad (11{,}969\quad-\quad 10{,}000)\quad\times\quad \$2.00\\
&=\quad \$3{,}938\ \textbf{U}
\end{aligned}
$$

The direct materials variances — from the beginning of this section — can be summarized as follows:

Price variance...	$838 F
Efficiency variance	3,938 U
Total flexible budget variance...	$3,100 U

Exhibit 24-6 summarizes the direct materials cost variance computations. Variance analysis begins with a total variance to be explained (in this example, the $3,100 flexible budget variance).

Note: In this example, we assumed all direct materials purchased in a month were also used in that month. Consequently, inventory levels for direct materials remain constant from month to month. If materials purchased are not equal to materials used, the price variance for direct materials should focus on actual units purchased rather than actual units used. This added provision ensures that direct

EXHIBIT 24-6 Bellmead Pools & Supply, Inc.
Direct Materials Variance Computations

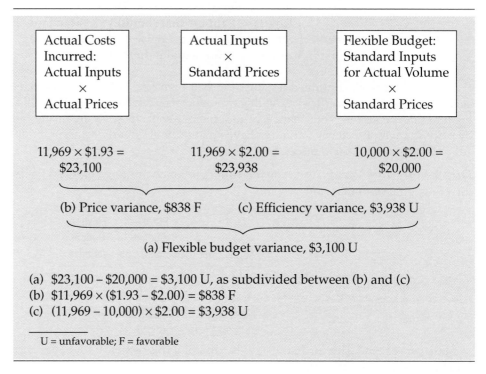

Actual Costs Incurred: Actual Inputs × Actual Prices	Actual Inputs × Standard Prices	Flexible Budget: Standard Inputs for Actual Volume × Standard Prices
11,969 × $1.93 = $23,100	11,969 × $2.00 = $23,938	10,000 × $2.00 = $20,000

(b) Price variance, $838 F   (c) Efficiency variance, $3,938 U

(a) Flexible budget variance, $3,100 U

(a) $23,100 – $20,000 = $3,100 U, as subdivided between (b) and (c)
(b) $11,969 × ($1.93 – $2.00) = $838 F
(c) (11,969 – 10,000) × $2.00 = $3,938 U

U = unfavorable; F = favorable

material price variances are isolated in a timely fashion, that is, when the materials are purchased, not when they are used (which is after the fact.)

Direct Labor Variances The relevant data for computing Bellmead Pools' direct labor variances are

	Actual Cost	Flexible Budget Standard Cost	Flexible Budget Variance
Hours....................................	3,800	4,000	
Hourly rate	× $11.00	× $10.50	
Total	$41,800	$42,000	$200 F

OBJECTIVE 4

Compute direct labor cost variances

$$\text{Price variance} = \begin{array}{c}\text{Difference between}\\ \text{actual and budgeted}\\ \text{unit prices of inputs}\end{array} \times \text{Actual inputs used}$$

$$\begin{aligned}\text{Price variance} &= (\$11.00 - \$10.50) \times 3{,}800 \text{ hours}\\ &= \$1{,}900 \text{ U}\end{aligned}$$

This variance is also called the *direct labor rate variance*.

$$\text{Efficiency variance} = \left(\begin{array}{c}\text{Inputs}\\ \text{actually}\\ \text{used}\end{array} - \begin{array}{c}\text{Inputs that should}\\ \text{have been used}\\ \text{for actual output}\end{array}\right) \times \begin{array}{c}\text{Standard}\\ \text{unit price}\\ \text{of input}\end{array}$$

$$\begin{aligned}\text{Efficiency variance} &= (3{,}800 \text{ hours} - 4{,}000 \text{ hours}) \times \$10.50 \text{ per hour}\\ &= \$2{,}100 \text{ F}\end{aligned}$$

EXHIBIT 24-7   *Bellmead Pools & Supply, Inc.*
Direct Labor Variance Computations

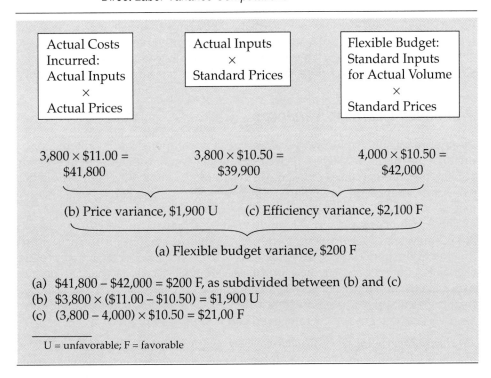

Actual Costs Incurred: Actual Inputs × Actual Prices	Actual Inputs × Standard Prices	Flexible Budget: Standard Inputs for Actual Volume × Standard Prices
3,800 × $11.00 = $41,800	3,800 × $10.50 = $39,900	4,000 × $10.50 = $42,000

(b) Price variance, $1,900 U   (c) Efficiency variance, $2,100 F

(a) Flexible budget variance, $200 F

(a) $41,800 − $42,000 = $200 F, as subdivided between (b) and (c)
(b) $3,800 × ($11.00 − $10.50) = $1,900 U
(c) (3,800 − 4,000) × $10.50 = $21,00 F

———————
U = unfavorable; F = favorable

The direct labor variances (from the beginning of this section) can be summarized as follows:

Price variance	$1,900	U
Efficiency variance	2,100	F
Total flexible budget variance	$ 200	F

To relate standard costing to the overall budget, trace these total flexible budget variances to Exhibit 24-5. In addition, Exhibit 24-7 summarizes the direct labor variance computations, providing an overall picture to aid your study.

Management Use of Variance Information

Variances do not identify problems or their solutions. But they often raise questions that deserve attention. For example, an unfavorable materials price variance may point to the need to shop around for a new supplier of raw materials. *Price* effects, though, may depend on market factors, which are hard or sometimes impossible to control. An unfavorable labor efficiency variance, however, may spur management to examine employee performance. The company certainly has greater control over its own people than it has over outside markets.

Managers sometimes trade off price and efficiency effects, accepting an unfavorable variance in one area in order to achieve a favorable variance in the other. In our example, Bellmead's favorable materials price variance may have resulted from using cheaper material. The unfavorable materials efficiency variance may have arisen because employees had to use more material than standard, perhaps due to its inferior quality. Thus the company's strategy failed. The overall materials cost variance was unfavorable by $3,100.

In another trade-off between price and efficiency, Bellmead used more expensive (better trained) labor than standard. But the company gained greater efficiency, and the company achieved a net labor cost saving of $200.

When should a variance be investigated? If significant variances are likely, hour-to-hour and day-to-day monitoring of quantities of materials and direct labor hours is desirable. When and how to investigate is often based on personal judgment. For example, a manager may believe that a 5 percent variance in a $1 million materials cost deserves more attention than a 20 percent variance in a $10,000 budget. Rules of thumb, such as "Investigate all variances above $5,000" and "Investigate all variances 25 percent or more above standard cost," are also common in practice.

Production Overhead Variances

Ideally, production overhead cost variances can be computed and monitored for individual overhead costs like property taxes, utilities and insurance, but many companies compute variances on total overhead. Many companies split production overhead variances into two parts: a *flexible budget variance* and a *production volume variance*.

The *flexible budget variance* for production overhead shows whether managers are keeping total overhead cost within the budgeted amount for the actual production of the period. The *production volume variance* arises when actual production differs from the level in the static (master) budget. The two variances combine to explain the difference between actual overhead cost and standard overhead cost that has been applied to production. Before discussing the computation of overhead variances, let us review how overhead is applied to production.

Applying Overhead to Production   In a system that uses standard costs, overhead is applied to production at a budgeted rate, as discussed in the two preceding chapters. Companies develop overhead standards based on past experience and budgets that reflect the business's goals. Suppose Exhibit 24-8 is Bellmead Pools' flexible overhead budget, which shows activity levels for 6, 8, 9 and 10 pools per month. We have highlighted the static (master) budget level of 8 pools and the actual production level of 10 pools, because these levels are useful for computing the overhead variances.

EXHIBIT 24-8   *Flexible Monthly Production Overhead Cost Budget*

		Static (Master) Budget		Flexible Budget for Actual Production
Bellmead Pools & Supply, Inc.				
Flexible Monthly Production Overhead Cost Budget				
Number of pools installed per month......................	6	8	9	10
Standard direct labor hours...	2,400	3,200	3,600	4,000
Budgeted production overhead cost				
Variable...	$ 4,800	$ 6,400	$ 7,200	$ 8,000
Fixed...	12,000	12,000	12,000	12,000
Total..	$16,800	$18,400	$19,200	$20,000
Standard variable overhead rate per direct labor hour		$6,400/3,200		
		= $2.00		
Standard fixed overhead rate per direct labor hour		$12,000/3,200		
		= $3.75		
Standard total overhead rate per direct labor hour		$18,400/3,200		
		= $5.75		

Exhibit 24-8 indicates that Bellmead applies $5.75 of overhead cost to production for each direct labor hour spent installing a swimming pool. Of this amount, $2.00 is for variable overhead, and $3.75 is for fixed overhead. These standards can be based on any level of production that is consistent with company goals. In this case, Bellmead's goal is static (master) budget volume of 8 pools per month.

Bellmead accountants assemble the data in Exhibit 24-9 for computing the overhead cost variances associated with actual production of 10 pools.

The total production overhead cost variance is the difference between actual cost and standard overhead applied to production. For Bellmead Pools & Supply, the total overhead cost variance is favorable by $1,700 ($21,300 – $23,000). Accountants break the total variance down further for management use.

Flexible Budget (Controllable) Production Overhead Variance   The **flexible budget production overhead variance** is the difference between total actual overhead (fixed and variable) and the flexible budget amount for actual production volume. Bellmead Pools' flexible budget variance for June is computed as follows (data from Exhibit 24-9):

Total actual overhead cost	$21,300
Flexible budget overhead for actual production	20,000
Flexible budget variance	$ 1,300 U

Total June overhead was $21,300, compared to the flexible budget amount of $20,000. The unfavorable variance raises questions regarding managers' control of costs. Often this variance is due more to variable costs than to fixed costs, and production managers exercise considerable control over variable overhead. Therefore, many accountants call this the **controllable overhead variance**. Because control often is not clear-cut, we prefer to label it simply as the flexible budget variance.

OBJECTIVE 5

Compute production overhead cost variances

Production Volume Overhead Variance   The **production volume overhead variance** is the difference between the flexible budget for actual production and standard overhead applied to production (data from Exhibit 24-9):

Flexible budget overhead for actual production	$20,000
Standard overhead applied to production	23,000
Production volume overhead variance	$ 3,000 F

EXHIBIT 24-9   *Data for Computing Production Overhead Cost Variances*

Bellmead Pools & Supply, Inc.
Data for Computing Production Overhead Cost Variances

	Actual Cost (Exhibit 24-5)	Flexible Budget for Actual Production (Exhibit 24-8)	Standard Overhead Applied to Production (Exhibit 24-8)
Variable overhead ..	$ 9,000	$ 8,000	4,000 direct labor hours × $2.00 = $ 8,000
Fixed overhead	12,300	12,000	4,000 direct labor hours × $3.75 = 15,000
Total overhead	$21,300	$20,000	4,000 direct labor hours × $5.75 = $23,000

Total production overhead cost variance
$1,700 F

When the flexible overhead budget amount is less than the standard overhead applied to production, the variance is favorable, as shown for Bellmead Pools. The increase in volume from 8 pools to 10 pools was favorable because productive capacity was more fully utilized than expected. Had the flexible budget amount exceeded the standard overhead applied to production, the variance would have been unfavorable because less than the full amount of the company's productive capacity was used.

Exhibit 24-9 reveals that variable overhead is (always) the same for the flexible budget and the amounts applied to production. Therefore, the production volume variance must be due solely to fixed cost effects. An alternative computation of this variance clarifies this point (all data from Exhibit 24-8):

Standard direct labor hours for actual production	4,000
Standard direct labor hours for static (master) budget	3,200
Actual production in excess of static budget.............................	800
Standard fixed overhead rate per direct labor hour	× $3.75
Production volume variance...	$ 3,000 F

The production volume variance is favorable because Bellmead installed more pools than the static budget called for. The sum of the two overhead variances explains the total favorable production overhead variance of $1,700:

Flexible budget (controllable) variance	$1,300 U
Production volume variance	3,000 F
Total overhead cost variance explained.......................................	$1,700 F

Exhibit 24-10 summarizes the computation of overhead cost variances, with amounts shown for Bellmead Pools & Supply.

Two-variance analysis as just described is the most common in practice. Some companies, however, perform a three-variance analysis that splits the flexible budget variance into spending and efficiency effects. A few companies divide overhead cost variances into four parts. These topics are covered in managerial accounting and cost accounting courses.

EXHIBIT 24-10   *Bellmead Pools & Supply, Inc.*
Production Overhead Variance Computations

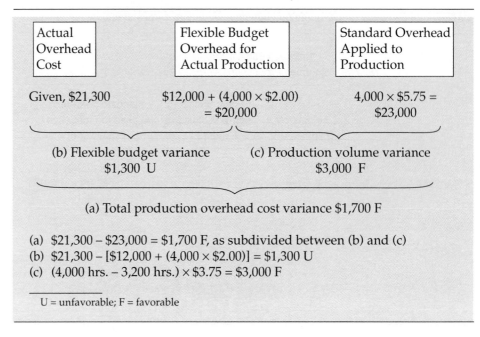

Actual Overhead Cost	Flexible Budget Overhead for Actual Production	Standard Overhead Applied to Production
Given, $21,300	$12,000 + (4,000 × $2.00) = $20,000	4,000 × $5.75 = $23,000

(b) Flexible budget variance   (c) Production volume variance
$1,300 U $3,000 F

(a) Total production overhead cost variance $1,700 F

(a) $21,300 – $23,000 = $1,700 F, as subdivided between (b) and (c)
(b) $21,300 – [$12,000 + (4,000 × $2.00)] = $1,300 U
(c) (4,000 hrs. – 3,200 hrs.) × $3.75 = $3,000 F

U = unfavorable; F = favorable

Standard Costs in the Accounts

Some companies use standard costing for control purposes without entering the standards in the accounts. Others make special standard cost entries.

Accounting systems differ among those companies that do record standard costs in the accounts. For example, one practice is to debit actual costs to Materials Inventory and Production Wages. When materials are used or when labor is applied to production, these accounts are credited for *actual* cost. However, Work in Process Inventory is debited for *standard* cost. Differences in these entries reveal the cost variances. In our Bellmead Pools illustration, the Materials Inventory, Production Wages, and Production Overhead accounts have been debited for actual costs incurred. The resulting account balances before applying costs to production and before introducing standard costs are as follows.

Materials Inventory	Production Wages	Production Overhead
Actual cost (assumed amount) 29,000	Actual cost 41,800	Actual cost 21,300

The entries to apply direct materials, direct labor, and production overhead to production and to record the cost variances are

> **OBJECTIVE 6**
>
> Record transactions at standard cost

Work in Process Inventory (standard cost)	20,000	
Direct Materials Efficiency Variance	3,938	
Direct Materials Price Variance		838
Materials Inventory (actual cost)..................................		23,100
Direct materials used in production.		
Work in Process Inventory (standard cost)	42,000	
Direct Labor Price Variance	1,900	
Direct Labor Efficiency Variance...................................		2,100
Production Wages (actual cost)		41,800
Direct labor applied to production.		
Work in Process Inventory (standard cost)	23,000	
Production Overhead Flexible Budget Variance	1,300	
Production Overhead Production Volume Variance..		3,000
Production Overhead (actual cost)...		21,300
Production overhead applied to production.		

After posting, the direct labor variance accounts appear as follows:

Direct Labor Price Variance

Unfavorable variance................. 1,900	

Direct Labor Efficiency Variance

	Favorable variance.................... 2,100

A debit balance in a variance account is treated as expense, and a credit balance is handled as a contra expense, or a reduction in expense. In this example, Direct Labor Price Variance's debit balance is expense, and Direct Labor Efficiency Variance's credit balance is a reduction in expense. These variance accounts are closed to Income Summary in the usual manner. Accounting for materials and overhead parallel these entries for labor.

Assume Bellmead sold all 10 pools that were installed during June. After posting, the Materials Inventory account shows the balance of materials on hand. Production Wages and Production Overhead have zero balances. Work in Process Inventory is stated at standard cost. The differences between actual costs credited to the accounts and standard costs debited to Work in Process Inventory identify the total cost variances, as follows:

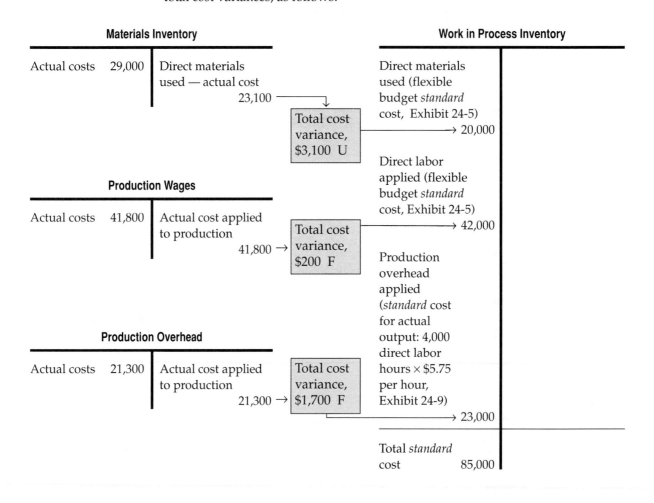

As goods are sold, standard costs flow through the accounts in the usual manner:

Standard Cost Income Statement for Management

OBJECTIVE 7

Prepare a standard cost income statement for management

Standard costing is a management tool, so the company does not usually report detailed variance information to investors, creditors and other outsiders. Managers, however, are vitally interested in the cost variances. Exhibit 24-11 illustrates an income statement the Bellmead president might use for planning and control purposes. We assume that Bellmead's sales for June were the 10 pools installed during the month.

EXHIBIT 24-11 *Income Statement*

Bellmead Pools & Supply, Inc.
Income Statement
for the month ended June 30, 19X5

Sales revenue (Exhibit 24-4: 10 pools at $12,000)				$120,000
Cost of goods sold at standard cost				
(preceding section)..		$85,000		
Cost variances*	Unfavorable	Favorable		
Direct materials	$ 3,100			
Direct labor..		$ 200		
Production overhead		1,700		
	3,100	1,900	1,200 U	
Cost of goods sold at actual cost..........................				86,200
Gross margin...				33,800
Selling and administrative expenses				
(Exhibit 24-5: variable, $9,100; fixed, $9,700)				18,800
Operating income..				$ 15,000

*Cost variance detail:	Unfavorable	Favorable	Total
Direct materials — price.................................		$838⎤	
(Exhibit 24-6) efficiency..........................	$3,938	⎦	$3,100 U
Direct labor — price......................................	1,900		
(Exhibit 24-7) efficiency..........................		2,100⎦	200 F
Production overhead —			
(Exhibit 24-10) flexible budget	1,300		
production volume........		3,000⎦	1,700 F
Total			$1,200 U

Variance analysis is also appearing in published annual reports when a forecast has been previously circulated. Exhibit 24-12 presents an example of variance analysis and management's explanation from the 1988 annual report of Air Canada.

Computers and Standard Costs

This chapter links together the master budget, flexible budgets, and standard costs. As the swimming pool example indicates, many calculations are needed to maintain the standard cost system. The advantages of a computer are obvious, especially if you want daily or weekly reports on operations.

The computer can help set the standard costs. A job order begins the process. The product's identification number and the quantity desired are entered into the computer. The computer then accesses the engineering specifications for that particular product to find out what materials are needed. It multiplies the needed materials by the quantity ordered. By repeating this process over a large number of similar jobs, management can develop the historical data for calculating standard costs.

In some manufacturing environments, the job order may trigger the computer to issue automatically the exact amount of required materials. Any materials not used on the job are shipped back to storage, with the unused quantity credited to the Materials Efficiency Variance account.

EXHIBIT 24-12 *Variance Analysis and Management Explanation*

Air Canada
Comparison of Actual to Forecast Consolidated Statement of Income
year ended December 31, 1988 (millions, except for per share information)

	Actual	Forecast	Variance
Total operating revenues	$3,426	$3,512	$ (86)
Total operating expenses	3,301	3,367	(66)
Operating income...	125	145	(20)
Total non-operating income (expense)	10	(2)	12
Income before income taxes, minority interest and extraordinary item...............	135	143	(8)
Provision for income taxes	(37)	(40)	3
Minority interest	1	—	1
Income before extraordinary item.................	99	103	(4)
Extraordinary item	(3)	(3)	—
Net income..	$ 96	$ 100	$ (4)
Net cash flow...	$ 131	$ 172	$ (41)
Per common share			
Net income before extraordinary item	$ 2.07	$2.13	$(0.06)
Net income	2.00	2.07	(0.07)
Net cash flow...	2.74	3.56	(0.82)

Comparison of Actual to Forecast Operating Statistics (all operations excluding subsidiaries)
six months ended December 31, 1988

	Actual	Forecast	Variance
Revenue passenger miles (millions)..............	7,993	8,099	(1)%
Available seat miles (millions)	11,254	11,300	—
Passenger load factor......................................	71.0%	71.7%	
Yield per revenue passenger mile..................	16.1¢	16.1¢	—
Available tonne miles (millions)	1,948	2,002	(3)%
Operating expense per available tonne mile	73.6¢	73.5¢	—

Management Discussion on Forecast

The reported net income of $96 million was $4 million below the forecasted amount in the common share prospectus of September 26, 1988. This was essentially the result of a $20 million underrun in operating income partially offset by a $12 million improvement in non-operating expense represented mainly by additional gains on sale of assets. The weakness in operating income was centered in Air Canada's subsidiaries, primarily Gelco Express Limited and Air Ontario Inc. Industry competition, stronger than forecast at the time of the prospectus, reduced both the passenger and cargo traffic levels and was the key factor in an $86 million revenue shortfall. Other elements in the decline in passenger revenue included heavy fourth quarter airport congestion at Pearson International Airport in Toronto and the lin-gering impact of Air Ontario's six-week strike which ended in the second quarter. Operating expenses decreased $66 million with the prime contributors being a $24 million reduction in depreciation expense and a decrease of $14 million in fuel expense from that forecast, arising from unanticipated further declines in world prices. The decline in depreciation expense was related to the adjustment of residual values as a result of the sale of the B-727 fleet, discussed previously. Although net income was comparatively close to target, net cash flow fell $41 million short of the forecast amount. Tougher industry conditions adversely affected the Corporation's cash generating ability. A greater proportion of the net income was derived from non-cash areas.

Summary Problem for Your Review

Exhibit 24-5 indicates that Bellmead Pools & Supply, Inc. installed 10 swimming pools during June. Suppose that June installations and sales were 7 pools instead of 10 and that actual expenses for the month were as follows:

Direct materials............................	7,400 cubic metres @ $2.00 per cubic metre
Direct labor..................................	2,740 hours @ $10.00 per hour
Variable production overhead	$5,400
Fixed production overhead.........	$11,900

Required

1. Given these new data, prepare two exhibits, similar to Exhibits 24-5 and 24-8. Ignore selling and administrative expenses in your first exhibit, and show budgeted overhead cost only for 7 and 8 pools per month in your second exhibit.
2. Compute the direct materials and direct labor price and efficiency variances.
3. Compute the total variance, flexible budget variance and production volume variance for overhead.
4. Prepare a June income statement through operating income for the president of Bellmead Pools & Supply. Report all cost variances, and assume selling and administrative expenses for the month were $17,700.

SOLUTION TO REVIEW PROBLEM

Requirement 1

Bellmead Pools & Supply, Inc.
Facts for Illustration of Standard Costing
Month of June

Panel A — Comparison of Actual Results with Flexible Budget:
Installed 7 Swimming Pools

	Actual Results at Actual Prices	Flexible Budget	Flexible Budget Variances
Variable expenses			
Direct materials.................................	$14,800[a]	$14,000[c]	$800 U
Direct labor.......................................	27,400[b]	29,400[c]	2,000 F
Variable production overhead.........	5,400	5,600[d]	200 F
Total variable expenses....................	47,600	49,000	1,400 F
Fixed expenses			
Fixed production overhead..............	11,900	12,000[e]	100 F
Total expenses	$59,500	$61,000	$1,500 F

---

a $14,800 = 7,400 cubic metres at actual price of $2.00 per cubic metre
b $27,400 = 2,740 hours at actual price of $10.00 per hour
c See Panel B
d Variable production overhead was budgeted at $2.00 per direct labor hour:
    $5,600 = 2,800 direct labor hours (7 pools × 400 direct labor hours) × $2.00
e Fixed production overhead was budgeted at $12,000 per month.

Panel B — Standards for Direct Material and Direct Labor Flexible Budget:
7 Swimming Pools

	(1) Standard Inputs Budgeted for 7 Finished Units (Swimming Pools Installed)	(2) Standard Price per Unit of Input	(1) × (2) Flexible Budget for 7 Finished Units of Output
Direct materials........................	1,000 cubic metres × 7	$ 2.00	$14,000
Direct labor	400 hours × 7	10.50	29,400

Bellmead Pools & Supply, Inc.
Flexible Monthly Production Overhead Cost Budget

Number of pools installed per month............................	7	8
Standard direct labor hours	2,800	3,200
Budgeted production overhead cost:		
Variable	$ 5,600	$ 6,400
Fixed...	12,000	12,000
Total...	$17,600	$18,400

Standard variable overhead rate per direct labor hour	$ 6,400/3,200 = $2.00
Standard fixed overhead rate per direct labor hour....	$12,000/3,200 = $3.75
Standard total overhead rate per direct labor hour.....	$18,400/3,200 = $5.75

Requirement 2

$$\text{Price variance} = \begin{array}{c}\textbf{Difference between}\\ \textbf{actual and budgeted}\\ \textbf{unit prices of inputs}\end{array} \times \textbf{Actual inputs used}$$

Direct materials:

Price variance =	($2.00 – $2.00)	×	7,400 cubic metres
=	$0		

Direct labor:

Price variance =	($10.00 – $10.50)	×	2,740 hours
=	$1,370 F		

$$\text{Efficiency variance} = \left(\begin{array}{c}\text{Actual}\\ \text{inputs}\\ \text{used}\end{array} - \begin{array}{c}\text{Inputs that should}\\ \text{have been used}\\ \text{for actual output}\end{array}\right) \times \begin{array}{c}\text{Standard}\\ \text{unit price}\\ \text{of input}\end{array}$$

$$= \left(\begin{array}{c}\text{Actual cubic}\\ \text{metres or}\\ \text{hours used}\end{array} - \begin{array}{c}\text{Standard number of cubic}\\ \text{metres or hours allowed}\\ \text{for actual output}\end{array}\right) \times \begin{array}{c}\text{Standard}\\ \text{unit price}\\ \text{of input}\end{array}$$

Direct materials:

Efficiency variance =	⎛ 7,400 ⎜ cubic ⎝ metres	–⎛ 1,000 cubic metres × 7 swimming pools ⎞	×	$2.00 per cubic metre
=	(7,400	– 7,000)	×	$2.00
=	$800 U			

Direct labor:

Efficiency variance = $\begin{pmatrix} 2,740 \\ \text{hours} \\ \text{used} \end{pmatrix}$ − $\begin{pmatrix} 400\ \text{hours} \\ \times\ 7\ \text{swimming} \\ \text{pools installed} \end{pmatrix}$ × $\begin{array}{c} \$10.50 \\ \text{per} \\ \text{hour} \end{array}$

= (2,740 − 2,800) × $10.50

= $630 F

Requirement 3

Total actual overhead cost (variable, $5,400 + fixed, $11,900)...............	$17,300
Standard total overhead cost applied to production, 7 pools	
(2,800 direct labor hours × $5.75)	16,100
Total overhead cost variance	$ 1,200 U

Flexible Budget Variance

Total actual overhead cost ($5,400 + $11,900)	$17,300
Total flexible budget overhead for actual production ($5,600 + $12,000)	17,600
Flexible budget variance	$ 300 F

Production Volume Variance

Flexible budget overhead for actual production	
(Requirement 1: variable, $5,600 + fixed, $12,000)............................	$17,600
Standard overhead applied to production	
[Requirement 1: 2,800 direct labor hours (for 7 pools) × 5.75]	16,100
Production volume variance..	$ 1,500 U

or

Standard direct labor hours for static (master) budget	
(Requirement 1: Master Budget)	3,200
Standard direct labor hours for actual production	
(Requirement 1: Flexible Budget)..	2,800
Difference in direct labor hours between flexible budget and	
master budget	400
Standard fixed overhead rate per direct labor hour	
(Requirement 1: Master Budget)	× $ 3.75
Production volume variance..	$ 1,500 U

Requirement 4

Bellmead Pools & Supply, Inc.
Income Statement
for the month ended June 30, 19X5

Sales revenue (7 pools at $12,000)...				$84,000
Cost of goods sold at standard cost (direct materials,				
$14,000 + direct labor, $29,400 + overhead, $16,100)...............			$59,500	
Cost variances*............................	Unfavorable	Favorable		
Direct materials.......................	$ 800			
Direct labor		$2,000		
Overhead.................................	1,200			
	$2,000	$2,000		
Net cost variance...			-0-	
Cost of goods sold at actual cost...				59,500
Gross margin..				24,500
Selling and administrative expenses...				17,700
Operating income				$ 6,800

*Cost variance detail:

	Unfavorable	Favorable	Total
Direct materials — price	$ -0-	$ -0-	
efficiency........................	800		$ 800 U
Direct labor — price...............................		1,370	
efficiency........................		630	2,000 F
Overhead — flexible budget..............		300	
production volume	1,500		1,200 U

Summary

A *static budget* is prepared for only one level of activity, usually the volume level that management expects for the period. A *flexible budget* is a set of budgets covering a range of volume. *Performance reports* compare actual and budgeted results for the sales volume achieved. Differences between actual and budgeted revenues and expenses are called *variances*. A variance is *favorable* if actual revenue exceeds budgeted revenue, or if actual expense is less than budgeted expense. An *unfavorable* variance occurs when actual revenue is less than budget or actual expense exceeds budget.

Costs are classified as *variable, fixed,* or *mixed*. The total amount of a variable cost fluctuates in direct proportion to changes in volume. By contrast, the total amount of a fixed cost does not change during a given period over a wide range of volume. A mixed cost has both variable and fixed components. These distinctions are important to flexible budgeting, which identifies costs and income for different levels of volume.

The heart of a flexible budget is the *budget formula*, which expresses the behavior of costs. A *flexible budget graph* provides a customized budget for any volume level.

Standard costs are the predetermined costs that managers believe the business should incur in producing an item. The standards are set low enough to spur employees to improve their performance but not so low as to discourage workers from reasonable effort. *Standard cost systems* are designed to control cost by analyzing differences between actual and standard cost. *Cost variances* are differences between actual cost and standard cost. In general, cost variances are divided into price and efficiency effects.

The *price variance* measures the effect price changes have on the cost of materials and labor. The *efficiency variance* gauges manager efficiency in using materials and labor.

Production overhead variances are divided two ways. The *flexible budget variance* is the difference between actual overhead cost and the flexible budget for actual output. It measures whether the company achieved its budgeted cost for the actual volume level achieved. The *production volume variance* arises when actual production differs from the level in the static (master) budget.

Some companies use standard costing for control purposes without recording standard costs in the accounts. Others journalize the standards and the related cost variances. The variance information is helpful in planning and control. It does not automatically identify excellence, or problems or cures, but points to areas of the business needing correction.

Self-Study Questions

Test your understanding of the chapter by marking the best answer for each of the following questions:

1. A flexible budget shows *(pp. 1058–59)*
   a. Expected results over a range of volume levels
   b. A single target level of volume
   c. Price variances
   d. Volume variances

2. Which is the most useful formula for budgeting expenses? *(p. 1060)*
   a. Expenses = Sales – Income
   b. Expenses = Fixed + Variable
   c. Expenses = Fixed + (Variable × Number of Units)
   d. Expenses = Standard + Variances

3. Flexible budget variances are differences between *(p. 1061)*
   a. Actual results and the static (master) budget
   b. Actual results and the flexible budget
   c. The static (master) budget and the flexible budget
   d. None of the above

4. Standard cost variances help managers identify *(p. 1064)*
   a. Ways of reducing cost   c. Both of the above
   b. Employees who control cost   d. None of the above

5. Cost variances for direct materials and direct labor are divided into *(pp. 1065–66)*
   a. Flexible budget effects and production volume effects
   b. Efficiency effects and flexible budget effects
   c. Controllable effects and master budget effects
   d. Price effects and efficiency effects

6. Krakow, Inc. paid $3 per kilogram for 10,000 kilograms of direct materials purchased and used. Standard cost was $2.80 per kilogram, and standard usage for actual production was 11,000 kilograms. How much is the price variance? *(p. 1066)*
   a. $800 favorable   c. $2,800 favorable
   b. $2,000 unfavorable   d. $3,000 favorable

7. How much is the efficiency variance in the preceding question? *(p. 1067)*
   a. $800 favorable   c. $2,800 favorable
   b. $2,000 unfavorable   d. $3,000 favorable

8. Cost variances for production overhead are divided into *(p. 1070)*
   a. Flexible budget effects and production volume effects
   b. Efficiency effects and flexible budget effects
   c. Controllable effects and master budget effects
   d. Price effects and efficiency effects

9. Actual overhead of Milstead Supply Ltd. is $540,000. Overhead for static (master) budget volume is $500,000, and flexible budget overhead for actual production is $510,000. The production volume overhead variance is *(p. 1071)*
   a. $10,000 unfavorable
   b. $30,000 unfavorable
   c. $40,000 unfavorable
   d. Not determinable from the information given.

10. Lemieux Manufacturing Inc. made the following entry for the use of direct materials in production:

Work in Process	380,000	
Direct Materials Efficiency Variance	35,000	
Direct Materials Price Variance		6,000
Materials Inventory		409,000

Which of the following statements is true? *(p. 1074)*

a. The price variance is unfavorable and the efficiency variance is favorable.
b. The price variance is favorable and the efficiency variance is unfavorable.
c. Both variances are favorable.
d. Both variances are unfavorable.

Answers to the Self-Study Questions are at the end of the chapter.

Accounting Vocabulary

budget formula *(p. 1060)*
controllable overhead
    variance *(p. 1071)*
efficiency variance
    (p. 1066)
flexible budget *(p. 1059)*
flexible budget overhead
    variance *(p. 1071)*

flexible budget variance
    (p. 1061)
performance report
    (p. 1058)
price variance *(p. 1066)*
production volume over-
    head variance *(p. 1071)*
quantity variance
    (p. 1066)

sales volume variance
    (p. 1061)
standard cost *(p. 1064)*
standard cost system
    (p. 1064)
static budget *(p. 1058)*
usage variance *(p. 1066)*
variance *(p. 1059)*

ASSIGNMENT MATERIAL _____

Questions

1. Which costs in total amount move in direct proportion to changes in volume? Which costs do not fluctuate in total amount with volume changes? How do total and unit amounts behave for these two categories of costs?

2. What is the relevant range, and why must it be considered in preparing a flexible budget?

3. How does a static budget differ from a flexible budget?

4. Identify how managers use variance information from a performance report.

5. McLaren, Inc. prepared its static (master) budget for a sales level of 35,000 for the month. Actual sales totaled 46,000. Describe the problem of using the master budget to evaluate company performance for the month. Propose a better way to evaluate McLaren's performance for the period.

6. What advantage does a flexible expense budget graph offer over a flexible expense budget that shows four levels of volume?

7. What do the sales volume variance and the flexible budget variance measure?

8. Describe the purpose of a standard cost system.

9. What two general categories of cost variances do most standard cost systems provide?

10. Identify the similarities and differences between a standard cost and a budgeted cost.

11. Suppose your company is installing a standard cost system. What sort of standard cost is most popular? For employees, what purposes does a standard cost fulfill?

12. What does a price variance measure? How is it computed?

13. What does an efficiency variance measure? How is it computed?

14. Consider price variance and efficiency variance. How do they relate to the total variance between actual and budgeted cost for direct materials and direct labor?

15. Describe a trade-off that a manager might make for labor cost.

16. When should a cost variance be investigated?

17. What causes a flexible budget overhead variance? What information does this variance provide?

18. What information is provided by the overhead production volume variance? How is this variance computed?

19. Scott & White, Inc., enters standard costs in the company accounts. The actual cost of direct materials used to manufacture inventory was $21,600. The direct materials price variance was $2,000 favorable, and the efficiency variance was $1,400 unfavorable. Make the journal entry to charge materials to production.

20. How does a standard cost income statement for management differ from an income statement reported to the public?

Exercises

Exercise 24-1 *Preparing a flexible budget for the income statement* **(L.O. 1)**

Antonelli & Salerno Ltd. sells its main product for $7 per unit, and variable cost is $1.60 per unit. Fixed expenses are $180,000 per month for volumes up to 55,000 units of output. Above 55,000 units, monthly fixed expenses are $240,000.

Required

Prepare a monthly flexible budget for the product, showing sales, variable expenses, fixed expenses and operating income or loss for volume levels of 40,000, 50,000 and 60,000 units.

Exercise 24-2 *Graphing expense behavior* **(L.O. 1)**

Graph the expense behavior of Antonelli & Salerno Ltd. in Exercise 24-1. Show total expenses for volume levels of 40,000, 50,000, 55,000, and 60,000 units.

Exercise 24-3 *Completing a performance report* **(L.O. 2)**

Stonegate Manufacturing Ltd. management received the following incomplete performance report:

Stonegate Manufacturing Ltd.
Income Statement Performance Report
for the year ended April 30, 19X3

	Actual Results at Actual Prices	Flexible Budget Variances	Flexible Budget for Actual Volume Achieved	Sales Volume Variances	Static (Master) Budget
Units................................	24,000		24,000		22,000
Sales................................	$192,000		$192,000		$176,000
Variable expenses.........	76,000		72,000		66,000
Fixed expenses..............	104,000		100,000		100,000
Total expenses..............	180,000		172,000		166,000
Operating income.........	$ 12,000		$ 20,000		$ 10,000

Required

Complete the performance report. Identify the employee group that should be praised and the group that may be subject to criticism. Give your reasons.

Exercise 24-4   *Preparing an income statement performance report (L.O. 2)*

Top managers of Black Bear Sporting Goods estimated 19X6 sales of 150,000 units of its product at a unit price of $6. Actual sales for the year were 140,000 units at $6.50. Variable expenses were budgeted at $2.20 per unit, and actual variable expenses were $2.15 per unit. Actual fixed expenses of $428,000 exceeded budgeted fixed expenses of $410,000.

Required

Prepare Black Bear's income statement performance report in a format similar to Exhibit 24-4. The bracketed amounts at the bottom are not required. What variance contributed the most to the year's favorable results? Explain what probably caused this variance.

Exercise 24-5   *Computing price and efficiency variances for direct materials (L.O. 3)*

The following direct materials variance computations are incomplete:

$$\text{Price variance} = (\$7 - \$?) \times 3{,}560 \text{ kg} = \$1{,}780 \text{ U}$$
$$\text{Efficiency variance} = (? - 3{,}600 \text{ kg}) \times ? = ? \text{ F}$$
$$\text{Total materials cost variance} = \$?$$

Required

Fill in the missing values and identify the total variance as favorable or unfavorable.

Exercise 24-6   *Computing price and efficiency cost variances for materials and labor (L.O. 3, 4)*

Broadmoor Limited, which uses a standard cost accounting system, manufactured 350,000 picture frames during the year, using 724,000 metres of lumber purchased earlier in the year at actual unit cost of $1.22. Production required 6,700 direct labor hours that cost $8.10 per hour. The materials standard was two metres of lumber per frame, at standard cost of $1.30 per metre. The labor standard was .019 direct labor hour per frame, at standard cost of $8.00 per hour.

Required

Compute the price and efficiency variances for direct materials and direct labor.

Exercise 24-7   *Journalizing standard costing transactions (L.O. 6)*

Make the journal entries to charge direct materials and direct labor to production in Exercise 24-6.

Exercise 24-8   *Explaining cost variances (L.O. 3, 4, 5)*

Walther Corporation managers are seeking explanations for the variances in the following report:

Walther Corporation
Income Statement for Managers
year ended December 31, 19X2

Sales revenue...		$541,000
Cost of goods sold — standard	$310,000	
Cost variances		
Materials: price	4,000 F	
efficiency	6,000 U	
Labor: price	8,000 U	
efficiency	3,000 F	
Overhead: flexible budget....................	9,000 U	
production volume...........	10,000 U	
Net cost variance	26,000 U	
Cost of goods sold — actual		336,000
Gross profit		205,000
Selling and administrative expenses......		181,000
Operating income.....................................		$ 24,000

Required

Explain the meaning of each of Walther Corporation's labor variances and each of the overhead variances.

Exercise 24-9   *Computing overhead cost variances* **(L.O. 5)**

Matsuko, Inc. charges the following standard unit cost to production, based on master budget volume of 30,000 units per month:

Direct materials..............	$3.20
Direct labor.....................	4.10
Overhead	1.00
Standard unit cost..........	$8.30

Matsuko used the following flexible overhead cost budget:

	Monthly Volume		
Number of units................................	27,000	30,000	33,000
Standard direct labor hours.............	2,700	3,000	3,300
Budgeted overhead cost			
Variable...	$13,500	$15,000	$16,500
Fixed	15,000	15,000	15,000

Actual monthly production was 27,000 units. Actual overhead cost was variable, $14,700, and fixed, $15,200.

Required

Compute the total overhead cost variance, the flexible budget variance, and the production volume variance for overhead cost.

Exercise 24-10 *Preparing a standard cost income statement for management* **(L.O. 7)**

TriStar Corporation revenue and expense information for the month of May follows:

| | Revenue or Expense | |
	Actual	Standard
Sales revenue...	$160,000	$160,000
Cost of goods sold	?	91,000
Information regarding		
Direction materials price variance	20,000	19,100
Direct materials efficiency variance................	19,000	20,600
Direct labor price variance	42,000	43,400
Direct labor efficiency variance	44,000	42,300
Overhead flexible budget variance.................	15,000	15,900
Overhead production volume variance	15,900	15,600

Required

Prepare a standard cost income statement through gross profit. Report all cost variances for use by management.

Problems

(Group A)

Problem 24-1A *Preparing a flexible budget income statement and graphing cost behavior* **(L.O. 1)**

Mueller Manufacturing Limited produces and sells prepackaged tests for certain infectious diseases. The company's master budget income statement for 19X7, based on expected sales volume of 110,000 units, follows:

Mueller Manufacturing Limited Master Budget Income Statement Year 19X7	
Sales...	$440,000
Variable expenses	
Cost of goods sold	$121,000
Sales commissions......................................	33,000
Shipping	24,200
Utilities...	11,000
Fixed expenses	
Salaries	73,000
Depreciation..	48,000
Rent	23,000
Insurance	17,700
Utilities...	12,400
Total operating expenses..............................	363,300
Income before income tax	76,700
Income tax expense (30%).............................	23,010
Net income	$ 53,690

Mueller's plant capacity is 125,000 units, so if actual volume exceeds 125,000 units, it will be necessary to expand the plant. In that case, salaries will increase by 15 percent, depreciation by 15 percent, rent by $11,000, and insurance by $2,800. Fixed utilities will be unchanged by the volume increase.

Required

1. Prepare a flexible budget income statement for the company, showing volume levels of 100,000, 110,000, 120,000, and 130,000 units.

2. Graph the total operating expense behavior of the company. Cost of goods sold is included.

Problem 24-2A   *Preparing an income statement performance report* *(L.O. 2)*

Refer to the Mueller Manufacturing situation of Problem 24-1A. The company sold 120,000 units during 19X7, and its actual income statement was as follows:

Mueller Manufacturing Limited Income Statement Year 19X7	
Sales	$487,000
Variable expenses	
Cost of goods sold	$133,000
Sales commissions	39,000
Shipping	27,000
Utilities	12,000
Fixed expenses	
Salaries	76,000
Depreciation	48,000
Rent	19,000
Insurance	15,000
Utilities	14,000
Total operating expenses	383,000
Income before income tax	104,000
Income tax expense (30%)	31,200
Net income	$ 72,800

Required

Prepare an income statement performance report for 19X7.

Problem 24-3A   *Preparing a flexible budget and computing cost variances* *(L.O. 1, 3, 4, 5)*

Pathbreaker Stereo Corp. manufactures compact disc players and uses flexible budgeting and a standard cost system. The company's performance report includes the following selected data:

	Master Budget 12,000 Units	Actual Results 13,300 Units
Sales	$948,000	$1,025,500
Variable expenses		
Cost of goods sold		
Direct materials (18,000 kg. @ $7.00)	$126,000	
(17,800 kg. @ $7.07)		$125,846
Direct labor (24,000 hr. @ $16.20)	388,800	
(27,700 hr. @ $16.15)		447,355
Variable overhead (24,000 hr. @ $2.10)	50,400	
(27,700 hr. @ $2.22)		61,494

Fixed expenses
 Cost of goods sold

Fixed overhead...	93,600	104,000
Total cost of goods sold..	658,800	738,695
Gross profit..	$289,200	$286,805

Required

1. Prepare a flexible budget based on actual volume.

2. Compute the price variance and the efficiency variance for direct materials and direct labor. Compute the total variance, the flexible budget variance, and the production volume variance for overhead.

3. Show that the sum of the price variance plus the efficiency variance equals the total cost variance for direct materials and for direct labor. Use Exhibit 24-6 as a guide.

Problem 24-4A *Using incomplete cost and variance information to determine the number of direct labor hours worked* **(L.O. 4)**

The city of Fredericton has a shop that manufactures street signs. The manager of the shop uses standard costs to judge performance. Recently a clerk mistakenly threw away some of the records, and the manager has only partial data for July. He knows that the total direct labor variance for the month was $680 — unfavorable, and that the standard labor price was $16.50 per hour. A recent pay raise caused an unfavorable labor price variance of $.30 per hour. The standard direct labor hours for actual July output were 2,500.

Required

1. Find the actual number of direct labor hours worked during July. First, find the actual direct labor price per hour. Then, determine the actual number of direct labor hours by setting up the computation of the total direct labor cost variance of $680.

2. Compute the direct labor price and efficiency variances.

Problem 24-5A *Computing and journalizing cost variances* **(L.O. 3, 4, 5, 6)**

Blue Wing Boots Ltd. manufactures hiking boots. The company prepares flexible budgets and uses a standard cost system to control manufacturing cost. The following standard unit cost of a pair of high-top boots is based on master budget volume of 14,000 pairs per month:

Direct materials (2.3 sq. m. @ $2.10 per sq. m.)............		$ 4.83
Direct labor (2 hours @ $14.50 per hour).......................		29.00
Overhead		
Variable...	$1.22	
Fixed (2 hours @ $2.06 per hour)..............................	4.12	5.34
Total unit cost..		$39.17

Transactions during November of the current year included these:

a. Actual production was 11,400 units.

b. Actual direct materials usage was 2.44 square metres per pair at actual cost of $2.17 per metre.

c. Actual direct labor usage of 22,600 hours cost $322,050.

d. Total actual overhead cost was $58,310.

Required

1. Compute the price and efficiency variances for direct materials and direct labor. Carry amounts to two decimal places.

2. Journalize the usage of direct material and the application of direct labor, including the related cost variances.

3. Compute the total variance, the flexible budget variance, and the production volume variance for overhead.

4. Blue Wing Boots' management intentionally purchased superior materials for November production. How did this decision affect the other cost variances? Overall, was the decision wise?

Problem 24-6A *Computing cost variances and reporting to management* **(L.O. 3, 4, 5, 7)**

Finkelstein Ltd. manufactures industrial plastics used in a variety of products. During April the company produced and sold 21,000 sheets of plastic and accumulated the following cost data:

		Standard Unit Cost	Total Actual Cost
Direct materials			
Standard (3 kg. @ $1.22 per kg.)		$3.66	
Actual (67,200 kg. @ $1.18 per kg.)			$ 79,296
Direct labor			
Standard (.1 hr. @ $17.00 per hr.).....................		1.70	
Actual (2,200 hr. @ $16.50 per hr.)			36,300
Overhead			
Standard			
Variable ($12.00 per direct labor hour)......	$1.20		
Fixed ($32,000 for master budget volume			
of 20,000 units and 2,000 direct			
labor hours)...	1.60	2.80	
Actual..			59,340
Total		$8.16	$174,936

Required

1. Compute the price and efficiency variances for direct materials and direct labor.

2. Compute the total variance, the flexible budget variance, and the production volume variance for overhead.

3. Prepare a standard cost income statement through gross profit to report all variances to management. Sale price of the plastic was $10.90 per sheet.

4. Finkelstein intentionally purchased cheaper materials during April. Was the decision wise? Discuss the trade-off between the two materials cost variances.

(Group B)

Problem 24-1B *Preparing a flexible budget income statement and graphing cost behavior* **(L.O. 1)**

Foster Kennedy Corporation manufactures solenoids for electronically controlled lawn sprinkler systems. The company's master budget income statement for 19X3, based on expected sales volume of 36,000 units, follows:

Foster Kennedy Corporation
Master Budget Income Statement
Year 19X3

Sales..	$756,000
Variable expenses	
Cost of goods sold.....................................	$288,000
Sales commissions......................................	37,800
Shipping	18,000
Utilities..	14,400
Fixed expenses	
Salaries..	110,000
Depreciation..	53,000
Rent	45,000
Insurance	11,000
Utilities..	9,000
Total operating expenses.............................	586,200
Income before income tax	169,800
Income tax expense (25%)............................	42,450
Net income	$127,350

Foster Kennedy's plant capacity is 38,000 units, so if actual volume exceeds 38,000 units it will be necessary to rent additional space. In that case, salaries will increase by 15 percent, rent will double, and insurance expense will increase by $2,200. Depreciation and fixed utilities will be unaffected by the increase in volume.

Required

1. Prepare a flexible budget income statement for the company, showing volume levels of 30,000, 36,000, 40,000, and 44,000 units.

2. Graph the total operating expense behavior of the company. Cost of goods is included.

Problem 24-2B *Preparing an income statement performance report* **(L.O. 2)**

Refer to the Foster Kennedy Corporation situation of Problem 24-1B. The company sold 44,000 units during 19X3, and its actual income statement was as reported below.

Foster Kennedy Corporation
Income Statement
Year 19X3

Sales	$928,000
Variable expenses	
Cost of goods sold	$361,000
Sales commissions	45,000
Shipping	27,000
Utilities	18,000
Fixed expenses	
Salaries...	127,000
Depreciation	56,000
Rent..	72,000
Insurance..	14,000
Utilities	8,000
Total operating expenses.............................	728,000

Income before income tax	200,000	
Income tax expense (25%)	50,000	
Net income	$150,000	

Required

Prepare an income statement performance report for 19X3.

Problem 24-3B *Preparing a flexible budget and computing cost variances* **(L.O. 1, 3, 4, 5)**

MasterCraft Furniture Inc. manufactures office furniture and uses flexible budgeting and a standard cost system. The company's performance report includes the following selected data:

	Master Budget 4,000 Units	Actual Results 3,800 Units
Sales	$800,000	$729,600
Variable expenses		
Cost of goods sold		
Direct materials (160,000 kg. @ $.80)	$128,000	
(164,000 kg. @ $.78)		$127,920
Direct labor (20,000 hr. @ $16.00)	320,000	
(19,300 hr. @ $16.25)		313,625
Variable overhead (20,000 hr. @ $4.00)	80,000	
(19,300 hr. @ $5.49)		105,966
Fixed expenses		
Cost of goods sold		
Fixed overhead	112,000	94,000
Total cost of goods sold	640,000	641,511
Gross profit	$160,000	$ 88,089

Required

1. Prepare a flexible budget based on actual volume.
2. Compute the price variance and the efficiency variance for direct materials and direct labor. Compute the total variance, the flexible budget variance, and the production volume variance for overhead.
3. Show that the sum of the price variance plus the efficiency variance equals the total cost variance for direct materials and for direct labor. Use Exhibit 24-6 as a guide.

Problem 24-4B *Using incomplete cost and variance information to determine the number of direct labor hours worked* **(L.O. 4)**

The province of Manitoba has a shop that manufactures road signs used throughout the province. The manager of the shop uses standard costs to judge performance. Recently a clerk mistakenly threw away some of the records, and the manager has only partial data for April. She knows that the total direct labor variance for the month was $900 — favorable, and that the standard labor price was $14.00 per hour. A recent pay raise caused an unfavorable labor price variance of $.25 per hour. The standard direct labor hours for actual April output were 2,900.

Required

1. Find the actual number of direct labor hours worked during April. First, find the actual direct labor price per hour. Then determine the actual number of direct labor hours by setting up the computation of the total direct labor cost variance of $900.
2. Compute the direct labor price of efficiency variances.

Problem 24-5B *Computing and journalizing cost variances* **(L.O. 3, 4, 5, 6)**

White Rock T-Shirts Corp. manufactures T-shirts that it sells to other companies for customizing with their own logos. White Rock prepares flexible budgets and uses a standard cost system to control manufacturing cost. The following standard unit cost of a basic white T-shirt is based on master budget volume 20,000 T-shirts per month:

Direct materials (3 sq. m. @ $.15 per sq. m.)................		$ .45
Direct labor (3 minutes @ $.20 per minute).................		.60
Overhead		
Variable..	$.12	
Fixed (2 minutes @ $.16 per minute).......................	.32	.44
Total unit cost		$1.49

Transactions during May of the current year included the following:

a. Actual production was 22,700 units.

b. Actual direct materials usage was 2.75 square metres per unit at actual cost of $.14 per square metre.

c. Actual direct labor usage of 69,200 minutes cost $14,532.

d. Total actual overhead cost was $10,107.

Required

1. Compute the price and efficiency variances for direct materials and direct labor. Carry amounts to two decimal places.

2. Journalize the usage of direct material and the application of direct labor, including the related cost variances.

3. Compute the total variance, the flexible budget variance, and the production volume variance for overhead. Evaluate the performance of the employee groups most responsible for the two overhead variances. Concentrate on the performance of the plant manager.

Problem 24-6B *Computing cost variances and reporting to management* **(L.O. 3, 4, 5, 7)**

Monarch Binder Ltd. manufactures ring binders used by college students. During August the company produced and sold 78,000 binders and accumulated the following cost data:

		Standard Unit Cost	Total Actual Cost
Direct materials			
Standard (1 kg. @ $.15 per kg.)............................		$.15	
Actual (74,900 kg. @ $.16 per kg.)			$11,984
Direct labor			
Standard (.02 hr. @ $10.00 per hr.)		.20	
Actual (1,600 hr. @ $10.10 per hr.).......................			16,160
Overhead			
Standard			
Variable ($6.00 per direct labor hour)	$.12		
Fixed ($12,000 for master budget volume of			
80,000 units and 1,600 direct labor hours)	.15	.27	
Actual...			21,440
Total		$.62	$49,584

Required

1. Compute the price and efficiency variances for direct materials and direct labor.
2. Compute the total variance, the flexible budget variance, and the production volume variance for overhead.
3. Prepare a standard cost income statement through gross profit to report all variances to management. Sale price of the binders to college bookstores was $1.25 each.
4. Monarch management purchased superior materials during August. Discuss the trade-off between the two materials cost variances.

Extending Your Knowledge

Decision Problems

1. Preparing a performance report and using it to evaluate company performance (L.O. 2)

The board of directors of Top Flite Golf Equipment Limited is meeting to evaluate the company's performance for the year just ended. Suppose the following report, which applies to Top Flite's basic line of golf clubs, has been prepared for use at the meeting.

The directors are disappointed at the net income results. They ask if the company maintained the price of its golf clubs at budgeted sale price of $120, and they are told yes. Moreover, the levels of beginning and ending inventories were unchanged.

Top Flite Golf Equipment Limited
Performance Report
year ended June 30, 19X7

	Actual Results	Master Budget	Variance	
Sales	$2,655,000	$3,240,000	$585,000	U
Variable expenses				
Cost of goods sold	$1,189,000	$1,546,000	$357,000	F
Promotion expense	126,800	110,000	16,800	U
Sales commissions	116,900	166,000	49,100	F
Shipping	64,000	87,000	23,000	F
Utilities	13,000	14,000	1,000	F
Fixed expenses				
Salaries	341,600	439,000	97,400	F
Depreciation	306,000	313,000	7,000	F
Rent	143,500	171,000	27,500	F
Utilities	11,200	13,000	1,800	F
Total operating expenses	2,312,000	2,859,000	547,000	F
Income before income tax	343,000	381,000	38,000	U
Income tax expense (30%)	102,900	114,300	11,400	F
Net income	$ 240,100	$ 266,700	$ 26,600	U

Required

1. Use the above information to prepare a more informative performance report.

2. A downturn in the economy was responsible for the company's inability to sell more golf clubs. How would you view company performance in light of this additional information? Would you decide to overhaul operations or keep the business operating on its present course?

2. *Variance analysis and reporting in a non-profit organization (L.O. 1, 2)*

St. Margaret's Church is a small congregation in Drummondville, Quebec. At the end of 1993, the church membership was 87 families. Each family donated an average of $400 per year to the Church's operating fund, and $100 per year to the mission and service fund.

At the beginning of 1994, the Church's Stewardship, Mission and Service Committee estimated that, due to the building of a new factory 10 kilometres outside Drummondville, the church membership would grow by 11 families. In addition, the committee planned a stewardship campaign for 1994 with the aim of increasing average donations to $450 for the operating fund, and $125 for mission and service.

During 1994, 7 new families became members at St. Margaret's; no families left the congregation. The 1994 receipts amounted to $44,864 for operations, and $11,152 for mission and service.

Required

1. Assume that you were the chair of St. Margaret's Church's 1994 Stewardship Campaign. Prepare an analysis for the Stewardship, Mission and Service Committee of the 1994 fund-raising efforts.

2. Write a one-paragraph report to summarize the results of the fund-raising campaign for the church's board of trustees.

Ethical Issue

Jurgens Products, Inc. budgets from the bottom up. Production workers prepare departmental goals, which are coordinated by supervisors. Top managers combine the departmental budgets into the company's overall flexible budget. Standard costs developed from the budget amounts are used for the full year.

Production workers have observed that the standard costs correspond closely to their own budget amounts. Accordingly, they have built a cushion for themselves by overestimating the quantities of materials and labor needed to manufacture a product.

Required

1. Are Jurgens's cost variances likely to be favorable or unfavorable? Why is this outcome likely to occur?

2. Whose behavior is unethical, and whose behavior is lax?

3. If this situation persists over several years, what is the likely outcome?

Answers to Self-Study Questions

1. a	6. b ($3.00 − $2.80) × 10,000 = $2,000 U
2. c	7. c (11,000 − 10,000) × $ 2.80 = $2,800 F
3. b	8. a
4. c	9. d Standard overhead applied to production is missing
5. d	10. b

Chapter 25

Responsibility Accounting: Departments and Branches

Consider the following article commenting on how Federal Industries Ltd., of Winnipeg, Manitoba is adapting its management style to overcome a $134 million loss in 1991:

"In a world where little is certain, companies must be flexible and continuously look for improvements. In response, Federal is flattening its management structure, holding fewer meetings and asking employees — not the bosses — to bring the company into the black," John Pelton, president and chief executive officer said. "You have to change the way in which you approach management at all levels."

In practical terms, that means employees and managers setting clear goals, and providing incentives to meet them. The roots of Federal's strategy does not fit the company's changing needs. With the new style, managers develop a so-called "soft bubble" approach to business tasks, where trust and teamwork replace turf protection and hierarchy.

Responsibility accounting meets one of the fundamental management challenges — that of empowering subordinates with responsibility and authority, yet ensuring that accountability and control are not lost in the shuffle. A properly designed information system is the critical link that allows this delegation process to succeed.

As Federal Industries, Labatt Breweries, Consumers Packaging, and many other firms are discovering, part of working smarter in the nineties requires the delegation of authority to a broader range of employees. As you read Chapter 25, consider how management accounting, with its focus on planning and control, facilitates this adjustment through a properly designed responsibility accounting system.

Source: Cathryn Motherwell, "Federal Discards Old Rules to Keep up with the Times." *The Globe and Mail* (May 19, 1992), p. B3.

LEARNING OBJECTIVES

After studying this chapter, you should be able to

1 Identify different types of responsibility centers, and specify the information they report.

2 Prepare a performance report for management by exception

3 Allocate indirect expenses to departments

4 Prepare a departmental income statement

5 Account for branch operations

The opening vignette describes how Federal Industries Ltd. has *empowered* its employees, and thereby expects to improve profitability. The challenge implied in increasing employees' autonomy is ensuring that accountability is not lost in the process. This management issue is called *responsibility accounting*.

Responsibility Accounting

Most businesses must divide the responsibility of management. Some companies are so geographically dispersed that one person cannot adequately oversee the entire operation. Other companies may have too many operations or too many employees for one person to handle all executive duties. To get the work done, executives must delegate authority over particular areas to middle-level managers. Depending on how complex or on how large the company is, this middle-level manager may in turn delegate authority to other employees to handle certain areas of operations under his or her responsibility. And so the responsibility chain grows.

How does the business measure each manager's performance? **Responsibility accounting** is a system for classifying financial data by defined areas in an organization in order to evaluate the performance of managers for activities under their supervision. Responsibility accounting is a key tool in managing all but single-person businesses. For example, automobile dealerships use responsibility accounting for separately measuring the performance of various activities such as new car sales, used car sales, parts sales, and the service department.

The basic unit in a responsibility accounting system is called a **responsibility center**, which is a part, segment, or subunit of an organization whose managers are accountable for specified activities. A center can be any subunit of an organization needing control. Each center works from a budget tailored to its particular activities. The three common types of responsibility centers are the cost center, profit center, and investment center.

OBJECTIVE 1

Identify different types of responsibility centers, and specify the information they report

1. *Cost center*   Responsibility center in which a manager is accountable for costs (expenses) only. Examples include a personnel department and a shipping department. It is important for these departments to control costs; they are not responsible for generating revenue. Consequently, only costs are reported for their activities. A shipping department manager is judged, for example, on the cost of shipping a certain volume of merchandise.

2. *Profit center*   Responsibility center in which a manager is accountable for revenues and costs (expenses). Examples are a McDonald's restaurant and a jewelry department in an Eaton's store. Managers of these subunits are responsible for generating income (revenues minus expenses). Both revenues and expenses are reported to show the income of a profit center.

3. *Investment center* Responsibility center in which a manager is accountable for investments, revenues, and costs (expenses). Investment in the business is reported in addition to revenues and expenses so that return on investment (income divided by investment) can be computed. Top managers as well as investors evaluate these centers by comparing their returns on investment.

Illustration of Responsibility Accounting

The simplified organization chart in Exhibit 25-1 illustrates how companies may use responsibility accounting in the fast-food industry. At the top level, a district manager oversees the branch managers, who supervise the managers of the individual restaurants (called stores). Store managers have limited freedom to make operating decisions. They may decide on how to handle local advertising, the number of employees and their schedules, and the store hours. Branch managers oversee several stores, evaluate store managers' performance and set store managers' compensation levels. In turn, district managers oversee several branches, evaluate branch managers' performance and compensation, and decide on district prices and sales promotions. District managers are accountable to regional managers, who answer to home-office vice-presidents.

Exhibit 25-2 provides a more detailed view of how responsibility accounting is used to evaluate profit centers. Examine the lowest level and move to the top. Follow how the reports are related through the three levels of responsibility. All variances may be subdivided for further analysis, either in these reports or in supporting schedules.

Trace the $54,000 operating income from the West Edmonton Mall manager report to the Edmonton branch manager report. The branch manager report summarizes the final results of the stores under his supervision. In addition, charges incurred by the branch manager office are included in this report.

Trace the $465,000 total from the Edmonton branch manager report to the Alberta district manager report. The report of the district manager includes data for her own district office plus a summary of the entire district's operating income performance.

EXHIBIT 25-1 *McDonald's Restaurants of Canada Ltd. Simplified Partial Organization Chart*

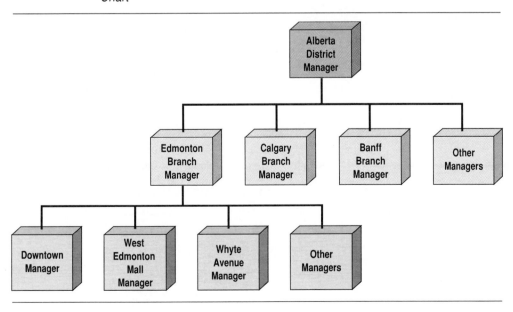

EXHIBIT 25-2 *Responsibility Accounting at Various Levels*

McDonald's Restaurants of Canada Ltd.
Responsibility Accounting at Various Levels
(in thousands of dollars for explanatory purposes)

Alberta District Manager
Monthly Responsibility Report

Operating income of branches and district manager office expense	Budget		Actual		Variance: Favorable (Unfavorable)	
	This Month	Year to Date	This Month	Year to Date	This Month	Year to Date
District manager office expense .	$ (150)	$ (600)	$ (158)	$ (620)	$ (8)	$ (20)
Edmonton branch.........................	→ 465	1,730	460	1,780	(5)	50
Calgary branch............................	500	1,800	519	1,890	19	90
Banff branch	310	1,220	341	1,330	31	110
Others...	600	2,560	647	2,690	47	130
Operating income.........................	$1,725	$6,710	$1,809	$7,070	$84	$360

Edmonton Branch Manager
Monthly Responsibility Report

Operating income of stores and branch manager office expense	Budget		Actual		Variance: Favorable (Unfavorable)	
	This Month	Year to Date	This Month	Year to Date	This Month	Year to Date
Branch manager office expense..	$ (20)	$ (306)	$ (25)	$ (302)	$ (5)	$ 4
Downtown....................................	48	148	47	143	(1)	(5)
West Edmonton Mall	→ 54	228	61	244	7	16
Whyte Avenue	38	160	42	170	4	10
Others...	345	1,500	335	1,525	(10)	25
Operating income.........................	$465	$1,730	$460	$1,780	$ (5)	$50

West Edmonton Mall Manager
Monthly Responsibility Report

Revenue and expense	Budget		Actual		Variance: Favorable (Unfavorable)	
	This Month	Year to Date	This Month	Year to Date	This Month	Year to Date
Revenue.......................................	$170	$690	$178	$702	$ 8	$12
Food expense..............................	50	198	45	184	5	14
Paper...	15	62	18	64	(3)	(2)
Wages...	24	98	28	103	(4)	(5)
Repairs..	5	19	4	20	1	(1)
General	12	45	12	47	—	(2)
Depreciation	10	40	10	40	—	—
Total expenses	116	462	117	458	(1)	4
Operating income.........................	$ 54	$228	$ 61	$244	$ 7	$16

Performance Report Format

Exhibit 25-2 stresses variances. This focus is a highlight of **management by exception**, a management policy in which executive attention is directed to the important deviations from budgeted amounts. For example, the Edmonton branch's operating income lagged behind the other branches during the current month and for the year to date. The district manager would concentrate her efforts on improving the Edmonton branch. Managers do not waste time investigating smoothly running operations.

The format for reporting operations used in Exhibit 25-2 may be expanded to highlight variances. The expanded performance report for the West Edmonton Mall manager follows:

OBJECTIVE 2

Prepare a performance report for management by exception

	Budget		Actual Results		Variance: Favorable (Unfavorable)		Variance: Percent of Budgeted Amount	
	This Month	Year to Date	This Month	Year to Date	This Month	Year to Date	This Month	Year to Date
Revenues	$170	$690	$178	$702	$8	$12	4.7%	1.7%

The complete performance report would likely include line-by-line presentations of other data. For example, a report for a restaurant will show the number of customers served and the average selling price per customer. In the hotel industry, managers report the percentage of rooms occupied and the average daily rental rate per room as performance measures.

No single format appeals to all users. Some managers prefer the greater detail shown in the eight-column format, but others prefer less detail. The choice is a matter of personal preference.

Design of a Responsibility Accounting System

A responsibility accounting system can be combined with whatever type of accounting system the company uses, such as a standard cost system, which highlights variances. The key to an effective accounting system is gathering and communicating information to assist the business in achieving its goals. Two factors are important: manager control over operations and manager access to information.

Consider a furniture manufacturer that uses a standard cost system to measure an efficiency (usage) variance and a price variance for the cost of lumber. The production supervisor is responsible for the quantity of lumber used to manufacture chairs. Good work in the factory wastes little lumber and holds costs down. Careless work wastes lumber and increases production cost. The supervisor must control operations. The efficiency (usage) variance is watched by the supervisor, often by personal observation.

Responsibility for the price variance is assigned to the purchasing manager who buys the lumber. The price of lumber may differ from standard cost because of droughts, crop disease and forest fires, which are beyond the purchasing manager's control. Nevertheless, the price variance is the responsibility of the purchasing manager because he or she has access to more price information than anyone else in the business. The *reporting* responsibility of any manager is to explain the outcome of an action regardless of personal influence over the outcome.

Responsibility accounting, budgets, standards and variances are aids to management. They help top managers to delegate decision-making to lower levels by assigning responsibility for action and establishing a way to evaluate performance.

Such a system frees top managers to work on broad issues affecting the whole organization.

Responsibility accounting systems can also be misused as a way of finding fault and placing blame. The question should not be: Who should be blamed for an unfavorable variance? The question should be: Which individual is in the best position to explain why a specific variance occurred? Or, who should be acknowledged and rewarded for the favorable variances, and what can the organization learn from this achievement so that such outstanding performance may be repeated?

Departmental Accounting

Departments are the most widely encountered responsibility centers. The department store is a familiar illustration. Top managers of a department store want more information than the net income of the store as a whole. At a minimum, they want to know each department's gross margin (sales minus cost of goods sold). In addition, they usually want to know each department's operating income. With these data, managers can identify their most profitable and least profitable departments. This information aids decisions such as whether to expand some departments and phase out others.

Departmental gross margins are easy to measure because sales and cost of goods sold records are kept by department. Departmental operating income (gross margin minus operating expenses) is not as easy to measure. Why? Primarily because of indirect expenses.

Direct expenses are those that are conveniently identified with and traceable to the department. The wages of sales clerks, salary of the department head, advertising of the shoe department and depreciation of display cases within a department are direct expenses.

OBJECTIVE 3

Allocate indirect expenses to departments

Indirect expenses are all those expenses other than direct expenses. Indirect expenses are not traceable to a single department. Examples are the costs of operating the receiving department and the stockroom. Often these activities serve more than one department simultaneously. For example, an incoming truck may be delivering merchandise to several departments. How does the business allocate this receiving cost? To what department does the business assign the expense of operating the stockroom, which holds inventory for several departments? How does the company allocate the expense of an advertising campaign that promotes the entire store, not just a single department? Although direct allocations of specific advertising can be made, most businesses regard general advertising as indirect expense.

Allocation of Service Department Expenses

Cost allocation is the assignment of various costs to departments. Cost allocation may also be called **expense allocation**, cost assignment, cost distribution and cost apportionment. (As you learned in Chapters 22 and 23, the term *cost allocation* applies to the costs of products also. In our present discussion, we are allocating the costs of service departments, not manufacturing departments.)

To allocate expense, the business must first set an **allocation base**, which is a logical common denominator for assigning a given cost to two or more departments. Consider a store that sells furniture and appliances. These two departments share the expense of warehousing the store's inventory. The business could allocate the expense of warehousing on the basis of the ratio of space taken up by each department's goods. If furniture occupies 80 percent of the warehouse, then the furniture department might be assigned 80 percent of warehouse expense. Similarly, the cost of the receiving department may be divided between the two departments on the basis of the number of hours spent unloading each department's goods. If unloading appliances takes 30 percent of the receiving employees' time, then the appliance department could be allocated 30 percent of receiving department expense.

EXHIBIT 25-3   *Bases for Allocating Costs to Departments*

Cost or Expense	Base for Allocating Cost to Departments
Direct material	Separately traced
Merchandise	Separately traced
Packaging materials	Separately traced, if feasible
Direct labor	Separately traced
Other labor	Time spent in each department
Supervision	Time spent or number of employees in each department
Equipment depreciation and rentals	Separately traced, hours used by each department
Building depreciation, property taxes and rentals	Square metres of space. Sometimes heavier allocations are made to departments that experience higher customer traffic.
Heat, light and air-conditioning	Square metres or cubic metres of space
Janitorial services	Square metres of space
Advertising	Separately traced, if possible. Otherwise, in proportion to newspaper space or radio or TV time in advertisement, or in proportion to budgeted sales or actual sales.
Payroll Department	Number of employees in each department
Personnel Department	Number of employees in each department
Purchasing Department	Number of orders or dollar amounts of purchases in each department

The costs of warehousing and receiving are examples of indirect expenses that are easy to assign to departments. Other indirect costs are more difficult to allocate. How do we assign factory overhead and home-office administrative costs to departments? The common denominator for allocating these expenses to departments is less clear. We will address this problem later in this chapter.

Companies use different allocation bases, and even within a single company several different bases may be used to allocate different expenses to the various departments. The list in Exhibit 25-3 offers common examples of allocation bases for selected costs and expenses.

Let us stress this point: the ideal guide for choosing an allocation base is the existence of a cause-and-effect relationship. That is, what are the cost drivers, the factors that cause costs? For instance, as Exhibit 25-3 shows, generally the more square metres of space, the higher the cost of janitorial services. Choosing an allocation base is largely a matter of common sense. No one "right" allocation base exists for each cost or expense. Managers use their experience and judgment in choosing these bases. Affected managers should participate in the choice of cost allocation bases. This will enhance confidence in the reasonableness of the cost allocations.

Illustration of Departmental Reporting

Exhibit 25-4 shows a simplified departmental income statement of a Computer Unlimited Store.

Supporting details can be shown in various ways. For example, gross sales, sales returns and allowances, and sales discounts can appear in the body of the statement

OBJECTIVE 4

Prepare a departmental income statement

EXHIBIT 25-4   *Departmental Income Statement*

Computer Unlimited Store
Departmental Income Statement
for the year ended December 31, 19X1
(in thousands)

		Department	
	Total	**Hardware**	**Software**
Net sales..	$10,000	$7,000	$3,000
Cost of goods sold	5,500	4,000	1,500
Gross margin...	4,500	3,000	1,500
Operating expenses			
Salaries and wages	1,100	660	440
Depreciation, equipment........................	100	80	20
Supplies...	200	140	60
Advertising..	1,000	400	600
Rent...	600	480	120
Heat, light, air conditioning.................	60	40	20
Purchasing department	300	230	70
General administration department....	200	160	40
Total operating expenses............................	3,560	2,190	1,370
Operating income...	$ 940	$ 810	$ 130

or in a separate schedule. Our discussion, however, focuses on the allocation of selected expenses to the store's two departments.

Salaries and Wages   These costs, which include each department manager's salary, are direct departmental expense.

Depreciation, Equipment   This expense is also direct departmental expense, related to the equipment used only by each specific department.

Supplies   If each department may request supplies as needed, supplies are a direct cost. However, suppose the personnel from both departments help themselves to a companywide pool of supplies without recording usage. In this case, the company must establish a base for allocating supplies expense to the individual departments. The company may use percentage of sales, illustrated as follows for total supplies expense of $200:

Department	Sales	Percent of Total Sales	Allocation of Supplies Expense of $200
Hardware	$ 7,000	70%	.70 × $200 = $140
Software................	3,000	30	.30 × 200 = 60
Total.......................	$10,000	100%	1.00 × $200 = $200

Advertising   Consider a $960 computer store ad that takes up 240 square centimetres in the Sunday newspaper: 150 square centimetres advertise hardware and 50 square centimetres promote software, and the remaining 40 square centimetres carry information about the company as a whole (its address, hours, and so forth). How does the business allocate the overall cost of advertising to the two departments?

Suppose each square centimetre of advertising costs $4. Then the $960 total cost (240 centimetres × $4 = $960) may be allocated in two steps, as the accompanying table shows:

Department	Step 1: 200 cm of Direct Advertising	Step 2: 40 cm of General Advertising	Steps 1 + 2: 240 cm of Total Advertising
Hardware	150 × $4 = $600 (75%)	75% × $160 = $120	$720
Software	50 × 4 = 200 (25%)	25 × 160 = 40	240
	$800 (100%)	$160	$960

Step 1 computes each department's direct cost, $600 and $200, respectively. Hardware's percentage of total direct costs is $600 ÷ $800, or 75 percent; Software's percentage is $200 ÷ $800, or 25 percent. Step 2 uses these percentages to allocate the $160 of general advertising costs ($960 – $800 = $160) to Hardware and Software.

If the computer store had three departments, we would simply total the individual departments' direct expense and use each department's percentage of that total to allocate the general advertising expense. We may allocate other general expenses, for example, salaries, wages and depreciation, among departments in this way.

Rent   Rent may be allocated on the basis of square area, as follows:

Rent for entire store $600,000
Total square metres 2,500
Rent per square metre ($600,000/2,500) ... 240

Suppose that the company considers each square metre of space in the store equally valuable and that the Hardware and Software Departments occupy 2,000 square metres and 500 square metres, respectively. The allocation of rent is

Hardware Department	2,000 sq. m.	×	$240 per sq. m.	= $480,000
Software Department	500	×	240	= 120,000
Total rent expense				$600,000

However, space in certain parts of the store may have different values because of varying potential to generate sales. For example, the space near the entrance may be the most valuable space in the store. The rear of the store may be the least valuable. Managers use judgment, combined with outside consultants, to arrive at an appropriate allocation of rent. One approach is to weight the square metre space. Suppose again that the Hardware and Software Departments occupy 2,000 and 500 square metres, respectively, and that Hardware's space is twice as valuable as Software's. In this case, rent of $600,000 is allocated to the two departments as follows:

Department	Space Occupied	Space Weighted by Value	Proportion of Weighted Space	Allocation of Rent of $600,000
Hardware	2,000	2,000 × 2 = 4,000	$\frac{8}{9}$	$\frac{8}{9}$ × $600,000 = $533,333
Software.................	500	500 × 1 = 500	$\frac{1}{9}$	$\frac{1}{9}$ × 600,000 = 66,667
Total.......................	2,500	4,500	$\frac{9}{9}$	$\frac{9}{9}$ × $600,000 = $600,000

Heat, Light, Air Conditioning   The most common allocation base is the square metres of space occupied. Cubic metres are used if ceiling height varies in different parts of the building.

Purchasing Department   Some of these expenses can be charged directly to specific departments. Any remaining expense is usually allocated in proportion to the dollar amount of purchases made on behalf of each department. Note that this assumes that the total cost of goods purchased is the cost driver. In some cases, the number of orders or the number of units purchased may be better measures of which departments used Purchasing Department resources.

General Administrative Expenses   This category includes depreciation on office furniture and equipment, office utilities, salaries of management and the office staff, and other expenses related to the organization as a whole. Some of these expenses may be charged directly. Others, such as payroll and personnel costs, may be allocated by the number of employees in various departments. The remainder is often allocated in proportion to departmental sales because this allocation base is convenient and no better base is apparent or feasible.

   Managers may want expense allocations refined beyond those in Exhibit 25-4. For example, they may desire a statement with the following format for the Hardware Department to emphasize the difference between direct departmental expense and indirect expense:

Net sales	$7,000
Cost of goods sold	4,000
Gross margin	3,000
Direct departmental expense.............	**1,800**
Margin before indirect expenses.........	1,200
Indirect expenses	**390**
Operating income.................................	$ 810

   The margin before indirect expenses may provide information for deciding whether to expand or cut back a department's operations. Accounting systems can be designed to fulfil these wishes.

Summary Problem for Your Review

Review the allocation of rent, as explained for the illustration of departmental reporting on p. 1103. Suppose the Hardware Department's space is three times as valuable as that of the Software Department. Total rent remains $600,000.

Required

1. Prepare an analysis to show how much total rent expense should be allocated to each department.
2. What is each department's rent expense per square metre?

SOLUTION TO REVIEW PROBLEM

Requirement 1

Department	Space Occupied	Space Weighted by Value	Proportion of Weighted Space	Allocation of Rent of $600,000
Hardware..........................	2,000	$2,000 \times 3 = 6,000$	$\frac{12}{13}$	$\frac{12}{13} \times \$600,000 = \$553,846$
Software	500	$500 \times 1 = 500$	$\frac{1}{13}$	$\frac{1}{13} \times 600,000 = 46,154$
Total..................................	2,500	6,500	$\frac{13}{13}$	$\frac{13}{13} \times \$600,000 = \$600,000$

Requirement 2

Rent expense per square metre
   Hardware: $553,846/2,000 = $276.93
   Software: $46,154/500 = $92.31

Note: Hardware's rent expense per square metre is indeed three times as high as Software's rent expense per square metre ($276.93 = $92.31 × 3).

Branch Accounting

Many companies establish branch offices or branch factories. Top managers may wish to take advantage of the particular benefits that a certain geographical area offers. Materials and labor may be cheaper at a location removed from the home office. Or the company may want to open a new sales market.

> **OBJECTIVE 5**
>
> Account for branch operations

Branches are responsibility centers — often cost centers if the branch is devoted to manufacturing or warehousing with no sales responsibility. A branch manager has responsibility for certain aspects of a branch's operations. In turn, he or she must report the branch's performance to a superior.

Who has the accounting responsibilities in a company that runs branch operations? The home office generally keeps most of the accounting records. The branch maintains only those records needed to manage its own operations. **Branch accounting** is a system for separating the accounts of a branch from those of the home office. The purpose is to establish accountability over the resources entrusted to the branch.

Consider a manufacturer that keeps cost records for direct materials, work in process inventory and factory overhead at its branch factory. Receivables, finished goods inventory, capital assets, payables, depreciation and other areas are accounted for in the corporate (home) office. This split of accounting between central headquarters and its branch means dividing the records between the two locations. With such a division, procedures are needed to ensure that all transactions are accounted for. Generally, two **reciprocal accounts** are used, one in the home office and one in the branch. Reciprocal accounts are two or more accounts that have exactly the same offsetting balances and are used to control a general ledger that is kept in two or more locations.

Branch Ledger and Journal

A **branch ledger** is that part of a general ledger kept by the branch, separate from the home-office ledger. The branch ledger contains only those accounts needed to manage its operations plus a special account used to handle its accountability to the home office. If the branch is a manufacturing plant, its ledger is often called a **factory ledger**. Each branch has its own branch or factory ledger.

The **home-office ledger** is that part of a general ledger kept by the home office, separate from the branch ledger. The home-office ledger is identical to the general ledger studied throughout this course except that it includes a special account for the branch and excludes the accounts kept by the branch. The home office and branch also maintain separate journals for recording transactions.

Suppose Appliance Company of Canada Inc. is headquartered in Windsor, but has its manufacturing plant in Hamilton. The home office makes all purchases and sales, handles cash payments and cash receipts and incurs all company liabilities. A separate factory ledger is maintained in Hamilton for managing the branch plant.

When the factory completes inventory, it transfers the finished goods to warehouses, which are managed directly by the home office. Upon transfer of merchandise to the warehouses, the home office debits inventory and credits the factory account for shipments at cost.

The general ledger accounts of the company follow, showing the link between the reciprocal accounts:

Home-Office Accounts	Branch-Factory Accounts
Cash	Direct materials inventory
Accounts receivable	Work in process inventory
Finished goods inventory	Factory overhead
Capital assets	Home-office ledger control
Accumulated depreciation	
Branch-factory ledger control	
Accounts payable	
Wages payable	
Common stock	
Retained earnings	
Sales revenue	
Cost of goods sold	
Selling expenses	
Administrative expenses	

The home office's **branch-factory ledger** control account can be viewed as an *investment in* or a *receivable from* the branch. Similarly, the branch's **home-office ledger control** account represents an *owner equity of* or a *payable to* the home office.

Illustrative Transactions and Related Journal Entries

Entries for the following transactions illustrate accounting for branch operations:

1. Direct materials purchased on credit	$230,000
2. Direct materials used in production	150,000
3. Factory payroll accrued	200,000
4. Miscellaneous factory overhead cost incurred (credit Accounts Payable, $150,000; and Accumulated Depreciation, $18,000)	168,000
5. Factory overhead applied	165,000
6. Cost of goods shipped to warehouse	425,000
7. Cost of goods sold	400,000
8. Sales (on credit)	600,000
9. Cash collected on account	440,000

Journal Entries   Illustrative journal entries and postings to the reciprocal accounts are given in Exhibit 25-5 (in thousands of dollars). The entries that would be made in a regular, unified journal are given first in the exhibit. Relating each pair of home-office/branch entries to the corresponding unified entry will help you see how branch accounting works. Keep in mind that the focus is on the home-office and branch entries. The regular, unified entries are presented solely to aid your understanding. Let us consider the first transaction and related entry — the credit purchase of direct materials by the home office for the branch factory (amounts in thousands of dollars).

EXHIBIT 25-5 Sample Journal Entries for Branch Accounting (in thousands of dollars)

Transaction	Entries That Would Be Made in a Regular, Unified Journal		Home-Office Journal		Branch-Factory Journal	
1. Direct materials purchases	Direct Materials Inventory Accounts Payable	230 230	Branch-Factory Ledger Control Accounts Payable	230 230	Direct Materials Inventory Home-Office Ledger Control	230 230
2. Direct materials uses	Work in Process Inventory Direct Materials Inventory	150 150	None		Work in Process Inventory Direct Materials Inventory	150 150
3. Factory payroll	Factory Wages Wages Payable	200 200	Branch-Factory Ledger Control Wages Payable	200 200	Factory Wages Home-Office Ledger Control	200 200
4. Miscellaneous overhead	Factory Overhead Accounts Payable Accumulated Depreciation	168 150 18	Branch-Factory Ledger Control Accounts Payable Accumulated Depreciation	168 150 18	Factory Overhead Home-Office Ledger Control	168 168
5. Overhead application	Work in Process Inventory Factory Overhead	165 165	None		Work in Process Inventory Factory Overhead	165 165
6. Shipments to warehouse	Finished Goods Inventory Work in Process Inventory	425 425	Finished Goods Inventory Branch-Factory Ledger Control	425 425	Home-Office Ledger Control Work in Process Inventory	425 425
7. Cost of goods sold	Cost of Goods Sold Finished Goods Inventory	400 400	Cost of Goods Sold Finished Goods Inventory	400 400	None	
8. Sales	Accounts Receivable Sales Revenue	600 600	Accounts Receivable Sales Revenue	600 600	None	
9. Collections on account	Cash Accounts Receivable	440 440	Cash Accounts Receivable	440 440	None	

Postings:

Branch-Factory Ledger Control

(1)	230	(6)	425
(3)	200		
(4)	168		
Bal.	173		

Home-Office Ledger Control

(6)	425	(1)	230
		(3)	200
		(4)	168
		Bal.	173

Home-Office Journal		
Branch-Factory Ledger Control	230	
Accounts Payable		230
Home-office purchase of direct materials.		

Branch-Factory Journal		
Direct Materials Inventory	230	
Home-Office Ledger Control		230
Home-office purchase of direct materials.		

The home office is responsible for paying the bill and so records the liability. The branch factory is responsible for using the direct materials and therefore records the inventory. Because accountability is split between the two locations, reciprocal accounts are used to assure that each transaction is fully accounted for. The home-office debit to the branch account counterbalances the branch's credit to the home-office account. We can regard the $230,000 debit in the first home-office entry as the home office's investment in, or receivable from, the factory. The branch's credit to the home-office account in the branch's entry shows the branch's obligation to the home office for the purchased materials.

Entries 2 and 5 are confined strictly to the branch-factory ledger because these transactions affect factory costs with no home-office involvement. Entries 3, 4 and 6 affect both home office and branch. Entries 7, 8 and 9 are recorded solely by the home office, because the branch has no responsibility for sales, cost of sales, or collections of receivables.

Entry 6 deserves special comment. Factory shipments of finished goods transfer inventory from the factory to the warehouses, which are under direct home-office management. Such shipments reduce the home-office investment in the factory because the home office receives inventory. Likewise, the branch decreases the owner equity of the home office by transferring inventory to the warehouses.

Reciprocal Balances   Exhibit 25-5 shows that the reciprocal accounts have identical, offsetting balances. Any difference between the balances signals the accountant to explain the imbalance. A common cause of imbalances is faulty communication. For example, a shipment of finished goods to the warehouse may be in transit at the balance sheet date. The home office may be unaware of the transaction until the goods arrive. At the same time, the factory may have already recorded the shipment. Progress in data processing via computers has reduced problems of this nature.

Accounting for a Sales Branch

Home-office and branch entries depend on the authority given to the branch. In the example shown in Exhibit 25-5, the home office pays branch bills, makes all sales and collects all cash. Many companies use sales branches to enter new markets. For instance, IBM Canada has sales offices throughout Canada. Sales branches may make sales, collect cash and make some of their own cash disbursements. Often the home office keeps control of the revenue and expense accounts. Assume a sales branch completed the following transactions:

1. Branch sold merchandise and received cash of $3,000.
2. Branch transferred $3,000 cash to home office.
3. Home office paid commission of $1,100 to salesperson who made the sale in 1.
4. Branch paid water bill, $90.
5. Branch recorded depreciation on office equipment, $300.

These transactions would be recorded by the home office and branch as follows:

Home-Office Journal			Branch Journal		
1. Branch Ledger Control.............	3,000		Cash	3,000	
Sales Revenue		3,000	Home-Office Ledger Control.............................		3,000
2. Cash	3,000		Home-Office Ledger Control........	3,000	
Branch Ledger Control ...		3,000	Cash		3,000
3. Sales Commission Expense......	1,100		None		
Cash...................................		1,100			
4. Utility Expense..........................	90		Home-Office Ledger Control........	90	
Branch Ledger Control ...		90	Cash		90
5. Depreciation Expense	300		Home-Office Ledger Control........	300	
Branch Ledger Control ...		300	Accumulated Depreciation — Office Furniture.............		300

After posting these entries, Branch Ledger Control's credit balance should equal the debit balance of Home-Office Ledger Control.

Computers, Responsibility Accounting, and Remote Processing

Recall Exhibit 25-2, Responsibility Accounting at Various Levels. This report gives managers information on the success of operations at different levels of the business. How might this report be prepared? Each McDonald's restaurant logs its revenues and expenses into its computer and transmits the information to central computer processing.

With complete information from each restaurant, the computer system can sort (that is, arrange in a useful grouping) the revenue and expense information. For example, district managers may want to know which restaurants are way off budget and need attention. The computer program can sort the information by size of budget variance — with additional breakdowns by restaurant, city, district, or region. A system for numbering accounts makes this sorting possible. All restaurant-level accounts have a certain number designation, all city-level accounts have another number designation, and so on. A computerized system like this is called a database management system. Managers and accountants can pull up whatever information they need for a particular decision. Ready access to the data enables managers to act on current information.

Consider responsibility accounting for McDonald's Restaurant of Canada Ltd. The company's system can provide the information for allocating indirect expenses to individual restaurants. Suppose corporate headquarters purchase much of the food centrally. The McDonald's accountant needs a base for allocating receiving-department costs to the various restaurants. The computer can sort receiving reports by restaurant. The more frequently a restaurant requests food from central headquarters, the higher is that restaurant's share of receiving-department cost. Periodic review of this information reveals any change in use patterns. Accountants can change the allocation base as needed to keep the cost allocation current. Restaurant managers can be evaluated fairly for the expenses under their supervision.

Summary Problem for Your Review

A general ledger may be divided between home office and branch in any manner whatsoever. Reconsider Exhibit 25-5. Suppose the branch factory, instead of the home office, keeps its capital asset accounts and the related depreciation records. The capital asset accounts would appear in the ledger of the factory but not the home office. Among the nine transactions in our example, what journal entry or entries would be changed? Prepare the changed entry or entries.

SOLUTION TO REVIEW PROBLEM

Entry 4 would be changed. Accumulated depreciation would appear in the branch-factory ledger but not in the home-office ledger. Moreover, the amounts recorded in the reciprocal accounts would be $150,000 instead of $168,000, as follows (amounts in thousands of dollars):

Home-Office Ledger		
4. Branch-Factory Ledger Control ...	150	
Accounts Payable.................		150

Branch-Factory Ledger		
Factory Overhead	168	
Accumulated Depreciation......		18
Home-Office Ledger Control ..		150

Summary

Responsibility accounting is a system for evaluating the progress of managers based on activities under their supervision. This system is especially important in organizations with scattered operations. Most companies are organized into *responsibility centers* to establish accountability. There are different types of responsibility centers: *cost center*, *profit center*, and *investment center*. The most critical factor in designing a responsibility accounting system is gathering and communicating information to help the business achieve its goals.

Performance reports show deviations from budgeted amounts. By focusing on important variances, managers can direct their attention to operations needing improvement and avoid wasting time investigating successful operations. This practice is called *management by exception*.

Departments are the most widely encountered responsibility centers. Gross margin and operating income are important measures of their performance. *Direct expenses* are conveniently identified with and traceable to the department. *Indirect expenses* are all those expenses other than direct expenses. Direct expenses are easy to allocate to departments because of their natural link to a particular department. Indirect expenses are allocated based on some logical relationship between the expense and departments.

Branch accounting is a system for separating branch accounts from home-office accounts. Its key feature is a set of *reciprocal accounts*. The home office has a *Branch Ledger Control* account for its investment in, or receivable from, the branch. The branch ledger has only those accounts needed to manage its own operations. Its special account, *Home-Office Ledger Control*, represents home-office equity in the branch or the branch payable to the home office. The debit balance in the Branch Ledger Control account should equal the credit balance in Home-Office Ledger Control.

Self-Study Questions

Test your understanding of the chapter by marking the best answer for each of the following questions:

1. Responsibility accounting is *(p. 1096)*
   a. An alternative to a standard cost system
   b. A system for assigning responsibility to managers and evaluating their progress
   c. A particular type of home-office/branch accounting system
   d. Designed without consideration of the business's organization structure

2. Which of the following departments is most likely to be a cost center? *(p. 1096)*
   a. Personnel Department
   b. Housewares Department of a Zellers store
   c. Sales office
   d. Manufacturing plant

3. Budgeted cost of goods sold was $30,000 and actual cost is $33,000. The variance is *(p. 1099)*
   a. 110 percent favorable
   b. 110 percent unfavorable
   c. 10 percent favorable
   d. 10 percent unfavorable

4. The key to the design of an effective responsibility accounting system is *(p. 1099)*
   a. Ability of the system to place blame when results are unfavorable
   b. Manager control over all aspects of the business in the department
   c. Gathering and communicating information to achieve the business's goals
   d. Use of a standard cost system

5. One of the more difficult accounting tasks in departmental accounting is *(p. 1100)*
   a. Measuring departmental gross margin
   b. Allocating direct costs to departments
   c. Allocating indirect costs to departments
   d. Assigning responsibility to department managers

6. Which of the following costs is the most difficult to allocate to departments? *(p. 1100)*
   a. Direct materials
   b. Janitorial services
   c. Merchandise purchases
   d. Direct labor

7. The most logical basis for allocating building depreciation to departments is *(pp. 1101–02)*
   a. Square metres of space
   b. Number of employees
   c. Hours used
   d. Building depreciation can be separately traced to each department

8. Which control device is a particular feature of branch accounting? *(p. 1105)*
   a. Responsibility assignment
   b. Reciprocal accounts
   c. Departmental accounting
   d. Cost allocation

9. Which of these accounts would be the most likely to appear in a branch-factory ledger? *(p. 1106)*
   a. Accounts Receivable
   b. Branch-Factory Ledger Control
   c. Common Stock
   d. Home-Office Ledger Control

10. A sales branch manages its own operations except for collections on account and cash payments for major expenses such as inventory purchases and salaries, which the home-office pays. Which entry would the branch make to record its salary expense? *(p. 1109)*

    a. Salary Expense   XXX
          Cash..   XXX

    b. Home-Office Ledger Control XXX
          Cash.. XXX
    c. Salary Expense XXX
          Branch Ledger Control XXX
    d. None of the above. The entry would appear on the home-office books only.

Answers to the Self-Study Questions are at the end of the chapter.

Accounting Vocabulary

allocation base *(p. 1100)*	expense allocation *(p. 1100)*	management by exception *(p. 1099)*
branch accounting *(p. 1105)*	factory ledger *(p. 1105)*	reciprocal accounts *(p. 1105)*
branch-factory ledger control *(p. 1106)*	home-office ledger *(p. 1105)*	responsibility accounting *(p. 1096)*
branch ledger *(p. 1105)*	home-office ledger control *(p. 1106)*	responsibility center *(p. 1096)*
cost allocation *(p. 1100)*		
direct expense *(p. 1100)*	indirect expense *(p. 1100)*	

ASSIGNMENT MATERIAL _____

Questions

1. Briefly describe responsibility accounting, giving examples of how managers use it in operating a business.

2. Which manager will control expenses better: Grant, whose performance is measured by his departmental sales, or Bruns, whose performance is gauged by her departmental income? Give your reason.

3. Identify three types of responsibility centers, giving examples of each and stating the information they report.

4. A company owns 13 Burger King restaurants in Fredericton, Moncton and Saint John, New Brunswick. In each city a local manager oversees operations. Starting at the individual store level, describe a likely flow of information based on responsibility accounting. What information would be reported?

5. What are the goals of management by exception?

6. What is the key to effective design of a responsibility accounting system?

7. What main question is a responsibility accounting system designed to answer? How can a responsibility accounting system be abused?

8. Distinguish between direct expenses and indirect expenses, giving examples of each type.

9. Identify a reasonable allocation base for the following indirect expenses: heating expense, depreciation of equipment used to manufacture products for three separate departments, and advertising expense.

10. Which of the following are likely to be direct expenses? Which are likely to be indirect expenses?
    a. Manufacturing labor
    b. Supervisor labor
    c. Advertising of a specific toy
    d. Cost of goods sold
    e. Depreciation of home-office building
    f. Janitorial services for a manufacturing plant
    g. Expenses of personnel department
    h. Advertising of a store-wide sale by a department store

11. Supplies are not charged to departments as used. Instead, supplies expense is allocated at the end of each period based on the period's sales. If a firm used supplies costing $900, and had sales of $5,000, $12,000 and $18,000 in departments X, Y and Z, respectively, how much supplies expense would be charged to each department?

12. How might rent be allocated in a department store with three floors, one of which is on ground level and opens onto a busy street?

13. Describe a plan for allocating the various components of general administrative expenses.

14. How does branch accounting differ from departmental accounting?

15. What are the special features of a branch accounting system?

16. How does the general ledger of a company with a branch accounting system differ from an ordinary general ledger?

17. What special account does a branch ledger contain? What special account does a home-office ledger contain? Indicate which account normally has a debit balance and which normally has a credit balance.

18. Consider the Branch-Factory Ledger Control account and the Home-Office Ledger Control account. Which account is more like an investment or receivable? Which is more like an owner equity account or payable? Which account is in the ledger of the home office? Which is in the branch ledger?

19. Briefly describe a branch accounting system for a company with two manufacturing plants in distant locations. Identify the special account on the books of the home office and the special account on the books of the branches.

20. A company manufactures its products at three plants. Which of the following transactions is likely to be recorded by the home office only, by the branch only, or by both the home office and the branch?
    a. Use of materials in production
    b. Sale of merchandise
    c. Payment of manufacturing payroll
    d. Purchase of direct materials
    e. Incurrence of overhead cost
    f. Collection of accounts receivable
    g. Shipment of finished goods to home-office warehouse

Exercises

Exercise 25-1   *Identifying different types of responsibility centers (L.O. 1)*

Identify each responsibility center as either a cost center, a profit center, or an investment center.

a. A branch manager's performance is judged by the ratio of the branch's net income to the home office's cost of the branch.

b. Accountants compile the cost of surgical supplies for evaluating the purchasing department of a hospital.

c. The sporting goods department reports both revenues and expenses.

d. The legal department of an insurance company prepares its budget and subsequent performance report based on its expected expenses for the year.

e. A charter airline records revenues and expenses for each airplane for each month. The airplane's performance report shows its ratio of operating income to average book value.

f. The manager of a Petro-Canada service station is evaluated based on the station's revenues and expenses.

Exercise 25-2 *Using responsibility accounting to report on profit centers at three levels* **(L.O. 2)**

Computer Concepts Ltd. has city managers for its Saskatoon, Prince Albert and Humboldt operations. These managers report to a provincial manager, who reports to the manager of the Prairies operations in Brandon, Manitoba. The Prairies manager has received the following data for June of the current year:

	The Prairies		
	Saskatchewan		
	Prince Albert and Humboldt	Saskatoon	The Prairies Totals Excluding Saskatchewan
Revenues, budget	$310,000	$1,800,000	$10,300,000
Expenses, budget	220,000	1,100,000	6,300,000
Revenues, actual	340,000	1,900,000	9,900,000
Expenses, actual..............	210,000	1,200,000	6,200,000

Required

Arrange the following data in a performance report similar to Exhibit 25-2. Show June results, in thousands of dollars, for Prince Albert, the province of Saskatchewan and the Prairies.

Exercise 25-3 *Preparing a four-column performance report* **(L.O. 2)**

Using the data of Exercise 25-2, prepare a performance report for June in the format illustrated on p. 1099. Show June results, in thousands of dollars, for Prince Albert and Humboldt, Saskatchewan and the Prairies. In each case, format your answer in four columns:

		Variance: Favorable	Variance: Percent of
Budget	Actual	(Unfavorable)	Budget

Exercise 25-4 *Allocating costs to departments* **(L.O. 3)**

The cost records of Cape Breton Manufacturing Corporation include the following selected indirect cost data for January of the current year:

Other labor..	$12,000
Equipment depreciation	6,000
Building depreciation..............................	3,600
Utilities	2,700
Selling expenses	24,000

Data for cost allocations:

	Department		
	A	B	C
Sales..	$60,000	$50,000	$90,000
Other labor — hours	400	500	100
Machine hours	300	450	150
Building — square metres...............................	9,000	3,000	1,500
Selling expense: allocate to departments in proportion to sales.			

Required

Show the allocation of these expenses to departments A, B and C for January.

Exercise 25-5 *Computing departmental rent expense (L.O. 3)*

Many department stores grant concessions to other companies to operate the store's shoe departments. Vogue Shoes Ltd. markets its shoes this way. Vogue sells ladies' shoes in a space occupying 50 square metres near the front door of a Zellers store. This location is three times as valuable as the average space in the store. Vogue's shoes for men occupy 20 square metres in a back corner of the ground floor, a space with average rental value. Children's shoes occupy 15 square metres on the third floor, which is only 30 percent as valuable as the average space in the store. The entire store has 5,000 square metres and monthly rent is $300,000.

Required

Compute Vogue's monthly rent expense.

Exercise 25-6 *Preparing a departmental income statement (L.O. 3, 4)*

Taylor Enterprises, Inc. has two departments, electronics and industrial. Taylor's income statement for 19X7 appears as follows:

Net sales..	$310,000
Cost of goods sold	116,000
Gross margin..	194,000
Operating expenses	
Salaries	70,000
Depreciation	15,000
Advertising...	6,000
Other..	10,000
Total operating expenses	101,000
Operating income....................................	$ 93,000

Cost of goods sold is distributed $42,000 for electronics and $74,000 for industrial products. Salaries are allocated to departments based on sales: electronics, $124,000; industrial, $186,000. Two thirds of advertising is spent on electronics. Depreciation is allocated based on square metre area: electronics has 2,800 square metres; industrial has 4,200 square metres. Other expenses are allocated based on number of employees, with an equal number working in each department.

Required

Prepare a departmental income statement showing revenues, expenses and operating income for Taylor's two departments.

Exercise 25-7 *Recording home-office and branch manufacturing transactions (L.O. 4, 5)*

McVey Lumber Limited manages operations from its home office in Chilliwack. Company sawmills, located in the province of British Columbia, are organized as branches. McVey uses a branch accounting system. The home office makes all purchases and sales, handles cash payments and cash receipts, and incurs all company liabilities. When a sawmill completes a custom job, it transfers the inventory to central warehouses, which the home office controls. On August 1 McVey Lumber's investment in the Prince George sawmill was $75,000. During August of the current year, the company completed the following transactions, certain of which related to the Prince George sawmill:

a. Direct materials purchased on account, $830.

b. Direct materials used in production, $1,090.

c. Sawmill payroll paid, $3,100.

d. Sawmill overhead applied, $4,600.

e. Goods shipped to central warehouse, $7,100.

f. Sales on account, $8,200.

g. Collections on account, $4,690.

Required

Journalize these transactions for the home office and the Prince George branch. Post to the reciprocal accounts and show that their balances at August 31 offset each other.

Exercise 25-8   *Recording home-office and branch sales-office transactions* **(L.O. 4, 5)**

Nye & Wheeler, Inc. has branch sales offices in Nova Scotia, Prince Edward Island and Newfoundland. The company uses a branch accounting system. The branches purchase and sell goods, pay bills, collect cash from customers, and incur selling expenses. The home office in Truro, Nova Scotia obtains outside financing as needed and advances cash to, and receives cash from, the branches. During a recent month, the company completed the following transactions:

a. Home office borrowed $7,000 from a bank, signing a note.

b. Home office advanced $2,250 to the Newfoundland branch.

c. Newfoundland branch purchased merchandise on account, $2,210 (debit Purchases).

d. Newfoundland branch paid selling expense, $60.

e. Newfoundland branch sold goods on account, $2,110.

f. Home office recorded depreciation of $1,040 on home-office building.

g. Newfoundland branch collected cash from customer, $930.

h. Newfoundland branch transferred $1,000 cash to home office.

Required

Journalize these transactions for the home office and the Newfoundland branch. Post to the reciprocal accounts and show that their balances offset each other.

Problems   *(Group A)*

Problem 25-1A   *Identifying different types of responsibility centers* **(L.O. 1)**

Identify by letter each of the following as being most likely a cost center, a profit center, or an investment center:

a. Surgery unit of a large dental practice

b. Personnel department of Bombardier

c. Accounts payable section of an accounting department

d. Proposed new office of a real estate firm

e. Branch warehouse of a carpet manufacturer

f. Marineland and Game Farm (a family amusement park)

g. Assembly-line supervisory employees

h. Service department of a stereo shop

i. Men's clothing in a department store

j. Canadian subsidiary of a Japanese company

k. Music director of a church or synagogue

l. Catering operation of an established restaurant

m. Executive director of a United Way agency

n. Different product lines of a gift shop

o. The CN Tower in Toronto

p. Work crews of a painting contractor

q. Investments department of a bank

r. Accounting department of a company

s. Eastern district of a salesperson's territory

t. Typesetting department of a printing company

Problem 25-2A   *Preparing a profit-center performance report* **(L.O. 2)**

Potpourri Gift Shops Corp. is organized with store managers reporting to a provincial manager, who in turn reports to the vice-president of marketing. The income statements of the Winnipeg store, all stores in Manitoba (including the Winnipeg store), and the company as a whole (including Manitoba stores) are summarized as follows for 19X6:

	Winnipeg	Manitoba	Companywide
Revenue and expenses			
Sales	$141,800	$1,647,000	$3,888,000
Expenses			
Provincial manager/ vice-president's office	—	59,000	116,000
Cost of goods sold	53,000	671,900	1,507,000
Salary expense	38,100	415,500	1,119,000
Depreciation	7,200	91,000	435,000
Utilities	3,800	46,200	260,000
Rent	2,400	34,700	178,000
Supplies	1,100	15,600	86,000
Total expenses	105,600	1,333,900	3,701,000
Operating income	$ 36,200	$ 313,100	$ 187,000

Budgeted amounts for 19X6 are as follows:

	Winnipeg	Manitoba	Companywide
Revenue and expenses			
Sales	$151,300	$1,769,700	$4,400,000
Expenses			
Provincial manager/ vice-president's office	—	65,600	118,000
Cost of goods sold	61,500	763,400	1,672,000
Salary expense	38,800	442,000	1,095,000
Depreciation	7,200	87,800	449,000
Utilities	4,700	54,400	271,000
Rent	2,800	32,300	174,000
Supplies	900	16,100	93,000
Total expenses	115,900	1,461,600	3,872,000
Operating income	$ 35,400	$ 308,100	$ 528,000

Required

1. Prepare a report for 19X6 that shows the performance of the Winnipeg store, all the stores in Manitoba and the company as a whole. Follow the format of Exhibit 25-2.

2. Identify the responsibility centers whose operating income exceeds budget and those whose operating income falls short of budget.

Problem 25-3A   *Preparing a profit-center performance report* **(L.O. 2)**

Maxwell Home Furnishings Ltd. is organized along product lines, with product managers reporting to department managers, who in turn report to the company vice-president. The vice-president, who has received the following data for August of the current year, needs a performance report to highlight the operating income of bedspreads, the bedding department and the company in total:

	Company Totals (amounts in thousands)		
	Bedding Department		
	Bedspreads	*Linens*	Other Departments
Revenues, actual..............	$3,700	$1,500	$6,500
Expenses, actual...............	2,100	800	3,100
Revenues, budget.............	3,300	1,400	7,100
Expenses, budget..............	1,600	700	3,600

Required

1. Prepare a performance report for August in a format similar to that on p. 1099. Show August operating income for bedspreads, the bedding department and the company as a whole.

2. Which responsibility centers exceeded budget? Which performed below budget?

Problem 25-4A   *Computing and allocating occupancy cost to a department* **(L.O. 3)**

Joske's Corp. occupies a six-story building (including the basement) in downtown Regina. Assume occupancy cost for a recent month included the following:

Depreciation — building........................	$ 93,200
Rent — store fixtures	24,700
Utilities..	21,300
Janitorial services	16,600
Total...	$155,800

Each floor of the building has 800 square metres, except for the second floor, which has 600 square metres. The company accountant computed the occupancy cost per square metre by dividing the total cost of $155,800 by 4,600 square metres. She charges occupancy to all company departments based on this $33.87 cost per square metre.

The manager of the Budget Buyer Department, located in the basement, objected. He cited a space-usage study conducted for the company by a real estate firm. It estimated that space in the basement is one fourth as valuable as street level space, one half as valuable as space on the second floor, and equal in value to the other floors.

Required

1. Based on the space-usage study, compute the occupancy cost of a square metre of space on each of Joske's floors. Round decimals to three places, and round the cost per square metre to the nearest cent.

2. The Budget Buyer Department occupies 550 square metres of the basement. How much occupancy cost should be charged to this department each month?

Problem 25-5A   *Preparing a departmental income statement* **(L.O. 3, 4)**

Adventure Travel Inc. is organized into a custom department and a group discount department. At August 31, the end of Adventure's fiscal year, the bookkeeper prepared the following trial balance, which includes the effects of year-end adjusting entries:

Cash	$ 1,300	
Receivables	24,600	
Supplies	3,800	
Prepaid expenses	1,700	
Building	70,500	
Accumulated depreciation — building		$ 20,900
Office furniture	38,100	
Accumulated depreciation — office furniture		7,300
Other assets	3,100	
Accounts payable		11,400
Accrued liabilities		6,900
Unearned service revenue		5,800
Long-term note payable		22,000
Owner equity		19,200
Custom travel service revenue		77,700
Group discount travel service revenue		107,300
Salary expense — travel agents	34,600	
Commission expense — travel agents	26,000	
Salary expense — office manager	25,000	
Salary expense — bookkeeper	16,800	
Lease expense — computer equipment	15,000	
Supplies expense	6,300	
Depreciation expense — office furniture	2,500	
Property tax expense	2,200	
Depreciation expense — building	2,100	
Interest expense	2,000	
Insurance expense	1,700	
Advertising expense	1,200	
Total	$278,500	$278,500

In January, Adventure hired a group travel specialist at an annual salary of $25,000. Remaining agent salaries of $9,600 go to part-time agents that handle custom travel plans. The office manager spends 60 percent of her time on group discount plans and 40 percent on custom travel planning. The bookkeeper spends approximately two thirds of his time on accounting for custom travel planning operations and the remainder on group discount plans. Adventure leases a computer that it uses 70 percent of the time for custom travel planning and 30 percent of the time for group discount packages. Insurance expense is evenly divided between the two departments. Interest expense relates to the note payable, which the company signed to purchase the building. The company allocates all other expenses based on relative service revenue.

Required

1. Prepare a departmental income statement through operating income.
2. Which department is more profitable? Was the decision to hire the group specialist wise? Give your reason.

Problem 25-6A *Preparing a budgeted departmental income statement* **(L.O. 3, 4)**

Chicosky's is a suburban hardware store with two departments. The most recent annual report to management follows:

Chicosky's
Departmental Income Statement
for the year ended January 31, 19X2

	Total	Dept. A	Dept. B
Sales revenue	$400,000	$300,000	$100,000
Expenses			
Cost of goods sold.........................	160,000	120,000	40,000
Sales salaries	41,000	28,000	13,000
Salary—store manager	35,000	17,500	17,500
Rent expense—building..............	16,000	8,000	8,000
Advertising	5,000	3,500	1,500
Property tax	3,000	1,500	1,500
Insurance.......................................	2,400	1,200	1,200
Depreciation—store fixtures.......	1,200	600	600
Supplies...	1,000	500	500
Interest..	800	400	400
Uncollectible accounts.................	600	300	300
Total expenses..............................	266,000	181,500	84,500
Operating income	$134,000	$118,500	$ 15,500

The company is considering opening a third department early in fiscal 19X3. To plan for the coming year, the store owner seeks your help in preparing a budgeted income statement. Your conversation with the owner reveals the following:

a. Management expects annual sales of the new department to be $90,000, with a gross profit percentage equal to that of the two existing departments.

b. Addition of a third department will also draw customers into Department A and should increase Department A sales by 25 percent. Sales of Department B are expected to increase by only 15 percent.

c. A salesperson can be hired for the new department at an annual salary of $16,000. Other salaries will increase by 5 percent.

d. Thus far, the company accountant has allocated all expenses except cost of goods sold, sales salaries and advertising equally to Departments A and B. The store owner decides that the equal allocation of indirect expenses to departments is inappropriate.

e. The store manager expects to spend equal amounts of time in the three departments during the coming year.

f. Department A is nearest the door and occupies 200 square metres of the most valuable space in the store. Department B also occupies 200 square metres, but its space is only half as valuable as that of Department A. The new department will take up 100 square metres with the same value per square metre as

Department A. Total rent expense under the long-term lease will be unchanged in 19X3.

g. Advertising expense will increase by 10 percent for the two existing departments. The company will commit $2,000 to advertising Department C merchandise.

h. Depreciation of new store fixtures for Department C will be $900. Other depreciation amounts will be unchanged.

i. Interest expense needed to finance Department C will be $1,000. The remaining 19X3 interest of $500 belongs equally to the other two departments.

j. All other expenses will increase by 8 percent and should be allocated to departments based on relative sales, except property tax, which is allocated on the same basis used for rent. Round percentages to three decimal places.

Required

1. Prepare a budgeted departmental income statement in multiple-step format for fiscal year 19X3 based on the preceding projections.

2. Based on your budget, would you recommend that Chicosky's add the new department? State your reasons.

Problem 25-7A *Recording home-office and branch transactions (L.O. 5)*

Empress Realty Ltd. has branch offices throughout Vancouver Island and uses a branch accounting system for control purposes. The home office has a separate Branch Ledger Control account for each branch, and the branches maintain branch ledgers. Branch ledgers contain only asset, liability and Home-Office Ledger Control accounts.

The home office advances cash to the branches. Branch managers have authority to purchase supplies and office furniture and equipment. They also pay utility and other branch-office expenses. However, only the home office records branch expenses. The branches collect commissions earned from their real estate sales and immediately transfer the cash to the home office. Only the home office records commissions revenue. The home office then pays half the commission directly to the agent who made the sale. During a recent month the following transactions occurred at the West Coast Branch of Empress Realty:

a. Home office advanced $6,900 to branch.

b. Branch sold a house, earning a commission and receiving cash of $4,000.

c. Branch transferred $4,000 to home office.

d. Home office paid commission to agent making sale in *b*, $2,000.

e. Branch paid office cleaning expense, $220.

f. Branch purchased office furniture on account, $1,400.

g. Branch paid cash for office supplies, $160.

h. Branch paid account payable, $700.

i. Branch transferred $2,300 cash to home office.

j. Branch recorded depreciation on office equipment, $380.

Required

1. Record these transactions in the home-office journal and in the branch journal.

2. Post the transactions to the reciprocal accounts. Show the balances of the reciprocal accounts after posting.

(Group B)

Problem 25-1B   *Identifying different types of responsibility centers* **(L.O. 1)**

Identify by letter each of the following as most likely being a cost center, a profit center, or an investment center:

a. Quality-control department of a manufacturing company

b. Top management of a company

c. Central region of Four Seasons Hotels

d. Editorial department of *The Financial Post*

e. A small clothing boutique

f. Payroll department of a university

g. Different product lines of a furniture manufacturer

h. Job superintendents of a home builder

i. A real estate firm

j. Fast-food restaurants under the supervision of a regional manager

k. European subsidiary of a Canadian company

l. Children's nursery in a church or synagogue

m. Lighting department in a Bay store

n. Personnel department of Coca-Cola Ltd.

o. Service department of an established automobile dealership

p. Proposed new office of a public accounting firm

q. Branch offices of a bank

r. Police department of a city

s. Canadian Airlines International Ltd.

t. Consumer Complaint Division of Canadian Tire Corp.

Problem 25-2B   *Preparing a profit-center performance report* **(L.O. 2)**

EyeCare Specialists Inc. is a chain of optical shops that dispense eyeglasses. Each store has a manager who answers to a city manager, who in turn reports to a provincial manager. The income statements of Store No. 24, all stores in the Toronto area (including Store No. 24), and all stores in the province of Ontario (including all Toronto stores) are summarized as follows for April:

	Store No. 24	Toronto	Province of Ontario
Revenue and expenses			
Sales...	$42,900	$486,000	$3,264,500
Expenses			
City/provincial manager office...	—	16,000	41,000
Cost of goods sold.........................	14,000	171,300	1,256,800
Salary expense	5,300	37,500	409,700
Depreciation..................................	3,000	26,100	334,000
Utilities...	2,700	19,300	245,600
Rent	1,900	16,400	186,000
Supplies	700	5,500	60,700
Total expenses.................................	27,600	292,100	2,533,800
Operating income.............................	$15,300	$193,900	$ 730,700

Budgeted amounts for April are as follows:

	Store No. 24	Toronto	Province of Ontario
Revenue and expenses			
Sales..	$42,000	$468,000	$3,143,000
Expenses			
City/provincial manager office ..	—	15,000	43,000
Cost of goods sold.........................	14,200	172,800	1,209,000
Salary expense	5,600	37,900	412,000
Depreciation..................................	3,500	25,400	320,000
Utilities	2,100	17,000	240,000
Rent	1,600	15,700	181,000
Supplies	800	5,900	60,000
Total expenses......................................	27,800	289,700	2,465,000
Operating income.................................	$14,200	$178,300	$ 678,000

Required

1. Prepare a report for April that shows the performance of Store No. 24, all the stores in the Toronto area, and all the stores in the province of Ontario. Follow the format of Exhibit 25-2.

2. Identify the responsibility centers whose operating income exceeds budget and those whose operating income falls short of budget.

Problem 25-3B *Preparing a profit-center performance report* (L.O. 2)

Software Designers Corp. is organized along product lines, with product managers reporting to division managers, who in turn report to the company vice-president. The vice-president, who has received the following data for November of the current year, needs a performance report to highlight the operating income of audio products, the audio-video division, and the company in total:

	Company Totals		
	Audio-Video Division		
	Audio Products	Video Products	Other Divisions
Revenues, actual.................	$212,000	$867,000	$788,000
Expenses, actual	138,000	516,000	374,000
Revenues, budget..............	218,000	907,000	760,000
Expenses, budget	147,000	505,000	368,000

Required

1. Prepare a performance report for November in a format similar to that on p. 1099. Show November operating income in thousands of dollars for audio products, the audio-video division, and the company as a whole.

2. Which responsibility centers exceeded budget? Which performed below budget?

Problem 25-4B *Computing and allocating occupancy cost to a department* (L.O. 3)

Modern Electric Company Ltd. occupies three floors in a building in downtown Halifax. Occupancy cost for a recent quarter included the following items and amounts:

Rent	$41,000
Utilities..	9,300
Janitorial services	8,200
Depreciation-building fixtures..............	3,500
Total..	$62,000

Modern occupies 500 square metres on the street level, 300 square metres on the second floor and 400 square metres of the basement. The company accountant computed the occupancy cost per square metre by dividing the total cost of $62,000 by 1,200 square metres. He charges occupancy to all company departments based on this $51.67 cost per square metre.

The manager of the industrial products department, located in the basement, objected. She cited an engineering study conducted for the company by a real estate firm. It estimated that space in the basement is one half as valuable as second-floor space and one fourth as valuable as space on the street level.

Required

1. Based on the engineering study, compute the occupancy cost of a square metre of space on each of Modern's three floors. Round decimals to three places, and round the cost per square metre to the nearest cent.

2. The industrial products department occupies 220 square metres of the basement. How much occupancy cost should be charged to this department each quarter?

Problem 25-5B *Preparing a departmental income statement* **(L.O. 3, 4)**

Mistletoe Express is organized into a printing department and a copy department. At May 31, the end of Mistletoe's fiscal year, the bookkeeper prepared the following trial balance, which includes the following effects of year-end adjusting entries:

Cash	$ 2,400	
Receivables..	3,600	
Supplies	25,400	
Prepaid expenses...	1,100	
Land	25,900	
Building...	41,200	
Accumulated depreciation — building		$ 16,200
Printing equipment..	33,700	
Accumulated depreciation — printing equipment.		9,600
Other assets..	4,700	
Accounts payable..		3,200
Accrued liabilities		1,600
Unearned printing revenue.......................................		2,200
Long-term note payable...		15,000
Owner equity...		61,400
Printing revenue...		67,100
Copy revenue		54,900
Salary expense — machine operators	23,600	
Salary expense — store manager...............................	22,900	
Salary expense — bookkeeper	18,300	
Lease expense — copy equipment	12,000	
Supplies expense..	9,000	
Property tax expense	2,300	
Insurance expense..	1,600	
Depreciation expense — building	1,400	
Depreciation expense — printing equipment..........	1,400	
Interest expense..	400	
Uncollectible account expense	300	
Total...	$231,200	$231,200

Mistletoe owns its printing equipment and leases a copier from Xerox Canada. Established printing customers do business with the company on a credit basis, but copy services are performed for cash only. Insurance expense is evenly divided between departments. The bookkeeper spends approximately two thirds of his time on accounts receivable and other printing department matters and the remainder on general accounting. Interest expense relates to the note payable, which the company signed to purchase the printing equipment. The store manager spends 60 percent of her time on printing and 40 percent on copy services. The company allocates all other expenses based on service revenue.

Required

1. Prepare a departmental income statement through operating income.
2. Which department has the higher operating income? What factor contributes most to the profitability difference between departments?

Problem 25-6B   *Preparing a budgeted departmental income statement* **(L.O. 3, 4)**

Goldwyn's Ltd. is a neighborhood clothing store with two departments. The most recent annual report to management appears in the following:

Goldwyn's
Departmental Income Statement
for the year ended January 31, 19X7

	Total	Men's	Women's
Sales revenue	$317,700	$141,800	$175,900
Expenses			
Cost of goods sold	152,500	68,050	84,450
Sales salaries	44,300	20,800	23,500
Salary — store manager	32,900	16,450	16,450
Rent expense — building	14,000	7,000	7,000
Advertising	8,000	2,400	5,600
Property tax	2,000	1,000	1,000
Insurance	1,800	900	900
Depreciation — store fixtures	1,700	850	850
Supplies	1,000	500	500
Interest	600	300	300
Uncollectible accounts	300	150	150
Total expenses	259,100	118,400	140,700
Operating income	$ 58,600	$ 23,400	$ 35,200

Goldwyn's is considering opening a children's department early in fiscal 19X8. To plan for the coming year, the store owner seeks your help in preparing a budgeted income statement. Your conversation with the owner reveals the following:

a. Management expects annual sales of the new department to be $75,000, with a gross profit percentage equal to that of the two existing departments.

b. Addition of a children's department will draw more women than men into the store and should increase sales of women's wear by 20 percent. Sales of men's wear are expected to increase by only 5 percent.

c. A salesperson can be hired for the children's department at an annual salary of $17,000. Other salaries will increase by 6 percent.

d. Thus far, the Goldwyn's accountant has allocated all expenses except cost of goods sold, sales salaries and advertising equally to the men's and women's departments. The store owner decides that the equal allocation of indirect expenses to the two departments is inappropriate.

e. The store manager expects to spend equal amounts of time in the three departments during the coming year.

f. The women's department is nearest the door and occupies 300 square metres of the most valuable space in the store. Men's wear also occupies 300 square metres, but its space is only two thirds as valuable as that of women's wear. The new children's department will take up 100 square metres with the same value per square metre as the women's department. Total rent expense under the long-term lease will be unchanged in 19X8.

g. Advertising expense will increase by 10 percent for the two existing departments. The company will commit $2,000 to advertising the children's department.

h. Depreciation of new store fixtures for the children's department will be $900. Other depreciation amounts will be unchanged.

i. Interest expense needed to finance the children's department will be $1,000. The remaining 19X8 interest of $600 belongs equally to the other two departments.

j. All other expenses will increase by 10 percent and should be allocated to departments based on relative sales, except property tax, which is allocated on the same basis used for rent. Round percentages to three decimal places.

Required

1. Prepare a budgeted departmental income statement in multiple-step format for fiscal year 19X8 based on the preceding projections.

2. Based on your budget, would you recommend that Goldwyn's open the new department? State your reasons.

Problem 25-7B   *Recording home-office and branch transactions* **(L.O. 5)**

South Shore Realty Corp. has branch offices throughout Nova Scotia and uses a branch accounting system for control purposes. The home office has a separate Branch Ledger Control account for each branch, and the branches maintain branch ledgers. Branch ledgers contain asset, liability and Home-Office Ledger-Control accounts.

The home office advances cash to the branches. Branch managers have the authority to purchase supplies and office furniture and equipment. They also pay utility and other branch office expenses. However, only the home office records branch expenses. The branches collect commissions earned from their real estate sales and immediately transfer the cash to the home office. Only the home office records commissions revenue. The home office then pays a commission directly to the agent who made the sale. During a recent month the following transactions occurred at the Chester Branch of South Shore Realty:

a. Home office advanced $5,000 to branch.

b. Branch purchased office supplies on account, $400.

c. Branch paid cash for a file cabinet, $700.

d. Branch paid account payable, $600.

e. Branch sold a house, earning a commission and receiving cash of $4,700.

f. Branch transferred $4,700 to home office.

g. Home office paid commission to agent making sale in *e*, $3,100.

h. Branch transferred $1,000 cash to home office.

i. Branch paid electricity expense, $300.

j. Branch recorded depreciation on office equipment, $600.

Required

1. Record these transactions in the home-office journal and in the branch journal.
2. Post the transactions to the reciprocal accounts. Show the balances of the reciprocal accounts after posting.

Extending Your Knowledge

Decision Problems

1. Evaluating cost allocation and departmental performance (L.O. 2, 3, 4)

Stuarts Inc. is a jewelry store located on the main floor of a four-star hotel in downtown Toronto. It opened in January of the current year. The store has two entrances, one off the lobby and the other off the street. Stuarts is one of many exclusive stores on the street. There are display windows beside both entrances.

Stuarts places particular departments close to each entrance. Customers entering the store from the street will see the watch department first. Entering from the lobby brings the customer into the diamond department. The watch and diamond departments occupy equal space in the store, and both have the same number of staff behind the counter. The silver and costume jewelry departments occupy relatively little space in the store compared to diamonds and watches.

It is now December, and the Stuarts accountant has prepared a departmental statement for presentation to George Stuart, the president.

	Diamonds	Watches	Other
Stuarts Inc.			
Departmental Income Statement			
for the year ended December 31, 19X7			
('000)			
Sales revenue..	$1,050	$675	$180
Expenses			
Cost of goods sold..........................	450	337	110
Sales commissions..........................	105	54	4
Salary — manager..........................	22	22	22
Rent expense	72	46	12
Advertising	70	0	0
Insurance	10	6	3
Depreciation — fixtures	8	8	8
Office expenses..............................	12	12	12
Income before interest and taxes.	$ 301	$190	$ 9

Required

Evaluate the presentation of the statement. If necessary, redraft the statement. Clearly state any assumptions you make. Analyze the profitability of Stuarts' departments.

2. Using departmental operating income to decide on an advertising campaign (L.O. 3, 4)

The accountant of Mazelli Oldsmobile-Cadillac Ltd. has produced the following annual summary of revenue and expense information for management:

	Oldsmobiles	Cadillacs
Units sold..	200	80
Average selling price per unit...............................	$25,000	$38,000
Average cost per unit	20,200	31,300
Average direct expense per unit...........................	1,900	2,320
Average variable indirect expense per unit........	500	1,200

Ron Mazelli, owner of the business, is considering an advertising campaign to increase sales and operating income. He estimates that additional advertising cost of $25,000 will increase sales of the automobile advertised by 30 automobiles each year. However, because Mazelli is the only Oldsmobile-Cadillac dealer in the area, any increase in Oldsmobile sales is likely to decrease sales of Cadillacs by an equal number. Likewise, an increase in Cadillac sales is likely to cause an equal decrease in Oldsmobile sales. Mazelli's fixed expenses, other than the $25,000 of advertising, will be unaffected by this decision.

Required

Prepare an analysis to show whether Mazelli should advertise Oldsmobiles or Cadillacs, or not undertake the advertising campaign at all. Base your decision on operating income (ignoring fixed expenses other than the $25,000 advertising) under three alternatives: (1) no new advertising, (2) advertise Oldsmobiles, or (3) advertise Cadillacs.

Ethical Issue

Bertha Bumiller manages the hosiery department of McRae's Department Store Inc. in the Metro Mall of Uxbridge, Ontario. Bertha buys merchandise, hires sales clerks, arranges displays, and takes the inventory. Her annual bonus depends on departmental income before income tax. The Bumiller family is planning a Christmas vacation to the Virgin Islands and is counting on Bertha's bonus. Sales for 1993 have been sluggish, so Bertha slightly overstates ending inventory.

Required

1. Specify the effect of the inventory overstatement on cost of goods sold, gross margin, income before income tax, and Bertha's bonus.
2. Is overstating ending inventory unethical? Who is helped and who is harmed by Bertha's action?

Answers to Self-Study Questions

1. b
2. a
3. d ($33,000 − $30,000 = $3,000;
    $3,000/$30,000 = 10 percent unfavorable)
4. c
5. c

6. b
7. a
8. b
9. d
10. d

Chapter 26

Special Decisions
and Capital Budgeting

Robert Echols, manager of the engineering department of Schaaf Tool Limited, closed his office door and strode over to his desk. He had only 48 hours to decide whether to recommend the purchase of a robotic stamping machine.
The stamping machine, designed to replace four-year-old general-purpose equipment, could be purchased for $850,000, delivered and installed. The older general-purpose equipment could be sold to a nearby company for $100,000.

Schaaf executives, Echols realized, demanded capital expenditures of this great an amount to generate at least a 15 percent return on a discounted basis. He believed that now would be a good time to buy the machine. The industry to which Schaaf sold its products and services was booming. Also, the prices of robotic stamping machines had dropped recently. It was likely that they would go up again within the next year. What should Echols recommend? Keep the old machine or purchase the new?

Should we sell 50,000 units of our product for $9 each — a price slightly below our cost? Should we make a special part used in our manufacturing process, or should we buy the part from an outside supplier? Should we drop the women's clothing line altogether? These are examples of special decisions that managers make. They are more far-reaching than day-to-day decisions, like whether to work overtime, to accept a rush job, or to change the schedule for repairing equipment. This chapter shows how to use accounting data to make special decisions with long-run effects on the business.

Relevant Information for Decision-Making

The main financial goals in business are to earn a profit, to achieve a positive cash-flow, and to have a strong financial position. Decisions center on how to achieve these goals. Decision-making includes choosing among several courses of action, which means managers must make comparisons. The process has two steps: (1) identifying the information useful for making the decision, and (2) analyzing the information to compare alternatives.

OBJECTIVE 1

Identify the relevant information for a special business decision

Relevant information is the expected future data that differ between the alternative courses of action. Which alternative will increase sales more? Which alternative will decrease expenses by a greater amount? By studying the expected future amounts resulting from the alternative actions, the manager can decide which action will help the business reach its goals.

Not all data influence a manager. Irrelevant data will not influence a decision. For example, in some situations the cost of fixed overhead will not change regardless of the action the manager takes. The manager, then, need not consider fixed overhead in making the decision. Determining which information is relevant — which data make a difference — is as important a skill as being able to analyze the information.

Let us consider an illustration of decision analysis using relevant information. Suppose Pringle Woolen Mills Ltd. is deciding whether to use pure wool or a wool-polyester blend in the manufacture of a line of sweaters. Pringle predicts the following costs under the two alternatives:

	Wool	Wool Blend	Cost Difference
Expected manufacturing cost per sweater:			
Direct material...	$10	$6	$4
Direct labor	2	2	—
Total cost of direct material and direct labor	$12	$8	$4

Assume cost is the chief consideration in this decision. The cost of direct material is relevant because this cost differs between alternatives (the wool costs more than the wool blend). The labor cost is irrelevant because there is no difference in its cost, whichever material is used.

We can compute the $4 cost difference between the alternatives either from the cost of direct material only or from total cost. It is helpful to know that there is a $4 total cost difference between the two alternatives. But it is more helpful for managers to know that the $4 cost difference results from the materials, not from labor. Failure to identify the reason for the difference may lead managers to make an unwise decision.

Let us emphasize this important point about special decision analysis: relevant information is *expected future data that differ between alternative courses of action*. Managers should base their decisions on the expected future data rather than on historical data.

Historical data are usually supplied by the accounting system and are often useful guides to predictions. However, bear in mind that historical data by themselves are irrelevant. They are useful only to the extent that managers use them to help predict future data.

This approach to making decisions is called the *relevant information* approach. This approach applies to a wide variety of decisions, regardless of the specific characteristics of the particular situation. We now turn to a number of special decisions.

Special Sales Order

Torino Limited, a manufacturer of automobile parts, ordinarily sells oil filters for $3.20 each. A mail-order company has offered Torino $35,000 for 20,000 oil filters. That works out to a special sale price of $1.75 per oil filter ($35,000/20,000 = $1.75). This sale will not affect regular business in any way, it will not change fixed costs, it will not require any additional variable selling and administrative expense, and it will put idle manufacturing capacity to use. Torino's total manufacturing cost of an oil filter is $2.00. Should Torino accept the special order and make the sale at $1.75? At first glance, the answer appears to be no, because each oil filter costs $2.00. But more thought must go into making this decision.

To set the stage for the analysis, let us examine Torino's income statement. Exhibit 26-1 presents the income statement in two different formats. The income statement on

> **OBJECTIVE 2**
>
> Make seven types of special business decisions

EXHIBIT 26-1 *Functional Format and Contribution Margin Format for the Income Statement*

Torino Limited
Income Statement
for the year ended December 31, 19X2

Functional Format		Contribution Margin Format		
Sales..............................	$800,000	Sales		$800,000
Less manufacturing		Less variable expenses		
cost of goods sold	500,000	Manufacturing..............	$300,000	
Gross margin..........................	300,000	Selling and		
Less selling and		administrative	75,000	375,000
administrative		Contribution margin.........		425,000
expenses............................	200,000	Less fixed expenses		
		Manufacturing..............	200,000	
		Selling and		
		administrative	125,000	325,000
Operating income..................	$100,000	Operating income.............		$100,000

the left is the standard format presented to shareholders, creditors and other parties outside the company. It is also called a *functional* income statement because it categorizes expenses by manufacturing and selling and administrative functions. The contribution margin format on the right categorizes expenses primarily as variable and fixed. The contribution margin format is more useful for special decision analysis because it highlights how costs and income are affected by decisions. Recall that the contribution margin is revenue minus all variable expenses.

In this illustration, assume that Torino made and sold 250,000 oil filters. Under the functional costing approach, the manufacturing cost per unit is $2.00 ($500,000/250,000 = $2.00). But the contribution margin approach shows that the variable manufacturing cost per unit is $1.20 ($300,000/250,000 = $1.20). We now answer the key question facing Torino: What difference would the special sale make to the company's operating income?

Correct Analysis: Contribution Margin Approach

The correct analysis concentrates on the differences in revenues, expenses, and operating income, as Exhibit 26-2 shows:

EXHIBIT 26-2   *Quick Summary of Special Sales Order Analysis*

Expected increase in revenues — sale of 20,000 oil filters × $1.75 each.	$35,000
Expected increase in expenses — variable manufacturing expenses:	
20,000 oil filters × $1.20 each..	24,000
Expected increase in operating income..	$11,000

This special sale is expected to increase revenues by $35,000. The only cost affected by the sale is variable manufacturing expense, which is expected to increase by $24,000. Torino management predicts that the special sales order will increase operating income by $11,000. Fixed expenses do not enter the analysis because they do not change. Variable selling and administrative expenses are unchanged because Torino has to make no special effort to get the sale. To make the decision, Torino should compare the special sale price to total variable cost of producing and selling the goods. As long as the increase in revenues exceeds the increase in variable expenses, there is a contribution to fixed expenses and profits.

Exhibit 26-3 gives Torino's income statements both without the special sales order (column 1) and with it (column 2). It shows operating income under both courses of action. Column 3 of Exhibit 26-3 repeats the quick summary by showing the differences caused by the special sales order. The quick summary presents the result of accepting the special sales order, an $11,000 increase in operating income.

You have just seen two correct ways of deciding whether to accept or reject the special sales order at a price less than total cost per unit: (1) a quick summary of differences (Exhibit 26-2) and (2) total revenues, expenses and operating income under both courses of action (Exhibit 26-3). Whether to use a quick summary or a total analysis depends on the question you are addressing. The summary answers this question: What will be the *difference* in revenues, expenses and operating income, if the business accepts the special order? The total analysis shows the summary of differences and answers an additional question: What will total revenues, expenses, and operating income be under the alternative courses of action? To accept or reject the special sales order can be decided from either analysis.

EXHIBIT 26-3   *Total Special Order Analysis: Income Statements Without and With the Special Order*

	Torino Limited Income Statement for the year ended December 31, 19X2			
	1 Without Special Order, 250,000 Units	**2** With Special Order, 270,000 Units	**3** Special-Order Difference, 20,000 Units	
			Total	**Per Unit**
Sales	$800,000	$835,000	$35,000	$1.75
Variable expenses				
Manufacturing	$300,000	$324,000	$24,000	$1.20
Selling and administrative	75,000	75,000	—	—
Total variable expenses	375,000	399,000	24,000	1.20
Contribution margin	425,000	436,000	11,000	.55
Fixed expenses				
Manufacturing	200,000	200,000	—	—
Selling and administrative	125,000	125,000	—	—
Total fixed expenses	325,000	325,000	—	—
Operating income	$100,000	$111,000	$11,000	$ .55

Incorrect Analysis: Ignoring the Nature of Fixed Costs

Let us look at an incorrect analysis of the Torino special sales order situation. Functional costing, shown on the left-hand side of Exhibit 26-1, leads to an incorrect measure of the change in expenses resulting from the sale.

> **OBJECTIVE 3**
>
> Explain the difference between correct analysis and incorrect analysis of a particular business decision

Total manufacturing costs	$ 500,000
Units produced	÷250,000
Total cost per unit ($500,000/250,000)	$ 2.00
Expected increase in revenues —	
sale of 20,000 oil filters × $1.75 each	$ 35,000
Expected increase in expenses — total manufacturing expenses:	
20,000 oil filters × $2.00 each	40,000
Expected decrease in operating income	$ (5,000)

A manager following this approach reasons that it costs $2.00 to make an oil filter. In this view, it is unprofitable to sell the product for less than $2.00. The flaw in this analysis arises from treating a fixed cost as though it changes in total like a variable cost. To manufacture one additional oil filter would increase Torino's cost only by the variable manufacturing expense of $1.20. Fixed expenses are irrelevant to the decision analysis because Torino will incur the fixed expenses whether or not the company accepts the special sales order. The addition of 20,000 oil filters will *not* add to *total* fixed expenses. As volume changes, manufacturing costs will increase at the rate of $1.20 per unit, not $2.00 per unit. In this analysis, the variable expenses are relevant, and the fixed expenses are irrelevant.

Short-Run versus Long-Run: Other Factors to Consider

The special sales order analysis focused on short-run factors — the expected effect on operating income. We must also consider long-run factors. What will be the impact on customers? Will acceptance of the order at $1.75 per unit hurt Torino's ability to make sales at the standard price of $3.20? Will regular customers find out about the special price and balk at paying the regular price? How will competitors react? Will they view this sale as the start of a price war?

Accepting the order yields an $11,000 advantage in operating income. Will potential disadvantages offset this $11,000? The sales manager may think so and reject the order. In turning away the business, the manager is saying that the company is better off passing up $11,000 now to protect its long-run market position. Rejecting the special sales order is like making an $11,000 "investment" in the company's long-run future.

Deletion of Products, Departments, Territories: Fixed Costs Unchanged _____

To analyze whether a company should drop a product line, a department or a territory, let us use the Torino Limited data. Assume that Torino is already operating at the 270,000-unit level, as shown in column 2 of Exhibit 26-3. Suppose Torino is considering dropping the air cleaner product line, which makes up $35,000 (20,000 units) of the company's sales. A manager is given an income statement divided by product line as follows:

		Product Line	
	Total	Oil Filters	Air Cleaners
Units	270,000	250,000	20,000
Sales	$835,000	$800,000	$35,000
Variable expenses.....................................	399,000	375,000	24,000
Contribution margin	436,000	425,000	11,000
Fixed expenses			
Manufacturing	200,000	185,185*	14,815*
Selling and administrative	125,000	115,741**	9,259**
Total fixed expenses	325,000	300,926	24,074
Operating income (loss)............................	$111,000	$124,074	$(13,074)

  * $200,000/270,000 units = $.74074 per unit; 250,000 units × $.74074 = $185,185; 20,000 units × $.74074 = $14,815

** $125,000/270,000 units = $.46296 per unit; 250,000 units × $.46296 = $115,741; 20,000 units × $.46296 = $9,259

In determining cost per unit, Torino, like many companies, allocates fixed expenses to units in proportion to the number of units sold. For example, the data show that Torino sold 270,000 units of its products altogether. Total fixed manufacturing expenses of $200,000 divided by 270,000 units equals fixed manufacturing cost of $.74074 per unit. Applying this unit cost to the 250,000 units of the oil filter product line allocates fixed manufacturing cost of $185,185 to this product. The same procedure allocates fixed manufacturing cost of $14,815 to air cleaners. Fixed selling and administrative expenses are allocated in the same manner. Using this allocation method, we see that air cleaners have an operating loss of $13,074. Should the air cleaner product line be dropped?

This illustration is basically the same example we studied for the special sales order. The relevant items are the changes in revenues and expenses. But now we are

EXHIBIT 26-4   *Deletion of a Product: Fixed Costs Unchanged*

Expected decrease in revenues		
Deletion of sales of air cleaners: 20,000 units × $1.75 each		$35,000
Expected decrease in expenses		
Deletion of variable manufacturing expenses:		
20,000 units × $1.20 each		24,000
Expected decrease in operating income		$11,000

considering a decrease in volume instead of an increase. The difference between the change in revenues and the change in expenses is the change in operating income, as shown in Exhibit 26-4. Again, only the variable expenses are relevant to the decision. In the short run, dropping air cleaners would decrease operating income by $11,000, the contribution margin of the air cleaners. This analysis suggests that Torino should not drop air cleaners.

The decision of whether to delete a product is based on the same analysis used for the special sales order. The only difference is that deleting products leads to decreases in revenues and expenses, whereas accepting a special sales order leads to increased revenues and expenses. Decisions in both cases are based on the expected change in operating income.

Deletion of Products, Departments, Territories: Fixed Costs Changed

In our two examples total fixed expenses have not changed. However, do not jump to the conclusion that fixed costs are always irrelevant. The following example illustrates the role of fixed costs in special decision analysis.

Suppose Torino Limited employs an engineer to improve the efficiency of the air cleaner product line. This employee is paid a fixed fee of $12,000, which can be avoided if the company phases out air cleaners. The question facing management is whether to drop air cleaners. To make this decision, Torino managers analyze all costs, fixed and variable, affected by the decision. Exhibit 26-5 shows the analysis.

EXHIBIT 26-5   *Deletion of a Product: Fixed Costs Changed*

Expected decrease in revenues		
Deletion of sales of air cleaners.....................................		$35,000
Expected decrease in expenses		
Variable manufacturing expenses...............................	$24,000	
Fixed expenses — engineer fee	12,000	
Expected decrease in total expenses..........................		36,000
Expected increase in operating income		$ 1,000

The analysis suggests that operating income will increase by $1,000 if Torino drops air cleaners. In this situation, fixed expenses are relevant, and so the change in the fixed cost must enter the analysis. Special decisions should consider all costs that management expects to be affected by the situation. Managers must ask, What costs — fixed *and* variable — will change?

Which Product to Emphasize

Companies must decide which products to emphasize and which to de-emphasize. This decision has a profound impact on profits. If salespersons push a product with a low profit margin, the company's operating income may decrease even though they succeed in selling the product. How should a manager decide which product to emphasize? Decisions like this are important because of limited sales staff, store display space, and advertising budgets.

Assume a clothing manufacturer has two products, shirts and slacks. The following data are relevant:

	Product	
	Shirts	**Slacks**
Per unit		
Selling price...	$15	$20
Variable expenses...	6	16
Contribution margin...	$ 9	$ 4
Contribution margin ratio		
Shirts: $9/$15...	60%	
Slacks: $4/$20...		20%

The data suggest that shirts are more profitable than slacks. But an important piece of information has been withheld — the time it takes to manufacture each product. This factor is called the *constraint*, *limiting factor*, or *scarce resource*.

The **limiting factor**, or **constraint**, is the item that restricts production or sales. In some companies, the constraint is production. The factory or the labor force may be unable to produce more than a specified maximum number of units. This constraint (the limit to how much the labor force can produce) may be stated in terms of labor hours, machine hours, materials, or square metres of shelf space. (For example, storage may be limited to 5,000 square metres of space in a warehouse.) These factors vary from company to company, depending on its line of business. Other companies are constrained by sales. Competition may be stiff, and the business may be able to sell only so many units. In other companies, the constraint is time, as we see in the following example: Suppose the company can produce three pairs of slacks or one shirt per hour. This company has 20,000 hours of capacity. Which product should the company emphasize?

The way to maximize profits for a given capacity is to obtain the highest possible contribution margin per unit of the limiting factor (in our example, direct labor

EXHIBIT 26-6   *Which Product to Emphasize*

	Product	
	Shirts	**Slacks**
(1) Units that can be produced each hour.................	1	3
(2) Contribution margin per unit...............................	× $9	× $4
(3) Contribution margin per hour (1) × (2)	$9	$12
Capacity: Number of hours	× 20,000	× 20,000
Total contribution margin for capacity................	$180,000	$240,000

hours). The analysis includes two steps. First, determine the contribution margin per unit of the limiting factor. Second, multiply this unit contribution margin by the company's capacity, stated in the number of units of the limiting factor.

Exhibit 26-6 shows how to decide which product to emphasize when there is a scarce resource. Slacks should be emphasized because they contribute more profit per hour. When the limiting factor is a part of the analysis, it is clear that this business should push slacks.

Make or Buy

Manufactured goods often include specialized parts. Overhead garage doors, for example, are activated by electronic controls. A garage door manufacturer may face this question: Should we manufacture the control device ourselves or buy it from an outside supplier? A furniture company may ask: Should we stain, lacquer and finish the furniture we manufacture, or should we hire an outsider for the finish work? Assuming quality is unaffected, at the heart of the make-or-buy decision is *how best to use available facilities.*

Let us see how to answer the make-or-buy question. Torino Limited's production process uses Part No. 4, which has the following manufacturing costs for 250,000 parts:

	Total Cost (250,000 Units)
Part No. 4 costs	
Direct material	$ 40,000
Direct labor	20,000
Variable overhead	15,000
Fixed overhead	50,000
Total manufacturing cost	$125,000
Cost per unit of Part No. 4 ($125,000/250,000)	$.50

Another manufacturer offers to sell Torino the same part for $.37 a unit. Should Torino make Part No. 4 or buy it from the outside supplier? Torino's $.50 unit cost of manufacturing the part is $.13 higher than the $.37 cost of buying it outside. At first glance, it appears that Torino should purchase Part No. 4 from the outsider. But the correct answer to a make-or-buy question is rarely as clear as this comparison suggests. The key to making the correct decision lies in analyzing the difference in expected future costs between the alternatives. Which costs listed above will differ depending on whether Torino makes or buys Part No. 4?

Assume that by purchasing the part from an outsider, Torino can avoid all variable manufacturing costs and reduce the fixed overhead cost by $10,000. (Fixed overhead will decrease to $40,000.) Exhibit 26-7 shows the difference in cost between the make-and-buy alternatives.

It would be cheaper to make the part than to buy it outside. Fixed overhead represents a significant amount of cost even in the buy alternative. The total cost savings from making 250,000 units of Part No. 4 is $7,500, which is $.03 per unit.

This example shows that fixed costs are relevant to a special decision if fixed costs differ between the alternatives. In this instance, fixed costs differ by $10,000. In these situations, this $10,000 amount is often called *avoidable* fixed overhead.

EXHIBIT 26-7 *Make or Buy*

	Make Part	Buy Part	Cost to Make minus Cost to Buy
Part No. 4 costs			
Direct material.................................	$ 40,000	$ —	$40,000
Direct labor	20,000	—	20,000
Variable overhead	15,000	—	15,000
Fixed overhead..............................	50,000	40,000	10,000
Purchase price from outsider			
(250,000 × $.37)	—	92,500	(92,500)
Total cost of Part No. 4	$125,000	$132,500	$(7,500)
Cost per unit: 250,000 units	$.50	$.53	$(.03)

Best Use of Facilities

The cost data in the make-or-buy decision indicate that making the part is the right decision. As we mention in that discussion, the focus is on making the best use of available facilities over a particular planning horizon. This decision is illustrated further with a make-or-buy decision that includes three alternative courses of action.

Assume that buying from an outside supplier releases factory facilities that can be used to manufacture another product. Suppose the expected annual profit contribution of this other product is $18,000. The three alternatives become (1) make, (2) buy and leave facilities idle, or (3) buy and use facilities to manufacture another product. The alternative with the lowest net cost indicates the best use of facilities. The comparison of *net* cost under the three alternatives is given in Exhibit 26-8.

This analysis of *net* cost indicates that buying the parts outside and using the vacated facilities to manufacture another product is the best choice. If the facilities remain idle, the company will forgo the opportunity to earn $18,000.

Special decisions often include nonquantitative factors. For example, Torino managers may believe they can better control the quality of Part No. 4 by manufacturing it themselves. Or they may fear that an outside supplier cannot deliver sufficient quantities of the part on time. These factors argue for Torino's making the part itself. However, Torino may not have the employees or the factory facilities to manufacture Part No. 4. Its manufacture may require raw materials that Torino cannot obtain economically, so Torino may decide to buy from the outside supplier. Managers consider nonquantitative factors as well as cost differences in making decisions.

EXHIBIT 26-8 *Best Use of Facilities*

	Make	Buy and Leave Facilities Idle	Buy and Use Facilities for Other Products
Expected cost of obtaining 250,000 units of Part No. 4 (amounts from Exhibit 26-7).	$125,000	$132,500	$132,500
Expected profit contribution from the other product...	—	—	(18,000)
Expected net cost of obtaining 250,000 units of Part No. 4....................................	$125,000	$132,500	$114,500

Sell As-Is or Process Further

Inventories become obsolete. Should the company incur the additional manufacturing cost to rework the inventory, or should the company try to sell the inventory as-is? Some companies hold inventory that is only partially finished. These businesses face the decision of whether to finish the inventory or sell it as-is. Of course, the finished inventory will bring a higher sale price, but management must consider the additional costs of completing the inventory. Whether the inventory is obsolete or incomplete, managers must decide if further work on it makes financial sense. For this decision, managers must know which costs to analyze. Historical costs are irrelevant to the "sell-or-process-further" decision.

Suppose a company has 1,000 obsolete computer parts that are carried in inventory at a manufacturing cost of $200,000. The alternatives facing the company are (1) process the inventory further at a cost of $40,000 with the expectation of selling it for $64,000, or (2) scrap the inventory for $17,000. Which alternative should the company select? The inventory's $200,000 historical cost is irrelevant to the decision. Such a cost is called a **sunk cost**. A sunk cost is an actual outlay that has been incurred in the past and is present under all alternatives. As the expenditure has already occurred, it cannot be reversed and is therefore sunk, or gone forever. It is irrelevant because it makes no difference to a current decision.

Exhibit 26-9 shows how to make the decision of whether to sell an asset in its present condition or to process it further.

Based on the expected revenues and costs, it appears best to process the inventory further. The historical cost (the sunk cost) of the obsolete inventory makes no difference to the decision of whether to scrap the inventory or to rework it for sale at a higher price.

The decision whether to replace a plant asset is analyzed the same way. The asset's book value (cost less accumulated depreciation) is a sunk cost and, therefore, is irrelevant to the replacement decision. The relevant data are the asset's current residual value minus the expected costs from (1) using the old asset or (2) using a new asset.

Residual value, also called *scrap value* and *disposal value,* is not a sunk cost. Residual value is the amount of cash to be received by selling an asset. It almost always differs among alternatives. Therefore, it is relevant. During the asset's life, residual or scrap value is an expected *future* amount, which is why it enters the analysis shown in Exhibit 26-9.

EXHIBIT 26-9   *Sell As-Is or Process Further*

	1 Process inventory Further	2 Scrap Inventory (Sell As-Is)	Difference (1) – (2)
Expected revenue	$64,000	$17,000	$47,000
Expected costs	40,000	—	40,000
Expected net revenue	$24,000	$17,000	$ 7,000

Opportunity Cost

The concept of opportunity cost is often relevant to special decisions. An **opportunity cost** is the maximum available profit contribution forgone (rejected) by using limited resources for a particular purpose. It is the cost of the forsaken next-best

OBJECTIVE 4

Use opportunity cost in decision-making

alternative. This definition indicates that opportunity cost is not the usual outlay cost recorded in accounting. An outlay cost requires a cash disbursement sooner or later. It is the typical cost recorded by accountants.

A common example of an opportunity cost is the salary forgone by an engineer who quits his job with IBM to start his own business. Suppose this engineer analyzes the two job opportunities as follows:

	Open an Independent Business	Remain an IBM Employee
Expected salary income from IBM		$60,000
Expected revenue......................................	$200,000	
Expected total expenses	120,000	
Expected net income................................	$ 80,000	$60,000

The opportunity cost of staying with IBM is the forgone $80,000 of net income that the independent business is expected to earn. The opportunity cost of starting a new business is the $60,000 salary that could be received from IBM for the next year.

The concept of opportunity cost applies to all business decisions that specify alternative courses of action. For example, in Exhibit 26-3, p. 1133, the opportunity cost of rejecting the special sales order is $11,000 of operating income. In Exhibit 26-6, p. 1136, the opportunity cost of manufacturing shirts is the $240,000 of contribution margin that could be earned on slacks. The opportunity cost of manufacturing slacks is the $180,000 contribution margin available on shirts. In Exhibit 26-9, p. 1139, the opportunity cost of scrapping the inventory in its present condition is the $24,000 that can be earned by processing the inventory further. The opportunity cost of processing the inventory further is $17,000, which can be received immediately by selling the inventory as-is.

Summary Problem for Your Review

1. Aziz, Inc., has two products, a standard model and a deluxe model, with the following per-unit data:

	Standard	Deluxe
Selling price.......................................	$20	$30
Variable expenses	16	21

The company has 15,000 hours of capacity available. Seven units of the standard model can be produced in an hour, compared to three units of the deluxe model per hour. Which product should the company emphasize?

2. Suppose Toshiba of Canada Ltd. has the following manufacturing costs for 20,000 of its television cabinets:

Direct material..	$ 20,000
Direct labor	80,000
Variable overhead	40,000
Fixed overhead	80,000
Total manufacturing cost	$220,000
Cost per cabinet ($220,000/20,000)................	$11

Another manufacturer has offered to sell Toshiba similar cabinets for $10, a total purchase cost of $200,000. By purchasing the cabinets outside, Toshiba can save $50,000 of fixed overhead cost. The released facilities can be devoted to the manufacture of other products that will contribute $60,000 to profits. Identify and analyze the alternatives. What is Toshiba's best decision?

SOLUTIONS TO REVIEW PROBLEMS

1. Decision: The company should emphasize the standard product because its contribution margin at capacity is greater by $15,000.

		Product	
		Standard	Deluxe
(1)	Units per hour that can be produced	7	3
(2)	Contribution margin per unit.........................	× $4*	× $9*
(3)	Contribution margin per hour (1) × (2).........	$28	$27
	Capacity: Number of hours	× 15,000	× 15,000
	Total contribution margin for capacity	$420,000	$405,000

* Contribution margins: Standard: $20 – $16 = $4; Deluxe: $30 – $21 = $9.

2.

		Alternatives	
	Make	Buy and Leave Facilities Idle	Buy and Use Facilities for Other Products
Cabinets for televisions			
Direct material	$ 20,000	—	—
Direct labor..	80,000	—	—
Variable overhead	40,000	—	—
Fixed overhead	80,000	$ 30,000	$ 30,000
Purchase price from outsider			
(20,000 × $10)......................................	—	200,000	200,000
Total cost of obtaining cabinets............	$220,000	$230,000	$230,000
Profit contribution from other products			(60,000)
Net cost of obtaining 20,000 cabinets	$220,000	$230,000	$170,000

Decision: Toshiba should buy the television cabinets from an outside supplier and use the released facilities to manufacture other products.

Capital Budgeting

A factory building may be used for 50 years. Equipment for successful products like Ivory soap and Coca-Cola may be used for decades. The term *capital asset* refers to an asset that is used over a long period of time. Assets such as land, buildings, machinery, equipment and furniture and fixtures are capital assets. The decisions for the purchase of such long-term assets often require long-range planning and large risks. Many uncertain factors, such as consumer preferences, manufacturing costs and government legislation, enter into the decisions on the purchase of capital assets. Successful organizations quantify as many of these factors as they can before making long-range decisions. In the chapter-opening vignette, Robert Echols is in the pressured position of having to make a long-range decision in a short period of time. The method, or technique, for evaluating and choosing among alternative courses of action is called a **decision model**.

Capital budgeting is a formal means of analyzing long-range investment decisions. Examples include plant locations, equipment purchases, additions of product lines, and territorial expansions. The following diagram shows where capital budgeting fits into the process of purchasing and using long-term assets:

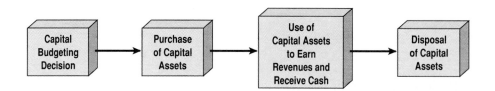

In the remainder of this chapter, we discuss four popular capital-budgeting decision models (methods of making choices): payback, accounting rate of return, net present value, and internal rate of return. In large measure, the models use net cash inflow from operations, which is covered in Chapter 18. Generally accepted accounting principles are based on the accrual accounting model, but capital budgeting focuses on cash because it takes cash to purchase assets.

Payback: Equal Annual Cash Flows

Payback is the length of time it will take to recover, in net cash inflow from operations, the dollars of a capital outlay. Suppose a business pays $24,000 for a machine with an estimated useful life of six years and zero estimated residual value. Managers expect use of the machine to generate net cash inflow from operations of $6,000 annually. This increase in cash could result from an increase in revenues, a decrease in expenses, or a combination of the two.

Payback is expressed as a period of time, as shown in Exhibit 26-10. The payback model measures how swiftly an investment dollar may be recovered. The shorter the payback period, the more attractive the asset will be.

A major criticism of the payback model is that it does *not* consider or measure profitability. Consequently, the payback technique can lead to an unwise decision. Suppose an alternative to the $24,000 machine is a comparable machine that also costs $24,000 but which will save $8,000 annually during its three-year life. The two machines' payback periods are computed as follows:

$$\text{Payback period for Machine 1} = \frac{\$24,000}{\$6,000} = 4 \text{ years}$$

$$\text{Payback period for Machine 2} = \frac{24,000}{\$8,000} = 3 \text{ years}$$

OBJECTIVE 5

Use and evaluate three capital-budgeting models

The payback criterion favors the second machine because it recovers the asset cost more quickly. But consider useful lives. Suppose the second machine's useful life is the same as its payback period, three years. Its use will merely cover cost and provide no profits. Machine 1, on the other hand, will be more profitable. It will generate net cash inflows for six years (two years beyond its payback period) which will give the company additional net cash inflow of $12,000 ($6,000 × 2 years).

EXHIBIT 26-10 *Payback: Equal Annual Net Cash Inflows*

$$\text{Payback period (P)} = \frac{\text{Amount invested (I)}}{\text{Expected annual net cash inflow from operations (O)}}$$

$$P = \frac{I}{O}$$

$$= \frac{\$24{,}000}{\$6{,}000} = 4 \text{ years}$$

Payback: Unequal Annual Cash Flows

The payback equation can be used only when net cash inflows are the same each period. When periodic cash flows are unequal, the payback computation has a cumulative form. Each year's net cash inflows are accumulated until the amount invested is recovered. Suppose Machine 1 in our example will produce annual net cash inflows of $10,000 in the first year, $8,000 in year 2 and $5,000 in years 3 through 6. Exhibit 26-11 shows the payback computation when annual cash flows are unequal.

Years 1, 2 and 3 bring in $23,000. Recovery of the amount invested ($24,000) occurs during year 4. We can compute that payback (P) occurs in 3.2 years:

$$P = 3 \text{ years} + \left(\frac{\$1{,}000 \text{ needed to complete recovery in year 4}}{\$5{,}000 \text{ net cash inflow during the year when recovery is completed}} \times 1 \text{ year} \right) =$$

$$= 3 \text{ years} + \qquad\qquad .2 \text{ year} \qquad\qquad = 3.2 \text{ years}$$

How does a manager use the payback model in capital budgeting? Managers often compare the payback period with the asset's useful life. The asset's payback period must be shorter than its useful life. Let us take an extreme example. If a machine has a payback period of five years and a useful life of three years, the company will never earn a profit from using the asset. How much shorter than the useful life the payback period must be is a matter of personal preference. When the business is deciding between two or more assets, the asset with the shortest payback period is preferable — if all other factors are the same.

The payback method highlights cash flows, an important factor in business decisions. Moreover, payback is easily understood. Advocates view it as a way to eliminate proposals (with lengthy payback periods) where the project is unusually risky. A major weakness of payback is that it ignores profitability.

EXHIBIT 26-11 *Payback: Unequal Annual Net Cash Inflows*

Year	Amount Invested	Net Cash Inflow	
		Each Year	Accumulated
0	$24,000	—	—
1	—	$10,000	$10,000
2	—	8,000	18,000
3	—	5,000	23,000
3.2	—	1,000	24,000

Accounting Rate of Return

A primary goal of business is to maximize profits. The most widely used measure of profitability is the **accounting rate of return** on investment. As we discussed in Chapter 19, a rate of return is computed by dividing income by the amount of the investment made to earn the income:

$$\text{Rate of Return} = \frac{\text{Income}}{\text{Investment}}$$

In capital budgeting, the income amount is income from operations (operating income) that results from use of the asset. Operating income on an asset can be computed as net cash inflow minus depreciation on the asset. Accounting rate of return is computed in Exhibit 26-12 for the machine in the payback illustration. Recall that the machine cost $24,000 and has a useful life of six years with no estimated residual value. Annual straight-line depreciation is, therefore, $4,000 ($24,000/6 years). Use of the machine is expected to generate annual net cash inflows of $6,000.

Accounting rate of return is an *average*. It measures the average rate of return from using the asset over its entire life. The computation is average annual operating income divided by the average amount invested in the asset. If annual operating income varies by year (as in the preceding payback illustration), compute the average annual operating income over the asset's life and use this amount (as O) to compute the accounting return. Also, the book value of the asset decreases as it is used and depreciated. Thus the company's investment in the asset declines. Average investment in the asset is computed as the average of its cost and estimated residual value.

When the asset's residual value is not zero, the average amount invested will not be half the asset's cost. For example, assume the asset's residual value is $3,000. Annual depreciation is $3,500 [($24,000 − $3,000)/6]. The accounting rate of return computation becomes

$$R = \frac{\$6,000 - \$3,500}{(\$24,000 + \$3,000)/2} = \frac{\$2,500}{\$13,500} = .185 = 18.5\%$$

Suppose a company is purchasing a machine. The company can use the accounting rate of return in two ways to make the capital-budgeting decision. Let us assume the machine under consideration is the one in Exhibit 26-12, with an accounting rate of return of 16.7 percent. Many companies demand a target rate of return on their investment projects. They invest only in assets with accounting rates of return equal to or greater than the target rate. Assume that the company's

EXHIBIT 26-12 *Accounting Rate of Return*

$$\begin{aligned}
\text{Accounting rate of return (R)} &= \frac{\text{Average annual operating income from investment*}}{\text{Average amount invested}} = \frac{\text{Average annual net cash inflow from operations (O)} - \text{Annual depreciation (D)}}{[\text{Amount invested (I)} + \text{Residual value (RV)}]/2} \\[2mm]
R &= \frac{O - D}{(I + RV)/2} \\[2mm]
&= \frac{\$6,000 - \$4,000}{(\$24,000 + \$0)/2} = \frac{\$2,000}{\$12,000} = .167 = 16.7\%
\end{aligned}$$

* Operating income can also be computed as revenues minus expenses.

target rate is 20 percent. Would managers approve an investment in the illustrated machine, which is expected to generate an average return of 16.7 percent? No, because the asset's average annual return is less than the company's target rate.

Discounted Cash Flow Models

Although the accounting rate of return model measures profitability, it has a major weakness. It does not recognize the time value of money. It fails to consider the timing of the cash outlay to purchase the asset and the timing of the annual net cash inflows. The discounted cash flow models are popular because they overcome this weakness. In the chapter-opening vignette, top management of Schaaf Tool Limited requires at least "a 15 percent return on a discounted basis." The reference to a "discounted basis" means that this company uses discounted cash flow models for capital budgeting.

Discounted cash flow models are conceptually superior to payback models and accounting models. They are used by over 75 percent of the large industrial firms in Canada. There are two main variations of discounted cash flow models: (1) net present value (NPV) and (2) internal rate of return (IRR). Both variations are based on the concept of compound interest.

Net Present Value

The appendix to Chapter 16 introduced the concept of present value. The present value of $1 to be received in the future is less than $1 today. The logic is this: to receive $1 a year from now, we would pay less than $1 today. Why? It is because if we pay $1 or more now to receive $1 a year later, we earn no income. Instead, we could deposit our $1 in a bank to earn interest of, say, $.08 during the year, and have $1.08 a year later. We would rather have $1.08 than $1.00. The fact that we can earn income by investing money for a period is called the **time value of money**.

The present-value concept can be applied to the acquisition of capital assets. For example, SaskTel, which provides terminal equipment, private line and mobile radio services throughout Saskatchewan, used net present value analysis when designing its new Customer Records and Billing system.

A company purchases an asset in order to earn revenues and receive cash. The excess of cash received for revenue over the cash paid for the costs associated with an investment is called the investment's net cash inflow. Ordinarily net cash inflow is stated in an annual amount. The advantage of analyzing net cash inflows instead of analyzing accounting income is that the focus is on the premier asset, cash. A company may be earning high income but be cash-poor. Moreover, the complexities of accrual accounting are avoided.

The timing of the net cash inflows from operations is important because of the time value of money. Consider two $10,000 investments. Both investments promise future cash receipts of $11,000. Investment 1 will bring in cash of $5,500 at the end of each of two years. Investment 2 will return the full $11,000 at the end of the second year. Which investment is better? Investment 1, because it brings cash home sooner, and so the cash can be invested for a longer period.

The **net present value (NPV)** model is a discounted cash flow approach to capital budgeting. It computes the expected net monetary gain or loss from a project by discounting all expected cash flows to the present value, using a desired rate of return. A positive NPV indicates that the investment should be purchased. A negative net present value indicates that the investment should be rejected. A zero NVP indicates the investment may be rejected, since investors would be no further ahead. If this model is used to compare several assets, the asset with the highest positive net present value is usually the best investment.

Assume that the business is considering the manufacture of two products, tape decks and VCRs. Each would require different specialized equipment costing the same amount, $1 million, and having zero residual value. Each piece of equipment is expected to have a five-year life. The two products have different patterns of expected net cash inflows:

	Annual Net Cash Inflows	
Year	Tape Decks	VCRs
1	$ 305,450	$ 500,000
2	305,450	350,000
3	305,450	300,000
4	305,450	250,000
5	305,450	40,000
Total	$1,527,250	$1,440,000

Total net cash inflows are greater if we invest in the manufacture of tape decks. However, these net cash inflows will occur in the future. In the net-present-value model, we base the capital budgeting decision on present value, not future values. In present-value language, we say that we discount these future cash flows to present value. Discounted cash flow is a representation of cash inflows and outflows at a common time so that they can be compared (added, subtracted, and so on) for decision-making.

Computation of present value requires an earnings rate. This rate, called the **discount rate**, is management's minimum desired rate of return on an investment. Synonyms are *hurdle rate, cutoff rate, required rate of return, cost of capital,* and *target rate of return.* The discount rate varies from company to company *depending on the risks undertaken.* The higher the risk, the higher the discount rate. Let us assume that an appropriate discount rate for these investments is 14 percent.

The manufacture and sale of tape decks is expected to generate $305,450 of net cash inflow each year — a total of $1,527,250. A stream of equal periodic amounts is called an **annuity**. The present value of an annuity is computed by multiplying the periodic amount ($305,450 annually, in this case) by the present value of an annuity of $1 from Table 26-2, p. 1132. The table indicates that the present value of an annuity of $1 for five periods discounted at 14 percent is 3.433. Exhibit 26-13 shows the computation of the present value of the net cash inflows from investing in the tape-deck project, $1,048,610.

The annual net cash inflows from investing in the manufacture of VCRs are unequal: $500,000 in year 1, $350,000 in year 2, and so on. Because these amounts vary by year, the present value of each annual amount is computed separately. For example:

Year	Find the Present Value Factor from Table 26-1 (p. 1148) 14% Column		Net Cash Inflow		Present Value of Net Cash Inflows
1	.877	×	$500,000	=	$438,500
2	.769	×	350,000	=	269,150

Exhibit 26-13 includes these present-value computations.

The exhibit indicates that the VCR project has a net present value of $78,910, compared to $48,610 for the tape-deck project. The analysis favors VCRs because an investment in that project will earn the company's target return of 14 percent plus an additional $78,910. This expected excess is greater than the net present value

EXHIBIT 26-13 *Net Present Value*

	Present Value at 14%		Net Cash Inflow		Present Value of Net Cash Inflows
Tape-Deck Project					
Present value of equal annual net cash inflows for 5 years	3.433*	×	$305,450 per year	=	$1,048,610
Investment..					(1,000,000)
Net present value of the tape-deck project..................					$ 48,610
VCR Project					
Present value of net cash inflow by year	**Year**				
	1	.877** ×	$500,000	=	$ 438,500
	2	.769 ×	350,000	=	269,150
	3	.675 ×	300,000	=	202,500
	4	.592 ×	250,000	=	148,000
	5	.519 ×	40,000	=	20,760
Total present value of net cash inflows					1,078,910
Investment...					(1,000,000)
Net present value of the VCR project					$ 78,910

*   Present value of annuity of $1 for 5 years at 14%, Table 26-2, p. 1150.
** Present value of $1 for 1 year, 2 years, 3 years, and so on, at 14%, Table 26-1, p. 1148.

of the tape-deck project, which also meets the target return of 14 percent but returns only an additional $48,610.

This example illustrates an important point about net-present-value analysis: the tape-deck project promises the greater total amount of net cash inflows. But the timing of the VCR cash flows (loaded near the beginning of the project) causes the VCR project to have a higher net present value. The VCR project is more attractive because of the time value of money. Its nearer dollars are worth more now than the more distant dollars of the tape-deck project.

Another important point about net-present-value analysis is this: Either project, considered alone, is acceptable because its net present value is at least zero. Thus, both projects earn at least the required rate of return of 14 percent.

Net Present Value of a Project with Residual Value

When the asset to be acquired is expected to have a residual value at the end of its useful life, that amount should also be considered in the NPV analysis. It must be discounted to its present value and added to the present value of the annual net cash inflows to determine the total present value of the project. The residual value is discounted as a single amount (not an annuity) because it will be received only at the end of the asset's useful life (for example, when the asset is sold).

Suppose the equipment to manufacture the tape decks (in Exhibit 26-13) is expected to be worth $100,000 at the end of its five-year life. To determine the tape-deck project's NPV, we discount $100,000 for five years at 14 percent, using Table 26-1 on p. 1148, and add its present value ($51,900), as shown in Exhibit 26-14.

Compare the tape-deck project's NPV's in Exhibits 26-13 and 26-14. The residual amount raises the project's NPV to $100,510, which is higher than the VCR project's NPV. If the VCR equipment is expected to have zero disposal value, then the

EXHIBIT 26-14 *Net Present Value of a Project with Residual Value*

Tape-Deck Project	Present Value at 14%		Net Cash Inflow		Present Value of Net Cash Inflows
Present value of equal annual net cash inflows for 5 years (from Exhibit 26-13)	3.433	×	$305,450 per year	=	$ 1,048,610
Present value of residual value	.519*	×	$100,000	=	51,900
Present value of the project's net cash inflows					$1,100,510
Investment					(1,000,000)
Net present value of the tape-deck project.......					$ 100,510

*Present value of $1 for 5 years at 14%, Table 26-1, below.

tape-deck project is more attractive. This illustrates the difference that residual value can make to a business decision.[1]

There is a slightly different way to use present-value analysis for making capital-budgeting decisions. Suppose the company starts the decision process by determining the present values of the expected future net cash inflows from the two projects: $1,048,610 for tape decks and $1,078,910 for VCRs. Managers may ask: What is the most we can invest in the tape-deck project and still earn our target rate of return of 14 percent? With zero residual values, the answer is $1,048,610. Similarly, the maximum acceptable investment for VCRs is $1,078,910. Negotiations

TABLE 26-1 *Present Value of $1*

				Present Value of $1					
Periods	4%	5%	6%	7%	8%	10%	12%	14%	16%
1	0.962	0.952	0.943	0.935	0.926	0.909	0.893	0.877	0.862
2	0.925	0.907	0.890	0.873	0.857	0.826	0.797	0.769	0.743
3	0.889	0.864	0.840	0.816	0.794	0.751	0.712	0.675	0.641
4	0.855	0.823	0.792	0.763	0.735	0.683	0.636	0.592	0.552
5	0.822	0.784	0.747	0.713	0.681	0.621	0.567	0.519	0.476
6	0.790	0.746	0.705	0.666	0.630	0.564	0.507	0.456	0.410
7	0.760	0.711	0.665	0.623	0.583	0.513	0.452	0.400	0.354
8	0.731	0.677	0.627	0.582	0.540	0.467	0.404	0.351	0.305
9	0.703	0.645	0.592	0.544	0.500	0.424	0.361	0.308	0.263
10	0.676	0.614	0.558	0.508	0.463	0.386	0.322	0.270	0.227
11	0.650	0.585	0.527	0.475	0.429	0.350	0.287	0.237	0.195
12	0.625	0.557	0.497	0.444	0.397	0.319	0.257	0.208	0.168
13	0.601	0.530	0.469	0.415	0.368	0.290	0.229	0.182	0.145
14	0.577	0.505	0.442	0.388	0.340	0.263	0.205	0.160	0.125
15	0.555	0.481	0.417	0.362	0.315	0.239	0.183	0.140	0.108
16	0.534	0.458	0.394	0.339	0.292	0.218	0.163	0.123	0.093
17	0.513	0.436	0.371	0.317	0.270	0.198	0.146	0.108	0.080
18	0.494	0.416	0.350	0.296	0.250	0.180	0.130	0.095	0.069
19	0.475	0.396	0.331	0.277	0.232	0.164	0.116	0.083	0.060
20	0.456	0.377	0.312	0.258	0.215	0.149	0.104	0.073	0.051

[1] The deductability of depreciation for tax purposes (which has been ignored for this discussion, since it is covered in more advanced courses) increases the cash flow and thus would affect the NPV decision.

with the seller of the tape-deck manufacturing equipment may drive the required investment down to only $850,000. This would increase the tape-deck project's attractiveness, especially if the cost of the VCR manufacturing equipment remains $1,000,000. In any event, managers would not want to pay more than $1,048,610 for the tape-deck equipment or more than $1,078,910 for the VCR equipment. At costs above these present-value amounts, the company would not be able to earn 14 percent on its investment.

Internal Rate of Return

Another discounted cash flow model for capital budgeting is the *internal rate of return (IRR)* model. The **internal rate of return** (the **IRR**) of an investment project is the rate of return that makes the net present value of the project equal to zero. As the name implies, a project's IRR is the rate of return that a company can expect to earn by investing in the project. The higher the IRR, the more desirable the project; the lower the IRR, the less desirable.

Exhibit 26-15 shows why 16 percent is the IRR of our tape-deck project. The 16 percent rate produces a net present value of zero. There are three steps:

1. Identify the expected net cash inflows ($305,450 for five years) exactly as you did in calculating the net present value in Exhibit 26-13.
2. Find the interest rate that equates the present value of the cash inflows to the present value of the cash outflows. If one outflow is followed by a series of equal inflows, use the following equation to solve for the value of the present-value (PV) factor:

Investment	=	**Expected annual net cash inflow**	×	**Annuity PV factor**
$1,000,000	=	**$305,450**	×	**PV factor**
PV factor	=	$\dfrac{\$1,000,000}{\$305,450}$	=	3.274

Scan the row in Table 26-2 that represents the relevant life of the project, the 5-period row in our example. Choose the column with the number closest to the annuity PV factor that was calculated. The 3.274 annuity factor is in the 16 percent column. Therefore, the IRR of the tape-deck project is 16 percent.

3. Compare the IRR with the minimum desired rate of return. If the IRR is equal to or greater than the minimum desired rate, the project should be accepted. Otherwise, it should be rejected.

EXHIBIT 26-15   *Internal Rate of Return, Tape-Deck Project*

	Present Value at 16%		Net Cash Inflow	Present Value of Net Cash Inflows
Present value of equal annual net cash inflows for 5 years	3.274	×	$305,450 =	$ 1,000,000*
Investment				(1,000,000)
Net present value of the tape-deck project				$ 0**

*   Slight rounding error.
** The zero difference proves that the rate of return is 16%.

TABLE 26-2   *Present Value of Annuity of $1*

	Present Value of Annuity of $1								
Periods	4%	5%	6%	7%	8%	10%	12%	14%	16%
1	0.962	0.952	0.943	0.935	0.926	0.909	0.893	0.877	0.862
2	1.886	1.859	1.833	1.808	1.783	1.736	1.690	1.647	1.605
3	2.775	2.723	2.673	2.624	2.577	2.487	2.402	2.322	2.246
4	3.630	3.546	3.465	3.387	3.312	3.170	3.037	2.914	2.798
5	4.452	4.329	4.212	4.100	3.993	3.791	3.605	3.433	3.274
6	5.242	5.076	4.917	4.767	4.623	4.355	4.111	3.889	3.685
7	6.002	5.786	5.582	5.389	5.206	4.868	4.564	4.288	4.039
8	6.733	6.463	6.210	5.971	5.747	5.335	4.968	4.639	4.344
9	7.435	7.108	6.802	6.515	6.247	5.759	5.328	4.946	4.607
10	8.111	7.722	7.360	7.024	6.710	6.145	5.650	5.216	4.833
11	8.760	8.306	7.887	7.499	7.139	6.495	5.938	5.453	5.029
12	9.385	8.863	8.384	7.943	7.536	6.814	6.194	5.660	5.197
13	9.986	9.394	8.853	8.358	7.904	7.103	6.424	5.842	5.342
14	10.563	9.899	9.295	8.745	8.244	7.367	6.628	6.002	5.468
15	11.118	10.380	9.712	9.108	8.559	7.606	6.811	6.142	5.575
16	11.652	10.838	10.106	9.447	8.851	7.824	6.974	6.265	5.669
17	12.166	11.274	10.477	9.763	9.122	8.022	7.120	6.373	5.749
18	12.659	11.690	10.828	10.059	9.372	8.201	7.250	6.467	5.818
19	13.134	12.085	11.158	10.336	9.604	8.365	7.366	6.550	5.877
20	13.590	12.462	11.470	10.594	9.818	8.514	7.469	6.623	5.929

If tape decks were the only investment under consideration, managers would invest in tape decks because their 16 percent IRR exceeds the 14 percent hurdle rate. In the situation of Exhibit 26-13, the VCR project has a higher net present value than the tape-deck project. The VCR investment also has a higher IRR. Computation of the VCR's IRR requires a trial-and-error procedure covered in more advanced courses. Many calculators can compute the IRR.

How do the net-present-value approach and the IRR approach compare? The net-present-value method indicates the amount of the excess (or deficiency) of a project's present value of net cash inflows over (or under) its cost — for a specified rate of return. Net present value, though, does not show the project's unique rate of return. The IRR, however, shows the project's unique rate of return but fails to indicate the dollar difference between the project's present value and its investment cost. In most cases the two methods lead to the same investment decision.

Comparison of the Capital Budgeting Models

The discounted cash flow models are the best of the four capital-budgeting models because they are based on cash flows and because they consider both profitability and the time value of money. The time value of money enters the analysis through the discounting of future dollars to present value. Profitability is also built into the discounted cash flow models. Managers specify the earnings rate that they demand of investment projects. Use of this target earnings rate, 10 percent, 15 percent, or whatever, as the discount rate for the computations produces the ideal price for the project. At this price, the project is expected to earn the specified level of profits.

EXHIBIT 26-16   *Capital-Budgeting Decision Models*

Model	Strengths	Weaknesses
Payback	Easy to understand Based on cash flows Highlights risks	Ignores profitability and the time value of money
Accounting rate of return	Based on profitability	Ignores the time value of money
Discounted cash flow models: Net present value Internal rate of return	Based on cash flows, profitability, and the time value of money	None of the above

Each of the other two capital-budgeting models ignores one or more of these factors. In actual practice, managers often use more than one model simultaneously to gain different perspectives on risks and returns. Exhibit 26-16 summarizes the strengths and weaknesses of the payback, accounting rate of return and discounted cash flow models.

Lease or Buy

The capital-budgeting decisions considered thus far have centered on which investment project to acquire. The first decision is whether to acquire a particular asset. After that decision is made, managers must decide how to finance the acquisition. There are several possibilities. The business may be able to purchase the asset with internally generated cash (cash flow from operations on the statement of changes in financial position) or with cash obtained by borrowing. In many cases managers can acquire the use of assets through leasing of capital assets, that is, renting on a long-term basis.

A recent survey of 600 companies indicated that only 45 companies did not acquire the use of some of their assets through leasing. Why is leasing so popular? One factor is rapid change in technology. Rather than buy a computer and risk getting stuck with a machine made obsolete by new developments, a company may prefer to lease one. Then if IBM, Control Data, or Compaq develops a new generation of computer, the company can let its lease expire and switch to a new, more powerful machine. For similar reasons, airline companies lease most of their aircraft.

The role of leasing should be kept in perspective. There are two steps: (1) whether or not to acquire an asset, which is an investment decision using a discounted-cash-flow model, and (2) whether to finance the acquisition by borrowing or leasing. The second step is not an investment decision. It is a financing decision that is covered in textbooks on finance.

Computers in Business Decision Analysis _____

Computers are ideally suited for decision analysis. They can compute the outcomes of alternative courses of action instantly and without computational error. Consider the net-present-value analysis of three possible investments. Suppose the assets under consideration promise irregular net cash inflows for 20 years. The 60 (3 × 20) present-value computations would be time consuming and present a great possibility for error. However, a computer can be programmed to handle these multiple computations. The manager can then use the program over and over. He or she can alter the annual cash flows, the earnings (discount) rate and timing of the cash flows. With a computer, the manager simply enters the data, and the entire analysis is performed in seconds.

Consider the special sales order decision. Many companies store their cost data in computers. The manager can enter the special sale price and call up the variable expenses and any fixed expenses that will change because of the special sale. The change in operating income is computed automatically. If the computed income is high enough, the manager can accept the order. If the income is too low, the manager can enter a revised sale price and compute the revised operating income. By trying different sale prices, he or she can come up with a range of acceptable options. Armed with this knowledge, the company may propose a different sale price to the buyer. More knowledge places the company in a stronger bargaining position. Microcomputers and spreadsheet programs like Lotus 1-2-3®, Excel, Quattro Pro, and AppleWorks bring this analytical power even to small companies.

The computer can greatly assist management in making capital budgeting decisions. Suppose a large manufacturer of lawn maintenance equipment, such as Toro, is considering opening a new production facility to meet increasing demands for its lawn mowers. Where will the new facility be? Company management has examined 25 possible sites and narrowed the choice to five. And which of the six alternative factory designs that management is considering is best? Analyzing the data with a spreadsheet allows the computer to quickly run through all the calculations to reach the optimal combination of site and design based on net present value and internal rate of return.

Summary Problem for Your Review

The data for a machine follow:

Cost of machine	$48,000
Estimated residual value	6,000
Estimated annual net cash inflow	13,000
Estimated useful life	5 years
Annual rate of return required	16%

Required

1. Compute the payback period.
2. Compute the accounting rate of return.
3. Compute the net present value (NPV).
4. Indicate whether each decision model leads to purchase or rejection of this investment. Would you decide to buy the machine? Give your reason.

SOLUTION TO REVIEW PROBLEM

Requirement 1

$$P = \frac{I}{O} = \frac{\$48,000}{\$13,000} = \textbf{3.7 years}$$

Requirement 2

$$R = \frac{O - D}{(I+RV)/2} = \frac{\$13,000 - \$8,400^*}{(\$48,000 + \$6,000)/2} = \frac{\$4,600}{\$54,000/2}$$

$$= \frac{\$4,600}{\$27,000} = .170 = 17\%$$

---

*D = ($48,000 – $6,000)/5 years = $8,400

Requirement 3

Present value of equal annual net cash inflows	
($13,000 × 3.274**)...	$42,562
Present value of residual value ($6,000 × .476***)..............	2,856
Present value of the machine...	45,418
Investment...	48,000
Net present value	$ (2,582)

** Present value of annuity of $1 for 5 years at 16%, Table 26-2, p. 1150.
*** Present value of $1 for 5 years at 16%, Table 26-1, p. 1148.

Requirement 4

Payback: Purchase machine because payback period (3.7 years) is less than useful life (5 years).

Accounting rate of return: Purchase machine because return on machine of 17 percent exceeds target rate of 16 percent.

Net present value: Reject machine because it has negative net present value.

Decision: Reject machine because of negative net present value. The net-present-value model considers cash flows, profitability and the time value of money. Each of the other models ignores two of these factors.

Summary

Special decisions are those with long-term consequences. In making these decisions, managers focus on differences among the alternative courses of action. Often historical data are irrelevant, except for helping to develop the *expected future data* for the decision analysis. The approach to making special decisions is called the *relevant information approach*.

Whether to *delete a product, which product to emphasize,* whether to *make or buy* a part, how to make the *best use of facilities,* and whether to *sell inventory in its present condition or process it further* are decisions with long-range effects. In each decision, the best alternative is the one that will produce the largest increase in income from operations.

A *contribution margin income statement,* which shows variable expenses and fixed expenses, is helpful to decision analysis. The change in *variable expenses* is always a factor because variable expenses change in direct response to changes in volume. Fixed expenses may or may not change, depending on the circumstances. Failure to account for *fixed expenses* correctly is a common mistake. When fixed expenses do not change, they do not enter the analysis. But when they do change, their effect must be considered.

In making special decisions, managers also consider nonquantitative factors, like the long-run effect on customers and competitors. Opportunity cost is another factor in special decisions. *Opportunity cost* is the maximum profit forgone by following a specific course of action. Thus it differs from ordinary accounting costs.

Capital budgeting helps managers make long-range decisions. *Payback, accounting rate of return* and *discounted cash flow* are three models for making capital budgeting decisions. Payback is the simplest. Discounted cash flow is the best of these because it is based on cash flows and also considers profitability and the time value of money. Two widely used variations are net present value and internal rate of return. Companies may use more than one method in practice. Computers are ideally suited for special decision analysis because they can help predict the outcomes of various courses of action.

Self-Study Questions

Test your understanding of the chapter by marking the best answer for each of the following questions:

1. Relevant information for decision analysis *(pp. 1130–31)*
   a. Remains constant regardless of the alternative courses of action
   b. Is used in some but not all business decisions
   c. Varies with the alternative courses of action
   d. Excludes direct materials and direct labor because they are fixed

2. Assume fixed costs remain unchanged. To decide whether to make a sale at a special price, compare *(p. 1132)*
   a. Expected change in gross margin (sales minus cost of goods sold) with and without the sale
   b. Expected change in revenue with expected change in fixed expenses
   c. Expected change in revenue with expected change in selling expenses
   d. Expected change in revenue with expected change in variable expenses

3. To decide whether to delete a product, a manager should *(pp. 1134–35)*
   a. Consider all costs that change
   b. Consider only variable costs
   c. Consider all costs that remain unchanged
   d. Consider only fixed costs

4. Hochelaga's $.47 cost per unit (incurred in manufacturing its inventory) includes fixed cost of $.19. Another company offers to sell the product to Hochelaga for $.35 per unit. The make-or-buy decision hinges on the comparison between Hochelaga's $.47 manufacturing cost and the total cost if the products are purchased from the other company. That total cost is *(p. 1137)*
   a. $.28   c. $.54
   b. $.35   d. $.66

5. Sunk costs are *(p. 1139)*
   a. Relevant to most business decisions
   b. The cost of the next-best alternative
   c. Equal to the residual value of a capital asset
   d. Irrelevant to most business decisions

6. Capital budgeting is a (an) *(pp. 1141–42)*
   a. Depreciation method
   b. Short-run decision
   c. Alternative to the payback method
   d. Way to make long-range investment decisions

7. A machine costs $45,000. It is expected to earn operating income of $6,000 and to generate $9,000 net cash inflow annually. Expected residual value is zero at the end of fifteen years. What is the asset's payback period? *(p. 1142)*
   a. 5 years   c. 7 years
   b. 6 years   d. 9 years

8. The accounting rate of return of the machine in the preceding question is *(p. 1144)*
   a. 15 percent
   b. 24 percent
   c. 26.7 percent
   d. 37.5 percent

9. The time value of money is an important part of *(p. 1145)*
   a. Payback analysis
   b. Accounting rate of return analysis
   c. Net-present-value analysis
   d. All capital-budgeting methods

10. Payback analysis and net-present-value analysis indicate that a particular investment should be rejected, but the accounting rate of return is favorable. What is the wisest investment decision? Give your reason. *(pp. 1150–51)*
    a. Reject because of net-present-value analysis
    b. Reject because of payback analysis
    c. Accept because of favorable accounting rate of return
    d. Cannot decide because of differences among the methods' results

Answers to the Self-Study Questions are at the end of the chapter.

Accounting Vocabulary

accounting rate of return *(p. 1144)*
annuity *(p. 1146)*
capital budgeting *(p. 1142)*
constraint *(p. 1136)*
decision model *(p. 1142)*
discount rate *(p. 1146)*

internal rate of return (IRR) *(p. 1149)*
limiting factor *(p. 1136)*
net present value (NPV) *(p. 1145)*
opportunity cost *(p. 1139)*

payback *(p. 1142)*
relevant information *(p. 1130)*
sunk cost *(p. 1139)*
time value of money *(p. 1145)*

ASSIGNMENT MATERIAL _____

Questions

1. How do special decisions differ from ordinary day-to-day business decisions? Give examples.

2. Briefly describe how relevant information is used in making special decisions.

3. Discuss the roles of expected future data and historical data in special decision analysis. On which set of data are special decisions based?

4. Identify two income statement formats. Which is more useful for deciding whether to accept a special sales order? Why?

5. Identify two income amounts on which special decisions are based.

6. What is "special" about a special sales order? How does a manager make a special sales order decision?

7. Identify two long-run factors to be considered in making a special sales order decision.

8. What is the similarity between a special sales order decision and a decision to delete a product? What is the difference?

9. Which type of cost is more likely to change in a special decision situation, a fixed cost or a variable cost? Can both costs change?

10. Outline how to decide which product to emphasize when there is a limiting factor. Give four examples of limiting factors.

11. Which is relevant to special decision analysis, an asset's sunk cost or its residual value? Give your reason including an explanation of each.

12. What is opportunity cost? How does it differ from an ordinary accounting cost?

13. Give an example of a decision that would be based on opportunity cost. Discuss the role of opportunity cost in making this decision.

14. What are decision models? Why are they helpful in capital budgeting?

15. What is capital budgeting? Are capital-budgeting decisions made before or after long-term assets are purchased?

16. Name three capital-budgeting decision models. State the strengths and the weaknesses of each model. Which model is best? Why?

17. Name the capital-budgeting model that fits each description: (a) based on operating income only; (b) based on cash flows without regard for their timing or for profitability; (c) based on the time value of money.

18. How is payback period computed? How does the estimated useful life of a capital asset affect the payback computation?

19. Your company is considering purchasing a manufacturing plant with an expected useful life of 15 years. What is the maximum acceptable payback period on this plant? Justify your answer.

20. How can managers use accounting rate of return in capital-budgeting decisions?

21. How can accounting rate of return be computed when the annual amounts of operating income are expected to vary each period?

22. State why a positive net present value indicates an attractive investment project and a negative net present value indicates an unattractive project.

23. Which capital-budgeting strategy is best? (1) Pick out the best model and use it exclusively. (2) Use all three models. Support your answer.

24. A company is investing in a 20-year project. The managers, who use the net-present-value model for capital-budgeting decisions, expect the net cash inflow amounts to vary considerably each year. How can a computer help the managers decide the amount to invest in this project?

25. How does the internal rate of return approach differ from the net-present-value approach? How are these approaches similar?

Exercises

Exercise 26-1 *Accept or reject a special sales order? (L.O. 1, 2)*

All-Star Marketing Inc. approaches MacDonald Manufacturing Corp. with a special offer. All-Star wishes to purchase 100,000 monogrammed golf balls for a special promotional campaign. All-Star offers $.38 per ball — a total of $38,000. MacDonald's total manufacturing cost per ball is $.40, broken down as follows:

Variable costs	
Direct material	$.06
Direct labor.........................	.03
Variable overhead	.11
Total variable cost..............	.20
Fixed overhead cost	.20
Total cost................................	$.40

Required

Prepare a quick summary to help determine whether or not MacDonald should accept the special sales order. Assume MacDonald has excess capacity and the order will not disturb other sales.

Exercise 26-2 *Retain or drop a product line (fixed costs unchanged)? (L.O. 1, 2, 3)*

Top managers of Muskrat Lumber Ltd. are alarmed that operating income is so low. They are considering dropping the building materials product line. Company accountants have prepared the following analysis to help make this decision:

	Total	Hardware	Building Materials
Sales..	$460,000	$290,000	$170,000
Variable expenses	240,000	140,000	100,000
Contribution margin	220,000	150,000	70,000
Fixed expenses			
Manufacturing	120,000	70,000	50,000
Selling and administrative	90,000	55,000	35,000
Total fixed expenses	210,000	125,000	85,000
Operating income (loss)	$ 10,000	$ 25,000	$ (15,000)

Fixed costs will not change if the company stops selling building materials.

Required

Prepare a quick summary to show whether Muskrat should drop the building materials product line. Explain the error in concluding that dropping building materials will add $15,000 to operating income.

Exercise 26-3 *Retain or drop a product line (fixed costs changed)? (L.O. 1, 2)*

Refer to the data of Exercise 26-2. Assume that Muskrat can avoid $35,000 of fixed expenses by dropping the building materials product line. Prepare a quick summary to show whether Muskrat should stop selling building materials.

Exercise 26-4 *Which product to emphasize? (L.O. 1, 2)*

Belvedere Fashions sells both designer and moderately priced women's wear. Profits have fluctuated recently, and top management is deciding which product line to emphasize. Accountants provide the following relevant data:

	Designer	Moderately Priced
Per item		
Average sale price...	$100	$60
Average variable expenses...........................	35	18
Average contribution margin	$ 65	$42
Average contribution margin ratio	65%	70%

The store, in Sudbury, Ontario, has 800 square metres of floor space. If moderately priced goods are emphasized, 300 items can be displayed in the store. Only 200 designer items could be displayed for sale.

Required

Prepare an analysis to show which product to emphasize.

Exercise 26-5 *Make or buy? (L.O. 1, 2, 3)*

The production process of Carswell Products Corp. uses an electronic control that has the following manufacturing cost per unit:

Direct material...	$2.45
Direct labor	.55
Variable overhead	.62
Fixed overhead..	2.04
Total manufacturing cost per unit........	$5.66

Another company has offered to sell Carswell the electronic control for $4.00 per unit. If Carswell buys the controls from the outside supplier, the manufacturing facilities that will be idle cannot be used for any other purpose in the business. Should Carswell make or buy the electronic controls? Show how you made this decision. Explain the difference between correct analysis and incorrect analysis of this decision.

Exercise 26-6   *Best use of facilities? (L.O. 1, 2)*

Refer to Exercise 26-5. Assume that Carswell needs 100,000 of the electronic controls. By purchasing them from the outside supplier, Carswell could use its idle facilities to manufacture another product that can be sold for a $42,000 profit. Identify the net costs that Carswell may incur to acquire 100,000 electronic controls under three alternative plans. Which alternative makes the best use of Carswell's facilities? Support your answer with analysis.

Exercise 26-7   *Scrap inventory or process further? (L.O. 1, 2, 4)*

Rotan Cabinet Works has damaged some custom cabinets, which cost the company $8,000 to manufacture. Raphael Rotan, the owner, is considering two options for disposing of this inventory. One plan is to sell the cabinets as damaged inventory for $1,400. The alternative is to spend an additional $600 to repair the damage and expect to sell the cabinets for $2,200. How should Rotan dispose of this inventory? Support your decision with an analysis that shows expected net revenue under each alternative. Identify the opportunity cost of each alternative.

Exercise 26-8   *Payback analysis of an investment: equal cash flows (L.O. 5)*

Chin & McQuade, Inc. is considering acquiring a manufacturing plant. The purchase price is $700,000. The owners believe the plant will generate net cash inflows of $95,000 annually. It will have to be replaced in five years. Use the payback model to determine whether Chin & McQuade should purchase this plant.

Exercise 26-9   *Payback analysis of an investment: unequal cash flows (L.O. 5)*

Skyhawk Manufacturing Ltd. is adding a new product line that will require an investment of $750,000. Managers estimate that this investment will generate net cash inflows of $110,000 the first year, $180,000 the second year, and $200,000 each year thereafter. What is the payback period for this investment? Compute a fraction of a year if necessary.

Exercise 26-10   *Accounting rate of return analysis of investments (L.O. 4, 5)*

FanMaster Corporation is shopping for new equipment. Managers are considering two investments. Equipment manufactured by Ling, Inc. costs $220,000 and will last for five years, with no residual value. The Ling equipment should generate annual operating income of $24,000. Equipment manufactured by Johnson Controls is priced at $310,000 and will remain useful for six years. It promises annual operating income of $32,000, and its expected residual value is $30,000.

Required

Which equipment offers the higher accounting rate of return? What is the opportunity cost of purchasing the Ling equipment? How would managers use the notion of opportunity cost in making their decision?

Exercise 26-11 *Net-present-value analysis of investments* **(L.O. 5)**

Use the net-present-value model to determine whether Rust Manufacturing Inc. should invest in the following projects:

    Project A costs $500,000 and offers 10 annual net cash inflows of $95,860. Rust demands an annual return of 12 percent on investments of this nature.

    Project B costs $330,000 and offers 7 annual net cash inflows of $81,700. Rust requires an annual return of 14 percent on projects like B.

Exercise 26-12 *Internal rate of return analysis of investments* **(L.O. 5)**

Refer to the data of Exercise 26-11. Compute the internal rate of return of each project, and use this information to identify the better investment.

Problems   (Group A)

Problem 26-1A *Accept or reject a special sales order?* **(L.O. 1, 2)**

Martin Fabricating Ltd. manufactures toys in Penticton, B.C. Martin's contribution margin income statement for the most recent month contains the following:

Sales — units	630,000
Sales	$ 63,000
Variable expenses	
Manufacturing	$ 12,600
Selling and administrative	14,900
Total variable expenses	27,500
Contribution margin	35,500
Fixed expenses	
Manufacturing	17,400
Selling and administrative	11,300
Total fixed expenses	28,700
Income from operations	$ 6,800

    Pacific Promotions, Inc. wishes to buy 120,000 toys from Martin. Acceptance of the offer will not increase selling and administrative expenses. Martin's plant has unused capacity to manufacture the additional toys. Pacific has offered $.07 per toy, which is considerably below the normal sale price of $.10.

Required

1. Prepare a quick summary to help determine whether Martin should accept this special sales order.

2. Prepare a total analysis to show Martin's operating income with and without the special sales order.

3. Identify long-run factors that Martin should consider in deciding whether or not to accept the special sales order.

Problem 26-2A *Retain or drop a product line?* **(L.O. 1, 2, 3)**

Members of the board of directors of Smoke Detector Corporation have received the following income statement for the year just ended:

	Total	Industrial Products	Household Products
Sales.	$866,000	$445,000	$421,000
Cost of goods sold			
Variable	$119,000	$ 64,000	$ 55,000
Fixed	327,000	241,000	86,000
Total cost of goods sold	446,000	305,000	141,000
Gross margin	420,000	140,000	280,000
Selling and administrative expenses			
Variable	178,000	86,000	92,000
Fixed	89,000	58,000	31,000
Total selling and administrative expenses	267,000	144,000	123,000
Operating income (loss)	$153,000	$ (4,000)	$157,000

Members of the board are shocked that the industrial products division is losing money. They commission a study to determine whether the company should delete the industrial products line. Company accountants estimate that dropping industrial products will decrease fixed cost of goods sold by $65,000 and decrease fixed selling and administrative expenses by $15,000.

Required

1. Prepare a quick summary to show whether Smoke Detector should drop the industrial products line.

2. Prepare a total analysis to show Smoke Detector's operating income with and without industrial products. Prepare the income statement in contribution-margin format.

3. Explain the difference between correct analysis and incorrect analysis of the decision whether to drop the industrial products line.

Problem 26-3A *Which product to emphasize? (L.O. 1, 2)*

Sutfin Manufacturing Ltd. produces two lines of household appliances in Camrose, Alberta: deluxe and standard models. The owners are expanding the plant, and they are deciding which product line to emphasize. To make this decision, they assemble the following data, which suggest that the deluxe product line is more profitable:

	Deluxe	Standard
Per unit		
Sale price	$40	$30
Variable expenses	12	10
Contribution margin	$28	$20
Contribution margin ratio	70%	66 ⅔%

After the plant expansion, the factory will have production capacity of 1,200 machine hours per month. By devoting the machine hours to deluxe appliances, the plant can manufacture 20 units of merchandise each hour. If standard appliances are emphasized, they can produce 30 units per hour.

Required

1. Identify the limiting factor for Sutfin Manufacturing.
2. Prepare an analysis to show which product to emphasize.

Problem 26-4A   *Make or buy/best use of facilities? (L.O. 1, 2)*

Duckloe Limited manufactures ski boats. Currently the company makes the seat covers. The cost of producing 1,000 seat covers each year is

Direct material	$1,100
Direct labor..	1,100
Variable overhead...	760
Fixed overhead..	2,210
Total manufacturing cost per unit................	$5,170

Belton Corporation can make the seat covers for $3 each. Duckloe would pay $.14 per unit to transport the seat covers to its manufacturing plant and add its own Duckloe label at a cost of $.05 per seat cover.

Required

1. Duckloe accountants estimate that purchasing the seat covers from Belton will enable the company to avoid $700 of fixed overhead. Prepare an analysis to show whether Duckloe should make or buy the seat covers.

2. Assume the Duckloe factory space freed up by the company's purchasing the seat covers from Belton can be used to manufacture another product that can be sold for a $1,610 profit. Fixed costs will not change. Prepare an analysis to show which alternative makes the best use of Duckloe's factory space: (a) make, (b) buy and leave facilities idle, or (c) buy and make another product.

Problem 26-5A   *Sell or process further? (L.O. 1, 2, 4)*

DuPont Canada manufactures a wide variety of chemical products. Assume that DuPont has spent $290,000 to refine 84,000 litres of acetone, which can be sold for $3.32 a litre. Alternatively, DuPont can process the acetone further and produce 77,000 litres of lacquer thinner that can be sold for $4.80 a litre. The additional processing will cost $.89 a litre. To sell the lacquer thinner, DuPont must pay a transportation charge of $.23 a litre and administrative expenses of $.16 a litre.

Required

1. Identify the sunk cost in this situation. Is the sunk cost relevant to DuPont's decision?

2. Prepare an analysis to indicate whether DuPont should sell the acetone or process it into lacquer thinner. Show the expected net revenue difference between the two alternatives.

3. Identify the opportunity cost of each alternative. State how managers use the notion of opportunity cost in making their decision.

Problem 26-6A   *Capital-budgeting decision by three methods (L.O. 5)*

Auburn Investments, Inc., operates a resort near Jasper, Alberta. The company is considering an expansion. The architectural plan calls for a construction cost of $5,200,000. Top managers of Auburn believe the expansion will generate annual net cash inflows of $700,000 for 10 years. Architects and engineers estimate that the new facilities will remain useful for 10 years and have a residual value of $2,400,000. The shareholders of Auburn Investments demand an annual return of 12 percent on investments of this nature.

Required

1. Compute the payback period, the accounting rate of return, and the net present value of this investment.

2. Make a recommendation to Auburn management as to whether the company should invest in this project.

Problem 26-7A   *Capital-budgeting decision by three methods* **(L.O. 5)**

Whole Foods Ltd. operates a chain of grocery stores that specialize in health foods. The company is considering two possible expansion plans. Plan A includes opening three stores at a cost of $4,800,000. This plan is expected to generate net cash inflows of $450,000 each year for 20 years, the estimated life of the store properties. Estimated residual value is $3,000,000. Under Plan B, Whole Foods would open eight smaller stores at a cost of $7,200,000. Expected annual net cash inflows are $860,000, with zero residual value at the end of 19 years. Whole Foods' top managers require an annual return of 8 percent.

Required

1. Compute the payback period, the accounting rate of return, and the net present value of these two investment plans.
2. Make a recommendation to Whole Foods owners as to whether the company should invest in these projects.
3. Estimate Plan B's internal rate of return (IRR). How does the IRR compare with the company's hurdle rate?

(Group B)

Problem 26-1B   *Accept or reject a special sales order?* **(L.O. 1, 2)**

Hillcrest Manufacturing Ltd. contribution margin income statement for the most recent month reports the following:

Sales — units	38,000
Sales	$95,000
Variable expenses	
Manufacturing	$19,000
Selling and administrative	27,000
Total variable expenses	46,000
Contribution margin	49,000
Fixed expenses	
Manufacturing	29,000
Selling and administrative	8,000
Total fixed expenses	37,000
Income from operations	$12,000

Canadian Marketing Limited (CML) wishes to buy 5,000 industrial belts from Hillcrest. Acceptance of the offer will not increase selling and administrative expenses. Hillcrest's plant has unused capacity to manufacture the additional belts. CML has offered $1.60 per belt, which is considerably below the normal sale price of $2.50.

Required

1. Prepare a quick summary to help determine whether Hillcrest should accept this special sales order.
2. Prepare a total analysis to show Hillcrest's operating income with and without the special sales order.
3. Identify long-run factors that Hillcrest should consider in deciding whether to accept the special sales order.

Problem 26-2B   *Retain or drop a product line? (L.O. 1, 2, 3)*

The income statement of Mazzio's Pasta Limited highlights the losses of the ravioli division:

	Total	All Other Products	Ravioli
Sales	$920,000	$630,000	$290,000
Cost of goods sold			
Variable	$170,000	$100,000	$ 70,000
Fixed	140,000	90,000	50,000
Total cost of goods sold	310,000	190,000	120,000
Gross margin	610,000	440,000	170,000
Selling and administrative expenses			
Variable	410,000	270,000	140,000
Fixed	150,000	80,000	70,000
Total selling and administrative expenses	560,000	350,000	210,000
Operating income (loss)	$ 50,000	$ 90,000	$(40,000)

Foge Mazzio, owner of the company, is considering deleting the ravioli product line. Accountants for the company estimate that dropping ravioli will decrease fixed cost of goods sold by $25,000 and decrease fixed selling and administrative expenses by $20,000.

Required

1. Prepare a quick summary to show whether Mazzio's should drop the ravioli product line.
2. Prepare a total analysis to show Mazzio's operating income with and without the ravioli division. Prepare the income statement in contribution-margin format.
3. Explain the difference between correct analysis and incorrect analysis of the decision whether to drop the ravioli product line.

Problem 26-3B   *Which product to emphasize? (L.O. 1, 2)*

Copeland Appliances is located in Corner Brook, Newfoundland. The business specializes in washers/dryers and televisions. Jim and Mary Sue Copeland, the owners, are expanding the store, and they are deciding which product line to emphasize. To make this decision, they assemble the following data, which suggest that televisions, with the higher contribution margin ratio, are more profitable:

	Washers/Dryers	Televisions
Per unit		
Sale price	$450	$320
Variable expenses	235	136
Contribution margin	$215	$184
Contribution margin ratio	47.8%	57.5%

After the renovation, the store will have 640 square metres of floor space. By devoting the new floor space to washers/dryers, the Copelands can display 35 units of merchandise in the store. If televisions are emphasized, they can display only 32 units.

Required

1. Identify the limiting factor for Copeland Appliances.

2. Prepare an analysis to show which product to emphasize. Round contribution margin per square metre to five decimal places.

Problem 26-4B *Make or buy/best use of facilities? (L.O. 1, 2)*

Western Corporation manufactures snowmobiles. Currently the company makes the seats. The cost of producing 2,000 seats each year is

Direct material	$ 3,900
Direct labor..	2,800
Variable overhead	1,040
Fixed overhead	5,110
Total manufacturing costs............................	$12,850

Regina Corporation can make the seats for $5 each. Western would pay $.17 per unit to transport the seats to its manufacturing plant and add its own Western insignia at a cost of $.03 per unit.

Required

1. Western accountants estimate that purchasing the seats from Regina will enable the company to avoid $1,800 of fixed overhead. Prepare an analysis to show whether Western should make or buy the seats.

2. Assume the Western factory space freed up by the company's purchasing the seats from Regina can be used to manufacture another product that can be sold for a $3,700 profit. Fixed costs will not change. Prepare an analysis to show which alternative makes the best use of Western's factory space: (a) make, (b) buy and leave facilities idle, or (c) buy and make another product.

Problem 26-5B *Sell or process further? (L.O. 1, 2, 4)*

The refining of crude oil by Imperial Oil Ltd. produces a variety of petroleum products. Assume that Imperial has spent $300,000 to refine 60,000 litres of petroleum distillate. Suppose Imperial can sell the distillate for $5.75 a litre. Alternatively, Imperial can process the distillate further and produce cleaner for tape heads in cassette decks. The additional processing will cost another $1.33 a litre. The tape-head cleaner can be sold for $7.50 a litre. To make this sale, Imperial must pay a sale commission of $.10 a litre and a transportation charge of $.15 a litre.

Required

1. Identify the sunk cost in this situation. Is the sunk cost relevant to Imperial's decision?

2. Prepare an analysis to indicate whether Imperial should sell the distillate or process it into tape-head cleaner for cassette decks. Show the expected net revenue difference between the two alternatives.

3. Identify the opportunity cost of each option. State how to use opportunity cost to make this decision.

Problem 26-6B *Capital-budgeting decision by three methods (L.O. 5)*

Lakeway Resorts, Inc., west of Calgary, is considering an investment. The architectural plan calls for a purchase price of $1,850,000. Top managers of Lakeway believe the new facility will generate annual net cash inflows of $385,000 for eight years. Architects and engineers estimate that the facility will remain useful for eight years and have a residual value of $600,000. The shareholders of Lakeway Resorts demand an annual return of 16 percent on investments of this nature.

Required

1. Compute the payback period, the accounting rate of return, and the net present value of this investment.

2. Make a recommendation to Lakeway management as to whether the company should invest in this project.

Problem 26-7B   *Capital-budgeting decision by three methods* **(L.O. 5)**

T.J. Cinnamon, Inc. features the original gourmet cinnamon roll. The company is considering two possible expansion plans. Plan A includes opening six stores at a cost of $2,100,000. This investment is expected to generate net cash inflows of $520,000 each year for seven years, which is the estimated life of the store properties. Because of the locations, estimated residual value is zero. Under Plan B, Cinnamon would open four stores at a cost of $1,600,000. Expected annual net cash inflows are $350,000, with residual value of $200,000 at the end of seven years, the estimated useful life of these stores. Cinnamon's top mangers require an annual return of 14 percent.

Required

1. Compute the payback period, the accounting rate of return, and the net present value of these two investment plans.

2. Make a recommendation to T.J. Cinnamon management as to whether the company should invest in these projects.

3. Estimate the internal rate of return (IRR) of Plan A. How does Plan A's IRR compare with the hurdle rate?

Extending Your Knowledge

Decision Problems

1. Selecting between two investment projects (L.O. 5)

The capital-budgeting committee of McBride Limited is evaluating two real estate investment projects. Project 1 is a shopping center in Sydney, Nova Scotia, and Project 2 is a parking garage in Vancouver. Estimated data for the two projects follow:

	Project 1			Project 2		
Year	Net Cash Inflow	Operating Income	Residual Value	Net Cash Inflow	Operating Income	Residual Value
1	$181,000	$ 80,000		$87,000	$32,000	
2	202,000	101,000		87,000	32,000	
3	234,000	133,000		87,000	32,000	
4	141,000	40,000		87,000	32,000	$30,000
5	116,000	15,000				
6	110,000	9,000	$94,000			

Project 1 requires an investment of $700,000, and Project 2 costs $250,000. McBride managers demand a 14 percent annual return on real estate investments.

Required

1. Compute the payback period, the accounting rate of return, and the net present value of the two investment projects.
2. Which capital-budgeting model is best? Give your reason.
3. McBride will invest in only one of these projects. Based on your analysis, make an investment recommendation to McBride managers.

2. Decision-making involving relevant, opportunity and sunk costs (L.O. 1, 4)

Sam Webb is a second-year business student at the University of Lethbridge. He will graduate in two years with an accounting major and a marketing minor. It is now April, and Sam is trying to decide where to work this summer. He has two choices: work full-time for a bottling plant, or work part-time in the accounting department of a meat-packing plant.

If Sam works part-time, he can take two courses toward his degree for no extra tuition. This will reduce his workload next year. It might even allow him to work part-time during the regular term in the bottling plant. In addition, the extra accounting credits this summer will qualify Sam for a full-time position with the meat-packing company next summer.

The meat-packing company and university are close enough to Sam's home for him to ride his bike. However, if he works at the bottling plant he must drive. Sam's car is a 1982 Dodge Swinger which he bought two years ago for $2,000; he is not sure how much longer the car will run.

Sam is able to work 12 weeks during the summer. This year the bottling plant is paying $300 per week; average annual increases have been 6 percent. At the meat-packing plant, Sam could work 20 hours per week at $7.90 per hour. Sam thinks he could work at the bottling plant again next summer. In a full-time position at the meat-packing company, he would earn $500 per week next summer.

Required

Advise Sam on the better course of action. Assume that the interest rate is 10 percent, and for convenience, assume Sam will receive each summer's earnings in a single amount at the end of the summer. Identify opportunity costs and sunk costs that enter your decision process. Also identify any assumptions that you make.

Ethical Issue

Missoula Construction Limited, a corporation, builds highways for the Northwest and Yukon Territories. Mike Duggins, company president, needs earth-moving equipment and is deciding among three vehicles. Vehicles 1 and 2 represent investments of equal risk, and their cash flows are both discounted at 14 percent. Vehicle 1 has a net present value of $12,500. Vehicle 2 has a net present value of –$6,000. Vehicle 3 is experimental, so its risk is higher than that of the other machines. Missoula's vice-presidents advise Duggins to apply a 16 percent interest rate to discounting cash flows for vehicle 3. At 16 percent, vehicle 3 has a net present value of –$22,000. However, a close friend owns the company marketing this machine, and Duggins wants him to get the business. When Duggins discounts vehicle 3's cash flows at 14 percent, that vehicle's net present value increases to $21,000.

Required

1. Which vehicle should Missoula purchase? Give your reason.
2. What is your opinion of Duggins' ethics if he buys vehicle 3? Who is helped and who is harmed by this action? How would your answer change if Missoula Construction Limited were a proprietorship instead of a corporation?

Answers to Self-Study Questions

1. c
2. d
3. a
4. c Fixed cost ($.19) + Cost of outside units ($.35) = $.54
5. d
6. d
7. a $45,000/$9,000 = 5 years
8. c Depreciation = $45,000/15 = $3,000 per year

$$\frac{\$9,000 - \$3,000}{\$45,000/2} = \frac{\$6,000}{\$22,500} = 26.6\%$$

9. c
10. a

Appendix A

We use accounting information for making economic decisions. Of course, these decisions can only be as good as the information we weigh in making them. Critics charge that accounting fails to provide the most accurate information possible because it fails to measure the effects of changing prices. How intelligent, then, can our economic decisions be?

We know that GAAP directs companies to assume the stable-monetary-unit concept when preparing financial statements. For accounting purposes, companies use the historical cost of the building throughout the building's lifetime. However, critics maintain that historical-cost accounting does not provide the necessary information to allow statement users to make intelligent decisions. Is it valid to assume a stable monetary unit when prices — and the dollar's value itself — change over time?

There are two forces simultaneously at work on the price of an asset over time. They are changes in the general price level and changes in specific prices of particular assets and liabilities. These are now discussed in turn.

Changes in the general price level, which is a weighted average of all the prices of goods and services in the economy, lead to changes in the purchasing power of the dollar. When the general price level increases and the purchasing power of the dollar decreases, we call it *inflation*; when the general price level decreases and the purchasing power of the dollar increases, we call it deflation. Since World War II, the world has seen almost steady inflation, that is, an almost continuous fall in the purchasing power of the dollar.

Changes in the general price level can be measured by a general price index that assigns a value of 100 to a base year. The price index tracks the movement of prices in the economy over time. A 6 percent price increase during year 1 would cause the price index to rise to a value of 106 (100×1.06) at the end of the year. A 50 percent increase in prices over a six-year period would result in a price index of 150 (100×1.50) at the end of six years.

The most widely used price index in Canada is the *Consumer Price Index* (CPI), published monthly by Statistics Canada. The CPI is based on a representative sample of food, clothing, shelter, transportation and other items purchased by an average consumer. The present base period for the CPI is 1981. Each month the average of these items' prices is compared to their prices the preceding month, and a new price index is computed. The CPI, based on 1981 as 100, was 33.1 in 1964, indicating that prices tripled from 1964 to 1981. The CPI was 154.3 at the end of 1989, an increase of 54.3 percent over 1981. Since 1989, the change in the CPI has slowed significantly and now is running at less than 2 percent a year.

As the CPI increases, the purchasing power of a dollar decreases, and it becomes more and more difficult to compare assets acquired in different years. For example, it is difficult to compare the cost of an asset bought in 19X1, when the CPI was at, say 120, with an asset that was purchased five years later in 19X6 when the CPI was at, say 140.

In order to make financial data comparable between years when inflation occurs, we restate amounts into *constant dollars*. We call dollars stated in terms of current purchasing power *nominal dollars*. We calculate constant dollars by using one year, for example, 19X1, as the base and deflating the dollars of the other year, for example, 19X6, by multiplying them by the CPI for 19X6 divided by the CPI for 19X1. Suppose Cathy Hanna bought 1 hectare of land for $2,000 in 19X1 (when the index was 120) and is considering buying a second hectare adjoining it in 19X6 (when the index is 140). The second hectare is for sale for $2,600. Hanna would compare the two prices by calculating the price of the second hectare in terms of constant or 19X1 dollars [$2,229 ($2,600 \times (120/140))$] and then comparing them; the first hecatre cost her $2,000 in 19X1 dollars.

Another way to describe inflation is in terms of decreases in the purchasing power of the dollar. A dollar today will buy less meat, less gasoline, less laundering for shirts and less of most other goods and services than a dollar would buy in 1981.

Changes in specific prices are caused by a variety of factors in addition to changes in the purchasing power of the dollar. The development of new technology can lead to falling prices for particular products. For example, computers and compact disc players have fallen in price over the past several years, in part, because of new technology. Market conditions can affect specific prices. A drought can lead to higher prices for grain because a shortage results, while a bumper crop can lead to a fall in prices.

The specific price of an asset may also be described as its current value. Specific prices can be measured in a variety of ways; two different ways that were suggested in Chapter 9 are *current replacement cost* and *net realizable value*. Current replacement cost is also called an entry or buying price, while net realizable value is an exit or selling price. An entry price is the amount of cash required to buy an asset that is similar to the asset being valued. An exit price is amount of cash that would be received from selling the asset, that is, the selling price less the cost of selling the asset.

Assume that Brehme Inc. bought land 20 years ago in June, 1970, for $500,000; the land was to be used for a planned expansion of the company's manufacturing facilities. Assume that inflation and an increase in demand for land have pushed the price of the land to $2,500,000. The specific price of the land increased by $2,000,000 ($2,500,000 – $500,000). The Consumer Price Index (based on 1981 as 100) was 41.0 in 1970 and is 157.8 in June, 1990.

The increase in the price of the land has two components: a *fictitious* component caused by inflation and a *real* component. The fictitious component is called fictitious because it is caused only by a decline in the purchasing power of the dollar; it represents no real change in the value of the asset. Thus you need $1.58 in 1990 dollars to buy what you could have bought for $.41 in 1970. The real increase is the difference between the increase in the specific price and the fictitious increase.

The fictitious gain is calculated by subtracting the historic cost from the inflation-adjusted cost:

$$[(\$500,000 \times (157.8/41.0)) - \$500,000] = \$1,424,390$$

The real gain is calculated by subtracting this amount from the increase in the specific price:

Specific price change..	$2,000,000
Fictitious gain caused by inflation.........................	1,424,390
Real Gain...	$ 575,610

By investing in the land in 1970, Brehme Inc. is $575,610, 1990 dollars better off in terms of general purchasing power than it was in 1970. Note that most of the specific price gain is illusory; it was caused by a decline in the purchasing power of the dollar.

Certain financial statement items, such as inventory, cost of goods sold, fixed assets and depreciation, are affected by changing prices more than others; providing information about the effects of changing prices on these items is helpful to users of the financial statements. However, not all assets, liabilities, revenues and expenses are affected by inflation to the same extent. For example, sales are made at a price that accurately reflects current value at the time of sale; the receivable arising from the sale reflects that same current value. Similarly, wages and salaries reflect the current value of the services performed at the time they are performed. For these financial statement accounts, current cost is historical cost.

In the remainder of this chapter, we discuss, first, issues related to the reporting of changing prices. Next, we illustrate the purchasing-power losses that accrue from holding net financial assets (and vice versa the gains from liabilities) when the purchasing power of the dollar is decreasing. The discussion concludes with a consideration of the components of the profit that arise from the sale of inventory when specific prices are increasing.

There are three issues that must be resolved when determining how to report the effects of changing prices:

1. Which attribute of the financial statement elements should be measured and reported?
2. Which capital maintenance concept should be followed?
3. What unit of measurement should be used?

The three issues are discussed below.

Attribute of Financial Statement Elements   You learned in Chapter 12 that the elements of financial statements include assets, liabilities, revenue and expenses. The attribute to be measured could be, among others, the historical cost of the element or its current value. Remember that among the possible definitions of the current value of an asset are its buying price or its selling price. As you learned in Chapter 1 and again in Chapter 12, accountants usually use historical cost in preparing financial statements according to GAAP.

Capital Maintenance   A company must maintain its capital (that is, owner's equity) if it is to continue in operation. In other words, it should not pay out to its owners more than it earns as income. This is especially true in a period of rapidly rising prices. As is illustrated below, the concept of *capital maintenance* suggests that income can be earned only after capital is maintained. In the three examples that follow we will consider measuring income under the three different capital maintenance concepts most commonly favored by accountants:

1. *Maintenance of financial capital in nominal dollars.* Financial capital is maintained in nominal dollars if the historical cost owner's equity is the same at the end of the period as it was at the beginning. Financial statements prepared under the historical cost principle are concerned with the maintenance of financial capital in nominal dollars. If they show owner's equity (ignoring dividends and capital transactions) at the end of the period is equal to owner's equity at the beginning of the period, financial capital has been maintained; if owner's equity at the end of the period is greater than owner's equity at the beginning of the period, income has been earned and is taken to be equal in amount to the increase.

    Suppose a company begins operations on January 1, 19X1 with cash of $10 and owner's equity of $10. The company buys one unit of product for $10 cash and sells the unit for $15 cash; income earned is $5. Following the historical cost principle, the company's balance sheet would be as follows after the transaction:

Assets		**Owner's Equity**	
Cash	$15	Owner's Equity	$15

    Opening owner's equity was $10 so income would be $5 ($15 – $10). A dividend of $5 could be paid and owner's equity would be maintained at $10. The company's income statement for the period would be as follows:

Sales..	$15
Cost of goods sold...	10
Income	$ 5

2. *Maintenance of financial capital in constant dollars.* The second capital maintenance concept is like the first except that the capital to be maintained is opening owner's equity adjusted for inflation during the period. If owner's equity (ignoring dividends and capital transactions) at the end of the period is equal to owner's equity at the beginning of the period adjusted for inflation during the period, financial capital has been maintained. If owner's equity at the end of the period is greater than owner's equity at the beginning of the period adjusted for inflation during the period, income has been earned and is equal in amount to the increase.

Suppose the Consumer Price Index (CPI) increased by 10 percent during 19X2. The price adjusted opening owner's equity would be $11 ($10 × 1.10). In order to maintain the purchasing power of its capital the company would have to retain $1 ($11 – $10) of the $5 excess of selling price over cost; the company's income would therefore be $4 ($5 – $1). The company's income statement for the period would be as follows:

Sales..	$15
Cost of goods sold...	10
Excess of sales over cost of goods sold....................	5
Amount required to maintain	
price-level-adjusted capital [($10 × 1.10) – $10]	1
Income...	$ 4

3. *Maintenance of operating capability or capital.* This capital maintenance concept requires the entity to maintain its *operating capability* or capacity (that is, the same level of operations as the previous year) before income can be earned. Suppose the purchase price of the product increased to $12 per unit during 19X2. To maintain its ability to operate, the company must be able to replace the unit of product sold during 19X2 at a price of $12. In order to maintain the operating capacity of its capital, the company would have to retain $2 ($12 – $10) of the $5 excess of selling price over cost; the company's income would then be $3 ($5 – $2). The company's income statement for the period would be as follows:

Sales..	$15
Cost of goods sold...	10
Excess of sales over cost of goods sold....................	5
Additional amount required to	
maintain operating capability at	
one unit of inventory ($12–$10)............................	2
Income...	$ 3

Income is earned only after operating capacity (in this case $12, the new cost of a unit of product) has been maintained. Note that the maximum amount the company will be able to pay out as a dividend and still maintain operating capacity is $3. The assumption underlying this discussion is that the company wishes to maintain the same level of operations.

The above illustrations are simple; the situation becomes more complex when the company's assets include other kinds of assets and when activities are financed by both debt and owner's equity.

Unit of Measurement   The information reported could be in nominal dollars or constant (price-adjusted) dollars. Recall that:

1. The attribute to be measured in historical cost financial statements is the historical cost of the asset, liability, revenue and expense.

2. The capital maintenance concept followed in historical cost financial statements is the maintenance of financial capital in nominal dollars.

Thus historical cost financial statements, which have been the kind traditionally compiled, use nominal dollars as the unit of measurement. Economists report national income accounts, for example, in both nominal and real or constant dollars.

After decisions have been made about the attribute to be measured, the capital maintenance concept to be adopted and the unit of measurement to be used, a decision must be made on what information should be reported and whether complete financial statements or elements from the financial statements should be reported taking into account changes in prices.

———

Until January 1983, with the exception of a few Canadian companies, annual reports contained only historical cost financial information, financial statements were prepared using the historical cost model. On that date, Section 4510 "Reporting the Effects of Changing Prices" was added to the *CICA Handbook*. Section 4510 suggested that companies whose shares were publicly traded and who met a size test (had inventories and fixed assets before depreciation of $50 million and total assets of $350 million) should issue information supplementary to the audited financial statements reporting the effects of changing prices. The information could be but did not have to be audited.

Companies meeting the size test could, but were not required to, provide the supplementary information about the effects of changing prices. Most companies elected not to provide it while those that did initially later discontinued the disclosure. The reasons that the Section 4510 experiment was not successful are not clear; two reasons put forward are the decline in the rate of inflation and the cost of the additional disclosures. The seventeenth, eighteenth, and nineteenth editions of the CICA publication, *Financial Reporting in Canada*, which is a survey of the financial statement reporting practices of 300 Canadian companies, cover the years 1983 to 1991. During that period, the percentage of companies that were covered by Section 4510 and did report information about changing prices in some form decreased from 57 percent in 1983 to 0 percent in 1990.[1] Section 4510 was withdrawn in 1991.

A company may have a purchasing-power gain from holding net monetary liabilities (that is, monetary liabilities exceed monetary assets) in a period of rising prices; if the company held net monetary assets during the same period, it would suffer a purchasing-power loss. The gain occurs during inflation because the company is able to pay its liabilities with dollars that are cheaper than the dollars borrowed.

What does the purchasing-power gain mean? Suppose you borrow $5,000 to purchase a sailboat. You repay the loan after two years, during which time prices have risen 20 percent. If you are obligated to pay only $5,000 (ignoring interest for the moment), you experience a *purchasing-power gain* of $1,000 ($5,000 multiplied by the inflation rate of 20 percent). The creditor who loaned you the money in-

---

[1] *Financial Reporting in Canada*, 17th edition, Toronto: CICA, 1987, p. 79; 18th edition, Toronto: CICA, 1990, pp. 92–93; and 19th edition, Toronto: CICA, 1992, pp. 68–70.

curs the corresponding *purchasing-power loss* of $1,000 because the dollars the creditor receives when you repay the loan are worth less than the dollars lent in terms of their command over goods and services. Interest rates are intended to compensate for this purchasing-power gain or loss, but interest is accounted for separately.

The purchasing-power gain or loss depends on the company's monetary assets and monetary liabilities. *Monetary assets* are assets whose values are stated in a fixed number of dollars. This amount does *not* change, regardless of inflation. Examples include cash and receivables. Cash of $1,000 remains cash of $1,000 whether inflation occurs or not. If you hold $1,000 cash during a period of inflation, your $1,000 will buy fewer goods and services at the end of the period. The result is a purchasing-power loss. Likewise, if you sell $1,500 of merchandise on account and you receive the cash after a period of inflation, you receive only $1,500. Holding the receivable results in a purchasing-power loss.

Nonmonetary assets are those assets whose prices do change during inflation. Examples include inventory, land, buildings and equipment. Holding nonmonetary assets does not result in a purchasing-power gain or loss.

Monetary liabilities are liabilities that are stated in a fixed number of dollars. Most liabilities are monetary. As discussed above in the sailboat example, you have a purchasing-power gain if you have a monetary liability during inflation.

The computation of the purchasing-power gain or loss is based on the company's *net monetary position* (monetary assets minus monetary liabilities). If the company has more monetary assets than monetary liabilities, it has *net monetary assets*. If its monetary liabilities exceed its monetary assets, it has *net monetary liabilities*. Most industrial corporations have net-monetary-liability positions and experience purchasing-power gains. Most financial institutions, such as banks, trust companies and insurance companies, have net-monetary-asset positions. They usually incur purchasing-power losses during inflation. A company's monetary assets and liabilities can be determined from its historical-cost balance sheet.

Exhibit A-1 illustrates one way to calculate a purchasing-power gain or loss. Dajol Ltd. had monetary assets of $450,000 in 19X8 and $520,000 in 19X9 at December 31, its year end. Monetary liabilities were $640,000 at December 31, 19X8 and $812,000 at December 31, 19X9. The CPI was 146.1 at December 31, 19X8 and 153.5 at December 31, 19X9.

At December 31, 19X8 (the beginning of 19X9), Dajol had a net-monetary-liability position of $190,000. During 19X9 the company increased its net monetary liabilities by $102 and ended 19X9 with a net-monetary-liability position of $292,000. These amounts are in the Historical Cost column. The net-monetary-liability positions are not comparable because they are stated in dollars of different purchasing power. The beginning position is stated in December 19X8 dollars, which are not comparable to the ending position, which is stated in December 19X9 dollars. The reason is that the general price level and the CPI in Canada increased during 19X9, that is, inflation occurred. To compute Dajol's overall purchasing-power gain or loss, it is necessary to compare the beginning and ending positions in dollars of equal purchasing power.

The inflation adjustments of Dajol's net monetary liabilities are in Exhibit A-1 under the columns Conversion Factor and Average 19X9 Dollars. The conversion factors are used to restate the beginning and ending net-monetary-liability positions to dollars of constant purchasing power. The Consumer Price Index (CPI) is used for the conversion. At the beginning of 19X9, when Dajol had net monetary liabilities of $190,000, the CPI was 146.1. For 19X9, the average was 149.8.

The beginning historical-cost balance is restated into average constant dollars of 19X9 by multiplying the ratio of the current-year average index (149.8) by the beginning price index (146.1). The numerator of the price-index ratio is the

EXHIBIT A-1   *Purchasing-Power Gain*

Dajol Ltd.
Gain from Purchasing Power of Net Amounts Owed
(Purchasing-Power Gain)
for the year ended December 31, 19X9
(thousands of dollars)

	Historical Cost	Conversion Factor	Average 19X9 Dollars
December 31, 19X8			
Monetary liabilities...........................	$640		
Monetary assets................................	450		
Net monetary liabilities	190	149.8	$194.8
		146.1	
Increase during year	102	149.8	102.0
		149.8	
			296.8
December 31, 19X9			
Monetary liabilities	$812		
Monetary assets	520		
Net monetary liability...................	292	149.8	285.0
		153.5	
Gain in general purchasing power from having net monetary liabilities during the year.			$ 11.8

Note: The change in dollar amount of net monetary liabilities during 19X9 is assumed to have occurred evenly over the year.

---

current-year average index, and the denominator is the price index that was in effect on the date of the balance. The adjustment of the beginning balance is (amounts rounded to the nearest thousand dollars):

Beginning Net Monetary Liabilities	×	$\dfrac{\text{Current-Year Average Consumer Price Index}}{\text{Beginning-of-Year Consumer Price Index}}$	=	Beginning Net Monetary Liabilities Stated in Average Constant Dollars of the Current Year
$190	×	$\dfrac{149.8}{146.1}$	=	$194.8

The change in net monetary liabilities during 19X9 ($102,000) is not adjusted because it occurred as the company transacted business all during the year. The average price index (149.8) is both the numerator and the denominator of the index ratio, resulting in a ratio of 1.

The subtotal in Exhibit A-1 ($296.8) is the sum of the adjusted beginning net monetary liabilities plus the increase (or minus the decrease) in net monetary liabilities that arose from the transactions of the year. During 19X9, Dajol increased its net monetary liabilities by $102,000. The subtotal of $295,000 is the amount of net monetary liabilities that Dajol would owe if the company's assets and liabilities had just kept pace with inflation during the year.

The ending historical-cost balance ($296.8) is restated into average constant dollars of 19X9 by multiplying it by the ratio of the current-year average index (148.9) to the ending price index (153.5). The adjustment of the ending balance is (amounts rounded to the nearest thousand dollars):

Ending Net Monetary Liabilities	×	Current-Year Average Consumer Price Index / End-of-Year Consumer Price Index	=	Ending Net Monetary Liabilities Stated in Average Constant Dollars of the Current Year
$292	×	$\dfrac{149.8}{153.5}$	=	$285.0

The purchasing-power gain can now be computed. Its amount is determined by subtracting the ending adjusted net-monetary-liability balance ($285,000) from the subtotal ($296,800). If Dajol had just kept pace with general inflation during 19X9, its net-monetary-liability position would have been $296,800. But at year end, the company's net monetary liabilities are only $285,000. The result is a purchasing-power gain of $11,800. Dajol's gain resulted primarily from (1) inflation during 19X9 and (2) the company's net-monetary-liability position during the year. If the company had had more monetary assets than liabilities during the year and there had been inflation, the company would have experienced a purchasing-power loss.

The purchasing-power gain computation is useful for determining how well the entity is managing its monetary position during inflation. Purchasing-power gain (or loss) can be applied to individual persons as well as businesses of all sizes.

In order to simplify the discussion in this section, we assume that there is no change in the purchasing power of the dollar in the illustrations provided below. In this way, we can focus on the trading gain and the holding gain.

A company that sells a unit of product for more than it paid for it in a period of rising prices earns a profit which has two components. Part of the profit arises from selling the product; it is called a *trading gain*. The balance of the profit arises from holding the product in inventory; it is called a *holding gain*. Todd's Cycle and Sports Ltd. buys one bicycle for $100, holds it for six months, and sells it for $180. During the six months, the cost to Todd of replacing the bicycle in inventory (or entry price) increases to $120; $120 is the amount Todd must pay to replace the bicycle that was sold. The total profit on the transaction was $80 ($180 − $100). The profit can be broken down as follows:

Selling price	$180	Trading gain	$60
Replacement cost	120		
Original cost	100	Holding gain	20

The trading profit arose from the sale of the bicycle while the holding profit arose from holding the bicycle while its replacement cost price rose from $100 to $120. The total profit ($80) is the amount we normally would recognize on the income statement; it is not broken down into components as we have done in the example.

The notion of earning a profit from simply holding an item in inventory may be difficult to grasp. Imagine two companies that sell Big Boom portable stereos. Company A buys one stereo on January 1, 19X1, from the manufacturer for $300, while Company B buys the same model from the same manufacturer for $350 on June 30, 19X1 (the cost price has increased to $350 because of an increase in the cost of components of the stereo). Both companies sell their stereos to customers on July 1, 19X1 for $500. Company A earns a total profit of $200; $50 ($350 − $300) is a holding profit, while the trading profit is $150 ($500 − $350). Company B earns a total profit of $150 ($500 – $350); there is no holding profit because Company B did not hold (own) the stereo while its cost price increased. You have probably noticed that we have assumed that the selling price increased as the cost price increased so that both companies sold the stereos for $500.

Companies that expect an increase in the replacement cost of inventory may try to earn a holding gain by purchasing more than is immediately needed. Of course, there are costs to buying the extra inventory, extra insurance coverage, extra storage costs and, perhaps, borrowing costs. If the holding gain exceeds these costs, then the decision to buy the extra inventory is sound. The situation may be complicated by the fact that there may be a change in general prices (inflation) during the holding period that may erode the potential holding gain.

Appendix B

This appendix provides present-value tables (more complete than those appearing in Chapter 16 and Chapter 26) and future-value tables.

Table B-1　*Present Value of $1*

Periods	1%	2%	3%	4%	Present Value 5%	6%	7%	8%	9%	10%	12%
1	0.990	0.980	0.971	0.962	0.952	0.943	0.935	0.926	0.917	0.909	0.893
2	0.980	0.961	0.943	0.925	0.907	0.890	0.873	0.857	0.842	0.826	0.797
3	0.971	0.942	0.915	0.889	0.864	0.840	0.816	0.794	0.772	0.751	0.712
4	0.961	0.924	0.888	0.855	0.823	0.792	0.763	0.735	0.708	0.683	0.636
5	0.951	0.906	0.883	0.822	0.784	0.747	0.713	0.681	0.650	0.621	0.567
6	0.942	0.888	0.837	0.790	0.746	0.705	0.666	0.630	0.596	0.564	0.507
7	0.933	0.871	0.813	0.760	0.711	0.665	0.623	0.583	0.547	0.513	0.452
8	0.923	0.853	0.789	0.731	0.677	0.627	0.582	0.540	0.502	0.467	0.404
9	0.914	0.837	0.766	0.703	0.645	0.592	0.544	0.500	0.460	0.424	0.361
10	0.905	0.820	0.744	0.676	0.614	0.558	0.508	0.463	0.422	0.386	0.322
11	0.896	0.804	0.722	0.650	0.585	0.527	0.475	0.429	0.388	0.350	0.287
12	0.887	0.788	0.701	0.625	0.557	0.497	0.444	0.397	0.356	0.319	0.257
13	0.879	0.773	0.681	0.601	0.530	0.469	0.415	0.368	0.326	0.290	0.229
14	0.870	0.758	0.661	0.577	0.505	0.442	0.388	0.340	0.299	0.263	0.205
15	0.861	0.743	0.642	0.555	0.481	0.417	0.362	0.315	0.275	0.239	0.183
16	0.853	0.728	0.623	0.534	0.458	0.394	0.339	0.292	0.252	0.218	0.163
17	0.844	0.714	0.605	0.513	0.436	0.371	0.317	0.270	0.231	0.198	0.146
18	0.836	0.700	0.587	0.494	0.416	0.350	0.296	0.250	0.212	0.180	0.130
19	0.828	0.686	0.570	0.475	0.396	0.331	0.277	0.232	0.194	0.164	0.116
20	0.820	0.673	0.554	0.456	0.377	0.312	0.258	0.215	0.178	0.149	0.104
21	0.811	0.660	0.538	0.439	0.359	0.294	0.242	0.199	0.164	0.135	0.093
22	0.803	0.647	0.522	0.422	0.342	0.278	0.226	0.184	0.150	0.123	0.083
23	0.795	0.634	0.507	0.406	0.326	0.262	0.211	0.170	0.138	0.112	0.074
24	0.788	0.622	0.492	0.390	0.310	0.247	0.197	0.158	0.126	0.102	0.066
25	0.780	0.610	0.478	0.375	0.295	0.233	0.184	0.146	0.116	0.092	0.059
26	0.772	0.598	0.464	0.361	0.281	0.220	0.172	0.135	0.106	0.084	0.053
27	0.764	0.586	0.450	0.347	0.268	0.207	0.161	0.125	0.098	0.076	0.047
28	0.757	0.574	0.437	0.333	0.255	0.196	0.150	0.116	0.090	0.069	0.042
29	0.749	0.563	0.424	0.321	0.243	0.185	0.141	0.107	0.082	0.063	0.037
30	0.742	0.552	0.412	0.308	0.231	0.174	0.131	0.099	0.075	0.057	0.033
40	0.672	0.453	0.307	0.208	0.142	0.097	0.067	0.046	0.032	0.022	0.011
50	0.608	0.372	0.228	0.141	0.087	0.054	0.034	0.021	0.013	0.009	0.003

Table B-1   *(cont'd)*

					Present Value						
14%	15%	16%	18%	20%	25%	30%	35%	40%	45%	50%	Periods
0.877	0.870	0.862	0.847	0.833	0.800	0.769	0.741	0.714	0.690	0.667	1
0.769	0.756	0.743	0.718	0.694	0.640	0.592	0.549	0.510	0.476	0.444	2
0.675	0.658	0.641	0.609	0.579	0.512	0.455	0.406	0.364	0.328	0.296	3
0.592	0.572	0.552	0.516	0.482	0.410	0.350	0.301	0.260	0.226	0.198	4
0.519	0.497	0.476	0.437	0.402	0.328	0.269	0.223	0.186	0.156	0.132	5
0.456	0.432	0.410	0.370	0.335	0.262	0.207	0.165	0.133	0.108	0.088	6
0.400	0.376	0.354	0.314	0.279	0.210	0.159	0.122	0.095	0.074	0.059	7
0.351	0.327	0.305	0.266	0.233	0.168	0.123	0.091	0.068	0.051	0.039	8
0.308	0.284	0.263	0.225	0.194	0.134	0.094	0.067	0.048	0.035	0.026	9
0.270	0.247	0.227	0.191	0.162	0.107	0.073	0.050	0.035	0.024	0.017	10
0.237	0.215	0.195	0.162	0.135	0.086	0.056	0.037	0.025	0.017	0.012	11
0.208	0.187	0.168	0.137	0.112	0.069	0.043	0.027	0.018	0.012	0.008	12
0.182	0.163	0.145	0.116	0.093	0.055	0.033	0.020	0.013	0.008	0.005	13
0.160	0.141	0.125	0.099	0.078	0.044	0.025	0.015	0.009	0.006	0.003	14
0.140	0.123	0.108	0.084	0.065	0.035	0.020	0.011	0.006	0.004	0.002	15
0.123	0.107	0.093	0.071	0.054	0.028	0.015	0.008	0.005	0.003	0.002	16
0.108	0.093	0.080	0.060	0.045	0.023	0.012	0.006	0.003	0.002	0.001	17
0.095	0.081	0.069	0.051	0.038	0.018	0.009	0.005	0.002	0.001	0.001	18
0.083	0.070	0.060	0.043	0.031	0.014	0.007	0.003	0.002	0.001		19
0.073	0.061	0.051	0.037	0.026	0.012	0.005	0.002	0.001	0.001		20
0.064	0.053	0.044	0.031	0.022	0.009	0.004	0.002	0.001			21
0.056	0.046	0.038	0.026	0.018	0.007	0.003	0.001	0.001			22
0.049	0.040	0.033	0.022	0.015	0.006	0.002	0.001				23
0.043	0.035	0.028	0.019	0.013	0.005	0.002	0.001				24
0.038	0.030	0.024	0.016	0.010	0.004	0.001	0.001				25
0.033	0.026	0.021	0.014	0.009	0.003	0.001					26
0.029	0.023	0.018	0.011	0.007	0.002	0.001					27
0.026	0.020	0.016	0.010	0.006	0.002	0.001					28
0.022	0.017	0.014	0.008	0.005	0.002						29
0.020	0.015	0.012	0.007	0.004	0.001						30
0.005	0.004	0.003	0.001	0.001							40
0.001	0.001	0.001									50

Table B-2 Present Value of Annuity $1

Periods	1%	2%	3%	4%	Present Value 5%	6%	7%	8%	9%	10%	12%
1	0.990	0.980	0.971	0.962	0.952	0.943	0.935	0.926	0.917	0.909	0.893
2	1.970	1.942	1.913	1.886	1.859	1.833	1.808	1.783	1.759	1.736	1.690
3	2.941	2.884	2.829	2.775	2.723	2.673	2.624	2.577	2.531	2.487	2.402
4	3.902	3.808	3.717	3.630	3.546	3.465	3.387	3.312	3.240	3.170	3.037
5	4.853	4.713	4.580	4.452	4.329	4.212	4.100	3.993	3.890	3.791	3.605
6	5.795	5.601	5.417	5.242	5.076	4.917	4.767	4.623	4.486	4.355	4.111
7	6.728	6.472	6.230	6.002	5.786	5.582	5.389	5.206	5.033	4.868	4.564
8	7.652	7.325	7.020	6.733	6.463	6.210	5.971	5.747	5.535	5.335	4.968
9	8.566	8.162	7.786	7.435	7.108	6.802	6.515	6.247	5.995	5.759	5.328
10	9.471	8.983	8.530	8.111	7.722	7.360	7.024	6.710	6.418	6.145	5.650
11	10.368	9.787	9.253	8.760	8.306	7.887	7.499	7.139	6.805	6.495	5.938
12	11.255	10.575	9.954	9.385	8.863	8.384	7.943	7.536	7.161	6.814	6.194
13	12.134	11.348	10.635	9.986	9.394	8.853	8.358	7.904	7.487	7.103	6.424
14	13.004	12.106	11.296	10.563	9.899	9.295	8.745	8.244	7.786	7.367	6.628
15	13.865	12.849	11.938	11.118	10.380	9.712	9.108	8.559	8.061	7.606	6.811
16	14.718	13.578	12.561	11.652	10.838	10.106	9.447	8.851	8.313	7.824	6.974
17	15.562	14.292	13.166	12.166	11.274	10.477	9.763	9.122	8.544	8.022	7.120
18	16.398	14.992	13.754	12.659	11.690	10.828	10.059	9.372	8.756	8.201	7.250
19	17.226	15.678	14.324	13.134	12.085	11.158	10.336	9.604	8.950	8.365	7.366
20	18.046	16.351	14.878	13.590	12.462	11.470	10.594	9.818	9.129	8.514	7.469
21	18.857	17.011	15.415	14.029	12.821	11.764	10.836	10.017	9.292	8.649	7.562
22	19.660	17.658	15.937	14.451	13.163	12.042	11.061	10.201	9.442	8.772	7.645
23	20.456	18.292	16.444	14.857	13.489	12.303	11.272	10.371	9.580	8.883	7.718
24	21.243	18.914	16.936	15.247	13.799	12.550	11.469	10.529	9.707	8.985	7.784
25	22.023	19.523	17.413	15.622	14.094	12.783	11.654	10.675	9.823	9.077	7.843
26	22.795	20.121	17.877	15.983	14.375	13.003	11.826	10.810	9.929	9.161	7.896
27	23.560	20.707	18.327	16.330	14.643	13.211	11.987	10.935	10.027	9.237	7.943
28	24.316	21.281	18.764	16.663	14.898	13.406	12.137	11.051	10.116	9.307	7.984
29	25.066	21.844	19.189	16.984	15.141	13.591	12.278	11.158	10.198	9.370	8.022
30	25.808	22.396	19.600	17.292	15.373	13.765	12.409	11.258	10.274	9.427	8.055
40	32.835	27.355	23.115	19.793	17.159	15.046	13.332	11.925	10.757	9.779	8.244
50	39.196	31.424	25.730	21.482	18.256	15.762	13.801	12.234	10.962	9.915	8.305

Table B-2   *(cont'd)*

					Present Value						
14%	**15%**	**16%**	**18%**	**20%**	**25%**	**30%**	**35%**	**40%**	**45%**	**50%**	**Periods**
0.877	0.870	0.862	0.847	0.833	0.800	0.769	0.741	0.714	0.690	0.667	1
1.647	1.626	1.605	1.566	1.528	1.440	1.361	1.289	1.224	1.165	1.111	2
2.322	2.283	2.246	2.174	2.106	1.952	1.816	1.696	1.589	1.493	1.407	3
2.914	2.855	2.798	2.690	2.589	2.362	2.166	1.997	1.849	1.720	1.605	4
3.433	3.352	3.274	3.127	2.991	2.689	2.436	2.220	2.035	1.876	1.737	5
3.889	3.784	3.685	3.498	3.326	2.951	2.643	2.385	2.168	1.983	1.824	6
4.288	4.160	4.039	3.812	3.605	3.161	2.802	2.508	2.263	2.057	1.883	7
4.639	4.487	4.344	4.078	3.837	3.329	2.925	2.598	2.331	2.109	1.922	8
4.946	4.772	4.607	4.303	4.031	3.463	3.019	2.665	2.379	2.144	1.948	9
5.216	5.019	4.833	4.494	4.192	3.571	3.092	2.715	2.414	2.168	1.965	10
5.453	5.234	5.029	4.656	4.327	3.656	3.147	2.752	2.438	2.185	1.977	11
5.660	5.421	5.197	4.793	4.439	3.725	3.190	2.779	2.456	2.197	1.985	12
5.842	5.583	5.342	4.910	4.533	3.780	3.223	2.799	2.469	2.204	1.990	13
6.002	5.724	5.468	5.008	4.611	3.824	3.249	2.814	2.478	2.210	1.993	14
6.142	5.847	5.575	5.092	4.675	3.859	3.268	2.825	2.484	2.214	1.995	15
6.265	5.954	5.669	5.162	4.730	3.887	3.283	2.834	2.489	2.216	1.997	16
6.373	6.047	5.749	5.222	4.775	3.910	3.295	2.840	2.492	2.218	1.998	17
6.467	6.128	5.818	5.273	4.812	3.928	3.304	2.844	2.494	2.219	1.999	18
6.550	6.198	5.877	5.316	4.844	3.942	3.311	2.848	2.496	2.220	1.999	19
6.623	6.259	5.929	5.353	4.870	3.954	3.316	2.850	2.497	2.221	1.999	20
6.687	6.312	5.973	5.384	4.891	3.963	3.320	2.852	2.498	2.221	2.000	21
6.743	6.359	6.011	5.410	4.909	3.970	3.323	2.853	2.498	2.222	2.000	22
6.792	6.399	6.044	5.432	4.925	3.976	3.325	2.854	2.499	2.222	2.000	23
6.835	6.434	6.073	5.451	4.937	3.981	3.327	2.855	2.499	2.222	2.000	24
6.873	6.464	6.097	5.467	4.948	3.985	3.329	2.856	2.499	2.222	2.000	25
6.906	6.491	6.118	5.480	4.956	3.988	3.330	2.856	2.500	2.222	2.000	26
6.935	6.514	6.136	5.492	4.964	3.990	3.331	2.856	2.500	2.222	2.000	27
6.961	6.534	6.152	5.502	4.970	3.992	3.331	2.857	2.500	2.222	2.000	28
6.983	6.551	6.166	5.510	4.975	3.994	3.332	2.857	2.500	2.222	2.000	29
7.003	6.566	6.177	5.517	4.979	3.995	3.332	2.857	2.500	2.222	2.000	30
7.105	6.642	6.234	5.548	4.997	3.999	3.333	2.857	2.500	2.222	2.000	40
7.133	6.661	6.246	5.554	4.999	4.000	3.333	2.857	2.500	2.222	2.000	50

Table B-3 Future Value of $1

Periods	1%	2%	3%	4%	5%	6%	7%	8%	9%	10%	12%	14%	15%
						Future Value							
1	1.010	1.020	1.030	1.040	1.050	1.060	1.070	1.080	1.090	1.100	1.120	1.140	1.150
2	1.020	1.040	1.061	1.082	1.103	1.124	1.145	1.166	1.188	1.210	1.254	1.300	1.323
3	1.030	1.061	1.093	1.125	1.158	1.191	1.225	1.260	1.295	1.331	1.405	1.482	1.521
4	1.041	1.082	1.126	1.170	1.216	1.262	1.311	1.360	1.412	1.464	1.574	1.689	1.749
5	1.051	1.104	1.159	1.217	1.276	1.338	1.403	1.469	1.539	1.611	1.762	1.925	2.011
6	1.062	1.126	1.194	1.265	1.340	1.419	1.501	1.587	1.677	1.772	1.974	2.195	2.313
7	1.072	1.149	1.230	1.316	1.407	1.504	1.606	1.714	1.828	1.949	2.211	2.502	2.660
8	1.083	1.172	1.267	1.369	1.477	1.594	1.718	1.851	1.993	2.144	2.476	2.853	3.059
9	1.094	1.195	1.305	1.423	1.551	1.689	1.838	1.999	2.172	2.358	2.773	3.252	3.518
10	1.105	1.219	1.344	1.480	1.629	1.791	1.967	2.159	2.367	2.594	3.106	3.707	4.046
11	1.116	1.243	1.384	1.539	1.710	1.898	2.105	2.332	2.580	2.853	3.479	4.226	4.652
12	1.127	1.268	1.426	1.601	1.796	2.012	2.252	2.518	2.813	3.138	3.896	4.818	5.350
13	1.138	1.294	1.469	1.665	1.886	2.133	2.410	2.720	3.066	3.452	4.363	5.492	6.153
14	1.149	1.319	1.513	1.732	1.980	2.261	2.579	2.937	3.342	3.798	4.887	6.261	7.076
15	1.161	1.346	1.558	1.801	2.079	2.397	2.759	3.172	3.642	4.177	5.474	7.138	8.137
16	1.173	1.373	1.605	1.873	2.183	2.540	2.952	3.426	3.970	4.595	6.130	8.137	9.358
17	1.184	1.400	1.653	1.948	2.292	2.693	3.159	3.700	4.328	5.054	6.866	9.276	10.76
18	1.196	1.428	1.702	2.026	2.407	2.854	3.380	3.996	4.717	5.560	7.690	10.58	12.38
19	1.208	1.457	1.754	2.107	2.527	3.026	3.617	4.316	5.142	6.116	8.613	12.06	14.23
20	1.220	1.486	1.806	2.191	2.653	3.207	3.870	4.661	5.604	6.728	9.646	13.74	16.37
21	1.232	1.516	1.860	2.279	2.786	3.400	4.141	5.034	6.109	7.400	10.80	15.67	18.82
22	1.245	1.546	1.916	2.370	2.925	3.604	4.430	5.437	6.659	8.140	12.10	17.86	21.64
23	1.257	1.577	1.974	2.465	3.072	3.820	4.741	5.871	7.258	8.954	13.55	20.36	24.89
24	1.270	1.608	2.033	2.563	3.225	4.049	5.072	6.341	7.911	9.850	15.18	23.21	28.63
25	1.282	1.641	2.094	2.666	3.386	4.292	5.427	6.848	8.623	10.83	17.00	26.46	32.92
26	1.295	1.673	2.157	2.772	3.556	4.549	5.807	7.396	9.399	11.92	19.04	30.17	37.86
27	1.308	1.707	2.221	2.883	3.733	4.822	6.214	7.988	10.25	13.11	21.32	34.39	43.54
28	1.321	1.741	2.288	2.999	3.920	5.112	6.649	8.627	11.17	14.42	23.88	39.20	50.07
29	1.335	1.776	2.357	3.119	4.116	5.418	7.114	9.317	12.17	15.86	26.75	44.69	57.58
30	1.348	1.811	2.427	3.243	4.322	5.743	7.612	10.06	13.27	17.45	29.96	50.95	66.21
40	1.489	2.208	3.262	4.801	7.040	10.29	14.97	21.72	31.41	45.26	93.05	188.9	267.9
50	1.645	2.692	4.384	7.107	11.47	18.42	29.46	46.90	74.36	117.4	289.0	700.2	1,084

Table B-4   *Future Value of Annuity of $1*

Periods	1%	2%	3%	4%	5%	Future Value 6%	7%	8%	9%	10%	12%	14%	15%
1	1.000	1.000	1.000	1.000	1.000	1.000	1.000	1.000	1.000	1.000	1.000	1.000	1.000
2	2.010	2.020	2.030	2.040	2.050	2.060	2.070	2.080	2.090	2.100	2.120	2.140	2.150
3	3.030	3.060	3.091	3.122	3.153	3.184	3.215	3.246	3.278	3.310	3.374	3.440	3.473
4	4.060	4.122	4.184	4.246	4.310	4.375	4.440	4.506	4.573	4.641	4.779	4.921	4.993
5	5.101	5.204	5.309	5.416	5.526	5.637	5.751	5.867	5.985	6.105	6.353	6.610	6.742
6	6.152	6.308	6.468	6.633	6.802	6.975	7.153	7.336	7.523	7.716	8.115	8.536	8.754
7	7.214	7.434	7.662	7.898	8.142	8.394	8.654	8.923	9.200	9.487	10.09	10.73	11.07
8	8.286	8.583	8.892	9.214	9.549	9.897	10.26	10.64	11.03	11.44	12.30	13.23	13.73
9	9.369	9.755	10.16	10.58	11.03	11.49	11.98	12.49	13.02	13.58	14.78	16.09	16.79
10	10.46	10.95	11.46	12.01	12.58	13.18	13.82	14.49	15.19	15.94	17.55	19.34	20.30
11	11.57	12.17	12.81	13.49	14.21	14.97	15.78	16.65	17.56	18.53	20.65	23.04	24.35
12	12.68	13.41	14.19	15.03	15.92	16.87	17.89	18.98	20.14	21.38	24.13	27.27	29.00
13	13.81	14.68	15.62	16.63	17.71	18.88	20.14	21.50	22.95	24.52	28.03	32.09	34.35
14	14.95	15.97	17.09	18.29	19.60	21.02	22.55	24.21	26.02	27.98	32.39	37.58	40.50
15	16.10	17.29	18.60	20.02	21.58	23.28	25.13	27.15	29.36	31.77	37.28	43.84	47.58
16	17.26	18.64	20.16	21.82	23.66	25.67	27.89	30.32	33.00	35.95	42.75	50.98	55.72
17	18.43	20.01	21.76	23.70	25.84	28.21	30.84	33.75	36.97	40.54	48.88	59.12	65.08
18	19.61	21.41	23.41	25.65	28.13	30.91	34.00	37.45	41.30	45.60	55.75	68.39	75.84
19	20.81	22.84	25.12	27.67	30.54	33.76	37.38	41.45	46.02	51.16	63.44	78.97	88.21
20	22.02	24.30	26.87	29.78	33.07	36.79	41.00	45.76	51.16	57.28	72.05	91.02	102.4
21	23.24	25.78	28.68	31.97	35.72	39.99	44.87	50.42	56.76	64.00	81.70	104.8	118.8
22	24.47	27.30	30.54	34.25	38.51	43.39	49.01	55.46	62.87	71.40	92.50	120.4	137.6
23	25.72	28.85	32.45	36.62	41.43	47.00	53.44	60.89	69.53	79.54	104.6	138.3	159.3
24	26.97	30.42	34.43	39.08	44.50	50.82	58.18	66.76	76.79	88.50	118.2	158.7	184.2
25	28.24	32.03	36.46	41.65	47.73	54.86	63.25	73.11	84.70	98.35	133.3	181.9	212.8
26	29.53	33.67	38.55	44.31	51.11	59.16	68.68	79.95	93.32	109.2	150.3	208.3	245.7
27	30.82	35.34	40.71	47.08	54.67	63.71	74.48	87.35	102.7	121.1	169.4	238.5	283.6
28	32.13	37.05	42.93	49.97	58.40	68.53	80.70	95.34	113.0	134.2	190.7	272.9	327.1
29	33.45	38.79	45.22	52.97	62.32	73.64	87.35	104.0	124.1	148.6	214.6	312.1	377.2
30	34.78	40.57	47.58	56.08	66.44	79.06	94.46	113.3	136.3	164.5	241.3	356.8	434.7
40	48.89	60.40	75.40	95.03	120.8	154.8	199.6	259.1	337.9	442.6	767.1	1,342	1,779
50	64.46	84.58	112.8	152.7	209.3	290.3	406.5	573.8	815.1	1,164	2,400	4,995	7,218

Appendix C

J.M. SCHNEIDER INC.

HORIZON POULTRY PRODUCTS INC.

CHARCUTERIE ROY INC.

MOTHER JACKSON'S OPEN KITCHENS LIMITED

NATIONAL MEATS INC.

SCHNEIDER CORPORATION

A new look for the 90's

CORPORATE PROFILE

Schneider Corporation of Kitchener, Ontario is one of Canada's largest producers of premium quality food products. The Corporation was founded in 1890 by John Metz Schneider who began making pork sausage in his home. Today, as a publicly owned corporation, Schneider Corporation has over 3,300 employees manufacturing and selling a wide variety of meat, poultry, cheese and baked goods products. These products are sold throughout Canada, and to the United States, Japan and other foreign markets.

The majority of the Corporation's meat processing is done through its subsidiary, J.M. Schneider Inc. which operates plants in Winnipeg, Manitoba, and Kitchener, Ontario. Meat products are also manufactured by the Corporation's subsidiary, Charcuterie Roy Inc. in St-Anselme, Quebec and by a joint venture company, National Meats Inc. in Toronto, Ontario

Cheese products are manufactured at J.M. Schneider Inc. processing plants in Millbank and Winchester, Ontario.

The Corporation has a 50% joint venture interest in Horizon Poultry Products Inc. Operations include a major hatchery in Hanover, Ontario, and manufacturing and processing facilities in Paris, Ayr and Kitchener, Ontario.

Mother Jackson's Open Kitchens Limited, also a subsidiary of the Corporation, manufactures a variety of baked goods products at its facility in Port Perry, Ontario. Schneider products are warehoused and shipped through major distribution centres in Vancouver, British Columbia, Calgary, Alberta, Winnipeg, Manitoba and Kitchener, Ontario.

In 1991, Schneider Corporation had sales of $630,966,000 and assets of $175,466,000. The Corporation's most valuable asset is its reputation for providing consumers with the finest quality food products available in the marketplace.

MANAGEMENT'S REPORT

Management of Schneider Corporation is responsible for the integrity and objectivity of the financial statements and all other information contained in the Annual Report. The financial statemetns have been prepared in accordance with generally accepted accounting principles and are based on management's best information and judgments.

In fulfilling its responsibilities, management has devleoped internal control systems and procedures designed to provide reasonable assurance that the Corporation's assets are safeguarded, that transactions are executed in accordance with appropriate authorization and that accounting records may be relied upon to properly reflect the Corporation's business transactions. To augment the internal control systems, the Corporation maintains an internal audit department which evaluates company operations and formally reports on the adequacy and effectiveness of the controls and procedures to the Audit Committee of the Board of Directors.

The Audit Committee of the Board of Directors is composed of a majority of outside directors. The committee meets periodically and independently with management, the internal auditors and the shareholders' auditors to discuss the Corporation's financial reporting and interanl controls. Both the internal auditors and the independent external auditors have unrestricted access to the Audit Committee.

Management recognizes its responsibility for conducting the Corporation's affairs in the best interest of its shareholders. The responsibility is characterized in the Code of Conduct signed by each management employee which provides for compliance with laws of each jurisdiction in which the Corporation operates and for observance of rules of ethical business conduct.

Douglas W. Dodds
President and Chief Executive Officer

Gerald A. Hooper
Vice-President and Chief Financial Officer

AUDITORS' REPORT

To the Shareholders

We have audited the consolidated balance sheets of Schneider Corporation as at October 26, 1991 and October 27, 1990 and the consolidated statements of earnings, retained earnings and changes in financial position for the years then ended. These financial statements are the responsibility of the Corporation's management. Our responsibility is to express an opinion on these financial statements based on our audits.

We conducted our audits in accordance with generally accepted auditing standards. Those standards require that we plan and perform an audit to obtain reasonable assurance whether the financial statements are free of material misstatement. An audit includes examining, on a test basis, evidence supporting the amounts and disclosures in the financial statements. An audit also includes assessing the accounting principles used and significant estimates made by management, as well as evaluating the overall financial statement presentation.

In our opinion, these consolidated financial statements present fairly, in all material respects, the financial position of Schneider Corporation as at October 26, 1991 and October 27, 1990 and the results of its operations and the changes in its financial position for the years then ended in accordance with generally accepted accounting principles.

Peat Marwick Thorne

Chartered Accountants, Kitchener, Canada, November 29, 1991

CONSOLIDATED BALANCE SHEETS

October 26, 1991 and October 27, 1990
(in thousands of dollars)

Assets	1991	1990
		(restated)
Current assets:		
Accounts receivable	$33,379	$29,556
Inventories	38,811	44,163
Income taxes recoverable	—	1,872
Current portion of loans receivable	463	—
Other	2,405	2,739
Total current assets	75,058	78,330
Property, plant and equipment	89,352	81,077
Other assets:		
Loans receivable	2,606	1,173
Production licences and rights	3,800	2,825
Intangible assets	4,650	3,115
Total other assets	11,056	7,113
Total assets	$175,466	$166,520

Liabilities and Shareholders' Equity	1991	1990
		(restated)
Current liabilities:		
Bank advances	$4,894	$22,695
Outstanding cheques	4,578	8,462
Accounts payable and accrued liabilities	34,808	31,109
Income taxes payable	4,458	—
Principal due within one year on debentures and loans	5,569	3,496
Total current liabilities	54,307	65,762
Debentures and loans	44,900	30,490
Other liabilities:		
Deferred income taxes	5,893	8,102
Deferred gains	1,814	—
Deferred pension liability	1,038	943
Minority interest	568	—
Total other liabilities	9,313	9,045
Shareholders' equity:		
Capital stock	11,529	9,668
Retained earnings	55,417	51,555
Total shareholders' equity	66,946	61,223
Total liabilities and shareholders' equity	$175,466	$166,520

The accompanying notes are an integral part of these statements.

On behalf of the Board:

Director   Director

CONSOLIDATED STATEMENTS OF EARNINGS

Years ended October 26, 1991 and October 27, 1990
(in thousands of dollars, except per share amounts)

	1991	1990
		(restated)
Sales $630,966	**$627,797**	
Expenses:		
Cost of products sold	**559,470**	567,411
Selling, marketing, and administrative	**46,091**	44,726
Depreciation and amortization	**9,419**	9,661
	614,980	621,798
Earnings from operations	**15,986**	5,999
Interest expense	**6,951**	7,910
Earnings (loss) before income taxes	**9,035**	(1,911)
Income taxes (recovery)	**3,971**	(234)
Net earnings (loss)	**$ 5,064**	$ (1,677)
Earnings (loss) per share	**$ 1.86**	$ (.62)

CONSOLIDATED STATEMENTS OF RETAINED EARNINGS

Years ended October 26, 1991 and October 27, 1990
(in thousands of dollars)

	1991	1990
		(restated)
Balance, beginning of year:		
As previously reproted	**$50,987**	$54,414
Adjustment of prior year's earnings	**568**	—
As restated	**51,555**	54,414
Net earnings (loss)	**5,064**	(1,677)
	56,619	52,737
Dividends:		
Class A shares	**1,037**	1,017
Common shares	**165**	165
	1,202	1,182
Balance, end of year	**$55,417**	$51,555

The accompanying notes are an integral part of these statements.

CONSOLIDATED STATEMENTS OF CHANGES IN FINANCIAL POSITION

Years ended October 26, 1991 and October 27, 1990
(in thousands of dollars)

	1991	1990
		(restated)
Operating activities:		
Cash from operations	$12,285	$ 8,327
Net change in non-cash working capital		
balances relating to operations	9,372	2,624
Cash provided by operating activities	21,657	10,951
Investment activities:		
Acquisition of subsidiaries and joint venture,		
less cash received of $1,104	(13,874)	—
Additions to property, plant and equipment	(5,475)	(15,952)
Proceeds on sale of equipment	168	205
Cash used in investment activities	(19,181)	(15,747)
Financing activities:		
Proceeds from loans	15,450	3,738
Transfer of assets to joint venture, net of deferred gains	3,060	—
Proceeds from issue of shares	1,861	1,229
Decrease (increase) in loans receivable	337	(80)
Decrease in debentures and loans	(4,181)	(2,397)
Dividends	(1,202)	(1,182)
Cash provided by financing activities	15,325	1,308
Increase (decrease) in bank advances	(17,801)	3,488
Bank advances, beginning of year	22,695	19,207
Bank advances, end of year	$ 4,894	$22,695
Cash from operations is derived as follows:		
Net earnings (loss)	$ 5,064	$ (1,677)
Adjustment for non-cash items:		
Depreciation and amortization	9,419	9,661
Deferred income taxes (reduction)	(2,692)	46
Loss on sale of equipment	387	93
Deferred pension liability	95	204
Minority interest in earnings of subsidiary	12	—
	$12,285	$ 8,327

The accompanying notes are an integral part of these statements.

NOTES TO CONSOLIDATED FINANCIAL STATEMENTS

Years ended October 26, 1991 and October 27, 1990
(tabular amounts only in thousands of dollars)

1. **Significant accounting policies:**

    (a) Basis of consolidation:
    The consolidated financial statements include the accounts of the Corporation and all of its subsidiaries and the Corporation's proportionate share of the assets, liabilities, revenues and expenses of joint ventures.

    (b) Inventories:
    Products are valued at the lower of cost and net realizable value. Since most products can be sold at any stage in their production, it is not practical to segregate them into raw materials, work in process or finished goods. Cost includes laid down material cost, manufacturing labour and certain elements of overhead to the stage of production completion. Net realizable value is based on the adjusted wholesale trading price at the balance sheet date.

    Certain raw materials and supplies, which include packaging, maintenance and manufacturing materials, are valued at the lower of cost and replacement cost.

    (c) Property, plant and equipment:
    Property, plant and equipment are stated at cost which includes capitalized interest incurred on major projects during the period of construction. Depreciation is provided on a straight-line bais to amortize the cost of the assets over their estimated useful life with estimated useful lives not to exceed certain limits. Depreciation is not provided on assets under construction.

	Maximum useful lives	Annual rates of depreciation
Buildings of solid constuction	40 years	2.5% to 5%
Buildings of frame construction and im proved areas	25 years	4% to 25%
Machinery and equipment	15 years	7% to 25%

    (d) Other assets:
    Production licences and rights and intangible assets are being amortized on a straight-line basis over their estimated lives, such amortization period not exceeding forty years. The Corporation recognizes permanent impairment in the value of these assets by additional charges against earnings.

    (e) Other liabilities:
    Deferred gains, which relate to asset transfers to joint ventures, will be included in income when amounts receivable from a joint venture partner are repaid or through amortization over the remaining estimated useful lives of the transferred assets.

    Pension obligations are determined by independent actuarial valuation using the accrued benefit method. Pension costs related to current service are charged to earnings as services are rendered, and past service costs, as well as variations between fund experience and the actuarial estiamtes, are amortized over the expected average remaining service life of each employee group.

    (f) Earnings per share:
    Earnings per share are calculated on the weighted average number of all classes of shares outstanding during the year.

2.   **Acquisitions:**

During 1991, the Corporation increased its investment in Mother Jackson's Open Kitchens Limited to a 72% interest and made the following acquisitions directly or through a 50% owned joint venture company:

Company name	Nature of business	Effective accquisition date	Voting interest acquired
Chickens, Inc. and Saville Food Products Inc.	Poultry slaughter	November 30, 1990	50%
Charcuterie Roy Inc.	Processed and speciality meats	August 2, 1991	100%
National Meats Inc.	Ground meats	August 6, 1991	50%
Mother Jackson's Open Kitchens Limited	Baked goods	August 31, 1991	22%

The Corporation acquired a 50% interest in a joint venture company, National Meats Inc., by contributing assets with a book value of $6,120,000. In addition to the joint venture interest, the Corporation received assets from the joint venture partner consisting primarily of cash and notes receivable. The fair value of the joint venture interest and the assets received exceeded the Corporation's share of the book value of the assets contributed and this difference has been recorded in the financial statements as a deferred gain.

Details of other acquisitions are as follows:

Net assets acquired at assigned values:	
Property, plant and equipment	$15,586
Other assets	1,126
Net working capital	1,770
Other liabilities	(7,652)
Excess cost of shares over assigned values of net assets	1,644
	12,474
Less minority interest	556
	$11,918
Consideration given at fair value:	
Cash	$ 8,345
Loans payable within one year	2,000
65,534 Class A shares	1,573
	$11,918

The acquisitions have been accounted for by the purchase method with the results of operations included in these financial statements from the dates of acquisition.

The Corporation is committed to paying additional consideration for the shares of Charcuterie Roy Inc. in each of the next five years based on earnings of that company during the period, with total additional consideration not to exceed $4,750,000. The additional consideration will be recorded as an additional cost of the purchase as it becomes determinable.

3.   **Joint ventures:**

The Corporation's joint venture investments include Schneider Horizon Inc., Mother Jackson's Open Kitchens Limited to the date of acquisition of control on August 31, 1991, and National Meats Inc., from the date of acquisition on August 6, 1991.

NOTES TO CONSOLIDATED FINANCIAL STATEMENTS

Years ended October 26, 1991 and October 27, 1990
(tabular amounts only in thousands of dollars)

Consolidated financial statements for the Corporation include a proportionate share of the assets, liabilities, revenues and expenses of these joint ventures as follows:

	1991	1990
Assets	$20,909	$21,817
Liabilities	14,718	14,564
Sales:		
Intercompany	40,254	25,727
Other	10,893	9,609
	51,147	35,336
Expenses, excluding income taxes	52,625	33,738

4. **Property, plant and equipment:**

	Cost	Accumulated depreciation	1991 Net book value	1990 Net book value
Land and improved areas	$ 5,162	$ 606	$ 4,556	$ 4,643
Buildings and leasehold improvements	66,214	28,856	37,358	32,278
Machinery and equipment	100,048	57,727	42,321	36,042
Assets under construction	5,117	—	5,117	8,114
	$176,541	$87,189	$89,352	$81,077

Interest capitalized on major projects during the period of construction was $nil in 1991 (1990 - $595,000). The Board of Directors has approved capital expenditures on future projects of $5,355,000.

5. **Loans receivable:**

	1991	1990
Loan receivable, interest at bank prime less 1/4%, maturing August 6, 1996	$2,213	$ —
Non-interest bearing loans receivable from companies which are related by virture of common management with joint venture companies, due on demand but not expected to be repaid prior to October 31, 1992	856	1,173
	3,069	1,173
Principal included in current assets	463	—
	$2,606	$1,173

6. **Debentures and loans:**

	1991	1990
Loans payable, interest at 7.875% to 12.15%, maturing at dates from December, 1991 to August, 1996	$30,053	$13,380
12.3% Sinking fund debentures, maturing Aug. 15, 1995	8,500	9,800
Bank term loans, interest at bank prime rate, repayable in monthly principal instalments	5,576	5,256
10.75% Sinking fund debentures, maturing Feb. 1, 1997	4,500	4,950
Mortgages payable at lender's cost of borrowing plus 2.25%, maturing July, 1999	920	—
Mortgages payable at bank prime rate plus 1.25%, maturing November, 1994	920	—
8.5% Sinking fund debentures, repaid during the year	—	600
	50,469	33,986
Principal included in current liabilities	5,569	3,496
	$44,900	$30,490
Interest for the year	$ 4,957	$ 3,602

Principal due within each of the next five years is as follows:

1992	$ 5,569
1993	3,911
1994	16,231
1995	6,439
1996	14,676

The debentures are secured by fixed and specific charges on certain assets and floating charges on all assets of the Corporation.

A trust indenture securing the sinking fund debentures contains certain covenants some of which limit the creation of additional debt and the entering into of long-term leases and restricts the use of proceeds from the sale of a substantial part of the Corporation's property, plant and equipment. The Corporation has undertaken not to declare or pay dividends or otherwise make changes in its capital which would have the effect of reducing the Corporation's equity below $50,000,000. In addition, the Corporation is required to maintain certain other financial ratios.

Bank term loans and certain bank advances are secured by an assignment of accounts receivable of a joint venture company as well as first fixed charge debentures, of which the Corporation's proportionate share is $9,500,000, covering all assets of the joint venture.

Loans payable of $5,600,000 and certain bank advances are secured by a fixed charge debenture in the amount of $3,500,000 covering property and plant of a subsidiary company, as well as an assignment of short-term investments and a general security agreement covering all assets of the subsidiary.

7. **Capital stock:**

	1991	1990
Authorized:		
5,401,000 Class A non-voting shares		
373,627 common shares		
Issued:		
2,418,722 Class A shares (1990 - 2,341,188)	$11,295	$9,434
373,627 common shares	234	234
	$11,529	$9668

The holders of the Class A shares are entitled toa 24¢ cumulative annual dividend and equal participation with the holders of common shares in annual dividends in excess of 24¢ and in any distribution of assets of the Corporation to its shareholders.

The Class A shares are restricted shares in that they are generally non-voting and only vote in very limited circumstances on matters respecting the attributes of the class itself, or in relation to the common shares where class approval is specifically required.

A "coat-tail" provision has been attached to the Class A shares which is designed to ensure that all holders of the Class A shares have an equal opportunity toarticipate with the holders of the common shares in any premium paid on a take-over bid.

During the year, the Corporation issued 12, 000 Class A shares to participants of its employee Share Purchase Plan for cash consideration of $288,000 and 65,534 Class A shares in connection with the acquisition of a company for consideration of $1,573,000. In 1990, the Corporation issued 63,660 Class A shares to participants of its employee Share Purchase Plan for cash consideration of $1,229,000.

NOTES TO CONSOLIDATED FINANCIAL STATEMENTS

Years ended October 26, 1991 and October 27, 1990
(tabular amounts only in thousands of dollars)

8. Income taxes:

	1991	1990
The Corporation's effective income tax rate on earnings (loss) is made up as follows:	%	%
Combined basic Canadian federal and provincial rate (recovery)	44.3	(44.3)
Adjustment in income tax rate resulting from:		
Manufacturing and processing deduction	(5.3)	4.3
Ontario manufacturing and processing current cost adjustment	(2.0)	(4.1)
Non-deductible expenses	2.9	12.5
Large corporations tax in excess of federal surtax	—	9.0
Other	4.0	10.4
Effective income tax rate (recovery)	43.9	(12.2)

9. Prior year's adjustment:

As a result of a ruling by the United States International Trade Commission during the year, countervailing duty charges on Canadian fresh, chilled and frozen pork exports to the United States were reversed. The effect of the change on the prior year, which has been included in retained earnings, amounted to $568,000, net of income taxes of $425,000. Comparative figures have been restated to reflect this change.

10. Pension plans:

The Corporation maintains defined benefit pension plans which provided pension benefits for most employees, based on years of service and contributions. The comparison of benefit obligations with assets of the pension plans is as follows:

	1991	1990
Pension plan assets at market value	$115,634	$ 96,667
Estimated present value of pension plan obligations	126,831	116,957

11. Commitments:

(a) The Corporation has issued letters of credit in the amount of $265,000 (1990 - $1,836,000).

(b) The following is a schedule of future rental payments required under operating leases as of the year end:

1992	$ 4,585
1993	2,380
1994	1,496
1995	803
1996	519
Later years	1,623
	$11,406

12. Segmented information:

The Corporation's principal business activity is the processing and distribution of meat and related food products. All of the Corporation's operations, employees and assets are located in Canada.

Sales to customers in foreign countries amounted to $47,520,000 in 1991 (1990 - $64,533,000).

13. Other information:

(a) The Corporation is incorporated under the laws of Ontario

	1991	1990
(b) Depreciation	$9,179	$9,423
Amortization	240	238

(c) Certain 1990 figures have been reclassified to conform with those presented in the 1991 financial statements.

(d) The Corporation has signed a letter of intent to study the feasibility of forming a national distribution joint venture with Maple Leaf Foods Inc. This study is now completed and is currently being reviewed by both companies.

Schneider Corporation

TEN YEAR STATISTICAL REVIEW

(thousands of dollars except where noted)

	1991	*1990	1989	1988	1987	1986	1985	1984	1983	1982
Operations:										
Sales	$630,966	627,797	619,168	597,932	683,934	648,468	648,598	645,558	590,074	581,071
Depreciation and amortization	9,419	9,661	8,195	7,543	6,688	6,458	7,072	5,960	5,978	5,861
Salaries, wages and employee benefits	138,491	132,688	134,549	122,372	121,780	117,129	126,791	128,316	108,508	100,515
Interest expense	6,951	7,910	4,861	4,182	4,774	4,285	5,303	4,502	3,557	5,375
Income taxes (recovery)	3,971	(234)	516	1,790	4,502	883	832	4,245	4,222	2,238
Earnings (loss) before extraordinary items	5,064	(1,677)	20	2,007	5,612	1,102	2,009	5,766	5,272	2,887
Earnings (loss) before extraordinary items as a percent of sales	0.80	(0.27)	0.00	0.34	0.82	0.17	0.31	0.89	0.89	0.50
Net earnings (loss)	5,064	(1,677)	20	2,007	5,612	1,102	(2,036)	5,766	5,272	2,887
Net earnings (loss) as a percent of sales	0.80	(0.27)	0.00	0.34	0.82	0.17	(0.31)	0.89	0.89	0.50
Cash flow:										
Cash from operations	12,285	8,327	8,291	11,160	16,484	5,357	8,053	11,067	10,834	8,337
Capital expenditures	5,475	15,952	16,722	10,249	8,001	5,072	6,983	5,254	5,741	3,329
Dividends paid	1,202	1,182	1,167	1,167	1,167	1,167	1,167	1,167	1,167	1,162
Financial position:										
Working capital	20,751	12,568	19,782	23,219	25,604	21,995	22,786	24,336	22,487	22,333
Working capital ratio	1.38	1.19	1.28	1.43	1.45	1.42	1.41	1.49	1.51	1.62
Total assets	175,466	166,520	171,749	144,338	146,942	137,245	143,814	136,811	126,867	119,715
Long-term debt	44,900	30,490	30,251	17,350	19,538	23,063	24,999	19,259	19,747	24,089
Shareholders' equity, end of year	66,946	61,223	62,853	64,000	63,160	58,715	58,780	61,983	57,384	53,279
Percent return on equity, beginning of year	8.27	(2.67)	0.03	3.18	9.56	1.87	(3.28)	10.05	9.90	5.62
Per share statistics, in dollars:										
Earnings (loss) before extraordinary items	1.86	(0.62)	0.01	0.76	2.12	0.42	0.76	2.17	1.99	1.10
Net earnings (loss)	1.86	(0.62)	0.01	0.76	2.12	0.42	(0.77)	2.17	1.99	1.10
Dividends paid	0.44	0.44	0.44	0.44	0.44	0.44	0.44	0.44	0.44	0.44
Equity, end of year	23.97	22.55	23.71	24.14	23.83	22.15	22.17	23.38	21.64	20.10

*1990 results restated

Glossary

Accelerated depreciation See Declining-balance method (438)

Account The detailed record of the changes that have occurred in a particular asset, liability or owner equity during a period (45)

Account format of the balance sheet Format that lists the assets at the left with liabilities and owner equity at the right (160)

Account payable A liability that is not written out. Instead, it is backed by the reputation and credit standing of the debtor (14)

Account receivable An asset, a promise to receive cash from customers to whom the business has sold goods or services (14)

Accounting The system that measures business activities, processes that information into reports and financial statements, and communicates the findings to decision-makers (2)

Accounting cycle Process by which accountants produce an entity's financial statements for a specific period (138)

Accounting information system The combination of personnel, records and procedures that a business uses to meet its need for financial data (256)

Accounting rate of return The remainder of average annual net cash inflow from operations minus annual depreciation, divided by average amount invested in the business. This is the most widely used measure of profitability. The higher the accounting rate of return, the better the investment (1144)

Accounting Standards Board (ASB) The ASB issues Recommendations on accounting (Volume 1 of the *CICA Handbook*) which are the basis of generally accepted accounting principles (GAAP) (527)

Accounts receivable turnover Ratio of net credit sales to average net accounts receivable.

Measures ability to collect cash from credit customers (853)

Accrual-basis accounting Accounting that recognizes (records) the impact of a business event as it occurs, regardless of whether the transaction affected cash (94)

Accrued expense An expense that has been incurred but not yet paid in cash (103)

Accrued revenue A revenue that has been earned but not yet received in cash (104)

Accumulated depreciation The cumulative sum of all depreciation expense from the date of acquiring a capital asset (102)

Acid-test ratio Ratio of the sum of cash plus short-term investments plus net current receivables to current liabilities. Tells whether the entity could pay all its current liabilities if they came due immediately. Also called the quick ratio (370, 852)

Activity-based costing A system that focuses on activities as the fundamental cost objects and uses the cost of these activities as building blocks for compiling the costs of products and other cost objects (1025-1026)

Adjusted trial balance A list of all the ledger accounts with their adjusted balances (108)

Adjusting entry Entry made at the end of the period to assign revenues to the period in which they are earned and expenses to the period in which they are incurred. Adjusting entries help measure the period's income and bring the related asset and liability accounts to correct balances for the financial statements (99)

Aging of accounts receivable A way to estimate bad debts by analyzing individual accounts receivable according to the length of time they have been due (357)

Allocation base Logical common denominator for assigning a given cost to two or more departments of a business (1100)

Allowance for doubtful accounts A contra account, related to accounts receivable, that holds the estimated amount of collection losses. Also called Allowance for uncollectible accounts (354)

Allowance for uncollectible accounts Another name for Allowance for doubtful accounts (354)

Allowance method A method of recording collection losses based on estimates prior to determining that the business will not collect from specific customers (354)

Amortization The term the *CICA Handbook* uses to describe the systematic changing of the cost of a capital asset; it is often called depreciation when applied to property, plant and equipment and depletion when applied to wasting assets. Also the term used to describe the writing off to expense of intangible assets (449)

Annuity Stream of equal periodic amounts (1146)

Appropriation of retained earnings Restriction of retained earnings that is recorded by a formal journal entry (661)

Articles of incorporation The document issued by the federal or provincial government giving the incorporators permission to form a corporation (611)

Asset An economic resource a business owns that is expected to be of benefit in the future (14)

Auditing The examination of financial statements by outside accountants, the most significant service that public accountants perform. The conclusion of an audit is the accountant's professional opinion about the financial statements (9)

Authorization of stock Provision in the articles of incorporation of a corporation that gives the issuing jurisdiction's permission for the corporation to use (that is, to sell) a certain number of shares of stock (618)

Average cost method Inventory costing method based on the average cost of inventory during the period. Average cost is determined by dividing the cost of goods available for sale by the number of units available (396)

Avoidable fixed overhead Fixed costs that are relevant to a special decision because they differ between the alternatives (1137)

Bad debt expense Another name for Uncollectible accounts expense (353)

Balance sheet List of an entity's assets, liabilities and owner equity as of a specific date. Also called the statement of financial position (19)

Balancing the ledgers Establishing the equality of (a) total debits and total credits in the general ledger, (b) the balance of the accounts receivable control account in the general ledger and the sum of individual customer accounts in the accounts receivable subsidiary ledger, or (c) the balance of the accounts payable control account in the general ledger and the sum of individual creditor accounts in the accounts payable subsidiary ledger (277)

Bank collection Collection of money by the bank on behalf of a depositor (311)

Bank reconciliation Process of explaining the reasons for the difference between a depositor's records and the bank's records about the depositor's bank account (309)

Bank statement Document for a particular bank account showing its beginning and ending balances and listing the month's transactions that affected the account (308)

Batch processing Computerized accounting for similar transactions in a group or batch (260)

Beginning inventory Goods left over from the preceding period (393)

Betterment Expenditure that increases the capacity or efficiency of an asset or extends its useful life. Capital expenditures are debited to an asset account (452)

Board of directors Group elected by the shareholders to set policy for a corporation and to appoint its officers (613)

Bond discount Excess of a bond's maturity (par) value over its issue price (693)

Bond indenture Contract under which bonds are issued (705)

Bond premium Excess of a bond's issue price over its maturity (par) value (693)

Bond sinking fund Group of assets segregated for the purpose of retiring bonds payable at maturity (705)

Bonds payable Groups of notes payable (bonds) issued to multiple lenders called bondholders (691)

Bonus Amount over and above regular compensation (485)

Book value of a capital asset The asset's cost less accumulated amortization (or depreciation or depletion) (102)

Book value of stock Amount of owners' equity on the company's books for each share of its stock (630)

Book value per share of common stock Common shareholders' equity divided by the number of shares of common stock outstanding (860)

Branch accounting System for separating the accounts of a branch of a business from the accounts of the home office (1105)

Branch-factory ledger control Account in the home-office ledger that represents the home-office investment in or receivable from a branch of the business (1106)

Branch ledger The part of a general ledger kept by a branch of the business, separate from the home-office ledger (1105)

Break-even analysis Another name for Cost-volume-profit analysis (933)

Break-even point Amount of unit sales or dollar sales at which revenue equals expenses (933)

Budget Management's tool for forecasting a business's future in amounts, including the quantities of products to be sold and their expected selling prices, the numbers of employees and their pay, and a host of other amounts that are ultimately expressed in dollars (890)

Budget committee Group that prepares the master budget; includes representatives from all departments of the business (890)

Budget formula The heart of a flexible budget; shows how to compute the budget amounts (1060)

Budgeted factory overhead rate Budgeted total overhead cost divided by the budgeted rate base (982)

Budgeting Setting of goals for a business, such as its sales and profits, for a future period (9)

Bylaws Constitution for governing a corporation (613)

Byproduct Output of a joint production process with minor sales value in comparison to the main product (1031)

Callable bonds Bonds that the issuer may call or pay off at a specified price whenever the issuer wants (706)

Canada (or Quebec) Pension Plan All employees and self-employed persons in Canada (except in Quebec where the pension plan is the Quebec Pension Plan) between 18 and 70 years of age are required to contribute to the Canada Pension Plan administered by the Government of Canada (488)

Capital Another name for the owner's equity of a business (14)

Capital asset Long-lived assets, like land, buildings and equipment, wasting assets and intangible assets used in the operation of the business (101)

Capital budgeting Formal means of making long-range decisions for investments such as plant locations, equipment purchases, additions of product lines, and territorial expansions (1142)

Capital cost allowance Depreciation allowed for income tax purposes by Revenue Canada; the rates allowed are called capital cost allowance rates (438)

Capital deficiency Debit balance in a partner's capital account (589)

Capital lease Lease agreement that transfers substantially all of the benefits and risks of ownership from the lessor to the lessee (709, 711)

Capital stock A corporation's capital from investments by the shareholders. Also called Share capital (614)

Cash-basis accounting Accounting that records only transactions in which cash is received or paid (95)

Cash budget Details the way a business intends to go from the beginning cash balance to the desired ending balance. Also called the Statement of budgeted cash receipts and disbursements (898)

Cash disbursements journal Special journal used to record cash disbursements by cheque (271)

Cash equivalent Highly liquid short-term investments that can be converted into cash with little delay (778)

Cash flows Cash receipts and cash payments (disbursements) (778)

Cash receipts journal Special journal used to record cash receipts (264)

Certified General Accountant (CGA) A professional accountant who earns this title through a combination of education and experience and the passing of national exams in certain subjects. A member of the Certified General Accountants Association of Canada (5)

Certified Management Accountant (CMA) A professional accountant who earns this title through a combination of education, experience, and acceptable scores on national written examinations. A member of the Society of Management Accountants of Canada (5)

Chartered Accountant (CA) A professional accountant who earns this title through a combination of education, experience, and an acceptable score on a written four-part national examination. A member of the Canadian Institute of Chartered Accountants (5)

Chairperson of the board Elected person on a corporation's board of directors, usually the most powerful person in the corporation (613)

Change in accounting estimate A change that occurs in the normal course of business as a company alters earlier expectations. Decreasing uncollectible account expense from 2 percent to 1½ percent of sales and changing the estimated useful life of a capital asset are examples (539)

Change in accounting principle A change in accounting method, such as from the FIFO method to the LIFO method for inventories and a switch from declining-balance depreciation to straight-line (538)

Chart of accounts List of all the accounts and their account numbers in the ledger (60)

Cheque Document that instructs the bank to pay the designated person or business the specified amount of money (308)

Cheque register Special journal used to record all cheques issued in a voucher system (323)

Closing entries Entries that transfer the revenue, expense, and owner withdrawal balances from these respective accounts to the capital account (152)

Closing the accounts Step in the accounting cycle at the end of the period that prepares the accounts for recording the transactions of the next period. Closing the accounts consists of journalizing and posting the closing entries to set the balances of the revenue, expense, and owner withdrawal accounts to zero (152)

Collection method Method of applying the revenue principle by which the seller waits until cash is received to record the sale. This method is used only if the receipt of cash is uncertain (534)

Commission Employee compensation computed as a percentage of the sales that the employee has made (485)

Common-size statement A financial statement that reports only percentages (no dollar amounts); a type of vertical analysis (845)

Common stock The most basic form of capital stock. In describing a corporation, the common shareholders are the owners of the business (616-617)

Comparability principle Specifies that accounting information must be comparable from business to business and that a single business's financial statements must be comparable from one period to the next (532)

Completed-contract method Method of applying the revenue principle by a construction company by which all revenue earned on the project is recorded in the period when the project is completed (535)

Conservatism Concept that underlies presenting the gloomiest possible figures in the financial statements (401)

Consignment Transfer of goods by the owner (consignor) to another business (consignee) who, for a fee, sells the inventory on the owner's behalf. The consignee does not take title to the consigned goods (395)

Consistency principle A business must use the same accounting methods and procedures from period to period (399)

Consolidated accounting A method of combining the financial statements of two or more companies that are controlled by the same owners (743)

Consolidated statements A combination of the balance sheets, income statements, and other financial statements of the parent company with those of the subsidiaries into an overall set as if the parents and its subsidiaries were a single entity (743)

Consolidation method for investments A way to combine the financial statements of two or more companies that are controlled by the same owners (743)

Constraint Item that restricts production or sales. Also called the Limiting factor (1136)

Contingent liability A potential liability (367)

Continuous budget Systematically adds a month or a quarter as the month or quarter just ended is deleted. Also called a Rolling budget (903)

Contra account An account with two distinguishing characteristics: (1) it always has a companion account and (2) its normal balance is opposite that of the companion account (102)

Contra asset An asset account with a credit balance. A contra account always has a companion account and its balance is opposite that of the companion account (102)

Contract interest rate Interest rate that determines the amount of cash interest the borrower pays and the investor receives each year. Also called the Stated interest rate (694)

Contribution margin Excess of sale price over variable expenses (931)

Contribution margin income statement Separates expenses into variable costs and fixed costs and highlights the contribution margin, which is the excess of sales over variable expenses (931)

Contribution margin percentage Sales of 100 percent minus the variable expense percentage (935)

Control account An account whose balance equals the sum of the balances in a group of related accounts in a subsidiary ledger (264)

Controllable variance Another name for the Flexible budget overhead variance (1071)

Controlling (majority) interest Ownership of more than 50 percent of an investee company's voting stock (743)

Conversion cost All manufacturing costs other than direct materials costs (direct labor and overhead) (1014)

Convertible bonds Bonds that may be converted into the common stock of the issuing company at the option of the investor (706)

Convertible preferred stock Preferred stock that may be exchanged by the preferred shareholders, if they choose, for another class of stock in the corporation (627)

Copyright Exclusive right to reproduce and sell a book, musical composition, film, or other work of art. Issued by the federal government, copyrights extend 50 years beyond the author's life (450)

Corporation A business owned by shareholders that begins when the federal government or provincial government approves its articles of incorporation. A corporation is a legal entity, an "artificial person," in the eyes of the law (11)

Cost Resources given up to achieve a specific objective (1057)

Cost accounting The branch of accounting that determines and controls a business's costs (9)

Cost allocation Assignment of various costs to the departments of a business (1100)

Cost application base A common denominator linking costs among all products. Ideally the best available measure of the cause-and-effect relationship between overhead costs and production volume (982)

Cost behavior Description of how costs change in response to a shift in the volume of business activity (928)

Cost center Responsibility center in which a manager is accountable for costs (expenses) only (1096)

Cost control Used to help plan and control the manufacturing function (966)

Cost driver Any factor whose change causes a difference in a related total cost (928)

Cost method for investment The method used to account for short-term investments in stock and for long-term investments when the investor holds less than 20 percent of the investee's voting stock. Under the cost method, investments are recorded at cost and reported at the lower of their cost or market value (738)

Cost object   Anything for which it is worthwhile to compile costs, such as an activity, a department, or a product (1025)

Cost of a capital asset   Purchase price, sales tax, purchase commission and all other amounts paid to acquire the asset and to ready it for its intended use (433)

Cost of goods manufactured   Manufacturers' counterpart to the Purchases account. Cost of goods manufactured takes the place of purchases in the computation of cost of goods sold (968)

Cost of goods sold   The cost of the inventory that the business has sold to customers, the largest single expense of most merchandising businesses. Also called Cost of sales (206)

Cost of sales   Another name for Cost of goods sold (206)

Cost principle   States that assets and services are recorded at their purchase cost and that the accounting record of the asset continues to be based on cost rather than current market value (533)

Cost-volume-profit (CVP) analysis   Expresses the relationships among a business's costs, volume and profit or loss. An important part of a budgeting system that helps managers predict the outcome of their decisions (928)

Coupon bonds   Bonds for which the owners receive interest by detaching a perforated coupon (which states the interest due and the date of payment) from the bond and depositing it in a bank for collection (692)

CPP   Abbreviation for Canada Pension Plan (488)

Credit   The right side of an account (48)

Credit memorandum   Document issued by a seller to indicate having credited a customer's account receivable account (273)

Creditor   The party to a credit transaction who sells a service or merchandise and obtains a receivable (352)

Cumulative preferred stock   Preferred stock whose owners must receive all dividends in arrears before the corporation pays dividends to the common shareholders (626)

Current asset   An asset that is expected to be converted to cash, sold, or consumed during the next 12 months, or within the business's normal operating cycle if longer than a year (159)

Current liability   A debt due to be paid within one year or one of the entity's operating cycles if the cycle is longer than a year (159)

Currently attainable standards   Standards that can be achieved but with difficulty. Serve as a significant positive motivational force for employees (1065)

Current portion of long-term debt   Amount of the principal that is payable within one year (479)

Current ratio   Current assets divided by current liabilities (161, 851)

Date of record   Date on which the owners of stock to receive a dividend are identified (625)

Days' sales in receivables   Ratio of average net accounts receivable to one day's sales. Tells how many days' sales remain in Accounts Receivable awaiting collection (371, 854)

Debentures   Unsecured bonds, backed only by the good faith of the borrower (692)

Debit   The left side of an account (48)

Debit memorandum   Business document issued by a buyer to state that the buyer no longer owes the seller for the amount of returned purchases (275)

Debt ratio   Ratio of total liabilities to total assets. Tells the proportion of a company's assets that it has financed with debt (161, 855)

Debtor   The party to a credit transaction who makes a purchase and creates a payable (352)

Decision model   A method or technique for evaluating and choosing among alternative courses of action (1142)

Declaration date   Date on which the board of directors announces the intention to pay a dividend. The declaration creates a liability for the corporation (625)

Declining-balance (DB) method of depreciation   A type of depreciation method that writes off a relatively larger amount of an asset's cost nearer the start of its useful life than does the straight-line method (438)

Default on a note   Failure of the maker of a note to pay at maturity. Also called Dishonor of a note (367)

Deferred revenue   Another name for Unearned revenue (479)

Deficit   Debit balance in the retained earnings account (615)

Defined benefits pension plan   Benefits to be paid to the employee upon retirement are specified (712)

Defined contribution pension plan   The contribution to the plan is defined and the benefits to be paid to the employee depend on what is available at retirement (712)

Depletion   That portion of a wasting asset's natural resource cost that is used up in a particular period. Depletion expense is computed in the same way as units of production depreciation (448)

Deposit in transit   A deposit recorded by the company but not yet by its bank (311)

Depreciable cost   The asset's cost minus its estimated residual value (435)

Depreciation   Expense associated with spreading (allocating) the cost of a capital asset over its useful life (101)

Direct expense   Expense that is conveniently identified with and traceable to a particular department of a business (1100)

Direct labor   Cost of salaries and wages for the employees who physically convert materials into the company's products (969)

Direct material   Material that becomes a physical part of a finished product and whose cost is separately and conveniently traceable through the manufacturing process to finished goods (968)

Direct method   Format of the operating activities section of the statement of changes in financial position that lists the major categories of operating cash receipts (collections from customers and receipts of interest and dividends) and cash disbursements (payments to suppliers, to employees, for interest and income taxes) (782)

Direct write-off method   A method of accounting for bad debts by which the company waits until the credit department decides that a cus-

tomer's account receivable is uncollectible and then records uncollectible account expense and credits the customer's account receivable (359)

Disclosure principle   Holds that a company's financial statements should report enough information for outsiders to make knowledgeable decisions about the company (536)

Discount rate   Management's minimum desired rate of return on an investment, used in a present value computation (1146)

Discounting a note payable   A borrowing arrangement in which the bank subtracts the interest amount from the note's face value. The borrower receives the net amount (475)

Discounting a note receivable   Selling a note receivable before its maturity (366)

Dishonor of a note   Another name for Default on a note (367)

Disposal value   Same as Estimated residual value (435)

Dissolution   Ending of a partnership (570)

Dividend yield   Ratio of dividends per share of stock to the stock's market price per share (859)

Dividends   Distributions by a corporation to its shareholders (616)

Dividends in arrears   Cumulative preferred dividends that the corporation has failed to pay (626)

Donated capital   Special category of shareholders' equity created when a corporation receives a donation (gift) from a donor who receives no ownership interest in the company (623)

Double taxation   Corporations pay their own income taxes on corporate income. Then, the shareholders pay personal income tax on the cash dividends that they receive from corporations (612)

Doubtful account expense   Another name for Uncollectible account expense (353)

Earnings per share (EPS)   Amount of a company's net income per share of its outstanding common stock (666)

Economic dependence   A company that is dependent on another company as its supplier or customer (544)

Effective interest rate   The rate that investors demand for loaning their money. Another name for Market interest rate (694)

Efficiency variance   Difference between the quantity of inputs (materials and labor) actually used and the quantity that should have been used (the flexible budget) for the actual output achieved, multiplied by the standard unit price of the input. Also called the Usage variance and the Quantity variance (1064)

Efficient capital market   One in which the market prices fully reflect all information available to the public (861)

Electronic fund transfer   System that accounts for cash transactions by electronic impulses rather than paper documents (326)

Ending inventory   Goods still on hand at the end of the period (393)

Entity   An organization or a section of an organization that, for accounting purposes, stands apart from other organizations and individuals as a separate economic unit. This is the most basic concept in accounting (11-12)

EPS   Abbreviation of Earnings per share of common stock (666)

Equity method for investments   The method used to account for investments in which the investor can significantly influence the decisions of the investee. Under the equity method, investments are recorded initially at cost. The investment account is debited (increased) for ownership in the investee's net income and credited (decreased) for ownership in the investee's dividends (742)

Equivalent units   Measure of the number of complete units that could have been manufactured from start to finish using the costs incurred during the period (1014)

Estimated residual value   Expected cash value of an asset at the end of its useful life. Also called Residual value, Scrap value and Salvage value (435)

Estimated useful life   Length of the service that a business expects to get from an asset; may be expressed in years, units of output, miles or other measures (435)

Expense   Decrease in owner equity that occurs in the course of delivering goods or services to customers or clients (17)

Expense allocation   Assignment of various expenses to the departments of a business (1100)

Extraordinary item   A gain or loss that is infrequent, not typical of the business and does not depend on a management decision (666)

Factory ledger   A branch ledger for a manufacturing plant (1105)

Factory overhead   All manufacturing costs other than direct materials and direct labor (969)

FIFO   The First-in, first-out inventory method (396)

Financial accounting   The branch of accounting that provides information to people outside the business (10)

Financial budget   Projects the means of raising money from shareholders and creditors and plans cash management (893)

Financial statements   Business documents that report financial information about an entity to persons and organizations outside the business (19)

Financing activity   Activity that obtains the funds from investors and creditors needed to launch and sustain the business. A section of the statement of changes in financial position (780)

Finished goods inventory   Completed goods that have not yet been sold (967)

First-in, first-out (FIFO) method   Inventory costing method by which the first costs into inventory are the first costs out to cost of goods sold. Ending inventory is based on the costs of the most recent purchases (396)

Fixed cost   Cost that does not change in total as volume changes (929)

Fixed expense   Expense that does not change in total as volume changes (929)

Flexible budget   Set of budgets covering a range of volume rather than a single level of volume (1058)

Flexible budget overhead variance   Difference between total actual overhead (fixed and variable) and the flexible budget amount for actual production volume. Also called the Controllable variance (1071)

Flexible budget variance   Difference between an amount in the flexible budget and the actual results for the corresponding item (1061)

FOB destination   Terms of a transaction that govern when the title to the inventory passes from the seller to the purchaser — when the goods arrive at the purchaser's location (394)

FOB shipping point   Terms of a transaction that govern when the title to the inventory passes from the seller to the purchaser — when the goods leave the seller's place of business (394)

Foreign-currency exchange rate   The measure of one currency against another currency (754)

Foreign-currency transaction gain or loss   This occurs when the exchange rate changes between the date of the purchase on account and the date of the subsequent payment of cash (755)

Franchises and licenses   Privileges granted by a private business or a government to sell a product or service in accordance with specified conditions (450)

Fringe benefits   Employee compensation, like health and life insurance and retirement pay, which the employee does not receive immediately in cash (485)

Gain   An increase in owner equity that does not result from a revenue or an investment by an owner in the business (547)

Generally accepted accounting principles (GAAP)   Accounting guidelines, formulated by the CICA's Accounting Standards Committee, that govern how businesses report their financial statements to the public (6)

General journal   Journal used to record all transactions that do not fit one of the special journals (262)

General ledger   Ledger of accounts that are reported in the financial statements (262)

Going-concern concept   Accountants' assumption that the business will continue operating in the foreseeable future (530)

Goods available for sale   Beginning inventory plus net purchases (393)

Goodwill   Excess of the cost of an acquired company over the sum of the market values of its net assets (assets minus liabilities) (451)

Gross margin   Excess of sales revenue over cost of goods sold. Also called Gross profit (199)

Gross margin method   A way to estimate inventory based on a rearrangement of the cost of goods sold model: Beginning inventory + Net purchases = Cost of goods available for sale. Cost of goods available for sale – Cost of goods sold = Ending inventory. Also called the Gross profit method (404-405)

Gross pay   Total amount of salary, wages, commissions, or any other employee compensation before taxes and other deductions are taken out (485)

Gross profit   Excess of sales revenue over cost of goods sold. Also called Gross margin (199)

Gross profit method   Another name for the gross margin method of estimating inventory cost (404-405)

Hardware   Equipment that makes up a computer system (259)

Hedging   This means to protect oneself from losing by engaging in a counterbalancing transaction (757)

High-low method   Method of separating a mixed cost into its variable and fixed components (943)

Home-office ledger   The part of a general ledger kept by the home office, separate from the branch ledger, which the branch keeps (1105)

Home-office ledger control   Account in the branch ledger that represents an owner equity of or branch payable to the home office (1106)

Horizontal analysis   Study of percentage changes in comparative financial statements (841)

Imprest system   A way to account for petty cash by maintaining a constant balance in the petty cash account, supported by the fund (cash plus disbursement tickets) totaling the same amount (320)

Income from operations   Gross margin (sales revenue minus cost of goods sold) minus operating expenses. Also called Operating income (214)

Income statement   List of an entity's revenues, expenses, and net income or net loss for a specific period. Also called the Statement of operations (19)

Income summary   A temporary "holding tank" account into which the revenues and expenses are transferred prior to their final transfer to the capital account (152)

Incorporators   Persons who organize a corporation (613)

Indirect expense   Expense that is not traceable to a single department of a business; an expense other than a direct expense. Often indirect expenses arise from activities that serve more than one department simultaneously (1100)

Indirect labor   Factory labor costs other than direct labor. Indirect labor costs, which are difficult to trace to specific products, include the pay of forklift operators, janitors and plant guards (969)

Indirect materials   Manufacturing materials whose cost cannot easily be traced directly to particular finished products (969)

Indirect method   Format of the operating activities section of the statement of changes in financial position that starts with net income and shows the reconciliation from net income to operating cash flows. Also called the Reconciliation method (795-796)

Information system design   Identification of an organization's information needs, and development and implementation of the system to meet those needs (9)

Installment method   Method of applying the revenue principle in which gross profit (sales revenue minus cost of goods sold) is recorded as cash is collected (534)

Intangible asset   An asset with no physical form, a special right to current and expected future benefits (449)

Interest   The revenue to the payee for loaning out the principal, and the expense to the maker for borrowing the principal (363)

Interest-coverage ratio   Another name for the Times-interest-earned ratio (856)

Interest period   The period of time during which interest is to be computed, extending from the original date of the note to the maturity date (363)

Interest rate   The percentage rate that is multiplied by the principal amount to compute the amount of interest on a note (363)

Internal auditing   Auditing that is performed by a business's own accountants to evaluate the firm's accounting and management systems. The aim is to improve operating efficiency and to ensure that employees follow management's procedures and plans (9-10)

Internal control   Organizational plan and all the related measures adopted by an entity to meet management's objectives of discharging statutory responsibilities, profitability, prevention and detection of fraud and error, safeguarding of assets, reliability of accounting records, and timely preparation of reliable financial information (257-258)

Internal rate of return   Rate of return that makes the net present value of a project equal to zero (1149)

Inventoriable cost   All costs of a product regarded as an asset under GAAP (971)

Inventory cost   Price paid to acquire inventory — not the selling price of the goods. Inventory cost includes its invoice price, less all discounts, plus sales tax, tariffs, transportation fees, insurance while in transit, and all other costs incurred to make the goods ready for sale (395)

Inventory turnover   Ratio of cost of goods sold to average inventory. Measures the number of times a company sells its average level of inventory during a year (853)

Investing activity   Activity that increases and decreases the assets that the business has to work with. A section of the statement of changes in financial position (780)

Investment center   Responsibility center in which a manager is accountable for investments, revenues and costs (expenses) (1097)

Invoice   Seller's request for payment from a purchaser. Also called a bill (201)

Issued stock   The stock that the corporation has issued to shareholders (618)

Job cost record   Document used to accumulate and control cost in a job order system (975)

Job order costing   Accounting system used by companies that manufacture products as individual units or in batches, each of which receives varying degrees of attention and skill (974)

Joint products   Goods identified as individual products only after a juncture in the production process called the split-off point (1030)

Journal   The chronological accounting record of an entity's transactions (50)

Just-in-Time (JIT) Production   A system in which each component on a production line is produced immediately as needed by the next step (1032)

Labor time ticket   Document that identifies an employee, the amount of time the employee spent on a particular job, and the employee's labor cost charged to the job (979)

Last-in, first-out (LIFO) method   Inventory costing method by which the last costs into inventory are the first costs out to cost of goods sold. This leaves the oldest costs — those of beginning inventory and the earliest purchases of the period — in ending inventory (396)

LCM rule   The Lower-of-cost-or-market rule (402)

Lease   Rental agreement in which the tenant (lessee) agrees to make rent payments to the property owner (lessor) in exchange for the use of the asset (709)

Leasehold   Prepayment that a lessee (renter) makes to secure the use of an asset from a lessor (landlord) (450)

Ledger   The book of accounts (45)

Lessee   Tenant in a lease agreement (709)

Lessor   Property owner in a lease agreement (709)

Leverage   Another name for Trading on the equity (858)

Liability   An economic obligation (a debt) payable to an individual or an organization outside the business (14)

LIFO   The last-in, first-out inventory method (396)

Limited liability   No personal obligation of a shareholder for corporation debts. The most that a shareholder can lose on an investment in a corporation's stock is the cost of the investment (612)

Limiting factor   Item that restricts production or sales. Also called the Constraint (1136)

Liquidation   The process of going out of business by selling the entity's assets and paying its liabilities. The final step in liquidation of a business is the distribution of any remaining cash to the owners (586)

Liquidation value of stock   Amount a corporation agrees to pay a preferred shareholder per share if the company liquidates (630)

Liquidity   Measure of how quickly an item may be converted to cash (158-159)

Long-term asset   An asset other than a current asset (159)

Long-term commitments   Commitments that involve making payments that may be unequal in amount over a series of years (542)

Long-term investment   Separate asset category reported on the balance sheet between current assets and capital assets (741)

Long-term liability   A liability other than a current liability (159)

Long-term solvency   The ability to generate enough cash to pay long-term debts as they mature (840)

Loss   A decrease in owner equity that does not result from an expense or a distribution to an owner of the business (547)

Lower-of-cost-or-market (LCM) rule   Requires that an asset be reported in the financial statements at the lower of its historical cost or its market value (current replacement cost or net realizable value) (402)

Mainframe system   Computer system characterized by a single computer (259)

Maker of a note   The person or business that signs the note and promises to pay the amount required by the note agreement. The maker is the debtor (363)

Management accounting   The branch of accounting that generates confidential information for internal decision-makers of a business, such as top executives (10)

Management by exception   Management strategy by which executive attention is directed to the important deviations from budgeted amounts (1099)

Margin of safety   Excess of expected sales over break-even sales (940)

Market interest rate   Interest rate that investors demand in order to loan their money. Also called the Effective interest rate (694)

Market value of stock   Price for which a person could buy or sell a share of stock (629)

Marketable security   Another name for short-term investment, one that may be sold any time the investor wishes (737-738)

Master budget   Budget that includes the major financial statements and supporting schedules. The master budget can be divided into operating budget, capital expenditures budget and financial budget (890)

Matching principle   The basis for recording expenses. Directs accountants to identify all expenses incurred during the period, measure the expenses and match them against the revenues earned during that same span of time (96-97)

Materiality concept   States that a company must perform strictly proper accounting only for items and transactions that are significant to the business's financial statements (545)

Materials inventory   Materials on hand and intended for use in the manufacturing process. Also called Raw materials inventory (967)

Materials requisition   Request for materials prepared by manufacturing personnel; the document that sets a manufacturing process in motion (976)

Maturity date   The date on which the final payment of a note is due. Also called the due date (363)

Maturity value   The sum of the principal and interest due at the maturity date of a note (363)

Microcomputer   A computer small enough for each employee to have his or her own (259)

Minicomputer   Small computer that operates like a large system but on a smaller scale (259)

Minority interest   A subsidiary company's equity that is held by shareholders other than the parent company (746)

Mixed cost   Cost that is part variable and part fixed (930)

Mixed expense   Expense that is part variable and part fixed (930)

Mortgage   Borrower's promise to transfer the legal title to certain assets to the lender if the debt is not paid on schedule (707)

Multiple-step income statement   Format that contains subtotals to highlight significant relationships. In addition to net income, it also presents gross margin and income from operations (217)

Mutual agency   Every partner can bind the business to a contract within the scope of the partnership's regular business operations (570)

Natural resources   Another name for wasting assets (432)

Net earnings   Another name for Net income or Net profit (17)

Net income   Excess of total revenues over total expenses. Also called Net earnings or Net profit (17)

Net loss   Excess of total expenses over total revenues (17)

Net pay   Gross pay minus all deductions, the amount of employee compensation that the employee actually takes home (485)

Net present value   Method of computing the expected net monetary gain or loss from a project by discounting all expected cash flows to the present value, using a desired rate of return. A zero or positive net present value indicates that the investment should be purchased. A negative net present value indicates that the investment should be rejected (1145)

Net profit   Another name for Net income or Net earnings (17)

Net purchases   Purchases less purchase discounts and purchase returns and allowances (204)

Net realizable value   Sales value less the cost of selling the item (1031)

Net sales revenue   Sales revenue less sales discounts and sales returns and allowances (206)

Nominal account   Another name for a Temporary account — revenues and expenses — that is closed at the end of the period. In a proprietorship the owner withdrawal account is also nominal (152)

No-par stock   Shares of stock that do not have a value assigned to them by the articles of incorporation (617)

Nonsufficient funds (NSF) cheque   A "hot" cheque, one for which the payer's bank account has insufficient money to pay the cheque (311)

Note payable   A liability evidenced by a written promise to make a future payment (14)

Note receivable   An asset evidenced by another party's written promise that entitles you to receive cash in the future (14)

NSF cheque   A nonsufficient funds cheque (311)

Off-balance-sheet financing   Acquisition of assets or services with debt that is not reported on the balance sheet (711)

On-line processing   Computerized accounting for transaction data on a continuous basis, often from various locations, rather than in batches at a single location (260)

Operating activity   Activity that creates revenue or expense in the entity's major line of business. Operating activities affect the income statement. A section of the statement of changes in financial position (779-780)

Operating budget   Sets the target revenues and expenses, and thus net income, for the period (893)

Operating cycle   The time span during which cash is (1) used to acquire goods and services and (2) those goods and services are sold to customers, who in turn pay for their purchases with cash. Usually a few months in length (159)

Operating expenses   Expenses, other than cost of goods sold, that are incurred in the entity's major line of business: rent, depreciation, salaries, wages, utilities, property tax and supplies expense (214)

Operating income   Another name for Income from operations (214)

Operating lease   Usually a short-term or cancelable rental agreement (709)

Opportunity cost   Maximum available profit contribution forgone (rejected) by using limited resources for a particular purpose. It is the cost of the forsaken next best alternative (1139)

Organization cost   The costs of organizing a corporation, including legal fees, taxes and charges by promoters for selling the stock. Organization cost is an intangible asset (624)

Other expense   Expense that is outside the main operations of a business, such as a loss on the sale of capital assets (214)

Other receivables   A miscellaneous category that includes loans to employees and branch companies, usually long-term assets reported on the balance sheet after current assets and before capital assets. Other receivables can be current assets (352-353)

Other revenue   Revenue that is outside the main operations of a business, such as a gain on the sale of capital assets (214)

Outstanding cheque   A cheque issued by the company and recorded on its books but not yet paid by its bank (311)

Outstanding stock   Stock in the hands of a shareholder. Also referred to as Issued Stock (614)

Overapplied overhead   Credit balance in the factory overhead account; results when applied overhead exceeds the actual overhead cost (984)

Owner's equity   The claim of an owner of a business to the assets of the business. Also called Capital (14)

Par value   Arbitrary amount assigned to a share of stock (617)

Parent company   An investor company that owns more than 50 percent of the voting stock of a subsidiary company (743)

Participating preferred stock   Preferred stock whose owners may receive (that is, participate in) dividends beyond the stated amount or stated percentage (627)

Partnership   An unincorporated business with two or more owners (10)

Partnership agreement   Agreement that is the contract between partners specifying such items as the name, location and nature of the business, the name, capital investment and duties of each partner, and the method of sharing profits and losses by the partners (570)

Patent   A federal government grant giving the holder the exclusive right for 17 years to produce and sell an invention (450)

Payback   Length of time it will take to recover, in net cash inflow from operations, the dollars of a capital outlay. The shorter the payback period the better the investment, and vice versa (1142)

Payee of a note   The person or business to whom the maker of a note promises future payment. The payee is the creditor (363)

Payroll   Employee compensation, a major expense of many businesses (485)

Pension   Employee compensation that will be received during retirement (711)

Percentage of completion method   Method of applying the revenue principle by a construction company by which revenue is recorded as the work is performed (535)

Performance report   Report that compares actual and budgeted results (1058)

Period cost   Operating expenses which are never traced through the inventory accounts (971)

Periodic inventory system   The business does not keep a continuous record of the inventory on hand. Instead, at the end of the period the business makes a physical count of the on-hand inventory and applies the appropriate unit costs to determine the cost of the ending inventory (406)

Permanent accounts   The assets, liabilities and capital accounts. These accounts are not closed at the end of the period because their balances are not used to measure income. Also called a Real account (152)

Perpetual inventory system   The business keeps a continuous record for each inventory item to show the inventory on hand at all times (407)

Petty cash   Fund containing a small amount of cash that is used to pay minor expenditures (319)

Postclosing trial balance   List of the ledger accounts and their balances at the end of the period after the journalizing and posting of the closing entries. The last step of the accounting cycle, the postclosing trial balance ensures that the ledger is in balance for the start of the next accounting period (154-155)

Posting   Transferring of amounts from the journal to the ledger (52)

Preferred stock   Stock that gives its owners certain advantages over common shareholders, such as the priority to receive dividends before the common shareholders and the priority to receive assets before the common shareholders if the corporation liquidates (617)

Prepaid expense   A category of miscellaneous assets that typically expire or get used up in the near future. Examples include prepaid rent, prepaid insurance, and supplies (99)

Present value   Amount a person would invest now to receive a greater amount at a future date (694)

President   Chief operating officer in charge of managing the day-to-day operations of a corporation (613)

Price-earnings ratio   Ratio of the market price of a share of common stock to the company's earnings per share (859)

Price variance   Difference between the actual unit price of an input (materials and labor) and a standard unit price, multiplied by the actual quantity of inputs used (1064)

Prime costs   Direct materials plus direct labor (969)

Principal amount   The amount loaned out by the payee and borrowed by the maker of a note (363)

Prior period adjustment   Correction to retained earnings for an error of an earlier period is a prior period adjustment (669)

Private accountant   Accountant who works for a single business, such as a department store or Northern Telecom (5)

Process costing   System for assigning costs to goods that are mass-produced in a continuous sequence of steps (1010)

Product cost   Cost identified with goods purchased or manufactured for resale (966)

Product costing   The computing of manufacturing product costs for financial statements and pricing and product-mix decisions (966)

Production cost report   Summary of the activity in a processing department for a period (1024)

Production volume overhead variance   Difference between the flexible budget for actual production and standard overhead applied to production (1071)

Profit center   Responsibility center in which a manager is accountable for revenues and costs (expenses) (1096)

Promissory note   A written promise to pay a specified amount of money at a particular future date (363)

Proprietorship   An unincorporated business with a single owner (10)

Proxy   Legal document that expresses a shareholder's preference and appoints another person to cast the shareholder's vote (613)

Public accountant   Accountant who serves the general public and collects fees for work, which includes auditing, income tax planning and preparation, management consulting and bookkeeping (5)

Purchase discount   Reduction in the cost of inventory that is offered by a seller as an incentive for the customer to pay promptly. A contra account to purchases (203)

Purchase returns and allowances   Decrease in a buyer's debt from returning merchandise to the seller or from receiving from the seller an allowance from the amount owed. A contra account to purchases (203)

Purchases   The cost of inventory that a firm buys to resell to customers in the normal course of business (200-201)

Purchases journal   Special journal used to record all purchases of inventory, supplies and other assets on account (269)

Quantity discount   A purchase discount that provides a lower price per item the larger the quantity purchased (202)

Quantity variance   Another name for the efficiency variance used to control materials and labor costs in a standard cost system (1066)

Quick ratio   Another name for the Acid-test ratio (370, 852)

Rate of return on common shareholders' equity   Net income minus preferred dividends, divided by average common shareholders' equity. A measure of profitability. Also called Return on common shareholders' equity (857)

Rate of return on net sales   Ratio of net income to net sales. A measure of profitability. Also called Return on sales (856-857)

Rate of return on total assets   The sum of net income plus interest expense divided by average total assets. This ratio measures the success a company has in using its assets to earn a profit. Also called Return on assets (628-629, 857)

Raw materials inventory   Another name for Materials inventory (967)

Real account   Another name for a Permanent account — asset, liability and capital — that is not closed at the end of the period (152)

Receivable   A monetary claim against a business or an individual, acquired mainly by selling goods and services and by lending money (352)

Reciprocal accounts   Two or more accounts that have the same offsetting balances and are used to control a general ledger that is kept in two or more locations (1105)

Reconciliation method   Another name for the indirect method of formatting the operating activities section of the statement of changes in financial position (795-796)

Redemption value of stock   Price a corporation agrees to pay for stock, which is set when the stock is issued (630)

Registered bonds   Bonds for which the owners receive interest cheques from the issuing company (691-692)

Relative-sales-value method   Allocation technique for identifying the cost of each asset purchased in a group for a single amount (434)

Relevant information Expected future data that differ between alternative courses of action (1130)

Relevant range Band of activity or volume in which actual operations are likely to occur. Within this range, a particular relationship exists between revenue and expenses (932)

Reliability principle Requires that accounting information be dependable (free from error and bias). Also called the Objectivity principle (532)

Repair Expenditure that merely maintains an asset in its existing condition or restores the asset to good working order. Repairs are expensed (matched against revenue) (452)

Report format of the balance sheet Format that lists the assets at the top, with the liabilities and owner equity below (160)

Repurchased capital stock Stock purchased by a corporation from its shareholders (656)

Residual value Same as Estimated residual value (435)

Responsibility accounting System for evaluating the progress of managers based on activities under their supervision (1096)

Responsibility center Any subunit of an organization needing control; the basic unit in a responsibility accounting system. The three common types of responsibility center are the cost center, the profit center, and the investment center (1096)

Retail method A way to estimate inventory cost based on the cost of goods sold model. The retail method requires that the business record inventory purchases both at cost and at retail. Multiply ending inventory at retail by the cost ratio to estimate the ending inventory's cost (405)

Retained earnings A corporation's capital that is earned through profitable operation of the business. The sum of profits less losses and dividends (615)

Return on assets Another name for Rate of return on total assets (628-629, 857)

Return on common shareholders' equity Another name for Rate of return on common shareholders' equity (857)

Return on sales Another name for Rate of return on net sales (856-857)

Revenue Increase in owner equity that is earned by delivering goods or services to customers or clients (16)

Revenue Canada rate The maximum depreciation rate, also called the Capital cost allowance rate, that Revenue Canada allows a taxpayer to use in calculating depreciation expense, also called capital cost allowance, in determining taxable income (438)

Revenue principle The basis for recording revenues, tells accountants when to record revenue and the amount of revenue to record (96)

Reversing entry An entry that switches the debit and the credit of a previous adjusting entry. The reversing entry is dated the first day of the period following the adjusting entry (155)

Rolling budget Another name for a Continuous budget (903)

Salary Employee compensation stated at a yearly, monthly or weekly rate (485)

Sales discount Reduction in the amount receivable from a customer, offered by the seller as an incentive for the customer to pay promptly. A contra account to Sales revenue (205)

Sales journal Special journal used to record credit sales (262)

Sales method Method of applying the revenue principle in which revenue is recorded at the point of sale. This method is used for most sales of goods and services (533-534)

Sales mix Combination of products that make up total sales (941)

Sales returns and allowances Decrease in the seller's receivable from a customer's return of merchandise or from granting the customer an allowance from the amount the customer owes the seller. A contra account to Sales revenue (205)

Sales revenue Amount that a merchandiser earns from selling inventory before subtracting expenses (205)

Sales volume variance Difference between a revenue, expense, or operating income amount in the flexible budget and the corresponding revenue, expense, or income amount in the static (master) budget (1061)

Salvage value Another name for Residual value or Estimated residual value (435)

Scrap value Same as Estimated residual value (435)

Segment of a business A distinguishable component of a company (665)

Serial bonds Bonds that mature in installments over a period of time (692)

Service charge Bank's fee for processing a depositor's transaction (311)

Share capital Another name for Capital stock (614-615)

Shareholder A person who owns the stock of a corporation (11)

Shareholders' equity Owners' equity of a corporation (614)

Short-term investments The investor must intend either to convert the investments to cash within one year or to use them to pay a current liability (737-738)

Short-term liquidity The ability to meet current payments as they become due (840)

Short-term note payable Note payable due within one year, a common form of financing (474)

Short-term self-liquidating financing Debt incurred to buy inventories that will be sold and with the cash collections used to pay the debt (902)

Single-step income statement Format that groups all revenues together and then lists and deducts all expenses together without drawing any subtotals (217)

Slide An accounting error that results from adding one or more zeros to a number, or from dropping a zero. For example, writing $500 as $5,000 or as $50 is a slide. A slide is evenly divisible by 9 (163)

Software Set of programs or instructions that cause the computer to perform the work desired (259)

Specific cost method Inventory cost method based on the specific cost of particular units of inventory (395-396)

Split-off point Juncture in the production process after which joint products are specifically identified (1030)

Spreadsheet Integrated software program that can be used to solve many different kinds of problems. An electronically prepared work sheet (146)

Stable monetary unit concept Accountants' basis for ignoring the effect of inflation and making no adjustments for the changing value of the dollar (531)

Standard cost Predetermined cost that management believes the business should incur in producing an item (1064)

Standard cost system Designed to control costs by analyzing the relationship between actual costs and standard costs (1064)

Stated capital The value assigned by the board of directors of a corporation to a share of no-par stock at the time of its issue and thus its issue price (615)

Stated interest rate Another name for the Contract interest rate (694)

Statement of budgeted cash receipts and disbursements Another name for the Cash budget (898)

Statement of changes in financial position Reports cash receipts and cash disbursements classified according to the entity's major activities: operating, financing and investing (777-800)

Statement of financial position Another name for the Balance sheet (19)

Statement of operations (Also called Statement of earnings) Another name for the Income statement (19)

Statement of owner's equity Summary of the changes in the owner equity of an entity during a specific period (19)

Static budget A budget prepared for only one level of activity (1058)

Stock Shares into which the owners' equity of a corporation is divided (611)

Stock dividend A proportional distribution by a corporation of its own stock to its shareholders (653)

Stock split An increase in the number of outstanding shares of stock coupled with a proportionate reduction in the book value per share of stock (655)

Stock subscription Contract that obligates an investor to purchase the corporation's stock at a later date at a specified price (619)

Straight-line method Depreciation method in which an equal amount of depreciation expense is assigned to each year (or period) of asset use (436)

Strong currency The exchange rate of this type of currency is rising relative to other nations' currencies (755)

Subsequent event An event that occurs after the end of a company's accounting period but before publication of its financial statements and which may affect the interpretation of the information in those statements (539)

Subsidiary company An investee company in which a parent company owns more than 50 percent of the voting stock (743)

Subsidiary ledger Book of accounts that provides supporting details on individual balances, the total of which appears in a general ledger account (264)

Sunk cost Actual outlay incurred in the past and is present under all alternative courses of action. Sunk cost is irrelevant because it makes no difference to a current decision (1139)

Temporary accounts The revenue and expense accounts which relate to a particular accounting period are closed at the end of the period. For a proprietorship, the owner withdrawal account is also temporary. Also called a Nominal account (152)

Temporary investments Another name for Short-term investments (737-738)

Term bonds Bonds that all mature at the same time for a particular issue (692)

Time and a half Overtime pay computed as 150 percent (1.5 times) the straight-time rate (485)

Time period concept Ensures that accounting information is reported at regular intervals (530)

Time value of money The fact that one can earn income by investing money for a period of time (1145)

Times-interest-earned ratio Ratio of income from operations to interest expense. Measures the number of times that operating income can cover interest expense. Also called the Interest-coverage ratio (856)

Total manufacturing cost Sum of direct materials used, direct labor, and factory overhead. Total manufacturing cost is used to compute cost of goods manufactured, which is part of cost of goods sold (970)

Trademarks and trade names Distinctive identifications of a product or service (450)

Trading on the equity Earning more income than the borrowed amount, which increases the earnings for the owners of a business. Also called Leverage (858)

Transaction An event that affects the financial position of a particular entity and may be reliably recorded (14)

Transposition An accounting error that occurs when digits are flip-flopped. For example, $85 is a transposition of $58. A transposition is evenly divisible by 9 (163)

Trial balance A list of all the ledger accounts with their balances (55)

UI Abbreviation of Unemployment Insurance (489)

Uncollectible account expense Cost to the seller of extending credit. Arises from the failure to collect from credit customers (353)

Underapplied overhead Debit balance remaining in the factory overhead account after overhead is applied; means that actual overhead cost exceeded the amount applied to jobs (984)

Underwriter Organization that purchases bonds or stocks from an issuing company and resells them to its clients, or sells the bonds or stocks for a commission, agreeing to buy all unsold bonds or stocks (691)

Unearned revenue A liability created when a business collects cash from customers in advance of doing work for the customer. The obligation is to provide a product or a service in the future. Also called Deferred revenue (105)

Unemployment Insurance   All employees and employers in Canada must contribute to the Unemployment Insurance Fund which provides assistance to unemployed workers (489)

Units-of-production (UOP) method   Depreciation method by which a fixed amount of depreciation is assigned to each unit of output produced by the capital asset (436)

Unlimited personal liability   When a partnership (or a proprietorship) cannot pay its debts with business assets, the partners (or the proprietor) must use personal assets to meet the debt (571)

Usage variance   Another name for the Efficiency variance used to control materials and labor costs in a standard cost system (1066)

Useful life   Same as Estimated useful life (435)

Value chain   Sequence of all business functions in which value is added to a firm's products or services (965)

Variable cost   Cost that changes in total in direct proportion with changes in volume or activity (928)

Variable expense   Expense that changes in total in direct proportion with changes in volume or activity (928)

Variance   Difference between an actual amount and the corresponding budget amount (1059)

Vertical analysis   Analysis of a financial statement that reveals the relationship of each statement item to the total, which is the 100 percent figure (844)

Voucher   Document authorizing a cash disbursement (321)

Voucher register   Special journal used to record all expenditures in a voucher system, similar to but more comprehensive than the purchases journal (323)

Voucher system   A way to record cash payments that enhances internal control by formalizing the process of approving and recording invoices for payment (321)

Wages   Employees' pay stated at an hourly figure (485)

Wasting assets   Capital assets that are natural resources (432)

Withheld income tax   Income tax deducted from employees' gross pay (488)

Work in process inventory   Cost of the goods that are in the manufacturing process and not yet complete (967)

Work sheet   A columnar document designed to help move data from the trial balance to the financial statements (138)

Weak currency   The exchange rate of this type of currency is falling relative to other nations' currencies (755)

Workers' compensation   A provincially administered plan which is funded by contributions by employers and which provides financial support for workers injured on the job (490)

Working capital   Current assets minus current liabilities, measures a business's ability to meet its short-term obligations with its current assets (851)

Index